The Wedding Present

sometimes these words just don't have to be said

Richard Houghton and David Gedge

All rights reserved. No part of this publication may be reproduced, stored in a retrieval system, or transmitted in any form or by any means, electronic, electrostatic, recording, magnetic tape, mechanical, photocopying or otherwise, without prior permission in writing from the publisher.

The publisher makes no representation, express or implied, with regard to the accuracy of the information contained in this publication and cannot accept any responsibility in law for any errors or omissions.

The rights of David Gedge and Richard Houghton to be identified as authors of this Work have been asserted by them in accordance with sections 77 and 78 of the Copyright, Designs and Patents Act 1988.

No part of this book may be reproduced in any form without permission from the publisher except for the quotation of brief passages in reviews.

A catalogue record for this book is available from the British Library

This edition © Red Planet Publishing Ltd 2017
Text © Red Planet Publishing Ltd 2017

ISBN: 978 1 9113 4616 6

Printed in the UK

Red Planet Publishing Ltd,
Tremough Innovation Centre,
Penryn, Cornwall TR10 9TA

www.redplanetzone.com
Email: info@redplanetzone.com

Contents

Foreword	5
Introduction	6
Acknowledgements	6
Early Days	7
The First Gigs	21
Word Gets Around	30
1986: These Boys Can't Wait	37
1987: My Favourite Band	56
1988: Nobody's Twisting Your Arm	81
1989: A Big Deal	108
1990: All Gigs And No Album	147
1991: *Seamonsters* And (Indie) Stardom	175
1992: Top Of *The Hit Parade*	201
1993–94: Island And *Watusi*	232
1995: Cooking On Vinyl	254

The Wedding Present

1996–1997: Cars And Planets	266
The Cinerama Years	279
2005: Return Of The Wedding Present	294
2006–2007: *Take Fountain* On Tour	318
2008: *El Rey* And A *George Best* Reboot	331
2009–2011: At The Edge Of The Sea	346
2012: *Valentina* And *Tales*	363
2013–2014: EPs And Re-Releases	385
2015–2016: *Going Going...* Still Here	402
Close Encounters	426
All The Songs Sound The Same...	429
End Credits	437

Foreword

When I was first approached about the idea of compiling people's thoughts on The Wedding Present, I was in two minds. Obviously, I felt flattered that someone believed there's enough interest in the band to warrant such a publication, and I became intrigued as I tried to imagine what people might say. But there was a nagging doubt that perhaps a series of stories about how people discovered the band might wear a bit thin after a few pages. When Richard sent me the first draft, I realised that my fears were unfounded.

It was, of course, initially humbling to read how much The Wedding Present means to people – and I thank everybody for their kind words – but I quickly realised that this book isn't actually about me! This is a collection of stories drawn from the lives – and, in some heart-breaking cases, deaths – of a diverse group of people who over the last three decades have become loosely connected through their interest in The Wedding Present or Cinerama. The songs and the records and the concerts are just a backdrop... just scenery for the performance of an absorbing drama. I was genuinely moved by the experience of reading these stories. I sighed nostalgically, remembering simpler days before smartphones, GPS, downloading and the internet and laughed out loud at some of the more ridiculous situations that people got themselves into by virtue of following the band. And I'm not ashamed to admit that I cried more than once at some of the tales of love and loss recounted in these pages.

Cinerama and The Wedding Present are, if I'm honest, selfish pursuits. I don't write songs for anybody other than myself, which is probably why I'm writing this from an airbnb near Calais and not my yacht in the Mediterranean and I don't really care what anybody else thinks about them. But I do care about these stories and I hope you get as much from reading this book as I have.

David Gedge
Bouquehault, 2016

Introduction

If someone else had done a shout out for stories I would have contributed two memories, because The Wedding Present have inadvertently been responsible for two major events in my life. On 22 June 1995 I was married and living and working in Preston. My wife worked in Oldham. The Wedding Present were playing the Citadel, St Helens and we planned to head off to the gig immediately she got home. But she got delayed by traffic, we didn't have tickets and suddenly a 27-mile drive to darkest St Helens didn't appeal. My son was born nine months later, on 22 March 1996. Scroll forward to 2006. I'm no longer married. In a new job, I meet an intriguing woman who's already admitted to being a Morrissey fan. I'm even more intrigued when she says she's making a midweek trip to Amsterdam with a man who's not her husband. It already has the makings of a David Gedge lyric. I ask who she's going to see. 'You won't have heard of them,' she assures me. 'Try me.' 'No, you really won't have heard of them.' It turns out I had heard of them, and Kate and I have now been together ten years and seen over sixty Wedding Present shows together since. So, thanks in part to David, I have a son and a fiancée. And, now, this book. It's been a pleasure to read people's stories and learn how much The Wedding Present mean to other people. I have enjoyed the ride. I hope you do too.

Richard Houghton
Manchester, 2017

Acknowledgements

The dates and venues of the concerts are taken from the information on the Scopitones website, although where discrepancies have arisen I have endeavoured to correct these in liaison with David.

I'd like to thank everyone who took the trouble to send me a Wedding Present memory or photograph or who encouraged and supported me. In particular, I'd like to thank Steve Albini, Patrick Alexander, Chris Allison, Darren Bugg, Shaun Charman, Simon Cleave, Stephanie Colledge, Andrew Collins, Gaz Coombes, Terry de Castro, Paul Dorrington, Steve Fisk, Mike Gayle, Ian Gelling, Andy Gillespie, Ian Gittins, Jeanne Hale, Simon Hale, Mick Houghton, Marcus Kain, Shaun Keaveny, Andy Kershaw, Charles Layton, Steve Lyon, Elesh Makwana, Martin Noble, Emma Pollock, William Potter, Graeme Ramsay, Andrew Scheps, Rachel Spivey (rachelspivey.com), Peter Solowka, Ian Tilton, Clare Wadd, Malcolm Wyatt and Catherine Wygal.

Finally, I'd like to thank Colin Young for his keen-eyed proofreading skills and Maria Forte for the same, David Gedge and Jessica McMillan for agreeing to do this book, and Kate Sullivan for her continued love and support.

Early Days

Born in Leeds, David Gedge went to secondary school in Middleton, Greater Manchester, which he attended from the age of 11. It was there that he met Peter Solowka...

PETER SOLOWKA
Wedding Present guitarist 1985–1991

I think we actually got on well together because, in that particular school (Hollin High School, Middleton), we were both quite geeky. The two of us were speccy kids at the age of eleven and I think we were both sort of outsiders. I was one of the few people there who had parents who weren't from England – I think Solowka was seen as a 'funny' name – and David had just come back from living in South Africa for a year.

I think that helped create a bit of a bond between us. And our humour was the same too – there were things that we could laugh about that others couldn't. So from then on we were

DAVID GEDGE

I've always been obsessed with music. I've always been fascinated by pop culture in general, actually... but, above all, music. I was in 'pretend bands' with my friends at school and we'd dance around the living room or the gymnasium with tennis racquets.

And then, as soon as we got to an age where we could have a go on *real* instruments, we started forming little bands. At first, I wanted to be a keyboard player so I got a little keyboard. But then I decided the guitar was cooler... a bit more rock 'n' roll, I suppose!

The Wedding Present

A school photo: David Gedge in the centre, with Peter Solowka (second from left)

close at school. Even then David came through as a very confident entertainer. He wasn't worried about doing things that would seem a little bit strange and off the rails. He was a bit of a leader for me in that way. One of the things that I remember was the wet lunchtimes when no one could go out to play at school. The teachers would say, 'It's going be a rainy lunchtime. Do you want to pay 2p and come to the school disco?' David and I went along... we were about 13 or 14... and we used to get out our tennis racquets and mime to pop songs of the time. And people at the disco would watch us do it and think it was great! We did things like 'Tiger Feet' and The Sweet and T.Rex... stuff like that. He'd pretend to sing and I'd pretend to play the guitar. It's amazing, really, when you think about it. It was kind of a game but it ended up being real, ten or twelve years later. It's funny, isn't it? From that start you'd probably never have predicted that something was going to happen but, looking back on it, you can see the tendency.

There was always music in our house. There was always a piano. When I was a kid my mum took me to get accordion lessons, which I hated. All that reading music didn't make any sense to me... and it still doesn't really, even though I can do it a little bit now. It's not fun. I've always wanted to just play by ear.

When I was about 12 or 13 I began to get excited by music and my brother-in-law had a guitar that he never played. That's how I

Early Days

David with Dave Fielding, a friend with whom he played music, and who went on to be in The Chameleons

SOMETIMES THESE WORDS **JUST DON'T HAVE TO BE SAID**

The Wedding Present

The Chameleons in their Eighties prime. Dave Fielding (left), Reg Smithies (second left) and singer Mark Burgess (second from right) were all school friends of David Gedge and Peter Solowka. Far right is drummer John Lever, who died in 2017

started. But actually playing songs in a band... that came later with David and a few other kids from school.

There were some other musicians at Hollins who ended up being pretty famous even before The Wedding Present came along. There was a band called The Chameleons... Mark Burgess was the singer. They were from the same year group as us. We all used to play music together. I wouldn't say we were that close or hung around together a lot, but we certainly knew each other and would talk about music and stuff. And when I went to university, Mark and the rest of the band would come over and stay with me sometimes and go to gigs in Liverpool. It's funny that two bands should come out of that one year group in school! Statistically that must be pretty rare. So, whatever was going on, even though it all seemed natural to us, there was probably something a little bit special happening. It just seemed to click for The Chameleons. They formed a band and had the drive to go forward and push themselves to radio stations and record companies and everywhere. In the early Eighties they were huge. I still love their music now. It was a great time in our lives. We were just playing music

Early Days

with people that we knew. We'd all talk about music... and it was getting exciting as well because the scene was changing from the glam rock thing and the Queen-type bands. When we were 16 or 17 it was all changing to punk. It was all very, very exciting. If you could get hold of a guitar and you wanted to play music with your mates... you could make it work!

MARK BURGESS
The Chameleons

I've known David since around the age of 12, having gone to the same school, although I had a closer bond with Pete Solowka to be honest – I think it was our mutual love of T. Rex.

When the name of the band comes up while talking to friends and folks in America, I always chime in with, 'I went to school with him, you know...' And the reaction is always the same. 'What? No fuckin' way!' Dunno why.

DAVID GEDGE

I had a friend at school called Dave Fielding. For as long as I'd known him he'd been this brilliant guitar player and I think that influenced me to be a guitarist too. I was never anywhere nearly as good as he was, though. I bought an acoustic guitar when I was a teenager and I played music with him for a bit. When I was in the sixth form I started a band with Peter Solowka, who I'd known since I was 11 and who was ultimately in The Wedding Present, of course. We both lived in Middleton, in Greater Manchester. The band was called Mitosis, as in the cell division. We rehearsed at Middleton Cricket Club and played a couple of local concerts.

And before that there was a band called Sen, which Dave Fielding was in for a short while. We did a couple of cover versions but I'd always wanted to write my own songs, really. There isn't a giant archive of unreleased material, though... Mitosis only did one demo tape. Maybe I'll release it one day. I played it the other week, actually. It's not great but it was better than I thought it would be! It's probably interesting from a historical point of view.

PETER SOLOWKA

Mitosis was when we were in the sixth form. I've got a cassette of that somewhere, six songs in a studio. I remember one song attempting to be radical and political.

One of the best songs was 'Thatcher The Snatcher'. It was our first go really. For our first-ever gig, we played in the sixth form room, for some parents in the evening.

The Wedding Present

DAVID GEDGE

When I was trying to decide which university to go to, Leeds was suggested to me as being particularly good for mathematics, which is the course I wanted to take. But I also do remember noticing that it had a great music scene, too. You'd look in *Sounds* and all the touring bands would be playing there. And, also, there seemed to be a hotbed of bands from the city itself. People like The Gang Of Four and The Mekons. So that also attracted me. When I was at university, I helped start a group called Meterzone with some student friends and we played at parties and stuff. We never recorded anything, though. The singer was this character called Tony Dardis and he wrote some very funny lyrics. I remember that we had an ironic song called 'Street Credibility'. In the early Eighties, the Leeds scene changed. The Sisters Of Mercy had become successful and I think they inspired bands like The March Violets and Skeletal Family, so Leeds became a bit of a 'Goth' city. There wasn't such an obvious scene when The Wedding Present started in the mid-Eighties

The Great Hall, Leeds University

Meterzone: David Gedge's university band; David is second from left

but there were still plenty of bands around... The 3 Johns, The Age Of Chance, Chumbawamba. So Leeds has always been a pretty vibrant city. Even though it's smaller, it's always given Manchester and London and Glasgow runs for their money. It always seemed to have loads going on... lots of venues, big and small... and Leeds University Union always booked a great selection of touring bands. Andy Kershaw was Ents Sec and probably had something to do with that.

PETER SOLOWKA

It was when I went to university that I really got into punk. I still had long curly hair because I was a bit of a Queen fan at that time – the early Queen. It took me a while to adapt to the New Wave.

It's funny because I used to dress like that but still go down and watch all the punk bands at Eric's (in Liverpool). It was music appreciation. I wasn't really into fashion. I never have been. Just be yourself and listen to what you want to listen to. I wasn't in a band at university in Liverpool, not a band that took anything seriously. The only time I did music was when I used to come back at weekends and occasionally go round to play with David or other

SOMETIMES THESE WORDS **JUST DON'T HAVE TO BE SAID**

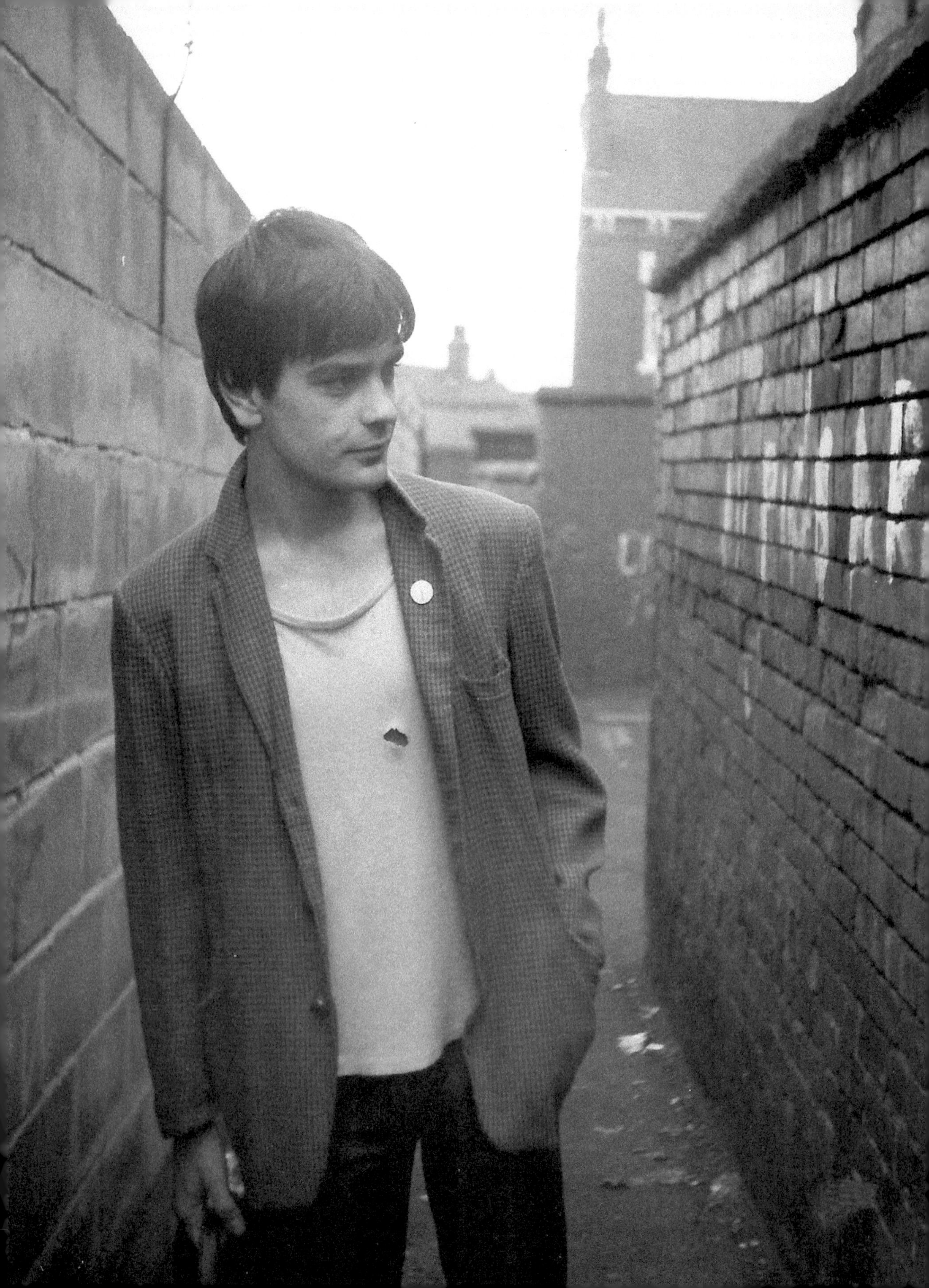

Early Days

Opposite: David Gedge in Leeds, 1980, looking dapper in torn T-shirt and houndstooth jacket

people. I used to have a guitar and play it but I didn't seem to want to be in a band in Liverpool. I don't know why. But I certainly did afterwards, because that was the reason I came to Leeds – it was a way of being with David and playing more music again. David said, 'Why don't you come up to Leeds?'

It was quite near to home, to Middleton, and also an opportunity for another year of a grant and not having to worry about working. That was quite exciting, going to a new city and going there specifically to do music. When I was there, in the first two or three years, I was in three or four bands. I just really threw myself into music.

DAVID GEDGE

I graduated from my BSc. course in 1981 and then I started doing a Master of Science degree in pure mathematics. My thinking was that I should probably get a good degree in case my musical career didn't work out. And that's about the time that The Lost Pandas started. My girlfriend at the time, Jaz Rigby, was the drummer and the bass player was Keith Gregory, who went on to be in The Wedding Present, of course.

I ended up not finishing the master's degree course because I decided to focus more on the group. You can probably blame Dave Fielding for that, too! He'd started a band back in Middleton called The Chameleons with two other school friends of mine, Mark Burgess and Reg Smithies. In 1981, while I was studying maths, they'd impressed John Peel enough to have been invited to record a Peel Session and had signed to Epic Records as a result. So that had me thinking, 'I could do that!'

MARK BURGESS

Around 1979 or 1980, I'd met up with David and Peter again, along with another couple of friends, Reg Smithies and Dave Fielding, with whom I eventually formed The Chameleons. Back then Dave and Reg had a band called Years and were playing various bars and clubs around the North West. That's how I got to know that Reg and Dave had played with Gedgey early on, and that Gedgey and Pete also had a band, Mitosis. As was the norm back then, we all supported each other by attending each other's gigs and I saw Mitosis play a few times. I recall one song Mitosis were playing, 'Thatcher The Snatcher', and I was very impressed with that. 'One of these days, she's gonna come atchya!' Ha! Anyway that provided the inspiration for one of our early songs, 'Singing Rule Britannia (While The Walls Close In)', which we still play to this day. We all became a tad closer through that, often staying

The Wedding Present

The Lost Pandas: Keith Gregory, David Gedge and Jaz Rigby

with Pete in Liverpool where he was attending Liverpool University, and once or twice with Gedgey in Leeds where he was a student. At the time I was just learning to play and had a three-piece punk 'send-up' band called The Clichés. My first ever live performance was at Holcombe Brook Tennis Club in Bury, Lancs, opening for a local student band that had set the whole thing up. Gedgey and Solowka were there along with Dave Fielding. It was a riot as it happens. I remember Gedgey was very taken with our homemade 'I AM A CLICHÉ' T-shirts and wanted to know where he could get one. They also taped the show that night and had it on cassette.

IAN GITTINS
Journalist, *Melody Maker*

I was at university in Leeds in the early Eighties, and there used to be a really quiet guy in my hall of residence, who sat in my tutorial group on my English degree course, called Keith Gregory. He hardly spoke; he hardly said a word in tutorials. And then, before the first year finished, he left to join this band. And I remember thinking, 'What a stupid thing to do! Chuck education to go and join a band...'

DAVID GEDGE

We played quite a few concerts as The Lost Pandas in Leeds... just in pubs and stuff... and we also intended to release a

Early Days

single. My dream at the time was to have John Peel play a record of mine on the radio and possibly record a Peel session. That was all I wanted, really! I was on the dole by this point. Jaz, my girlfriend, was working for the council and Keith was still at university. So the plan was to carry on playing live and recording demos with a Lost Pandas single being the eventual target. The Lost Pandas recorded a few demos and I could probably release them, I suppose. They're probably better than the Mitosis one and you can hear the roots of The Wedding Present in them. Peter Solowka helped me out by lending me money to buy a decent guitar. It was a lovely Ibanez Artist semi-acoustic guitar that I ended up selling on eBay a few years ago. After we left school in Middleton, Peter had gone to Liverpool University while I went to Leeds but we still did music together. After he'd finished his degree I persuaded him to come and join me over the Pennines to do his postgraduate teaching qualification so that he could be in the band with me and Jaz. But Jaz didn't get on with him and so he ended up coming to Leeds for no reason, really... until I asked him to be in The Wedding Present a couple of years later, that is.

PETER SOLOWKA

Whether Jaz liked me or didn't like me made no difference really; I think it's partly to do with the relationships that you're in. She's with him 24/7 and there was still that thing with me and David – a certain comedy, a certain way of speaking – which was pretty exclusive to us. If I was talking to him in a certain way it would make her feel excluded. Other people in the band wouldn't mind, but when it's your girlfriend I can imagine that would be a problem. I never got any positive vibes from her. When we used to come over sometimes – if we were having a long rehearsal weekend, we'd sit around for two days in the house – sometimes that could be quite uncomfortable. We would have been taking a bit of the personal space up that she had with him. Now I'm a bit more mature I can see that. At the time I probably couldn't. I don't think I was in The Lost Pandas ever. Or was I? At the time I was with two or three bands, perhaps even four. The actual history of when I was asked to play in The Wedding Present at various different times... I couldn't say.

Keith Gregory, the quiet guy in English Literature tutorials

> **"They always say you shouldn't really have girlfriends and boyfriends in bands..."**
>
> Peter Solowka

SOMETIMES THESE WORDS **JUST DON'T HAVE TO BE SAID**

The Wedding Present

DAVID GEDGE

Keith, Jaz and I had this band, The Lost Pandas, which was just a three-piece and, to be honest, never really sounded quite right. But then Jaz and I split up. That was really upsetting for me because she was my first proper girlfriend. I was heartbroken. But it was also inspiring in some ways – for me as a songwriter, I mean.

We still kept the band together though, and her new boyfriend, Michael, ended up being in the group! We thought that a four-piece band would sound better than a three-piece because we'd have two guitarists. Then Jaz and Michael went off on holiday to Cyprus but, while they were there, they had a car accident and Michael injured his hand. He was a graphic artist and when they returned home he couldn't work. So they came back saying, 'We're going to get loads of money out of the travel insurance and use it to pay for the single.' And Keith and I thought, 'Great! We're sorted!' Michael was off work for a long time and, after prolonged negotiations with the insurance company, they eventually got a settlement.

But then he and Jaz came round and said, 'Erm, we've decided that we're not going to pay for the single after all... we're off to New York!' And I thought, 'OK. Thanks a lot.' So Keith and I were back to square one. Half the band had upped and left and we didn't have any money. So it was a case of, 'Now what do we do?!' And the answer was that we formed The Wedding Present! I went back to Peter and said, 'I'm really sorry about all this but do you mind being in my group after all?' He agreed. And then we just needed to find a drummer...

This page and opposite: early Wedding Present gig clippings and demo tapes from the period in which Mike Bedford was the drummer

---

THE Wedding Present unveil their new line-up at the Adelphi in Leeds on Friday, with new drummer John Turner, formerly of the Dance Chapter, who recently released a solo LP of his poetry.

The Wedding Present are planning to release a single of their own in the spring.

Debut gig

NEW Leeds band The Wedding Present makes its live debut at the Astoria on October 19.

□ □ □

The band was formed when two members of Leeds band The Lost Pandas went to live in America leaving guitarist - vocalist David Gedge and bassist Keith Gregory out on a limb. Now they have recruited drummer Mike Bedford through a Pop Post plea and have guitarist Pete Solowka on loan from The Chorus.

□ □ □

"As a result the music, although retaining a strong emphasis on melodies has become more powerful than the old Pandas songs," said David.

THE WEDDING PRESENT, a Leeds band who will soon be releasing their first single, have a local gig at the Adelphi on January 25.

Early Days

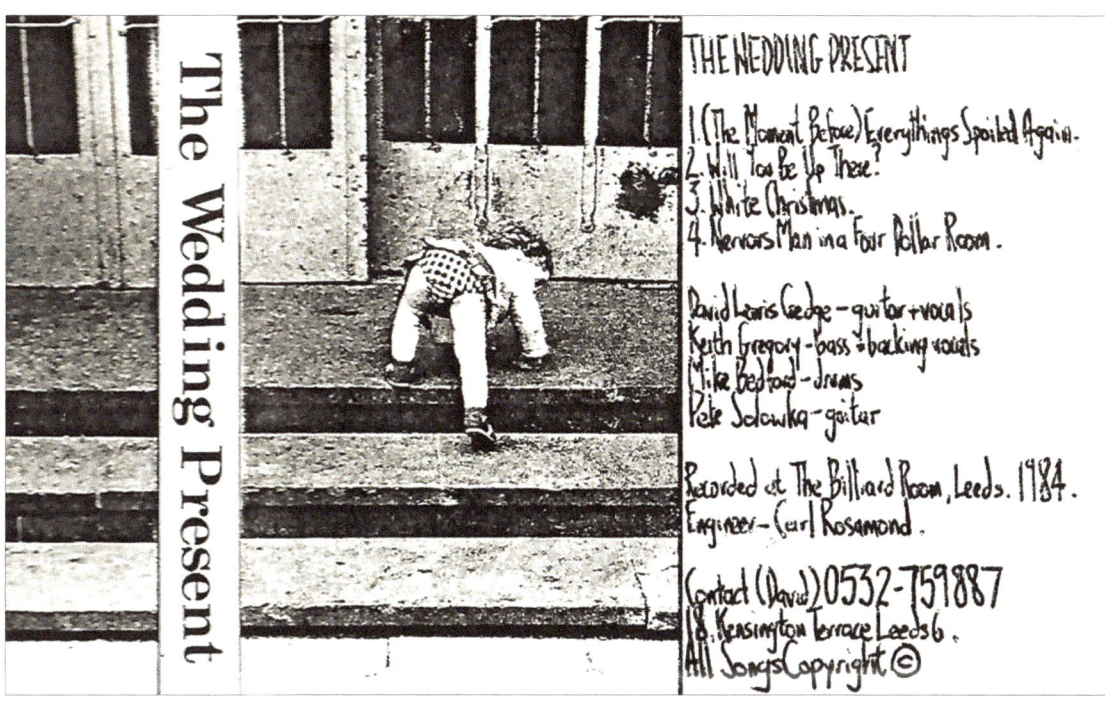

A: GO OUT AND GET 'EM, BOY!
B: PRETTY BLUE HIGH

The Wedding Present

Vocals – David.
Guitars – David + Pete.
Bass – Keith.
Drums – Mike.
Chants – David, Keith, Pete.
Knobs – Cad.

Recorded at The Billiard Room, Leeds
19th November 1984
All songs copyright

THE WEDDING PRESENT

1. (The Moment Before) Everything's Spoiled Again.
2. Will You Be Up There?
3. White Christmas.
4. Nervous Man in a Four Dollar Room.

David Lewis Gedge – guitar + vocals
Keith Gregory – bass + backing vocals
Mike Bedford – drums
Pete Solowka – guitar

Recorded at The Billiard Room, Leeds. 1984.
Engineer – Carl Rosamond.

Contact (David) 0532-759887
18 Kensington Terrace Leeds 6.
All Songs Copyright ©

the strawberry match

The Wedding Present

"Will You Be Up There?"

TAPE REEL
A
STICK IT IN YOUR EAR TAPES!

Actually an untitled demo, but the second track is an
irresistable question. The Wedding Present don't seem
so concerned about 1984 with a feel that hark back
to 1968 or '70 - Velvet Underground, Joseph K respect-
ively. This is not a criticism. I admire them for it.
The tape only serves to remind me how tepid so much
'contemporary' music is.
   Wedding Present make me feel comfortable. Apart
in their attitude, the tunes evident on tape would
cate possibilities for a great future.
Lyrical content was hidden beyond a dreadful mix
h the few words I did hear and the song titles
t indicate that anything of a revolutionary
e is being discussed: (The Moment Before) Every-
's Spoiled Again; Will You Be Up There?; Whit-
mas; Nervous Man In A Four Dollar
got to find someone
many new

The First Gigs

And so began The Wedding Present, its first line-up complete, thanks to the supercharged drumming of fellow Peel devotee Shaun Charman…

SHIRES CLUB
1 MARCH 1985, ALLERTON BYWATER, UK

DAVID GEDGE

I consider the 'debut' Wedding Present concert to be the Allerton Bywater Shires Club one because that was the first show we did with Shaun Charman in the line-up. Before that The Wedding Present did do some concerts with other drummers… there was a year when we had ten different drummers, in fact… but those concerts were more like The Lost Pandas, really.

When Shaun joined something definitely changed. We clicked with him and it transformed the group. It became a lot more aggressive… more punky. Quicker tempos. Fast guitars. It was more exhilarating. The pre-Shaun Wedding Present shows aren't in the Concertography page on the Scopitones web site because I don't count them as Wedding Present concerts. It was difficult to find a drummer who liked the same kind of music… we wanted someone who enjoyed listening to John Peel and alternative or independent music or whatever it was called back then. They all liked metal or funk or stuff. And it's still true today; for some reason drummers are hard to find.

SHAUN CHARMAN
Wedding Present drummer 1985–1987

We played this gig in Allerton Bywater and I was really nervous. It was my first gig. But I got through it and we went down really well. We got an encore as the support band, which was pretty good really.

But even then I wasn't sure whether I could do it because I couldn't play very well. So I was always a bit insecure. Even now, having been in lots of bands, I don't regard myself as

Below: a new drummer for The Wedding Present and a new bass player for Dik Dik Dimorphic, the headline act at the Shires Club gig in Allerton Bywater

DIK DIK Dimorphic, now with a new bass player, play the Shire Club at Allerton Bywater, Leeds on Friday supported by The Wedding Present.

The Wedding Present

a drummer. But we got through that gig and it took off. The atmosphere changed too, which I think had been quite serious. We started playing 'Felicity' at practices, and having more fun. With the same favourite bands, we were all coming from the same place.

COOKRIDGE STREET SQUAT

1 MAY 1985, LEEDS, UK

SHAUN CHARMAN

Early on we played a lot of punky gigs. We did go to quite a punky place for a while, in between 'Go Out And Get 'Em, Boy!' and 'Once More'. It wasn't really *C86*. It was Leeds indie but on the edge of being punky – we even did a couple of gigs where people were spitting, which was really horrible.

We played these squat gigs sometimes. We played with Chumbawamba when they sounded like Crass rather than 'Tubthumper'. I remember us playing a squat gig in an office with dogs roaming about. Punks liked us for being loud and fast. Goth music was definitely important for Leeds. We'd all liked that type of music. We used to go down to the Phono in the Merrion Centre on Mondays and they'd play Sisters Of Mercy type stuff and all that. We were very aware that Goth had just been and that it was part of the Leeds heritage.

Left to right: David, Peter and Keith, at the Adelphi pub in Leeds, 1985

22 SOMETIMES THESE WORDS JUST DON'T HAVE TO BE SAID

The first gigs

David and Keith used to talk about the time they had walked the 14 miles back from Wakefield after seeing The March Violets and they'd missed their train. If you've been to that area of Leeds 6, with the back-to-backs around the Brudenell Road, that period had the atmosphere of that area. We all lived about two or three hundred yards from each other. We would go to gigs all the time, even when we weren't playing. It had that feeling of slight drizzle of that area of Leeds and just going to loads of gigs in places like the 1 in 12 Club in Bradford or the University bars and all that kind of stuff. And we didn't play that many gigs anyway in those days. When we did play, often we'd have like four people at the beginning, though gradually that changed. It was an exciting period and obviously when things started to happen with the band that was exciting as well – being played on the radio for the first time, getting the vinyl for the first time.

An early Wedding Present rehearsal: Keith Gregory, David Gedge, Shaun Charman and Pete Solowka

The Wedding Present

OLD BELL

8 MAY 1985, DERBY, UK

DAVID GEDGE

At those first concerts we were getting maybe 50 people if we were lucky! We played in Derby once and there was, like, six people there. That's because nobody had heard of us until after the first single came out. Derby was the only place we played outside of Yorkshire during that time; we were just playing in pubs around Leeds, really. I think we got good reactions... there just wasn't a lot of people there. It was the kind of person who was interested in seeing a 'new' band regardless of what they sounded like.

GO OUT AND GET 'EM, BOY!
THE DEBUT SINGLE
24 MAY 1985

SHAUN CHARMAN

The reason why I don't play on the A-side of 'Go Out And Get 'Em, Boy!' is because I couldn't play the drums well enough, and thought it would be a better single if I got somebody else in – I still think so. I asked the drummer of the band that I played the bass in to play for me, as I thought it would sound better.

The B-side, '(The Moment Before) Everything's Spoiled Again', has a slow bit in the middle. The reason I could play that song is because it had that slow bit. I ran out of puff, had a bit of a rest and then launched off into the second half of it. That's how the first single came out like it did. Basically I learnt how to play the drums between 'Go Out And Get 'Em, Boy!' and 'Once More'. I don't think there was any compromise needed in terms of our music taste. I had the same music tastes as them, particularly David and Keith. And it meant that we could

The First Gigs

just do what we wanted to do. It meant that we did get louder, and faster. I was always playing as fast as I could. And, as I learnt how to play, I was still playing as fast as I could. As a result it got faster. It got faster organically. And as I got to play the drums a bit better I think it sped the band up.

David went to school with The Chameleons. And when I joined, they sounded more like The Chameleons. The guitars were a bit more 'jig jig jig' in that Chameleons style. I remember David giving Peter a tape of 'The Missionary' by Josef K, suggesting he played more like that, and I was very happy with that idea. If I was a catalyst for the band gelling, I think it was just that I was the last piece in the jigsaw. It meant that we all had the same music taste. I got the impression at the time that it all clicked.

PETER SOLOWKA

When you're a little bit unsure as a drummer or even as a guitar player, if your timing's not perfect, then the faster a song is, the less you see the percentage error in timing. I think playing fast is an easy option for somebody who's got stamina and is young and is playing the drums.

And of course we were all younger. Having fast guitars was great, and a lot more exciting than all the slow power chords that people were playing at the time.

MARK BURGESS

I first became aware of The Wedding Present when Dave Fielding came into the studio at Cargo in Rochdale while we were recording. He had a 12" copy of 'Go Out And Get 'Em, Boy!' tucked under his arm, which I thought was fuckin' brilliant. Post-punk music had gone up its own arse a little bit by then so it was totally refreshing to hear such a raw record presenting such a great song at breakneck speed with that fantastic chord interplay. I thought the record was actually going to melt. I understood and liked the ethos around the band.

The cover of the debut single, 'Go Out And Get 'Em, Boy!'

SOMETIMES THESE WORDS **JUST DON'T HAVE TO BE SAID**

The Wedding Present

They had their own sleeve style, much like we did but more urban, which they kind of made their own, as did The Smiths. Titling the album *George Best* was absolute genius in my view. They even used my favourite photo of him – the one that I still have in my *Park Drive Book Of Football*.

I saw them play a few times in those early years but, as much as I liked the band, it was difficult for me to relate to the audience, to be honest. It was kind of like being at a massive student rave and I always felt like a fish out of water really. But I managed to see them here in the UK, in LA, New York. I was really pleased that everywhere I saw them the rooms were packed, the response ecstatic and the band was on fire.

It was always great when our paths crossed, at least for me. I remember being asked to play an acoustic set as an opener for one of David's shows in New York City and I was struck by the surrealism of it, you know, both of us coming through Hollin High School and Moorclose Comprehensive in Manchester, and here we were playing shows together in the centre of Manhattan.

I remember another time I played a show with David in Lyon. In our set that night was a cover of The Fall's 'Frightened', and I'd introduced it by saying how Mark E. Smith and The Fall were one of the reasons I was there at all. Toward the end of his set Gedgey namechecked me and paid me a huge compliment. I thought that was really cool of him.

I'd always admired him and when someone you admire professionally gives you that kind of courtesy – well, it was very generous and a moment I'll never forget. Unfortunately, one of his crew wrecked his hire van the next day so that was his deposit up the Swanee River. Well, at least they got out of Lyon. An airport strike meant we were there trying to leave for the best part of the day.

I also remember bringing up the subject of 'Brassneck'. Now when we were at Hollin High School I dated a girl called Tracy Bassnett. She was a pretty little girl but an absolute bitch. Her nickname round the school was – yep – 'Brassneck'.

So I hear the lyrics, 'Brassneck, I don't love you anymore.' I said to David that night in Lyon, 'That was about Tracy Bassnett, wasn't it?' His eyes flickered while he totally denied it. He can deny it all he wants. I know the truth!

Promo badge for the 'Brassneck' single (1990): Mark Burgess recalls having spoken to Gedge about whether or not it might have been about, or perhaps inspired by, a girl Mark went out with when they were all at school together

26 SOMETIMES THESE WORDS JUST DON'T HAVE TO BE SAID

The First Gigs

FIRST JOHN PEEL AIRPLAY
BBC RADIO 1
5 JUNE 1985

DAVID GEDGE

I was driven by this burning ambition to be on John Peel's radio show. People say, 'You're very lucky to have had Peel's patronage' and that's obviously true but, at the same time, because I was so influenced by that programme and the music he was playing, I think that informed what we did as a group and it was kind of obvious that we'd end up being a 'John Peel band', in a way. We ticked all the right boxes. People often say, 'What's the most exciting thing that's ever happened to you? Was it playing in America or Japan... or going on *Top Of The Pops*?' or whatever... but my answer is always, 'Hearing John Peel playing 'Go Out And Get 'Em, Boy!' on the radio.' That was such a memorable night.

But then, doing Peel Sessions and stuff... that was always brilliant, too. It's a bit ridiculous, really, because it's all just based on my liking of that one programme. But it obviously affects you as a person.

At that time, John Peel's support was absolutely crucial for the success of a band of our type. He was the target for everybody from the alternative scene, really.

We noticed the effect during the summer of 1985. Before then we'd play all these little concerts that we'd arranged but then, as soon as the single came out, it was so much easier because people would contact us and say, 'I heard your record on Peel last night and I want you to come and play at our venue.' It was a massive change! He played that first single about ten times and, over that period, you could feel the profile of the group lifting after each play, such was his status.

He was almost too important, in a way. Obviously, we benefitted from his support but, even at that time, I felt like he had too much influence. John Peel's patronage could make or break a band like The Wedding Present. It's much more disparate today; there

The Wedding Present

are many more outlets for music. But Peel was the be all and end all. If he played your record and you were from that kind of area of music, it was a lot more likely that you'd have some success. I really would have been heartbroken to have found myself in John Robb's position, say... having made Peel-type records that John Peel wasn't playing. I loved The Membranes and I always thought that they sounded like an archetypal Peel band. But Peel hardly ever played them. I remember John Robb asking me, 'Why doesn't Peel play us? Have I upset him in some way?!' And so there was me, desperately trying to offer support by saying, 'I don't understand why he doesn't play your records. You're brilliant!' And I think it probably did hold them back. The Membranes could have been more successful had Peel championed them but he didn't, for some reason. He was quirky like that.

Another example is that he never really used to play records by Blur. And then they released that 'American' sounding album... the one with 'Song 2' on it... and suddenly he was playing them all the time and they performed live at Peel Acres and all that.

Seven years after their first single, they were suddenly a Peel band! He was sometimes unpredictable in his tastes, I think... which was part of his appeal in many ways.

JOHN ROBB
The Membranes

The first time I met David Gedge was when he came to see The Membranes play a gig at a student hall of residence in Leeds in about 1983. We had gone down in a minibus driven by a couple of members of A Witness who hadn't quite formed yet but were about to – so it was a bit of a proto-Eighties indie underground micro-event. At that time we were in the post-punk zone – all possibilities were wide open and noise and dislocated rhythms were part of the language.

The young Gedge liked all that kind of stuff and I remember chatting to him that night – an earnest and quite shy young man. He was already a crafted songwriter but also knew how to make it into a sort of noise music, as he was soon to prove when he turned up at another Membranes gig a few months later, armed with his first single and his own fanzine. The single sounded astonishing – it had all the fire and brimstone of The Membranes but somehow he had turned this into perfect pop music – a perfect pop that must have been a relief to John Peel with his ears bleeding from the amassed army of noiseniks sending him countless high-decibel cassettes. Peel made The Wedding Present firm faves and the band became sort of second to The

The First Gigs

John Robb, early Eighties. While they were fellow travellers, The Membranes never quite received the same level of patronage from John Peel that The Wedding Present did

Smiths in dealers of classic mid-Eighties indie pop. They were selling lots of records and would have sold more if Gedge had been a pushy calculating type. But his modesty saw him swap the flash bang of insta-success for a longevity that has been far more worthwhile. Moulding the band into many different shapes, he's allied his classic songwriting with a cutting-edge exploration of the possibilities of guitar music and that's why I still love them.

SHAUN CHARMAN

I was excited when Peel played the single, but even more so when he turned it over and played the B-side once! It was all exciting, really.

The Wedding Present

Word Gets Around

After John Peel played 'Go Out And Get 'Em, Boy!' (and its B-side), The Wedding Present started to get gigs further afield. There were the beginnings of a buzz about them; they were a band taking their first tentative steps towards indie stardom.

GRAHAM HOLLIDAY

'Go Out And Get 'Em, Boy!' by The Wedding Present came out in 1985. I heard it when it was first played on the John Peel Show. I liked the Orange Juice motifs, feedback and that gorgeously mangled opening guitar riff. A riff that always reminded me of the sound of a Seventies ice cream van. I immediately decided that it was the best thing I'd heard since 'Upside Down' by The Jesus And Mary Chain. I wrote to the band straight away to ask them some questions for a fanzine I put together with friends in the small town of Rugby. They wrote back with a tape recording of their answers, some photos, a letter and a copy

An early interview with the band from Sounds, promoting their first single

FOR BETTER OR FOR WORSE
PETE PICTON grabs his invite and chooses The Wedding Present

"KNACKERED," IS how drummer Shaun describes The Wedding Present's sound. Good enough, however, for their self-financed debut seven-inch, 'Go Out And Get 'Em Boy', to be hailed as single of the year in certain critical quarters, and for City Slang label to re-release it this month along with a new 12 inch four track 'Once More' (through The Cartel).

"All the bands we like are exciting and loud," explains singing guitarist David. His list of faves veers from The Postcard set and The Buzzcocks to The Membranes and The Three Johns, which all helps to outline The Wedding Present — a chaotic collapse of jangling guitars protecting the sweetest of melodies.

"Pop brains and punk art" is the band's slogan. Their noise aims for the raw nerve.

"We've had trouble with engineers trying to sneak down the levels in the studio," says Dave. "But we like that live sound. I'm not that good a singer anyway, but that way it gets hidden in the row."

Together since January, the Leeds band also include Pete on guitar and Keith on bass. No surnames, no pack drill. They hope, like a lot of the cottage industry indie bands, to maintain their independence, preferring to staple record sleeves in their bedrooms than be swallowed up by the big companies' large factories.

"We're not pretending to be anything special or even the greatest thing to come out of Leeds," says Dave. "We're bold but nice, all punk rockers at heart."

With their feet firmly on the ground...

"When the record came out we were scared to talk to Red Rhino" (the distributors) "in case they'd only managed to get rid of eight or something," Shaun declares. "But they phoned us last week. They'd sold the lot."

30 SOMETIMES THESE WORDS JUST DON'T HAVE TO BE SAID

of the single. We tried to get the band to play at the Reverberation Club in Rugby, a club run by Spacemen 3. From memory, The Wedding Present were too expensive (£200?) at the time and the Spacemen had to turn them down. However, they did submit a track (a live version of 'This Boy Can Wait') for us to include on a compilation tape we put out called *The Holy Bible*. This tape also featured Inspiral Carpets, Spacemen 3, Jazz Butcher and Loop among other bands. Not a bad line-up for a couple of 16-year-olds from a small town to assemble on tape in the mid-Eighties.

To thank him, I sent Gedge a tape of some live recordings of bands from Rugby. It seems quaint today, but back then mailing tapes to acquaintances was one of the only ways of sharing music. From memory, most of the tape was taken up with early live recordings of Spacemen 3. I remember Gedge thought he could hear the influence of Rema Rema in the Spacemen. It was an influence I never heard myself.

MARTIN CALLAGHAN

Early March, 1985. It was over for the striking miners and it was over for me and her. She said I couldn't make her happy; disentangled herself from the front of the car and walked in the rain to her front door. She didn't look back. I drove off feeling like I'd just featured in a scene from a soap opera, or a three-minute classic by a minor indie band.

A few months later I started renting a house elsewhere in the city, closed the curtains and started living on tinned food. Off work one day I wandered into an independent record store that my mate ran.

I was a bit out of touch, but I knew from reading the *NME* that John Peel had been playing stuff by a band called The Wedding Present. That they were part of some amorphous, dishevelled movement called 'shambling'; the premise (subsequently denied when I spoke to David Gedge) being that it took two or three goes to start every song.

'Go out and get 'em' indeed. Nowt to lose, kid. Buy it. Straightaway I was hooked. Guitars flailing at about 300 miles-an-hour, a defiant northern voice, articulating lyrics that sounded just how I felt.

The girl might not have been getting out of his car for the last time, but he could see her new partner through his window, reminisce about ham-fisted DIY when they'd first got together and, in the end, find humour in it all.

It was like listening to someone on the phone trying to persuade his girlfriend not to leave him, or thinking out loud whilst writing a letter. The sound of punctured dreams; hope escaping in a disbelieving howl.

They did great cover versions as well: 'Getting Nowhere Fast' by Girls At Our Best! and Orange Juice's

The band in Leeds, some time in between the first two singles: Gedge, Solowka, Gregory and Charman

'Felicity'. Someone got me a tape of a gig they did in East Berlin where they performed 'It's Not Unusual', preceded by David Gedge painstakingly trying to explain all about Tom Jones. Within a few months I'd been to the gigs, bought the records, and oh, most definitely, got the T-shirt. I must have had about five of them. The gigs I went to were mainly in Leeds, but I also saw them in Hull, Huddersfield, and at an open-air gig at the Piece Hall in Halifax, in September 1986, with Ghost Dance and The Shop Assistants. We also went to Manchester one lovely sunny Saturday where we turned up hoping to pay on the door and couldn't get in. Their fans seemed mainly to be an unhealthy mix of spotty students and lairy football herberts. The former effected quirky, self-contained dance moves in their two-bob market-stall anoraks. The latter just glowered and, apart from one ugly night at the Astoria on Roundhay Road, that's as bad as they got. By now I was co-editing a fanzine and sending copies to David Gedge, asking for an interview. He was

SOMETIMES THESE WORDS JUST DON'T HAVE TO BE SAID

Word Gets Around

always top value for between-songs rapport with the crowd and I knew he'd have something to say. Turned out he was indeed a good lad. Spoke to him for the best part of an hour and he kindly sent us some publicity photos that Ian Tilton had taken of the band, in the snow on Woodhouse Moor.

ROYAL PARK PUBLIC HOUSE
20 SEPTEMBER 1985, LEEDS, UK

DIANE FINLAYSON

Sally, a friend of mine from school, was going out with Peter Solowka, guitarist with the band. My boyfriend at the time was also called Pete, had a music degree and was running the Early Music Shop in Bradford. Sally thought we'd be good people to give informed feedback on one of the band's performances. I have a vague memory that someone with a van didn't turn up and so we got roped in as impromptu roadies and headed off to Headingley with the band's gear loaded into Pete's clapped out Chrysler Alpine. As a sign of how clapped out the Alpine was, the headlights were half-filled with water. We sat through the set, which seemed to be mainly loud one-chord one-note thrashing. At the end, Sally came over to see what we thought. My ears were still ringing and Pete just said thoughtfully, 'Well, it was very loud!' Needless to say, we didn't get invited again. The Wedding Present got famous. Pete still runs the Early Music Shop.

AMBULANCE STATION
2 NOVEMBER 1985, LONDON, UK

ROBERT LILLY

The first time I saw The Wedding Present was their debut in London. They were third on the bill but there was a noise about them that made us get there to see them, as well as the headliners who were the main draw. A good friend at the time was a music journo working for *Sounds* and he told

SOMETIMES THESE WORDS **JUST DON'T HAVE TO BE SAID**

The Wedding Present

us about the fuss and played us a tape he'd got hold of. It's funny but, while I remember The Wedding Present, I could not remember who we had gone to see as the headliners until David reminded me in a recent Twitter exchange that it was The June Brides and The Wolfhounds. We knew the latter, being fellow Romfordites.

The Wedding Present were brilliant. I recall David had a very loud shirt on. It started a phase where The Wedding Present became a 'must see and must buy output' band. I also remember my music journo mate had just started promoting a few gigs at the downstairs of the Clarendon. His journo contacts meant he got some good names.

I remember him talking to David and the band to see if he could book them. Sadly, it didn't come off. But he was a bit too clever at this promoting, this mate. He booked Sonic Youth and, fearing a mass turnout at this tiny venue, advertised it by using a codename – something related to their record label. Trouble was, few deciphered it and it was only a third full.

ANDY KERSHAW SESSION
BBC RADIO 1
26 NOVEMBER 1985

DAVID GEDGE

Andy Kershaw was at the University of Leeds around the same time as I was. Then he became the Entertainments Secretary at the Union, so he was in charge of booking bands.

The first time I met him was when I nervously took a demo tape in to try and get concerts at the union. I can't remember if he booked us or not. Later, he went on to work at Radio Aire, which was the local commercial radio station, and I pestered him with tapes while he was there, too.

The Wedding Present actually recorded our first BBC radio session for Andy towards the end of 1985, by which time he'd joined Radio 1.

Word Gets Around

ANDY KERSHAW
Broadcaster

When I was Ents Sec at Leeds University, David hadn't yet formed The Wedding Present. Back then, he was in a group called The Lost Pandas, which I liked.

But I couldn't give them a gig back then, as the venue I had to fill (the famous University Refectory) had a capacity of 2,200. But I had a lot of time for David – a very nice bloke. I remember him approaching me to give me a Lost Pandas demo cassette as I was eating a curry in an Indian in Headingley. And when I was given a weekly show on the local station, Radio Aire, I remember playing Lost Panda songs from that demo tape. I next saw David when I was presenting the Old Grey Whistle Test on BBC2 (1984 onwards) and had a show on Radio 1. By then, he'd formed The Wedding Present. I played their stuff quite a bit on Radio 1, and – of course – they did sessions for John Peel.

PRIESTHORPE SCHOOL

DECEMBER 1985, LEEDS, UK

PETER SOLOWKA

Whenever I was short of money, one of the benefits of having done the teaching degree was that I could go and get four or five weeks' work and save up to buy a new guitar or something like that, which other people couldn't do. I never had a permanent job. It was always a temporary thing. Those were the days when you could live off your dole money and get housing benefit and that's exactly what I did.

> "I had no desire at all to welcome the riches that other people were supposedly getting. What I wanted was time. That's what I still look for in my life now to be honest. It's far more important than those other things"
>
> Peter Solowka

SOMETIMES THESE WORDS **JUST DON'T HAVE TO BE SAID**

The Wedding Present

I never thought I could make a living out of being a musician at the time. Never. Never. Never. You always look at the next step. The next gig, the next record, the next whatever it is you have to do. You do every step you do as well as you possibly can. You get the best sound you can. Play the chords in the best way you can. You make the best record you can. You take it to the best places you think you can take it to. It's only ever that. There's no five-year plan.

IAN BRITTON

We were in fifth form at Priesthorpe School in Leeds and had a slightly 'odd' supply teacher. He'd already got in trouble from the deputy head as he had an earring in school. He admitted to us that he was a bit tired and hungover, as the band he was in had driven to Brighton the night before for a gig – £80 fee, had a bag with a load of stuff stolen, razors, etc. – and then had driven back overnight and straight into school. He had ended up being worse off than not going, but that was not the point.

PETER SOLOWKA

That was the morning when I got into school and I'd had no sleep and I turned up late and it was absolutely crazy. I just decided then that that was absolutely my last session of teaching because I couldn't do both at once. And the band were having to drive back overnight just so that I could get back to work – that was crap. That was probably my one flash of grown-upness in the whole thing. I just couldn't do it. It was absolutely stupid, just so that I could do what I wanted to do. When that week's contract finished that was it. I didn't do it again. Not until I went back to it again in about 1999!

DAVID PERIGO

Peter Solowka was my physics teacher for a short while before running away from Priesthorpe School to live the life of a rock star. I remember watching, open-mouthed, when they were on *The Chart Show* a couple of months later. Wasn't it us kids who were supposed to leave school to join a band?

> "You think when you're in your twenties you're invincible but I just couldn't do it. It was too much and I was letting people down"
>
> Peter Solowka

1986: These Boys Can't Wait

1986 saw The Wedding Present record their first John Peel session, with the band being carried along on the wave of the C86 movement, championed by the *NME*.

1-IN-12 CLUB

10 APRIL 1986, BRADFORD, UK

NICK SPENCE

My college flatmate Hitch wrote to the band after we saw them live, when they were still very much a local indie band, up in Bradford, at the 1-in-12 Club. I remember thinking they sounded a little like Orange Juice, only with the jangly guitars turned up to 11. As a result of that letter, very early on Hitch started designing cover artwork for the band. I got in on the act with the 'You Should Always Keep In Touch With Your Friends' artwork, which was used on posters and T-shirts to promote the single, much to my delight.

Liberty, equality, solidarity (and indie guitar bands) since 1981: The 1-In-12

The Wedding Present

FIRST JOHN PEEL SESSION
BBC RADIO 1
11 FEBRUARY 1986

The Wedding Present achieved one of their ambitions early in the year: they recorded their first John Peel session for the BBC at Maida Vale studios in London on 11 February 1986. The session was broadcast on 26 February and included: 'Felicity', 'What Becomes Of The Broken Hearted?', 'You Should Always Keep In Touch With Your Friends' and 'This Boy Can Wait'. It was the start of a long-term association with the legendary radio DJ that would continue until his untimely death in 2004.

The band turned up en masse to OK the artwork in our small kitchen. It was a painless process. We'd been illustration/graphic design students at Liverpool Polytechnic together so I was grateful for the nod, although prior to computers most of the budget was taken up employing a typesetter to create the lettering. We saw them many times during the late Eighties and early Nineties, and got invited backstage at various venues – some more attractive and enticing than others. 'Free drinks anyone?'

TOWN HALL
16 APRIL 1986, WALTHAMSTOW, UK

CHRIS WILLIAMS

My mate, Tony from Leeds, dragged me along to see them supporting Half Man Half Biscuit. It was life changing. At the tube station a lad was sporting a cartoon T-shirt of the band – so they were bound to be good, right? The sound was so muddy you couldn't hear the words from Half Man Half Biscuit, which kind of defeated the object, but The Wedding Present stole the show. I was taken by the paisley shirts and leather jackets,

1986: These Boys Can't Wait

the nervous looks when they got to the end of a song without breaking a string and the sheer majesty of the music. Peter had that glint of mischief in his eye and a guitar strap made from a Leeds United scarf. Keith looked like they'd had to forcibly drag him on stage, while Shaun somehow seemed to tie it all together, through gritted teeth and flailing arms. Meanwhile David just looked like the politest pop star in the world. You could invite him home to meet your sister, provided you didn't mind her breaking his heart and him singing about it. I was hooked.

ROYAL PARK PUBLIC HOUSE
25 APRIL 1986, LEEDS, UK

The Wedding Present, April 1986, *NME*

WILLIAM POTTER
Bass player, CUD

Without The Wedding Present it's unlikely anyone outside of Leeds would have heard of my band, CUD.

We had seen The Wedding Present live and about in the city several times. I particularly recall a brilliant, breakneck, intimate gig with The Wedding Present and Age Of Chance upstairs at the Royal Park pub soon after The Wedding Present's debut Peel session.

IAN GITTINS
Journalist, Melody Maker

I started doing *Melody Maker* in 1985. The next year I moved down to London and I got sent to interview The Wedding Present. By then they were doing quite well – with John Peel supporting them, they were getting a bit of a push behind

The Wedding Present

Cover of the 1986 'Once More' single

them – and Keith was in the band. And I remember thinking, 'Ah, great. Keith's in the band. That'll help the interview, somebody that I know.' And he didn't say a word in the interview. It was the university tutorial group all over again.

Melody Maker didn't really like The Wedding Present. Many *Melody Maker* people didn't like them at all. One reason I interviewed them so many times was that, whilst I was never a huge fan, I liked David a lot. Over five or six years I probably interviewed David four or five times. And what I always found with him was that he doesn't give a lot away. At the time, I had this big thing about asking people, 'Are you spilling your heart and soul? Is it heart on sleeve, what you're doing in your music?' And he'd always go, 'No, not really' and play everything down. He wasn't a quote machine, that's for sure. He's not Morrissey. He's very guarded and very private, which interviewers don't really want. When I was transcribing a tape I'd be going, 'Come on, say something.' I recall long hours sitting backstage or in bars and me saying things like, 'Do you feel The Wedding Present is really important, that it's making a difference to the world?' and he would laugh and go, 'No, no.' It was as if any big idea I had he would want to squash and, if you tried to say they were important, he'd laugh you down. That was very much his attitude.

Being the age Gedge is, he totally held and bought into the punk ethic, very DIY fanzine, where bands didn't really go into great depth about their lyrics. It was, 'Take it or leave it, this is us.' I think he bought into that ethos to a large degree and, whether that was a conscious or a subconscious thing, I think that certainly shaped his interview technique. He didn't go off on long poncey explanations of what The Wedding Present meant.

SHAUN CHARMAN

It was heading into 1986 when I started to feel that something was going on, just before the *C86* thing. People did start to come and we started

40 SOMETIMES THESE WORDS JUST DON'T HAVE TO BE SAID

to play more gigs in other towns and in Germany and Holland. Between 'Go Out And Get 'Em, Boy!' and 'Once More', in the first four or five months, we would play local pub gigs in Leeds, but after that, gigs gradually got bigger.

TROPIC CLUB
12 JUNE 1986, BRISTOL, UK

CLARE WADD
Sarah Records

Despite being local – I grew up in Harrogate ten miles north and a half hour train ride away from Leeds – I was a bit slow discovering The Wedding Present. Perhaps Peel was playing them too late in his show for me to be up on (literally) a school night? But, by the summer of 1986 and the time I'd done my A-levels, bedtime and curfews were relaxed. I was working on my fifth fanzine and they were very much on my radar.

I'm pretty sure I hadn't seen them play at the time when I interviewed them. But I definitely did that summer – there was something at the Poly with Age Of Chance and Big Flame I can remember quite distinctly. And then a gig at the Tropic in Bristol, where I moved for University that autumn, at the point when my latest fanzine was out and needed selling. My last ever moshpit – I was limping for a week after.

My vague memory of that Leeds gig is that I rang Red Rhino and they gave me the number. No data protection or star protection or 'We can't give it out, but we can pass your number to them' in those days.

I think it was David I rang. I remember it being remarkably easy to fix up an interview for one afternoon in Leeds. I didn't interview many bands like that. It was usually backstage before or after a gig, or by post in true fanzine-writer style.

We met in the Hyde Park pub, which I'd never been in before and have never been in since. Sometime around exactly thirty years ago. The music in the pub was phenomenally loud – no way could we do an interview in there – so David called Shaun and we walked round the corner to do the interview at his house. I interviewed three of them – David, Shaun and Keith – Grapper had a job, I think. There's little preamble to the printed interview, and then, at the end, it just stops – no wrap-up. And there's

The Wedding Present

an OK photo of them I took in the street outside the house on black and white film. Reading the interview now is as skin-crawling as revisiting anything you did as a teenager. If you're not in a band, and you ever wonder why people don't want to sing songs they wrote when they were really young, or aren't chuffed to bits when you tell them the first thing they ever did was their best, try reading something you wrote when you were a teenager. It's just mortifyingly cringe-worthy.

I wrote my first fanzine when I was 16, never expecting people would still be asking me about it in my late forties. I couldn't really figure out what I was into at this point – as comes across in the wide-ranging questions I asked The Wedding Present – about The Sisters of Mercy, sanctions on South Africa, the music press and benefit gigs.

A year before I co-set up Sarah Records, seen so widely as incredibly musically narrow and twee, I was writing fanzines with the Jarrow March on the cover and including articles on Greenpeace, Amnesty and Traidcraft and an interview with Ivor Cutler (he rang to thank me when I sent him a copy and told my mum she should be proud of me). For the next one I interviewed Ewan MacColl. I wonder if it was interviewing The Wedding Present that led to me going down to London for the *C86* week that summer, though I didn't think we'd be able to get in to see them?

Three of us travelled to London for a week of gigs without advance tickets, staying with a grandparent in Eynsford. We managed to get into two of the three we were there for – if you ever thought *C86* was a big phenomenon, remember there were walk-up tickets most nights. I sent David a copy of the fanzine when it came out, and he sent me a couple of postcards from exciting European tour destinations.

Shaun and Peter at The Tropic Club, Bristol

1986: These Boys Can't Wait

A Wedding Present promo postcard, sent by David Gedge to Clare Wadd

KENTISH TOWN BULL & GATE

18 JUNE 1986, LONDON, UK

DAMON BROWN

It was billed as a *C86* night. It was a fantastic night with support from Close Lobsters, The Chesterfields and more. England were also playing in the World Cup and updates were read out in between the bands. Because I lived in Kent at the time, I had to leave after four songs to get the last train home, but it was a great night – despite the early finish.

The Wedding Present

Left: David Gedge, Keith Gregory and Shaun Charman, outside Shaun's house in 1986. Below: 'Don't Try And Stop Me, Mother' was a compilation of The Wedding Present's first two singles. 'This Boy Can Wait' was the band's third single
Photo: Clare Wadd

BOARDWALK
28 JUNE 1986, MANCHESTER, UK

PAUL STAGG

I remember playing five-a-side football on the waste ground next to the venue against DLG, Keith, Grapper (Pete Solowka), Shaun and Mike Stout (their sound engineer). Me and Nige, from Shrewsbury, put in a fantastic performance but had just conceded the lead when the venue manager called a halt because the band were due on stage in five minutes.

44 SOMETIMES THESE WORDS JUST DON'T HAVE TO BE SAID

1986: These Boys Can't Wait

THE C86 CASSETTE
NME
JULY 1986

SHAUN CHARMAN

We were asked to be involved in that *C86* thing. [In July 1986, The Wedding Present's 'This Boy Can Wait' was featured on the *C86* cassette, available from *NME*.] I remember taking the call from Neil Taylor at the *NME* talking about an update to the previous *C81* tape. So we played all the gigs in London with other bands, like The Close Lobsters and McCarthy. Before that, we hadn't felt part of a scene, but it definitely gave everyone some publicity and impetus.

We felt right in the middle of the styles too. We liked the clankier Fall-type bands as well as the janglier side.

IAN GITTINS

There were two reasons why *Melody Maker* didn't like David very much. The agendas were that people either liked this really avant-garde, noise-based music like the Young Gods, Skinny Puppy and so forth. Or there was the movement where people liked fun, giddy soaraway pop.

And The Wedding Present were seen as meat-and-potatoes dreary indie, which wasn't particularly popular in the office. And I think the other problem was that people knew that Gedge was a really hard interview and that you were going to have to really slog away to get your few pearls of wisdom out of him.

If you interviewed Morrissey, form a queue and he'll give you stuff to work with. But Gedge was so grudging and gave so little away, he didn't do himself any favours on that front. Whereas the *NME* always loved him. They were seen as part of the *C86* scene, and when that came along, the *NME* went with it a bit for a year or two, whereas the *Melody Maker* had a backlash straight away. We'd review a gig and say, 'These people can't play. This is self-indulgent middle-class nonsense.' So The Wedding Present went down slightly with that ship as far as *Melody Maker* was concerned. I'd quite

The Wedding Present

often review their shows. They did one big show at the Town And Country Club and I basically said, 'Well, this is quite stodgy fare. This is quite plain. They do their best and seem likeable but there's nothing here to lift you to the stars.' I got sent to interview David shortly after and he was as nice as could be. He didn't seem to take bad reviews badly, on the surface at least. He was always very friendly to me. He thought Morrissey was the bee's knees but he wouldn't begin to think about behaving in that sort of way himself. I think he thought that The Wedding Present were the ones in the kitchen at the party. He used to write in a book every single Wedding Present gig they'd played, and I think he used to write down the indie chart positions as well. He was quite trainspottery about the whole thing.

And that was probably why he wasn't loved at the *Maker*. The ethos at the *Maker* was all audacious, mindblowing music and unbridled genius. David Gedge writing his gigs down in a spiral-bound notebook didn't really fit the agenda.

MICK HOUGHTON
Wedding Present PR

I don't think they were ever press darlings, even within the *NME*, but they definitely had Danny Kelly firmly on side; Danny was the editor at the time and he saw what they represented – they were almost the archetypal indie group and the epitome of that *C86* generation.

It's no coincidence that the *C86* tape was parenthesised by its two biggest groups: Primal Scream opened it and The Wedding Present closed it. *C86* was a major boost for The Wedding Present because it created a genre that said 'We're going to do things our way.'

It summed up an attitude that said as much about self-expression as punk had – but without the piss and vinegar. By and large, most of the *C86* bands were quite anonymous. It was never styled in any way and nobody was ever going to style The Wedding Present.

The Escape Club, Brighton, 22 July 1986. Note the football on in the background

1986: These Boys Can't Wait

Lure of Leeds uncool

POP

JOHN PEEL

'LOUDER,' came the cry from the dance floor. 'Louder and faster.' The Wedding Present, fronted by David Gedge, a man with one of those pale, sad faces you see looking solemnly at you from photographs of First World War volunteers awaiting embarkation, redoubled their efforts before a hundred or so of Bedford's young, who had gathered together in the upper room of the George and Dragon pub to see two of Britain's most highly regarded independent bands, The Wedding Present and The Age of Chance.

Playing at floor level, so that non-dancers had to stand on chairs to see what was going on, over haircuts poised precariously between style and alopecia, and using a PA that boomed throughout in an other-worldly manner, the Wedding Present, all ringing guitars and hot tempos, scurried through a set of their own songs. Most of these were known to the audience from the three singles—the first 1,000 copies of the latest, 'You Should Always Keep in Touch with Your Friends,' had the same track on both sides, making them either a waste of money or collectors' items—and a range of Radio One sessions.

It is the melancholy fate of our younger, snappier groups to be compared with American bands from the 1960s, usually the Doors, Velvet Underground, or, in the Wedding Present's case, The Byrds. In 1966 I compered a Byrds concert in San Bernardino, California, and found them a peculiarly repellent bunch of lads, so caught in LA cool that none of them would even speak to me. The Wedding Presents suffer, if suffer is the right word, from Leeds uncool, pausing between songs to talk with the dancers, and to check on the welfare of one seeker after truth who had pranced with such abandon that he had developed a nose bleed.

The Age of Chance, who recently and most successfully covered Prince's 'Kiss' on a Radio One session, have released a couple of exhilarating singles which owe less to those Yank groups listed above than they do to the Velvelettes' 'Needle in a Haystack.' They play a sort of disassembled Motown but with the edginess of the ages, and although the PA developed problems it was still a pleasure to hear them.

ENOT'S SOCIAL CLUB

29 JULY 1986, LICHFIELD, UK

DALE FARRINGTON

A review, in The Observer, *by John Peel of The Wedding Present's gig at the George And Dragon, Bedford on 17 July 1986*

I fell in love with The Wedding Present the first time I heard 'Go Out And Get 'Em, Boy!' on Peel. It wasn't just the guitars – there was a certain quality to David's voice that appealed to me. It was at the Leadmill in Sheffield, on a triple bill with Pigbros and Age Of Chance, that we first approached them with a view to appearing at Enot's. Peter Solowka was watching a World Cup match on a tiny telly behind the bar so I sidled up to him and struck up a conversation about football.

I finally got around to asking him if they'd fancy coming to Lichfield. He was more than keen so we swapped phone numbers and shook hands. I think that it only took one call to sort everything out.

The Wedding Present

We had a date in mind and they were free. It was that simple. I posted them a map and we set about promoting the gig. The posters we made were simple black-and-white affairs with the cover from 'Once More' being prominent. All the details had been carefully added with Letraset – nobody owned a computer in those days. I don't even think any of us had access to a typewriter. The posters

On gigs and money...

When you reach a certain level, you do need assistance and so we have a booking agent. We tend to work with established promoters with whom I've had a relationship for years and I don't usually have any problems at all with those people. If it's a new promoter, our agent will typically make sure we get half the fee up front before we even arrive at the venue. He'll tell me a month in advance of the show if it's not arrived and he'll start chasing it up. He might say, 'I'm a bit worried because so-and-so's not paid the deposit. Do you still want to do it?' And then it's a matter of assessing people, really... and deciding whether to take the risk.

In the last twenty years, there's only been a couple of times when we haven't been paid in full. There was this one bloke in Scotland in 2010. It was snowing and we'd driven all the way up to Aberdeen. It was quite an effort. We played in Edinburgh the night before and there was literally three feet of snow. People were asking, 'Where are you playing tomorrow?' and when I told them they'd say, 'Oh, well, you'll be cancelling that then, won't you? They're closing the bridge. You'll have go all the way round. There's going to be blizzards.'

But that was like a red rag to a bull for me! 'I'm from Yorkshire! A bit of snow's not going to stop me!' So we did it. I drove the van up there and we played the gig. And it was sold out. I felt pleased and quite proud that we hadn't let people down.

But then the promoter didn't pay me a few hundred pounds out of the fee, even though he'd obviously made a fair bit because it was a sold out concert. And, until very recently, I've been chasing him. It became more a matter of principle than anything. And he always fobbed me off. 'Sorry, I really thought that had been paid. You'll have to speak to my assistant. We'll definitely have to get that sorted.' And I would say, 'Thanks, that's great' and another year would go past. 'Yeah... hello. Me again. Did you ever sort that out?' 'Oh, wasn't that arranged? Really sorry... let me do that right now.' He finally paid up in 2016 but only because I threatened to pull out of another concert, to which he was vaguely connected, at the last minute.

And there was a venue in Shrewsbury that stiffed us. But I think they offered us too much money, based on an optimistic expectation of how many people would come! So we only got the deposit... half the fee. But I think that was probably an appropriate amount for the event. I half-heartedly pursued them through the Musicians Union for a while but gave up in the end. Those two are the only ones I can think of from the past twenty years.

David Gedge

1986: These Boys Can't Wait

Shaun and David, Melkweg, Amsterdam, 1986

SOMETIMES THESE WORDS **JUST DON'T HAVE TO BE SAID**

The Wedding Present

looked great. On the day of the gig we all arrived early at the venue because we were so excited. There was no one around and everything was locked up but we weren't worried as there were still another five hours or so before the doors were due to open. The band arrived about an hour later to find a still locked venue and the promoters munching Milky Bars and sunbathing on the car park. One of The Wedding Present's entourage produced a football from somewhere and a match to rival any in that summer's World Cup ensued. I can't remember the score but it was an enjoyable way to pass the time until the caretaker eventually showed up.

Once inside we set up all the gear and the band soundchecked. Happy with what they heard, they retired to a local chippy for some tea and we started readying ourselves for the influx of punters. One of the great things about those gigs was how friendly everyone was. It was more like a party than a public event and there was always a fantastic atmosphere. The usual pre-performance stuff went on. I played some records, people danced and the old blokes who were playing dominoes in the next room wandered in to see what all the fuss was about.

The Wedding Present were brilliant that night, Gedge was on fine form, trading banter with the crowd and the sound was magnificent. The whole crowd was up dancing at the front. We were also privileged to get a Wedding Present encore – possibly the only one ever!

However, there was a problem brewing. It was becoming pretty apparent that we wouldn't have enough money to pay the band. We'd paid for the room and the P.A. but we were still a fair way short of the £250 we needed for the band's fee. Our friend Claire went around everyone in the venue, including the domino players, to explain the situation and ask

1986: These Boys Can't Wait

Pump action! David Gedge, feeling a bit deflated, on tour in Germany, September 1986. Opposite: Shaun Charman and David Gedge, having been wheel-clamped in Amsterdam, where they played the Melkweg venue on 17 September 1986 (top); live at the Forum in Enger, West Germany on 20 September (bottom)

SOMETIMES THESE WORDS **JUST DON'T HAVE TO BE SAID** 51

The Wedding Present

for a donation. The response was terrific. Everyone started throwing bits of loose change into her bag and there wasn't a single complaint or refusal. When we counted the collection, we were still about thirty quid shy of our total but we couldn't put the moment off any longer.

Rather sheepishly, we approached the band. Our opening line was, 'Well, have you enjoyed yourselves?' 'Fantastic. Brilliant. We've loved it!' they replied. 'That's good because we can't afford to pay you all the money!'

The lads were really good about it. They offered to take £200 instead of the agreed figure and told us to spend the other twenty quid we had left over on drinks for everyone. A lovely gesture, and the perfect way to end a perfect night. For years afterwards, whenever I went to see The Wedding Present, I'd make a point of asking David Gedge if he remembered Enot's. He must have been pretty bored of me doing so but he always replied cheerily, 'That is one of my favourite ever gigs.'

PIECE HALL FESTIVAL

27 AUGUST 1986, HALIFAX, UK

IAN TILTON
Photographer

I first photographed them quite early on. They were playing with The Shop Assistants in Halifax. James Brown was writing for *Sounds* at the time. James said, 'This is going to be a great band.' But it was very early days. He and I had teamed up because I'd been to see *Sounds* and they said, 'Yeah, we really like your work, we'll give you work' but it wasn't forthcoming. Unbeknown to each other, James had done the same and work was unforthcoming for him as well because we were in the north and all the magazines were based in the south. So we got together and agreed that we would do a few pieces and just submit them for free.

And they took three of the four pieces and published them and we got paid for those.

That was marvellously encouraging but, even better, *Sounds* then trusted us; they knew that we were good at what we did and that we were a good team. We did a good job and we did it on time and that's what they wanted. We wanted the editor to go, 'This is happening in Birmingham' or, 'This is happening in Manchester. James! Ian!' Rather than, 'Oh Steve, you're in the office. Just go up to Manchester and cover this, will you?' And soon after we'd managed to get their attention, this commission at the Piece Hall came up. It was quite exciting for it

1986: These Boys Can't Wait

to be one of my first commissioned gigs – one which I was going to get paid for. I didn't know the band and I didn't know The Shop Assistants either. But I ended up photographing The Wedding Present many times after that for themselves, mostly for magazines.

JOHN DOIDGE

I'd heard 'Once More' and I was hooked. Fortunately they played it that evening. This was only my second-ever gig, following on from Half Man Half Biscuit at Leeds Poly earlier that year. I was blown away; this would be the first of well over 100 Wedding Present gigs.

JAMES FRYER

I don't recall my first Wedding Present gig, but as soon as I had seen them I knew I had to see them again soon. It turned out they were playing an open-air festival in me and my mates' home town at the historic Piece Hall, an 18th century building with a cobbled courtyard. They were great, and cemented themselves as this 18-year-old's new favourite band.

BRUCE ANTELL

This was a mini-festival featuring The Wedding Present, Shop Assistants, Pop Will Eat Itself, Ghost Dance, Rose Of Avalanche, The Psycho Surgeons and a few more. Me and a couple of friends drove up from Suffolk on the day, attracted by the line-up and also the price, which I remember as being £2.50. I've read elsewhere it was £3.50. Either way, it was a snip for that line-up at that time. Sadly the weather was the biggest let-down; it didn't rain but it was the coldest August day I have ever endured and putting up with it for eight to ten hours was a

Two boys in Berlin: David and Shaun on tour in Germany, September 1986

SOMETIMES THESE WORDS **JUST DON'T HAVE TO BE SAID**

The Wedding Present

test of stamina for a bunch of southern softies used to blazing sunshine all year round. The Wedding Present weren't headlining. That honour went to The Shop Assistants, whose rendition of 'Somewhere In China' was brought to a halt by Alex bursting out laughing as Pop Will Eat Itself held cigarette lighters aloft in the crowd. The Wedding Present were something like fourth support but they gave a typically full-on energetic set for about half an hour or so. I still remember someone in the crowd shouting out, 'Play faster, ya bastard!' and David replying, with as much dignity as he could muster, 'I'm not a bastard, you know?'

DAVID GEDGE

The Piece Hall in Halifax was a big deal for us at the time. The stage was set up inside a quadrangle. It was like a huge building with no roof or insides... an open-air courtyard with the stage at one end... but I can't remember the capacity of it. It might have been the first festival we played.

BIRMINGHAM POLYTECHNIC

14 NOVEMBER 1986, BIRMINGHAM, UK

LEE THACKER

The first time I saw The Wedding Present playing live I almost burned down my halls of residence! I first heard the band on the John Peel Show playing a cover version of an Orange Juice song. The song was called 'Felicity' and for some reason I'd always thought that Edwyn Collins sang 'blues today' on the original. It was only upon hearing this version that I realised he had been singing 'Felicity', hence the title of the song – duh!

The jangly guitars seemingly played at a hundred miles an hour and the gravelly yet soulful vocals appealed to me immediately. Actually, the guitar sound reminded me of one of my favourite songs, 'The Crunch' by The Nightingales, and that's what initially made my ears prick up.

I'll often get into new music through association with the familiar. I first listened to The Birthday Party when I was into Altered Images (who had a song called 'Happy Birthday'). Just the word 'birthday' was enough to make me sit up and pay attention. It happens a lot.

1986: These Boys Can't Wait

At the Carousel Bar in Ilfracombe, with Sara Catt on bass and Mike Stout on guitar on 11 October, 1986

I think The Wedding Present were about to release their fourth single, so most of their set was unknown to me. Earlier that evening, I went over to the JCR (Junior Common Room) to check if I had any post and The Wedding Present were in the process of going through their soundcheck. I ran back to the halls of residence to tell Mark (the guy who'd moved into the room next to mine and who also had great taste in music) and we stood and watched them run through a couple of songs.

Then I suddenly remembered I'd left my beans and toast cooking in the communal kitchen! I got back to a smoke-filled kitchen, blackened toast and congealed beans and had to start my regular dinner from scratch. One of my neighbours had taken to calling me Heinz because all I ever ate was beans on toast.

According to the diary I kept at the time, 'The Wedding Present came on and played a stunning, noisy but incomplete set. A good gig.' I can't remember why it was 'incomplete' but I do remember most of the audience were made up of the same disco crowd I'd seen on my first night of college and most of them left about halfway through.

Some were heard complaining that 'all the songs sound the same', which was the title of a 10" single the band released a few years later. They did sound a bit 'samey', but they would be one of the few bands I saw that year whose album didn't disappoint me.

SOMETIMES THESE WORDS **JUST DON'T HAVE TO BE SAID**

The Wedding Present

1987: My Favourite Band

1987 saw The Wedding Present release their anthemic single 'My Favourite Dress'. A re-recorded version was to appear in October on the band's debut album, *George Best*.

IAN TILTON

I did a photo session with them in the centre of Leeds in 1987 and then David (we called him Dave back then) said to me, 'Have you got anything that would go on a record cover? Something that you like, that you feel good about?' And he said, 'It doesn't even have to be relevant to the title or to the song.' I said, 'What is it?' He said, 'Well, it's called 'My Favourite Dress'. But as long as it looks good.'

And I'd been doing these shots of a bonfire that I'd had in my garden and there was lots of paper all curled up and charred. So I showed him this and he went, 'Yeah! That's really good. We'll use that.' And they did. They didn't look at anything else.

The cover of 'My Favourite Dress', with the remnants of Ian Tilton's bonfire looking artfully abstract

1987: My Favourite Band

SINGLE OF THE WEEK

THE WEDDING PRESENT 'My Favourite Dress' (Reception) It doesn't take a genius to work out that 1987 is going to be a year when Leeds scoops up all the awards for furthering mankind through the development of impulsive, brilliant records.

Age Of Chance's close proximity to Manchester moguls The Smiths at the top of Peel's Festive 50 was the most obvious sign, but whittling away at the nether regions of the chart were The Wedding Present. Their four songs – 'Once More' (number 16), 'This Boy Can Wait' (18), 'You Should Always Keep In Touch' (28), and a cover of Orange Juice's 'Felicity' (36) – made them the third most popular group in the chart, only beaten by The Fall and The Smiths.

'My Favourite Dress' provides little ammunition for the weapons of criticism. Although producer Chris Allison could be accused of scraping a little from the edges, the three songs (on the 12-inch) still carve a straight line between commerciality and credibility. 'My Favourite Dress' itself is a song that captures all the emotions and images that crush your lungs when you see someone a month after they've chucked you. (I imagine that if played near a poster of George Michael, it would cause the corners to curl as the paper spontaneously combusted.)

On the flipside, 'Every Mother's Son' tries to make amends for man's reluctance to see woman as anything other than the weaker vessel (I'll have W please, Bob), and 'Never Said' takes another ride along the road of the wrecked relationship.

"Sometimes these words just don't have to be said."

Time for another shot of this melancholy on the rocks.

THE WEDDING Present touch wood

MICK HOUGHTON

I was aware of The Wedding Present but I'm almost certain I hadn't knowingly heard them till I was approached by Red Rhino, who sent me all the singles so far with a view to my looking after the next one, which was the 'My Favourite Dress' single. The group had been more or less looking after the PR themselves until then and felt they had taken things as far as they could. The other factor was that they were looking to record their debut album, which would inevitably raise their game and need a much wider press platform. I had a history of looking after independent groups, and not only groups who were perceived as independents but who all actually had major label deals by the time I was involved (The Jesus And Mary Chain, Teardrop Explodes, Bunnymen, for example).

I met them in London where they were playing. What struck me was that they were much better live than the singles I'd heard had led me to believe. It was a relatively short set (50 minutes) with no frills and no encores – just unbridled energy. And the audience loved them. So I could tell they had something going for

Single of the week in Sounds *for 'My Favourite Dress'*

SOMETIMES THESE WORDS **JUST DON'T HAVE TO BE SAID** 57

The Wedding Present

them because you really can't fool fans. There was a commitment there on both sides. I was also aware that they had a strong regional fanbase, particularly in the North and North West, and the singles thus far had done well in the indie charts. It was the kind of fanbase that could easily propel a band into the pop charts in time.

I was even more impressed by their attitude off-stage and how self-contained they were. It was just the four of them, no roadies, no entourage; they all had their roles and just got on with it. Meeting bands for the first time is always difficult. They tend to be quite wary of outsiders coming in and it always takes a while to earn their trust and respect. I only remember talking to David and Peter but I must have come away thinking, 'I can work with this lot, they are smart and they know what they want.' If I hadn't liked them or thought they were going to be impossible I would have turned the job down. Their independence was still something of a badge of honour and a good calling card with the press.

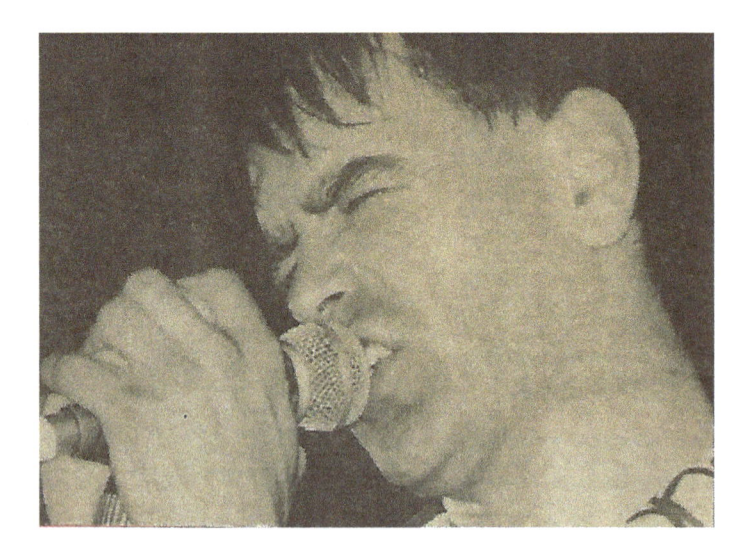

Ready for his close-up: David onstage in May 1987

STALLONE'S
19 FEBRUARY 1987, LEEDS, UK

JOHN DOIDGE

Being only 16, the first challenge was getting through the door. We made it in successfully, and saw This Poison!, the support band with whom we later became good friends and who subsequently got us on many a Wedding Present guest list.

The gig was incredible. I spent half of it on my mate's shoulders and the place was one huge moshpit. A lot of the Leeds United fans followed the band in those days and they were out in force that night. The Wedding Present played very late and afterwards I asked David and Keith whether they'd put us up for the night. I slept on Leeds City Station before going to school the next morning.

1987: My Favourite Band

MAJESTIC BALLROOM

25 FEBRUARY 1987, READING, UK

MALCOLM WYATT

I was 18 when I first became aware of The Wedding Present, courtesy of John Peel's championing of the band.

I can't recall how soon I started snapping up the singles, but I soon had copies of the 'Don't Try And Stop Me, Mother', 'My Favourite Dress' and 'Peel Sessions' 12"s as well as that seminal *NME* cassette, *C86*. Yet it took a while before I finally clapped eyes on them.

HUDDERSFIELD POLYTECHNIC

13 MAY 1987, HUDDERSFIELD, UK

NIGEL PRESTON

My standout gig memory is Huddersfield Polytechnic, when I first heard 'Take Me!' live. [David Gedge: 'That's interesting, because it wasn't written until 1988!'] As an impressionable 18-year-old I was stood at the front, right in front of David, as he was bent over his guitar, grimace of pain on his sweat dripping face, thrashing away at a quadzillion miles per hour. I remember looking up in awe and thinking, 'He's killing himself for me.' After all these years I still get goosebumps thinking about it.

Wedding Present concert poster, May 1987

SOMETIMES THESE WORDS **JUST DON'T HAVE TO BE SAID**

The Wedding Present

SHEFFIELD UNIVERSITY

11 MAY 1987, SHEFFIELD, UK

TIM MORTON

It's 1987. I've wrapped up secondary school and have recently started attending design school in Sheffield with a weekend and odd weekday job in a supermarket at Manor Top where I'm sanitized with Sixties and Seventies gentrified pop covers pushed through the supermarket speakers as I align biscuit packets diligently.

It's 6.30pm on a Monday and I'm out like a shot, switching the grey overcoat and nylon slacks for denim jacket and black Levis – I'm off to see The Wedding Present for the first time! I hop on the bus, meet up with four school friends and surge to Sheffield University. A sweaty ear-thudding couple of hours or so later we emerge electrified into the chilled night air, T-shirts in hand, with tales of lost shoes and our hearing muted.

Team Wedding Present, including two girlfriends, The Netherlands, May 1987

GLASTONBURY FESTIVAL

20 JUNE 1987, GLASTONBURY, UK

STEPHEN WARD

I was 19 and went with my 16-year-old sister. I hired a car for my dad to drive down from County Durham and drop us off at the top of the campsite road.

He then drove to his aunt's in Slough and came back and picked us up. We didn't have a watch, and lived on crisps and chocolate and chips for the weekend. Oh to be young again!

1987: My Favourite Band

KEVIN PAPWORTH

I was at Glastonbury, waiting for Red Lorry Yellow Lorry to come on stage. I wasn't really into them. Then an announcement: Red Lorry Yellow Lorry had cancelled and been replaced by The Wedding Present. On stage in one minute! I exploded with happiness and had a complete blast bouncing around to my favourite songs. The best band of the festival.

LEEDS POLY

26 JUNE 1987, LEEDS, UK

REV TIM GOODBODY

It's all a bit of blur, really. The support band was claiming their guitarist was Jim Reid out of Jesus And Mary Chain. Maybe it really was him. This was around the 'Ukrainian' period. I remember getting a T-shirt with the Ukrainian text. Funnily enough, when it was all kicking off in Ukraine the other year, I revisited that part of the canon to assist in my prayers for that country – I'm a vicar now.

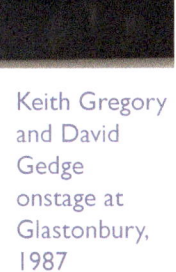

Keith Gregory and David Gedge onstage at Glastonbury, 1987

STUART BAIRD

I first heard The Wedding Present on John Peel at my mate's house in 1987. It was just such a fabulous sound and we went up to Leeds Poly to see them live. I thought I loved them on the radio, but live was just like nothing else I had seen – the 'wall of sound' guitars were just phenomenal. The first single I remember buying was 'Nobody's Twisting Your Arm' at Crash Records in Leeds. Up until The Wedding Present it had all been a bit of a mishmash of music – The Mission and The Cult, The Smiths,

SOMETIMES THESE WORDS **JUST DON'T HAVE TO BE SAID**

The Wedding Present

New Order, a bit of Clash and post-punk. I was just a 17-year-old wannabe indie kid in a Yorkshire mining village where the tunes down the local pubs were Stock, Aitken & Waterman stuff.

We were square pegs in round holes – Pulp's 'Misfits' song summed it up. When my mate's brother turned 14 we filled a telephone box full of balloons, like the promo vid of 'Nobody's Twisting Your Arm', and stuffed him in it to take pictures. People walked past us like we were barking mad. The Wedding Present for me were the stand out. They proved there was another life, another way of doing stuff. For me, they became part of that 'finding your own identity' thing. Although I liked the music, I wasn't old enough to remember punk, or for it to have a significant influence on me or my mates. I guess the North's indie scene was our punk. When we went off to uni, we congregated around like-minded souls into the indie scene, from London or Newcastle, Plymouth or Brighton. We spoke a common language.

WILLIAM POTTER

In spring 1987, CUD had just a few local gigs under our belt and a portastudio demo recorded at Leeds Poly. This happened to reach the Wedding Present tour bus. A short time later, wearing my self-printed CUD T-shirt, I bumped into Wedding Present drummer Shaun Charman outside the Poly and he astonished me by recognising our band logo and admiring our rough-and-ready songs. We were offered a support slot and chance to release a record on The Wedding Present's Reception label on the spot. (I still have a cool cassette collection of Wedding Present songs the

William Potter (far left), bass player with CUD. They played several Wedding Present support slots (see flyers opposite) and their first single, 'You're The Boss', was released on The Wedding Present's Reception record label

1987: My Favourite Band

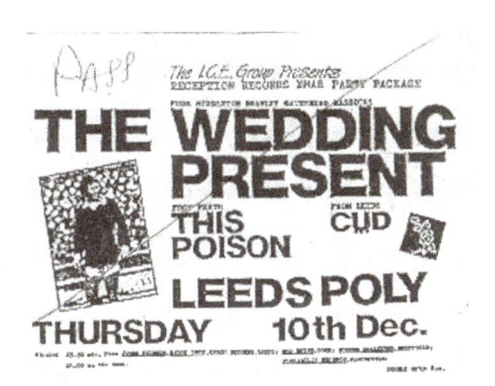

generous Shaun gave me.) Scrambling together £50, the eager CUD bashed out three tracks at Leeds' tiny Lion Studios for our first release. In another case of good fortune, John Peel had just announced he was clearing the decks and listening to all new demos to be sent in. We posted this trio of tracks and were rewarded with a Peel session of our own, which was aired just four days after our gig with The Wedding Present at Leeds Poly. It was a mind-blowing month. We splurged our Peel session money on, admittedly, inferior 24-track recordings for our Reception Records 12", but it fared well enough for us to continue making records. And we played a couple more shows with The Wedding Present now we had a bit of a name ourselves. Thanks to The Wedding Present's early mentorship, CUD had a fair crack at the music business. We supported the band again on their 1989 *Bizarro* tour and, following our reunion, we enjoyed a couple of sets at The Wedding Present's excellent At The Edge Of The Sea festivals and Gigantic. We owe a great deal to the band, who gave us such a break, and it's been an absolute pleasure to watch them live from the front and side of stage for three decades now.

MILKY BAR
11 SEPTEMBER 1987, CARDIFF, UK

PAUL WIGLEY

A small club on Charles Street. I was sceptical as I did not like many *C86* type bands. But I ended up being blown away. Aged 19, I had a very

The Wedding Present

poor first year in university and this gig cheered me up hugely, followed a few months later at ULU for the *George Best* tour. The band left a big impression on the young men of the Upper Rhondda, who would roam from pub to pub singing songs from *George Best* and *Bizarro*. I got to interview David Gedge in Oxford in 1992, and Amelia Fletcher (who did some backing vocals for the band) a few weeks later. I still love the band nearly 30 years later and when I saw them in Manchester not so long ago, I drank far too much for an overweight, middle-aged professor – and was even jumping around.

PAUL WARMAN

The Milky Bar was my first time, and they're probably my second 'most seen' band. I've seen them live every time they come to Cardiff, in London, at festivals and also in New York. But even then I was too shy to speak to David, as I didn't know what to say.

PETER SOLOWKA

Every single thing we did in the early days was really exciting. The first time you make a single. The first time you're playing London. The first time you tour Britain. The first time you do an album. In the early days we did it all ourselves. It was only when we got to the first album that we involved a manager, because there were too many things to do. When you're only doing a few shows yourself, you can ring up the venues, organise it, get it all sorted, get all the transport done. But if you're doing more than 30 shows a year you can't do it. Or someone's got to help you do it in some way, because you just can't keep track of everything. We were very organised – there's no doubt about that. We were very independent. This idea of being an indie band – it's not that you do every single thing yourself. But you can do a lot more than, traditionally, you might think you can. Indie for me is deciding how you want to sound. We could work things out for ourselves. If we were going to do a video, we decided what it looked like. We decided what the album artwork would be. We took all the decisions that record labels in the past had done for the artist.

1987: My Favourite Band

GEORGE BEST
THE DEBUT ALBUM
RELEASED 12 OCTOBER 1987

PETER SOLOWKA

Chris Allison was somebody that our new manager suggested as a producer, because we definitely didn't want to use a producer who was established in a style.

It's all right saying you shouldn't work with a producer, but if you're recording in a high-tech recording studio and you don't have a lot of experience of working in those environments, you need to have somebody who knows what they're doing otherwise you just make a mess of it.

So we sought somebody who was relatively young. He'd only worked on a couple of small projects before. It had to be somebody who wasn't tainted by the business too much.

Chris was the producer who made our sound interesting. But I don't think it's interesting because he wanted it to be that way. He actually set a very, very strong foundation and sometimes he's not given credit for this.

He did things with the drums that had never been done before, the way he sequenced them. He had computer sequencing of our drums so that we could actually make sure that the tempo changes, the timing, absolutely everything, was spot on to get the right dynamic in the song. And then we put the sound on top of it.

CHRIS ALLISON
Producer, George Best

I started off at SARM Studios in 1984 in London, which was owned by Trevor Horn. There I was introduced to the 'new gods' of the studio: the Fairlight and the Synclavier. These were programming and sampling tools which Trevor Horn and Steve Lipson used to great effect on sessions that they were working on at the time – Frankie Goes To Hollywood, ABC, Yes, Art Of Noise, Propaganda. Nowadays you can get a sampler and sequencer for virtually nothing but back then the Fairlight was £60,000 or £70,000, so there were probably fewer than a hundred of them in the country.

The Wedding Present

I got pretty familiar with it and I went freelance, programming them and working on projects in studios in the UK and Europe. I did all sorts of stuff, from Iggy Pop and The Triffids to *The Kingdom Of The Ice Bear*, a three-part BBC TV series.

In the majority of these sessions you'd be asked to come up with the same sort of sounds that Trevor Horn had been coming up with – the classic brass stabs and the Fairlight voices. I was paid well, but it wasn't particularly creative – I was being asked to come up with the same thing over and over again. I really wanted to work with some live bands. I met The Wedding Present's first manager Brian Hallin. He took me on as a music producer, and my first gig was 'My Favourite Dress'!

The programming skills I had developed were quite relevant to the situation that The Wedding Present found themselves in when recording their first record inasmuch as, while the ethic that they had of the loud guitars and the DIY nature was a really good ethic to have, it was a little too shambolic in terms of the actual drumming and the tuning and they didn't pay too much attention to it. Some of the great punk and new wave bands retained that indie DIY ethic in their sound but made sure that they played in time and in tune because it's just more listenable.

David and the band had their own very strong vision as to how they wanted to sound so it was difficult to make many inroads in making suggestions on that front whether it be in the studio recording or when we came to mix. I think that was fine for the *George Best* album. I think it was a strong album with some good tunes and great lyrics.

The added pressure that bands don't often feel because the producer usually takes it off them is the financial pressure that, 'This has got to be done under a certain budget in a certain time.' So we had a certain budget to do it and come up with a great result and this was the best way I could think of doing it within that time and budget.

What we had was a problem with the timekeeping of the drums and what I proposed wasn't a normal thing to do. It was a fairly drastic idea. I was not going to say, 'Use another drummer.' They're a band. That is all-important.

So I had to devise a way of helping

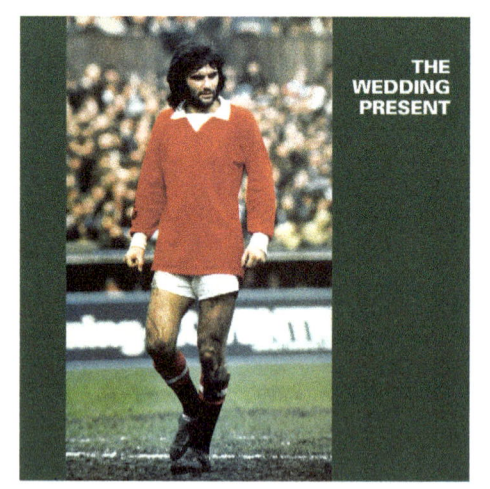

George Best: one of football's greatest players adorned the cover of one of indie music's greatest albums

1987: My Favourite Band

HAVING A BALL

THE WEDDING PRESENT 'George Best' (Reception LEEDS 1)*****

AT LAST, pop pickers, you can throw your despondency out of the window because it is here, it has finally arrived, the all new, all powerful, debut Wedding Present album, 'George Best'. Forget The Shop Assistants' and The Lemon Drops' first albums, 'George Best' is the one, simply because it refuses to be anything but a blistering racket of sheer exhilarating pop noise.

I know enthusiasm was last year's thing, but I can't help it with 'George Best'. Other critics will probably hate it for being totally unlike the 'post modern pop' that is all the rage at the moment. They'll no doubt blab on about The Wedding Present being too monochrome and they'll try to connect this music with tweeness, anoraks and frustrated virginity to underline their arguments. Well, stuff 'em! I know what I like and I like this and you will too.

So what makes it so special? Firstly, and ultimately, the guitars. They're always right up there, showering down in torrents and emphasising the emotions behind Dave Gedge's simply phrased lyrics. I'm not sure whether this is the closest pop has come to hardcore or vice-versa, but the last time I heard such a spectrum of monumental guitars was on the latest Hüsker Dü album.

Every guitar intro, especially in the classic 'My Favourite Dress' and 'You Can't Moan Can You', leaves you with the anticipation of a changed world.

Beside the rattling, shimmering, vibrating melodies that skittle merrily through 'George Best', there's a sombre world weariness that cries from the back of Gedge's voice. Meanwhile, the songs have the same down to earth, boy next door feel that made Billy Bragg such a genius with love songs.

'George Best' is a great album, packed with great songs, great guitars and great lyrics. It's an album to cuddle up to this winter and recollect past moments with.

SOUNDS   **RON ROM**

THE WEDDING Present: well, Gary Lineker's a bit pricey these days.

Back of the net: George Best scores with Sounds

the band in a way that they would be happy with. The way I did it was to use a Simmons drum kit, which was made up of hexagonal electronic drum pads with MIDI outputs that could be connected to a MIDI device. A Fairlight would have been way over the top, so I used Steinberg sequencer software running on an Atari ST computer, meaning you could record the playing of the Simmons drum kit into this sequencer so it would record not the sounds but the notes. The sounds would be generated by the Akai S900 sampler, which was one of the first samplers with a reasonably quick trigger time.

The Wedding Present

We did this in a rehearsal room, not a studio. We had Shaun and the band play so he was playing this Simmons kit connected up to the sequencer. We would record each track into the sequencer keeping the swing of the tempos. After they'd got a good take, I would go painstakingly through correcting the obvious bits that were out and which were making it too shambolic.

Overall, we're talking about hundreds of corrections per track, not just with the timing but the velocity at which the drum samples were being triggered in order to keep it authentic sounding. Throughout this process it was essential to keep the style in which Shaun was drumming preserved.

We sampled Shaun's drum kit or other drums into the Akai S900 sampler and triggered these sounds on snare drum, bass drum and each tom from the sequencer. When we were in the studio and the band was all playing together again, Shaun would play his hi-hat and other cymbals to the sequencer.

So this way we were able to get some sort of consistency through the record that I think really helped getting a good end result. I think it made the record more listenable. It's no fun for a drummer to be put in this position. I think it's going to affect anyone. There was tension, and it was understandable, I was essentially undermining Shaun's ability. I was trying to iron out the issue of the drum timekeeping in the most sensitive way, in the best way I could think of that was going to get a positive result for everyone.

I probably got a bit more flak than necessary, but in some ways it was understandable. That's what happens when you walk into a studio with a band that's been together for a certain period. You're becoming a temporary member and it's best not to tread on too many toes while making it work for everybody.

How a dodgy curry could have killed *George Best*

The album was recorded at Easy Studios. We also spent two weeks at the Strongroom Studios near Brick Lane in London. We were only a few days into the *George Best* album session and the whole band and I ordered a takeaway from an Indian restaurant nearby. Within twenty minutes we were all queuing up for the studio toilets.

It was quite a serious case of food poisoning. We had to cancel the sessions for us all to recover, which in some cases took two weeks as the poisoning had been serious. Studio owner Richard Boot was very understanding, allowing us to reschedule a few weeks later and not charging us for the missed studio time.

Chris Allison

1987: My Favourite Band

A George Best *plastic bag is for life, not just a debut album*

Many gigging band's thoughts are that they want a recording to sound the same as a listener hears in the front row at a gig. But how you go about that is a different matter. In theory, it would be great to just set up the recording equipment, invite an audience and just have them play. But you just end up overdubbing a lot of stuff because of mistakes, timing or tuning and having to do retakes because not every single version that they're going to do live is going to be how they want it. In an ideal world, it'd be great to capture a live sound perfectly, but it's just not quite as simple as that if you want to create a great sounding record that can be played over and over. With technology now it would be even easier and one could probably make the drum sounds even better. I don't think anyone at the time picked up on the fact that those drums were done with the aid of a sequencer and drum samples. And Shaun shouldn't feel too bad about it because he still ultimately played it all.

We had to constantly reassess the tuning because, when they're playing their guitars that hard and fast, the tuning goes out quite rapidly. At a gig, you don't really notice it so much but on a record it's easier for the ear to detect. So we would constantly be tuning the guitars in the studio. I think Peter ended up using one of my guitars as it was holding its tuning a bit better – he eventually bought it off me and used it for gigs!

SOMETIMES THESE WORDS **JUST DON'T HAVE TO BE SAID**

The Wedding Present

SHAUN CHARMAN

We took a step up with every single: a step up with 'Once More', a step up with 'You Should Always Keep In Touch With Your Friends' and 'My Favourite Dress'. And then, obviously, when the album came out it was something completely different altogether.

When I talk to Wedding Present fans now, there are different camps. Indie kids still like *George Best*, though some of the more diehard fans prefer *Seamonsters*. Often it depends on the album they heard first, though people can also be quite insensitive about telling me.

When it came to Chris Allison producing that album, the way that they recorded some of it – the drums and stuff – I was really deeply suspicious of it. I always wanted to make a first album that sounded like a first album. I've always had a thing about first albums, and I just wanted ours to be a classic, exciting first album. I didn't mind the idea of experimenting afterwards, with the second or third or whatever, but I wanted the first album to be like we sounded live.

We had a manager (Brian Hallin) who wanted us to use his producer, and the drums were recorded on an electronic kit, with the cymbals put on afterwards, and I really didn't like that. I still think it sounds like a drum machine on the album.

PETER SOLOWKA

It's the first big project. When you realise you've got enough tracks and you can do something better, you think of making an album. I don't think it was put together with the idea of putting together an album. Some bands have a theme or an idea, a style they want to portray. But I think we were just putting together all of the songs we had at the time.

We used to write songs so fast in those days. They did tend to be the same because we'd write all of them in the space of a few months.

It was good to work with producers that were forward thinking as well. Surprisingly, on *George Best* and on other albums too, we used quite a lot of technology at the time. We did a lot of sampling of drums. It wasn't just the band in a room with a couple of microphones. It was a quite technical procedure.

Chris wanted to be a bit more traditional-rocky with loud vocals and guitars in the background so you could hear every word and we were having none of it. There was quite a lot of discussion. I suppose from Chris Allison's point of view, he wants to produce a record that he thinks is going to show him in a good light as well. His idea of a well-produced record was not the same as ours. There were discussions about that,

1987: My Favourite Band

> "Fast lifestyle. Fast band. Loads of gigs. Living together, writing a song, just recording it as we played it. We enjoyed it"
>
> Peter Solowka

certainly, very heated discussions on many occasions. And in the end I think it's all right saying it's exactly our sound but if it wasn't for Chris Allison doing some things to it… it's still a team effort even though it's not recognised as such, although we had to push Chris a long way away from where he wanted to be.

STEVE LYON
Engineer, *George Best*

I'd just turned 23 and I'd come back from the States. I was working at George Martin's AIR Studios in London, above Oxford Circus. I'd been headhunted by one of the engineers that I knew called John Jacobs. I'd been assisting and then I started to engineer at AIR, which was a prestigious studio.

I'd worked there about a year. Everyone was using SSL consoles, of which there were two at the studio, and there was this Neve V3 console in one of the little rooms and no one used it very much.

Thanks to the management there, I'd done a couple of things on my own and I'd brought in some work and I'd done a bit of mixing. And they said, 'Listen, this band called The Wedding Present want to come in and want to mix.' I think the budget was relatively small at the time – no one really talked to us about budgets, we just worked there – and they asked me if I wanted to do it. And I said, 'Yeah, sure.'

I did, as one could do through *NME* or *Sounds* or whatever, a bit of research on them and they came in with Chris Allison, who was their producer. And they threw the stuff at me and said, 'Well this is what we want it to sound like.' They were playing all this indie kind of stuff; some of it was The Pixies.

The guy who trained me was Glyn Johns. He's worked with The Who and one thing and another. So I'd already decided that if they wanted a sound that was edgier and rougher there were certain things you'd do on the two-track tape to make it, not distorted, but a little bit edgy depending on how hot you would print it, how much level you would

The Wedding Present

Steve Lyon, the man who mixed George Best and who worked with the band again on Bizarro, then with EMF, The Cure, Drugstore, Depeche Mode and many others

put onto the tape. Everyone was happy and that was the end of that.

We'd get to the end of what Chris had decided what he wanted with the mix and then Chris would leave the room and the band would come in, sit down with me and go 'Well actually, what we want is this'. Which was lots of guitars really up front. I was 'OK, that's cool' because I came from a punk listening background.

And they wanted the drums not so ambient, a bit straighter, and a bit more distortion on the bass. That was it. So we would come up with a version. I wasn't privy to any – let's call them 'discussions' – between band and producer. There were times when there were some discussions and I wasn't in the room. And basically that's how it went with the whole thing. I really loved the record. I thought the songs were great and I really, really liked the guys. I was quite young and they were very young.

DAVID GEDGE

I wouldn't say *George Best* didn't reflect the way the band sounded because I think we did sound like that at the time. I think it's more of a case of, when I listen to it now, that it sounds quite one-dimensional. And that's our fault, I think. Or my fault, as the main songwriter. Since then, we... or I... have learnt how to write songs and

1987: My Favourite Band

> "There was kind of a difference between what Chris wanted and what the band wanted and I was thrown in the middle"
>
> Steve Lyon

arrange songs and record songs better. I appreciate that there's a certain charm and naivety to *George Best* but it still sounds disappointing to me now. I think there should probably be more variety in it, more depth to it. It's fantastic to play live, though! It's an energetic live set, *George Best*. But it's definitely my least favourite album.

MICK HOUGHTON

What really won the *NME* and the music press in general round – although bar one or two hard core fans, *Melody Maker* hated The Wedding Present – was the genius move of calling their album *George Best* and using that classic image on the front.

It was an album that was far better than the sum of its parts; it established David as a songwriter whereas, before that, The Wedding Present signified a sound, a harder-core, fast paced variant on jangly indie pop. They did become the band that indie fans who didn't like The Smiths loved. They were the band for anybody who wanted a more down-to-earth frontman, who was less lyrically fanciful than Morrissey. David was fast becoming the indie Everyman.

PETER SOLOWKA

George Best is the passion of youth, finally finding something new you can do and doing it differently. It was done with a great smile on your face and a great 'Hurrah! Look at what we do. This is who we are' and that definitely makes a statement. It was 120 gigs a year and no sleep.

And every single person in every town that you met, you ended up sleeping on their floor because you couldn't afford anything else. That sort of lifestyle is what we were doing for *George Best*. It was rough and harsh and fast and furious. You can hear it on the album.

The Wedding Present

WEST INDIAN CENTRE

12 OCTOBER 1987, MANCHESTER, UK

EDWARD BOWEN

I'd already seen the band a few times, but this was going to be a really special gig. It was only a quarter of a mile from my digs on Great Western Street, Rusholme. I was still pretending to be at university even though I'd crashed out really badly that summer.

It was also just three days before my birthday and, to cap it all, it was the day that *George Best* was released. I'd been to Piccadilly Records that morning – or afternoon, more likely – and bought the vinyl LP in its special *George Best* carrier bag.

The West Indian Centre was a strange choice of venue, a bit like a community centre with quite a low ceiling. I'd managed to strike up a bit of a rapport with Keith Gregory at earlier gigs and sought him out as soon as I arrived. I told him I'd been playing the LP all day and he asked where I bought it from. 'Piccadilly Records.' Keith: 'Ah, did you get the free 7" single with it?' Me: 'No!' 'How about the free fanzine?' Me: 'Er, no!' Keith: 'Follow me.'

He then took me to the 'backstage' area where he produced the *Invasion Of The Wedding Present* fanzine and 'My Favourite Dress' 7" on white vinyl.

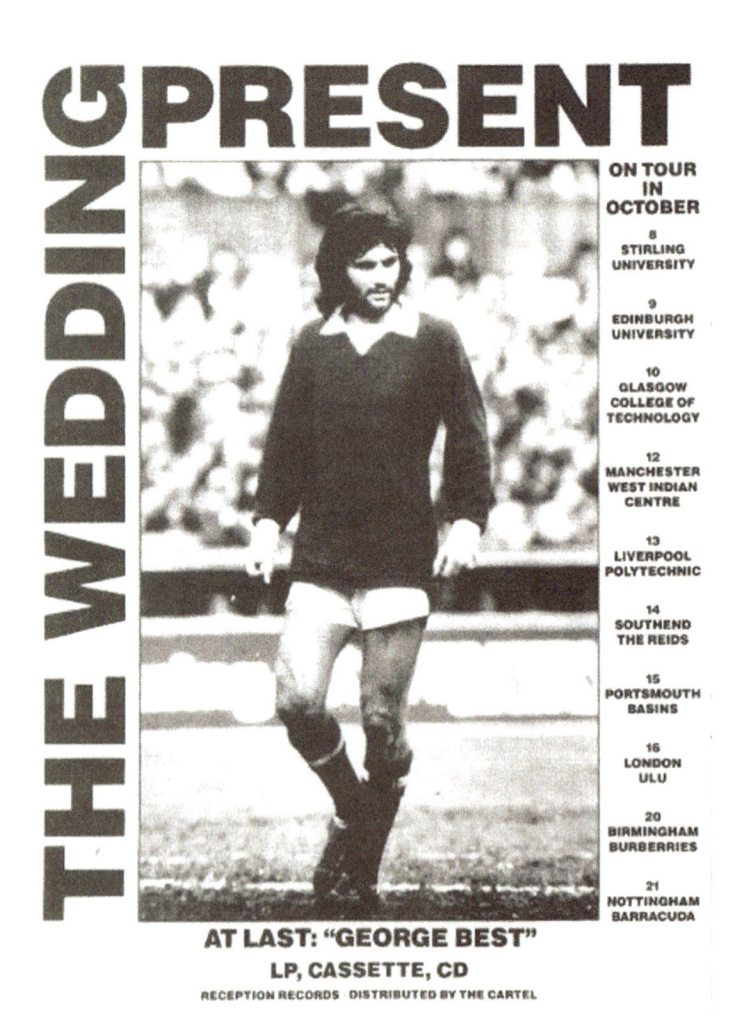

There'd been some sort of cock-up with the distribution or something. Then he says, 'Here you go, have this as well' and gave me a white label single of two tracks from the LP! To my shame, I can't remember what they are.

Poster for The Wedding Present's UK tour promoting their mighty, influential debut album

1987: My Favourite Band

ULU
16 OCTOBER 1987, LONDON, UK

ROBERT LILLY

I had fallen in love with *George Best* – 'Everyone Thinks He Looks Daft' and 'A Million Miles' in particular. But the previous night had brought that fantastic storm. We feared it would be called off. Fortunately our fears were groundless. By the time of *Seamonsters*, I had recruited a few friends to the cause who wouldn't normally go near indie. Still to this day, a mate who loved the song 'Dare' will recount 'And Gedgey walked on stage and said, "Good evening, we're The Wedding Present – and there's just one more thing…"' before launching into the tour de force that was that song. Personally I used to love, love, love the way they would just extend and extend the riffs to particular songs so they went on for ages once all the singing had been done, in particular 'My Favourite Dress' (that driving bass line) and 'Flying Saucer'.

MALCOLM WYATT

I still remember the heady excitement of my first few plays of that debut album, many of the songs already well known to us by the time they were committed to vinyl. That gave us a real sense of ownership… and pride. From 'Everyone Thinks He Looks Daft' onwards, we had an instant classic that really resonated with this late teen – those clanging guitars and songs of love lost and found seeming to address me personally.

LEEDS POLYTECHNIC
10 DECEMBER 1987, LEEDS, UK

SHAUN CHARMAN

George Best made the biggest difference. There was one particular gig at Leeds Poly in December 1987 where, when we played 'A Million Miles', you could hear the crowd singing over the top. It was one of those moments where

The Wedding Present

George Best makes it into HMV Oxford Street

I was flat out at AIR – I'd not really been in touch with the guys and I was too busy to go and see them play. So it only seemed like a couple of weeks later when I was walking down Oxford Circus, past the front window of HMV on Oxford Street. I remember seeing *George Best* by The Wedding Present in the window. And I was like, 'You gotta be kidding me!' because you never know where these things are going to go. I was like, 'Wow, that's amazing' and I was really made up for the guys. 'That's brilliant.' It was Record Of The Month. I was blown away and I actually went in and bought a copy of the vinyl, because very early on in my career I'd made a promise to myself that whatever I worked on I would actually go and physically buy a copy of. And I've still got it.

Steve Lyon

you felt a shiver down your spine. And whatever it felt like for me I wonder what it must have felt like for David – everyone singing the lyrics back to him. We'd never been particularly popular in Leeds above other places, but as the lights went down, there were 'We are Leeds' football chants and the gig was amazing. It is still weird for me to go to a gig where *George Best* is being played from beginning to end, watching it from the audience. I even supported them doing that set with my current band The Fireworks. I was really nervous because it felt so strange. It's an odd thing, but a good thing though. A mixture of weird and 'it's great people still want to hear that album after so long'.

JON PINDER

It was the Reception Records 1987 Christmas bash. I was in the fifth year of secondary school. Me and my friend Knighty were giddy about seeing the band for the first time and were right at the front of the stage getting crushed by the crowd.

Carl Puttnam of CUD must have seen how excitable we were and pushed the mic into Knighty's face for him to shout 'art!' in the song of the same name. Although he didn't know the tune, it was pretty obvious what the lyric was and what was expected of him.

When The Wedding Present came on Peter Solowka was sporting a rather fetching plastic face mask, one

1987: My Favourite Band

of those solid things you don't really see much anymore which was held on by a piece of white elastic. It was a Star Wars stormtrooper, or Darth Vader, but had been customised with a purple-and-black paint job. Those things encourage your face to sweat, so it was quickly dropped by the monitor and my quick hands were straight there to grab me a piece of Wedding Present ephemera. It's still in my ex-wife's loft.

PAVILION THEATRE
18 DECEMBER 1987, BRIGHTON, UK

JON LEET

The first time I ever saw The Wedding Present I was 17. Every Sunday evening on BBC Radio Sussex and immediately after the Top 40, the second finest programme championing music from the independent scene was broadcast: *Turn It Up*. With its mix of records, interviews and competitions, it was essential weekly listening for two hours. The rota of volunteer presenters included one Richard Osman, a former student at Hayward's Heath sixth form college and regular indie kid. He went on to play bass in Suede.

Every year, *Turn It Up* hosted a Christmas party. This year it was The Wedding Present. What a signing. *George Best* had been on our record decks continuously in the preceding weeks, having been released in October, and now we'd get to see the boy Gedge and co. for real.

And so it was that myself, Big Al and Hasley were in attendance that evening. It was the first of many Wedding Present experiences but the

The 'Anyone Can Make A Mistake' single sleeve, 1987

The Wedding Present

only one where we witnessed – and took part in – a stage invasion. I remember being onstage during 'You Should Always Keep In Touch With Your Friends'. Many years later, at Exeter Phoenix 2009, I chatted with David during one of his stints on the merchandise stall and recalled my first Weddoes gig. Quick as a flash he made the link – 'That was the night of the stage invasion.' I confessed to being part of it and he didn't look too impressed. Well, anyone can make a mistake!

In December 1987, drummer Shaun Charman was asked to leave the band...

DAVID GEDGE

Although he learned the drums to be in the band, Shaun was never really that comfortable with being a drummer. Ultimately he began to hold the group back a bit, I think. He was always threatening to leave and in the end we asked him to. But it wasn't because of the playing.

Removing someone from the band is always distressing. A group is a tight knit organization so it's an upsetting time for them and for you. But then you acquire a new person who has a whole new set of ideas and enthusiasm and you move on. That's exactly what happened when Simon Smith joined.

MICK HOUGHTON

Shaun leaving wasn't unusual; drummers always seem to be the first to go.

PETER SOLOWKA

We were all amazingly young and hot-headed. And to be honest, looking back on the way we behaved with each other, we were all – I hate saying this – pretty immature.

There's nothing adult about the way we behaved with each other. If you think about the lifestyle we were all leading: by the time I was travelling around in bands and stuff, most of the people I'd grown up with at school

1987: My Favourite Band

had already had nine-to-five jobs for ten years. They were married and had kids and stuff and a completely different relationship pattern. For us, all in our mid-to-late twenties, we were still extended teenagers. I think we looked at life and relationships very, very much that way as well. I don't think for one minute, if we were all in a band together now, that we'd in any way behave towards each other like we did then. We were in each other's faces 24/7. Even for adults you'd have to find ways to try and get personal space.

Now, when I'm on tour with The Ukrainians, even though the line-up I'm in has been stable for eight years or so and we're all older blokes – we're all in our late forties or our fifties – there's still the desire to find personal space. You know when you've got to do it and people just wander off for a couple of hours sometimes. Or get a book and bury themselves in it while they're in the van for three or four hours.

And you just know they don't want to speak to you. It's that understanding, that people know that, which I don't think we had when we were that young. It would be David driving back after the gigs. He was the only driver at the time. If it was London we'd stay overnight on people's floors. But anywhere in the Midlands or around there we'd drive back home overnight and unload all the stuff at three or four in the morning. And of course because we had nothing else to do there was tons of tension and a lack of sleep. Everything was passionate. Everything was intense. Everything had to be at that moment. That's how it had to be.

SHAUN CHARMAN

It was my address on the back of the singles, so I was doing the mail and organising gigs, and practices, but I think I lost sight of the group as being David's band with his songs. I didn't handle the transition very well.

I understand a bit more of David's position these days. I realise that the songwriter must ultimately be happy with their songs, so true democracy isn't possible.

I think you have to take it back to the context of the time, because when I say I was worried about selling out, that seems a bit ridiculous when you think about what came afterwards... but at the time we were releasing 'Nobody's Twisting Your Arm'. Things were getting poppier and I was very suspicious of our management trying to water us down, trying to crack the charts. In the end they cracked the charts anyway... but it looked very different in the autumn of 1987.

We played about 150 gigs in 1986, which also affected how I felt. Paul Dorrington later commented about his experience of being in The Wedding Present as 'four years in a van'. I like travelling, but I was one of those people

The Wedding Present

who did get homesick. 150 gigs in a year is a lot. I remember bursting into tears in Switzerland once because I just wanted to go home. I just wanted to do my laundry, watch telly, see my friends, have a pint, not be told where to be all the time. And then there were 120, 130 gigs or something in 1987. I was pretty worn out, and agents didn't always seem to have a map when they arranged the tours! Some of the gigs were hundreds of miles apart, especially in Europe. My style was not very economical with energy. At the end of gigs, it would generally be David at one end of the dressing room, me at the other, steaming with sweat, while Peter and Keith were able to talk to people. So I think I was a bit worn out as well.

By the time that Christmas came around (1987) relations between us were not good. But the letter telling me I was out of the band came totally out of the blue, though I had thought about leaving.

My parents did say afterwards, 'But we thought you wanted to leave?' If we'd been older, I think a chat would have sorted it out, one way or the other. If we'd had that conversation I might well have left of my own accord, but if I hadn't, we would have at least understood what was going on.

1988: Nobody's Twisting Your Arm

1988 was a quieter year in terms of Wedding Present gigs, as they recruited a new drummer to replace Shaun Charman and found themselves performing Ukrainian music for John Peel. There was also the fact that their record label's distributor was going into liquidation…

TRENT POLYTECHNIC

17 FEBRUARY 1988, NOTTINGHAM, UK

ROB FLEAY

As a 17-year-old, I wrote to David Gedge after buying *George Best* to tell him how much I liked the album and asking if they would ever play in my home town of Derby. He wrote back and said that they had already played Derby a couple of years earlier, and that it was their first non-Leeds gig. He said if I could make the Nottingham gig in February 1988 he would put me on the guest list. I blagged a lift with my friend Woody to find that my name was very much not on the guest list. I ended up paying to get in and hung around outside afterwards to have it out with David! He apologised profusely and gave me four cans of Holsten Pils from their rider as a gift. I kept those then empty cans on top of the wardrobe for years.

BIERKELLER

18 FEBRUARY 1988, BRISTOL, UK

PAUL WARMAN

I was down at the front for the Bristol Bierkeller gig, and being young and foolish and dancing away, I lost my watch. Now, a Wedding Present gig

The Wedding Present

Ballooning outward: The Wedding Present on *NME*'s cover in February 1988, without Shaun Charman.

82 SOMETIMES THESE WORDS JUST DON'T HAVE TO BE SAID

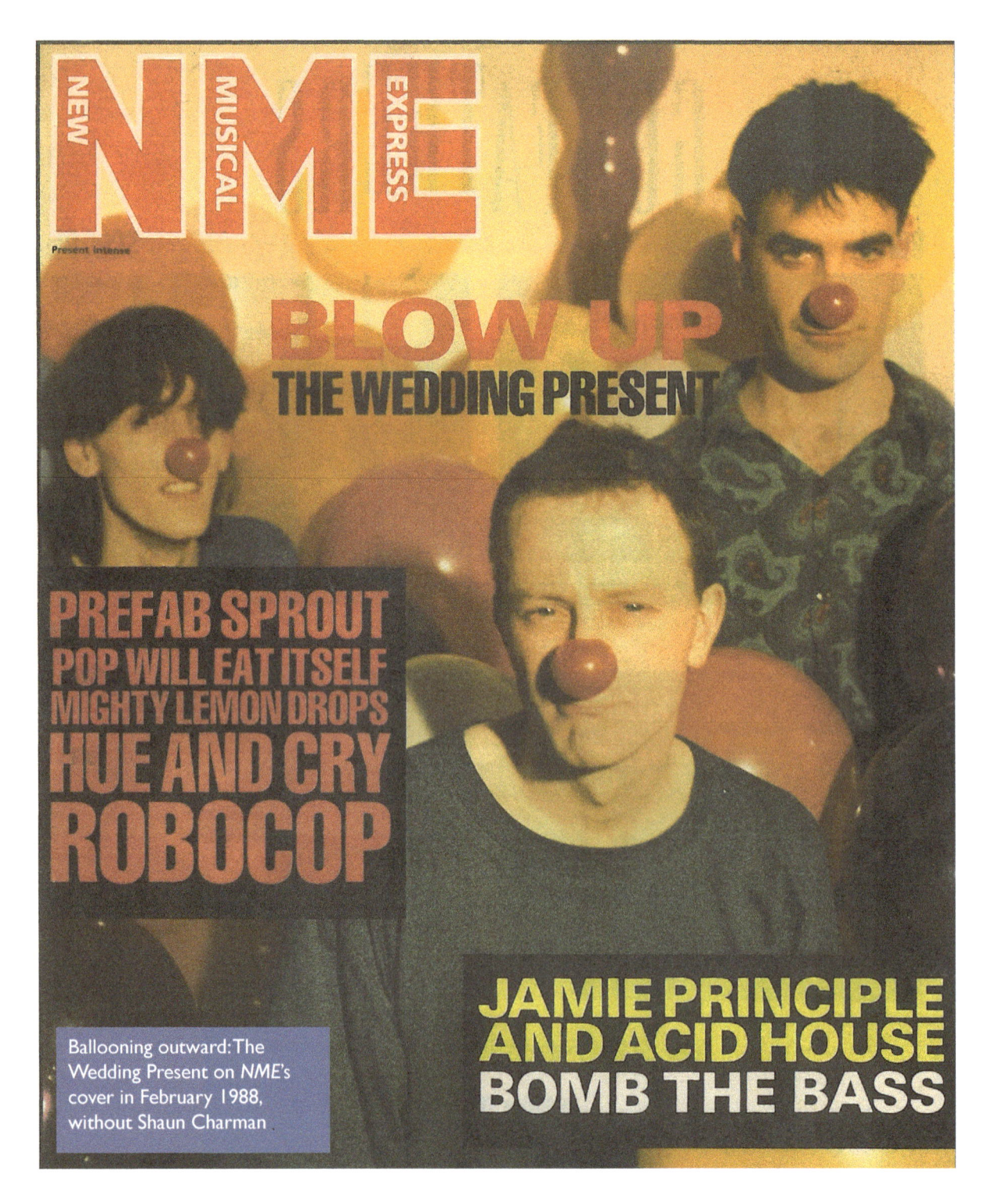

1988: Nobody's Twisting Your Arm

is like a family reunion. I have so many mates I hardly see but they all turn out at Wedding Present gigs and it's like we were never apart. You should always keep in touch with your friends!

DOMINIC O'GRADY

I was queuing up to get my copy of *Invasion Of The Wedding Present* (fanzine) signed when I spotted some other items for sale on the merchandise stall. Being ever so cool and right on, I needed to have the small badge sporting the image of one of most iconic bearded figures in history. Obviously, it took pride of place on the lapel of my long Eighties tramp mac. Some months later, I was wearing the coat – probably in the height of summer, being a youngish indie dude – when I was challenged by some friends. Why, being a Chelsea fan, was I parading around sporting a picture of George Best? 'Don't you squares know nothing?' I said. 'That's not George Best, it's the Marxist revolutionary Che Guevara.' 'Really, where did you get it from?' 'From a Wedding Present gig I went to.' 'Who?' 'Oh man, The Wedding Present. They have a great album out called...' The penny drops!

Marxist revolutionary or legendary footballer? It's an easy mistake to make

TOWN AND COUNTRY CLUB

19 FEBRUARY 1988, LONDON, UK

MIRANDA MAGUIRE

I was 15-years-old and massively excited to see them for the first time. Having bopped along to The Close Lobsters and The Flatmates, I was enthralled when The Wedding Present came on stage. I was down at the front. Balloons fell from the skies – I seem to remember a recent *NME* cover had pictured them with balloons – and the crowd surged forward to reach for the balloons.

I got a bit crushed and the bouncer pulled me out from the moshpit, put me backstage by the doors and then promptly shut them as he wasn't a big fan of The Wedding Present. I was too scared to ask him if I could go back in. My brother brought me back a playlist from another Wedding Present gig in my hometown, which I missed. I've still never seen them live!

The Wedding Present

PAUL WHITE

David handed out free biscuits to everyone in the front row from a selection box. There was a bit of a crush and several people, me included, ended up watching the gig from the side of the stage. The crush, I should add, wasn't because of the demand for biscuits.

MANCHESTER UNIVERSITY
20 FEBRUARY 1988, MANCHESTER, UK

RICHARD FARNELL

I remember the thrill of going all the way from Sheffield to Manchester to buy *George Best* the week it was released. We had record shops in Sheffield but I'd heard that Piccadilly Records in Manchester had the limited edition carrier bag and were also giving away a bonus 7" (in this case the 'My Favourite Dress' single).

My girlfriend and I boarded a National Express coach in Stocksbridge and weaved our way across the Pennines for about an hour. Luckily, they still had some left and I got my prize!

Within a few days of buying *George Best*, I wrote to them asking if they could print and send me a lyric sheet as I wanted to hear all the words – for some reason I couldn't work out all the lyrics! Gedge replied and said he was thinking about writing out a lyric sheet that people could send off for but he might not find the time – I guess he never got round to it but it seems odd to me now that I ever asked as I can hear every word as clear as a bell.

Whenever I listen to the album, which is still a lot all these years later, I can vividly recall poring over the fairly scant sleeve notes on the journey home and trying to glean as much info as possible about my new favourite band. Later on we went back over to see them play live, supported by the equally superb

Sleeve of the 'Nobody's Twisting Your Arm' single

84 SOMETIMES THESE WORDS JUST DON'T HAVE TO BE SAID

1988: Nobody's Twisting Your Arm

Flatmates, for the 'Why Are You Being So Reasonable Now?' tour and I recall the incredibly exciting atmosphere. In a moment of pure teenage abandon my friend Marcus ripped off his shirt and dived into the moshpit, and the band released hundreds of balloons over the crowd just like in the video.

ASSEMBLY ROOMS
23 FEBRUARY 1988, EDINBURGH, UK

TIM ABRAHAMS

We'd seen the London show a few nights before and enjoyed it so much we decided to take advantage of the Young Persons Railcard offer (£10 return anywhere in the UK). After also taking in Manchester, we got the train from Surrey to Scotland.

Our main memory of London had been the giant balloons being batted around to celebrate the Technicolor 'Why Are You Being So Reasonable Now?' video release. I was only 16 so these were exciting times for me.

One of my friends, Glen, had earlier embarrassed himself in the sweaty Town And Country Club. Some topless (male) students – a weird Nineties gig trend that I've always hated; only at Psychic TV did the ladies join in – literally ripped the shirt from his back. And he'd demonstrated terrible Wedding Present ignorance: in those days they did encores, although never 'Getting Nowhere Fast', and when some people shouted for them to play the extra LP track 'All About Eve', Glen laughed out loudly, thinking it was some Goth hippy reference to the band All About Eve. My mate Andrew managed to keep hold of a balloon and asked me to hold it for him at Chalk Farm tube station while he pissed up the wall. Unfortunately at that point a train came in and, while my Snakebite eyes were watching the tube mice, the wind gust from the train blew the balloon from my grip to an untimely death.

In Edinburgh we had no plans for where to stay. Perhaps the band would let us sleep on their floor? After all it's cold in Edinburgh in February. The flyer says The Shop Assistants were supposed to play but I guess they were busy splitting up or something as they didn't show.

Archbishop Kebab stole the show with an immense sax-soaked version of the 'Hokey Cokey'. Keith, meanwhile, had forgotten to bring the big balloons.

My chance of redemption with Andrew had gone. They'd been out and bought some masks, one of which

The Wedding Present

I nabbed at the end, but Andrew didn't want it. The gig finished at about 1am. Although we chatted to the band after, there were no sympathy offers of floors to sleep on so we spent the night in an underpass talking to Glaswegian tramps. There are lots of other gigs of theirs I can't really remember due to alcohol consumption. The oddest one was the Brixton Fridge gig and playing football on the dance floor with the band, kicking around a crushed beer can.

GRANT ORMSBY

I was totally gutted when I heard The Wedding Present had been drafted in as late replacements for a reformed line-up of my favourite band of the time, The Shop Assistants. I only found out about it by overhearing some people on the bus discussing it on the way to the gig. But The Wedding Present won me over that night and I couldn't believe I'd never gone to see them before. They also acknowledged the original headliners by doing an improvised cover of 'Safety Net', with David reading the lyrics from a piece of paper.

The sleeve for the single 'Why Are You Being So Reasonable Now?'

ASTORIA
18 MARCH 1988, LEEDS, UK

DARREN BUGG

In the very early days, they had more of a local audience than a studenty one. There were also some football hooligans, Leeds United fans, following them about. And then, once they became a bit trendy and had been on John Peel a few times, they got a massive student audience. They were famously described as a Smiths fan's second-favourite band. It was quite a

1988: Nobody's Twisting Your Arm

violent gig. It wasn't full of students in glasses. At about the fourth song, a guy got up on stage and punched David. It was just weird and all of a sudden it was mayhem. Pandemonium broke out, with bouncers everywhere, and it looked like there was going to be a riot. The band went offstage for about ten minutes. In the end it all calmed down. Somebody from the venue came on stage and was trying to identify who had hit David. The audience picked on a guy near the front and started pointing at him. I don't think it was him who had gone on stage but they were all chanting, 'You fat bastard!' and he was saying, 'It wasn't me, it wasn't me!'

I was quite new to Leeds at the time. I'd only been there a few months. I got completely lost afterwards and it must have taken me about three hours to get home. I walked round and round and round in circles in this really dodgy area of Leeds. And I only lived a mile away.

JAMES FRYER

The 'fighting in lumps' gig! It was a particularly nasty stop-start show with Gedge and the boys having to curtail a few songs mid-thrash due to the proper scrapping going on in the audience. Before the gig Keith complimented me on my home-customised black baseball jacket, onto the back of which I had lovingly painted the Reception Records rose.

Stills from the 'Why Are You Being So Reasonable Now?' video

SOMETIMES THESE WORDS **JUST DON'T HAVE TO BE SAID**

The Wedding Present

BRIXTON FRIDGE

9 JUNE 1988, LONDON, UK

ANDY SHEARER

For most of the first half of 1988, I had been wearing out an album called *George Best* by The Wedding Present and so, when I saw they were due to play in London in June, I was very excited. But the Brixton Fridge sounded a world away from Wembley Arena and Hammersmith Odeon and it was during my A-levels. Being a conscientious teenager, I thought I'd write to the band to see if there were any more gigs planned for the summer after my exams had finished. Grapper (guitarist Pete Solowka) wrote back to me very promptly and confirmed my worst fears. Unless I was able to get to Berlin or Copenhagen, I'd have to risk screwing up my A-levels or wait for a longer UK tour in October. Five months was pretty much a lifetime at that age so I decided to risk my future by buying tickets for me and my friend Graham Burgess, who was a veteran gigger by this stage – he had even seen The Smiths, which he still tells me about today. Grapper could have clearly had a career in health and safety as he finished the letter with a suggestion that I avoid standing too close to the speakers.

So on a Thursday night in June, I picked up Graham in my clapped out Renault 5 and drove to Hatton Cross tube station where I abandoned my car and we got the tube to Brixton. I can remember the excitement of arriving at Brixton station and walking to the Fridge. It felt like a whole different world.

We got there pretty early and had time for a drink before heading to the front, ready for the band to come on. The next hour or so was an exhilarating, sweaty blur as the band rattled through most of the songs from *George Best* and their latest EP, 'Nobody's Twisting Your Arm'.

Sage words of advice from Peter Solowka to a young fan

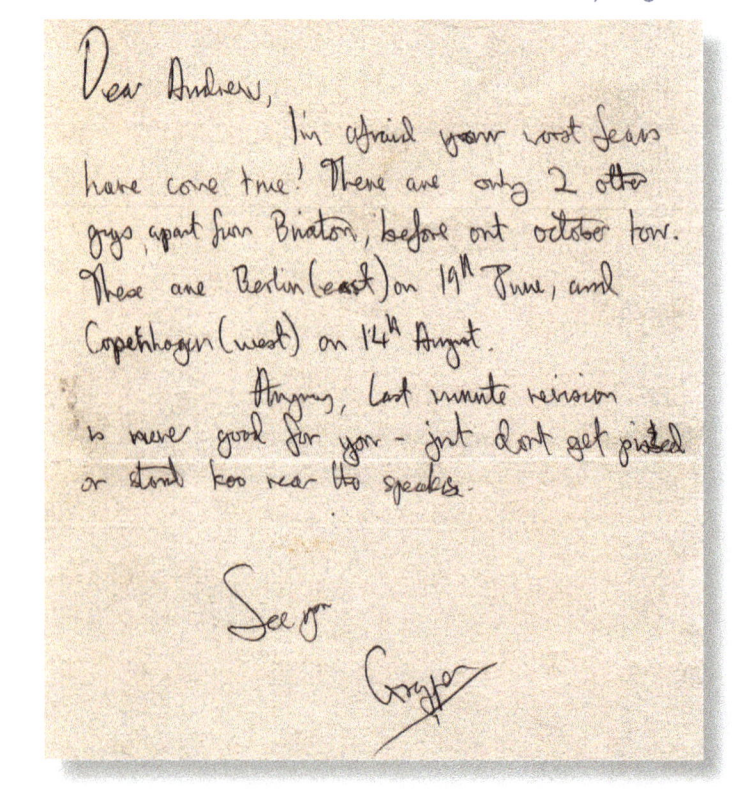

1988: Nobody's Twisting Your Arm

They mucked up 'Anyone Can Make A Mistake' and had to play it again. The following week's *NME* joked 'How could you tell?', playing on a common criticism of the band that all the songs sounded the same. My life was changed by that night, and not just because I failed my economics A-level the next day. The gig ignited a passion for music in me that I previously hadn't realised and over the next few years I would go to hundreds of gigs. Now I only go to the occasional one and when I do, I still get reminded of that feeling of the band coming out on stage at the Brixton Fridge all those years ago. And I have to end this with a little confession. I did stand too near to those speakers.

BLACKBIRD LEYS PARK

11 SEPTEMBER 1988, OXFORD, UK

CHRIS WILLIAMS

I saw them every time they played in London over a year or so, the venues growing in size by the month – North London Poly, Middlesex Poly, Hammersmith Clarendon, ULU. Onwards and upwards. They played in a field in Oxford and a back room in Wendover. I was there. They still broke strings with alarming frequency but just ploughed on. They had silly dances for each song – spinning for 'A Million Miles', kicking for the bridge bit. They even had their own secret sign. It never caught on. I've seen them over 50 times and my son is named after the singer. And yet I have only ever spoken to David on rare occasions, despite him being the most approachable rock star in the world. I don't want to know him. I just want to know the music. My favourite band? By a million miles.

LISTER PARK

24 SEPTEMBER 1988, BRADFORD, UK

WENDY SHARPE

I remember there was a big lake between us and them. They were on some sort of island. People were wading in the lake to get closer to the stage! It took us about two buses, one train and two hours to get there.

The Wedding Present

Setting up at Rock Roads Festival, Italy, in July 1988. Opposite: Gedge graces the cover of the much-loved London institution that was *City Limits* magazine

JOHN DOIDGE

It was a warm evening. The stage was erected in the middle of a big lake, and the terrain sloped gently down to the lake's edge, creating a natural amphitheatre.

The Wedding Present were on fire, but the thing that sticks in the memory was 'Kennedy'. David announced it as a new song and the first play had an instant impact, the crowd latching on to the lyrics almost immediately.

They played an encore that evening, as they did regularly in those days, but one thing's for certain – they played 'Kennedy' again! On hearing that intro, a number of us ran straight into the lake fully clothed and, standing waist deep in the water, danced like crazy to this new song.

A few nutters got as far as the stage and tried to climb onstage. The remainder of us stayed in the water and I distinctly remember the stage lighting illuminating us as we flailed around in the lake. That night my mates went for a curry in Bradford and I had to stay shivering in the car, wet through, whilst they ate.

A few days later we bumped into Grapper at the Duchess Of York in Leeds and he told us how he'd been scared that they were going to be electrocuted in Bradford by the mad few who had made it onto the stage wet through!

CITY LIMITS MAGAZINE

JOBS IN THE CAPITAL

FESTIVAL SPECIAL • FULL DETAILS

MERCHANDISING THE BLOCKBUSTERS

STAFFORD-CLARK AT THE ROYAL COURT

POLICING LONDON'S RIVERS

WIN VIP TICKETS TO SEE BROS

ON READING WRITING & KENNEDY

WEDDING PRESENT

The Wedding Present

JON PINDER

That Saturday I was full of a cold, the type where not only my nose but my eyes were running. The sort of illness I would have played on and taken a week off sixth form college for, but there was no way I was going to let that get in the way of a free Wedding Present gig.

For me and my friends to get to the event from the village of Crofton was a three-bus journey on West Yorkshire day rover tickets – half an hour from Crofton to Wakefield then over an hour from Wakefield to Bradford. None of us had a clue where Lister Park was. A rather friendly bus driver stopped and agreed to shout us when we arrived at the required stop; it must have taken us about three hours to get there. It was dark when we got there and we quickly found a spot on the hill to watch the event. After the band had been on for a few songs, they played a new tune, 'Kennedy'. Halfway through, some knobheads jumped into the lake and started splashing about, which duly brought the song and the gig to a halt. Electric guitars and water aren't a great combination. The splashing stopped and the song was attempted again, so we got two chances to savour the delights of that now much-loved classic.

Fast-forward 25 years and me and my fiancée push our children around Lister Park in a double-buggy, so I recall this tale on a regular basis. And although I hate to use the phrase 'it's a small world', it turns out one of those knobheads is a bloke I work with and we car-share for the journey to Leeds. It also turns out he's not a knobhead.

KEVIN O'ROURKE

Me and two friends got the bus there from Leeds. The band had set up on an island in the middle of the lake. The fans were amassed on the grass banking in front of the lake. When the band came on, about twenty people jumped in the lake and were splashing about in front of the stage.

This caused the band to stop playing for fear of electrocution. They wouldn't continue until the people got out of the lake. All the wet bodies on the grass banking coupled with other people jumping in the lake and getting back out again made the grass banking a mud bath. People were falling about in the mud, throwing it at each other and jumping back into the lake. We were covered from head to toe in mud but we still tried to get back in the local pub afterwards. The bouncer said he wouldn't let us in unless we washed our hands – classy joint! So we went back to the park, washed our hands and he actually let us in. The bus driver back to Leeds was less accommodating, and we had to walk all the way back to the city centre.

Opposite: a review in the local press of a potentially shocking open-air Wedding Present gig

1988: Nobody's Twisting Your Arm

Bradford Festival
Almost a shocker!

COMBINE an impressive stage on the lake, the best and least complex pop group in the world and a horde of followers and the results are spectacular.

Just as the very excellent Wedding Present launched into the favourite number, Everyone Thinks He Looks Daft, the inevitable happened.

A few dozen tanked-up fanatics threw caution to the wind and themselves into the murky Lister Park lake.

They comically splashed and half-swam their way to the stage and did their best to clamber on, blissfully forgetting that wet fans and high voltage electrical instruments and lights are not perfect partners.

"If you don't get off the stage we'll all be electrocuted and die," Pressies' singer David Gedge calmly explained.

They got off.

The Wedding Present, the finest band in Leeds, perform sad and funny songs about love-gone-wrong.

Wedding Present at Lister Park, Bradford.

Manic guitars play furiously and the mock Shadows dancing routines sum up the band's sense of humour.

Scores of devoted fans had travelled from Leeds, Manchester and Birmingham just to be part of the Festival's pop musical highlight.

The atmosphere was friendly and fun and the acoustics in the park — the only venue where the roadies need a rowing boat — surprisingly good. So was the weather.

The Fabulous Dirt Sisters, however, were not. You don't have to be a woman to enjoy their largely feminist lyrics, but it obviously helps.

Thankfully, The Futons and the Don Weller Quartet proved improvised jazz can be enjoyed by all.

All this and fireworks too. The best free show in West Yorkshire.

David Ford

The Wedding Present

JAMES FRYER

This was a celebration marking the reopening of Lister Park in Bradford. The band played at the far end of the park's water feature as the light faded. With a day's drinking under their belts and the band's emotive songs stirring passions, it wasn't long before some of the more plucky Wedding Present fans started wading out, then swimming the lake in an effort to reach the stage.

As the first soaking-wet fan (idiot) climbed onto the stage, dripping all over the monitors, David famously announced – with an increasing air of panic – that 'water and electricity don't mix!'

SIMON SHELDON

Four or five of us drove up especially to see The Wedding Present. The stage was in the middle of a lake in a park in Bradford. We got drunk and danced a lot.

DAVID GEDGE

Ah... the 'infamous' Stage On The Lake gig? I didn't really invite people into the water... did I?! The stage was surrounded by a lake and faced a hill where the fans were sat. Possibly because they were all a little... refreshed... by then, some of them decided to wade through the lake and clamber up onto the stage. That's when it got a bit dicey because of all the electrical equipment. You had all these soaking people splashing around and extremely worried looking technicians trying to stop them. It was hilarious, really. That reminds me of a concert in France, too. It was an outdoor festival in Rennes in 1994 and it was absolutely pouring down. Rain was coming in through the roof of the tent and onto our amplifiers. We said, 'Isn't this dangerous?' And they said, 'Oh, don't worry, we'll put some towels on the amps.' I said, 'I'm not sure that's going to stop it!'

But we've never had any electrocutions on stage. So far, anyway! When we first started there were definitely still stories going around about musicians having accidents at rock concerts. And we did play some venues where you felt, 'It's a death trap, this place!' You'd be walking around in the dark and there'd be a big hole in the stage or wires hanging out of the wall.

Health And Safety would be all over that, these days. But most of those issues were all sorted out by the end of the Eighties, I think... especially for The Wedding Present because we were bigger by then. If anything untoward is happening with the electrical circuitry these days, it all just cuts out.

1988: Nobody's Twisting Your Arm

MAYFAIR SUITE
2 OCTOBER 1988, SOUTHAMPTON, UK

KEVIN CAMPBELL

As a kid I'd fall asleep listening to John Peel on a small transistor radio under my pillow, a habit which I carried with me as my teenage years ended, got a job and moved out of the family home.

Peel's world seemed at once strange and familiar; he knew people and places I'd never seen, yet presented them in a way that was obvious and accessible. Of course he'd play a track from Extreme Noise Terror immediately after one from Ladysmith Black Mambazo – all music was equally considered by Peel. So it was that I first saw The Wedding Present live at the Mayfair Suite.

I'd never been one for clubs or concerts; they both seemed a bit alien to a middle-class suburbanite lad like myself. I heard about the tour on Peel and persuaded my flatmate John to go with me. Three days later, the tinnitus had almost completely gone…

ELEANOR WILLIAMSON

Being young and having way too much spare time, me and my mate spent the day hanging about the venue. David and the guys came out to say 'Hi' and spent an hour or so chatting. A few days later they were playing in Cambridge.

Me and my mate rang the venue and asked to speak to David, never expecting him to come to the phone. But come to the phone he did and we spent ages chatting to him about his music, his influences, our plans for the future and so on. I think we wrote to him to say thanks after that call and, from then on, he'd send us a postcard every few months to say 'Hi' and let us know what he was up to.

This, as you can imagine, was very impressive to a 16-year-old music obsessive like me. We met up again a few times when they were playing at Portsmouth Uni.

I even got to go onstage with them for their soundchecks and have a beer with them before the gig. Amazing times. I was obsessed with their music growing up. I still am. Seeing them live, even now, is as exciting as it always was.

The Wedding Present

CORN EXCHANGE
3 OCTOBER 1988, CAMBRIDGE, UK

KARL KATHURIA

I'd just turned 16 and was somewhat muddled in my musical tastes. In the past year I'd been to see Howard Jones, Anthrax, Prince and Bryan Adams. I'd got into The Wedding Present after hearing a scratchy medium wave playing of 'My Favourite Dress' on a Sunday evening drive in my parents' car.

Slowly, over the course of those twelve months, I picked up all of their releases and played them constantly. When I finally got to see them live for the first time, 'Why Are You Being So Reasonable Now?' had just been released and its posters and T-shirts were all over the merchandise stand. David Gedge was standing there too, elevating him instantly into a legend in my mind. Prince certainly hadn't been selling his own T-shirts at Wembley Arena. David asked if I'd bought the new single yet and then told me in great detail how the CD wasn't eligible for the charts because they'd recently changed the rules and it had too many tracks. As with many fans of the band, I've spoken to David many times since and couldn't tell you what ninety percent of the conversations were about. For some reason, the one about chart eligibility stuck with me and I kept up with the changing rules for many years afterwards. The concert itself must have really amazed me at the time. It started with the new single, sung partly in French, and carried on with most of the songs I would have considered my favourites.

They didn't play as long as I'd thought they might, or as long as I'd been used to seeing bands play for but, unlike Anthrax, they didn't fill it out with a ten minute guitar solo followed by a ten minute bass solo and equally lengthy drum solo!

UNIVERSITY OF EAST ANGLIA
8 OCTOBER 1988, NORWICH, UK

SIMON HALE

In 1978, I moved north from the Midlands to study mathematics at the University of Leeds. I became good friends with a lad on my course called

1988: Nobody's Twisting Your Arm

BEST BAND
1. THE WEDDING PRESENT
2. R.E.M.
3. THE FALL
4. U2
5. THE SMITHS
6. NEW ORDER
7. PUBLIC ENEMY
8. THE HOUSE OF LOVE
9. THE POGUES
10. SONIC YOUTH
11. THE SUGARCUBES
12. THE JESUS AND MARY CHAIN
13. THE CURE
14. THE PET SHOP BOYS
15. THE WONDER STUFF

SOLO ARTIST
1. MORRISSEY
2. PRINCE
3. BILLY BRAGG
4. NICK CAVE
5. JULIAN COPE
6. MICHELLE-SHOCKED
7. TRACY CHAPMAN
8. SINEAD O'CONNOR
9. MARC ALMOND
10. DANIELLE DAX
11. TOM WAITS
12. KIM WILDE
13. TANITA TIKARAM
14. IGGY POP
15. VAN MORRISON

BEST NEW BAND/ACT
1. THE HOUSE OF LOVE
2. THE WONDER STUFF
3. THE DARLING BUDS
4. TRACY CHAPMAN
5. INSPIRAL CARPETS
6. THE PIXIES
7. THE SUGARCUBES
8. MORRISSEY
9. THE LA'S
10. TANITA TIKARAM

Nobody does it better: *NME*'s 'Best Band' in 1988's end-of-year poll

Stephen from Middleton, Greater Manchester. A schoolmate of Stephen's was also studying mathematics and he tried to persuade me to listen to a post-punk band called The Chameleons from their hometown. Sadly his words fell on deaf ears as I was more likely to go to the Refectory to see John Martyn or Roy Harper than The Ramones or Iggy Pop.

My musical tastes began to change, however, during my third year at Leeds after seeing local bands Delta 5 and The Gang Of Four. Seven years later I was back in Northamptonshire and teaching mathematics to often reluctant teenagers. The prog rock albums were collecting dust and it was The Sugarcubes, Sonic Youth and The Jesus And Mary Chain that were being played instead.

Although a lifelong Leeds United fan, I was drawn to an album cover in the Peterborough branch of HMV and convinced that, although I'd never heard of them, a band called The Wedding Present must be quite good.

At £6.49, it was worth a gamble and I returned home with a copy of *George Best*. The jangly guitars and stories of lost love were reminiscent of The Smiths, but this band was even better. The album sleeve gave little away. There were no lyrics and even the names of the band members were missing. This was not your usual arrogant, posturing bunch of rock musicians. The only clue was Middleton, Bramley, Gateshead, Hassocks on the record label and a writing credit to Gedge.

In October 1988 my wife and I drove to Norwich for our first Wedding Present concert. We were way too early and chatting in a half empty concert hall we heard some people near us say, 'Look,

The Wedding Present

there's Gedgey.' Turning in the direction they were pointing, David saw us, smiled and started walking our way. Puzzled initially by his reaction, by the time he'd reached us and said, 'Good to see you, how are you?' I'd recognised him as the Chameleon-loving friend of a friend.

We talked for about a quarter of an hour about dysfunctional mathematics lecturers and our very divergent career paths since graduating. It's not been difficult to remain friends. We meet David once or twice a year for a chat at the merchandise stall.

VICTORIA HALL
10 OCTOBER 1988, HANLEY, UK

IAN BRADSHAW

I first saw them on the tour to coincide with the release of 'Why Are You Being So Reasonable Now?' The venue held 1,600 people but only the downstairs part was open and not the balconies. I think the promoter was a bit optimistic about the band filling the venue. They did 'This Boy Can Wait' as an encore – they used to do them then. David Gedge is a gentleman with a dry wit. When my wife took a photo of the two of us he asked if I was going to send it to *Heat* magazine.

TOWN AND COUNTRY CLUB
11–13 OCTOBER 1988, LONDON, UK

STEVE LYON

They were in their element live. That was *them* – live. I went to many a show of theirs. It was that reaction with the audience as well, which seemed to play off one another, which got them going even more. They seemed to love that interaction.

I remember seeing them at the Forum (then known as the Town And Country Club) in Kentish Town where they were playing for three nights running. The sound at that gig was absolutely extraordinary. It's not so much the level of it. It's the EQ, because David really liked that searing guitar sound and when you're listening on a big PA system in a venue like that, it's just unbelievably deafening. And everyone loved that aspect of it. It was part of the charm.

1988: Nobody's Twisting Your Arm

REDCAR BOWL
16 OCTOBER 1988, REDCAR, UK

The French-language single 'Pourquoi Es Tu Devenue Si Raisonnable?' by Cadeau De Mariage

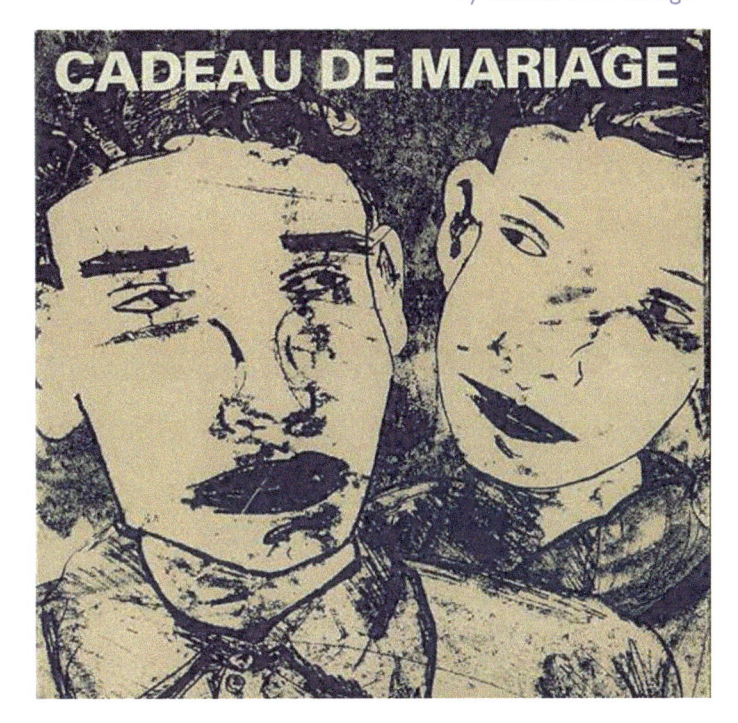

PETER ROWE

I was 15 years old and just into my last year of school. My best friend Chris got hold of a cassette with lots of bands we'd never heard of, featuring artists like The Wolfhounds, The Primitives, The June Brides, Dog Faced Hermans and several home-taped Peel session tracks from The Wedding Present.

Not having ventured outside of the Top 40 before, we had never heard anything like this and The Wedding Present were the least accessible of any of the featured bands. Nevertheless I recall buying both the 12" of 'Why Are You Being So Reasonable Now?' and an accompanying 7" by the enigmatic 'Cadeau De Mariage' shortly afterwards.

Bearing in mind that LPs were well outside of our normal price range and had to wait for special occasions like birthdays or Christmas, we still didn't know that many songs, so it was a bit of a gamble shelling out for tickets. In retrospect a Sunday night in Redcar was probably a risky gig for the band too, but it was packed.

The Redcar Bowl was basically a sports hall just along from the seafront. From the Sixties to the early Nineties it had bands on practically every week and gave Middlesbrough and Stockton a run for their money in drawing touring bands into Teesside. There was a separate bar that was strictly out of bounds for us but some older lads that Chris knew were happy to pass out drinks – not that we were serious drinkers by any means. I'm sure we necked no more than one or two pints,

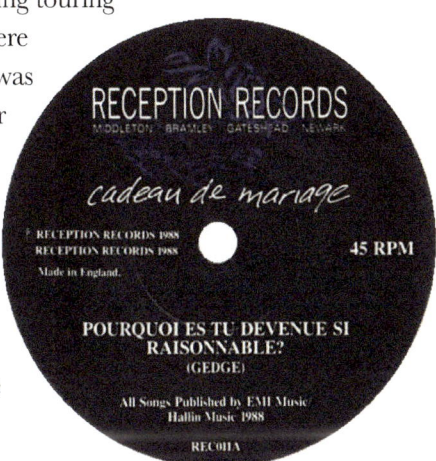

SOMETIMES THESE WORDS **JUST DON'T HAVE TO BE SAID**

The Wedding Present

albeit as fast as possible to avoid being spotted by the bouncers.

Being a good head shorter than everyone else, we were down the front to get a decent view of The Heart Throbs providing the support slot to a fairly sober crowd. This in no way prepared us for what was to come next. The first song that exploded from the amps as The Wedding Present took to the stage sent the crowd into a frenzy. I was knocked to the ground and spent the next couple of songs scrabbling around on the parquet floor trying to find my specs whilst avoiding boots and elbows.

I recall some breathing space as David paused the proceedings a couple of songs in to allow new recruits such as myself to gather ourselves and move to a less zealous area of the crowd.

Most of the gig passed in a bit of a blur. I recall hearing some of the songs I knew from the taped Peel sessions and the singles I had bought. Dare I suggest that they might even have played an encore?

Of course, no Wedding Present gig is complete without a trip to the merchandise stall. My purchases that night were a rose T-shirt which to my delight came in a band-branded carrier bag and a copy of the *Invasion Of The Wedding Present* fanzine. That plastic bag became a good luck talisman and was at my side throughout my GCSE exams the following summer. Despite the bruises and ringing in my ears, that gig was pretty much the start of a life long obsession. So much for 'home taping killing music'.

JULIE LIDDELL

I was 15 and had an older brother with impeccable music taste and, more importantly, the ability to drive. I tagged along with him and mates to a number of gigs at Redcar Bowl in that period – Voice Of The Beehive, Transvision Vamp and – at odds with these bands – The Proclaimers. It was, however, The Wedding Present that had the most significant impact on me. The heavy guitars, the lyrics that spoke to my soul and the boy Gedge himself. I think I fell a little bit in love that night.

Songs were largely from the *George Best* album and I became convinced 'My Favourite Dress' was written for me alone. My tartan skirt and Doc Martens are long gone but my love for The Wedding Present remains. They have provided the soundtrack to my life. I have probably seen them another twenty times since 1988 but that gig, in the shabby glamour of Redcar Bowl in a lost seaside town on the North East coast, was where it all began.

1988: Nobody's Twisting Your Arm

LIVERPOOL UNIVERSITY
19 OCTOBER 1988, LIVERPOOL, UK

JON PINDER

When it was announced that The Wedding Present were to play Liverpool University, I quickly convinced my parents that I should get a train over the Pennines and visit my brother Steve who was studying there. So The Wedding Present were the reason I got my first night away without my parents, a quite significant event for an over protected 17 year old. The La's were the surpise support act, just as they were about to break into the big time. I would have been happy with just The Heart Throbs. That night was also my first introduction to the wonders of Newcastle Brown Ale and the unpleasant hangovers that stuff can cause. I slept on an inflatable mattress on the floor of my brother's room in halls of residence. The mattress had a slow puncture and after half an hour I ended up on a hard floor with just a rubber under sheet for padding. A very uncomfortable night, but a great gig!

CONFETTIS
20 OCTOBER 1988, DERBY, UK

MALCOLM SCHOFIELD

Having had *George Best* for around a year, I was looking forward to going to the gig at the legendary Confettis (now an 'all you can eat' Chinese restaurant) in Derby with my new found friends from Wilmorton College (now razed to the ground).

But disaster struck and I got chicken pox. Despite being pretty spotty and sick as a dog, I was determined to attend. But my mother intervened. My mate Gaz (now playing bass for Jesus Jones, weirdly) got to meet David Gedge and all I had was chicken pox where no man should get them. It would be another two years before I finally got to see them, this time at the Assembly Rooms (now closed due to a fire).

It was one of the most violent moshpits I've ever been in, but worth every bruise and bleeding toe.

The Wedding Present

ROB FLEAY

We blagged our way in as fanzine editors wanting to do an interview. It quickly became apparent that there was no fanzine. The band were very polite about it and we sat round having a good old chat instead. They played 'Never Said' that night as a request for us and gave us an onstage dedication beforehand. I live in Derby but I went to uni and lived in Leeds for a few years in the late Eighties and early Nineties – specifically so I could see more Wedding Present gigs!

MIKE HARRIS

I had just got hold of a free tape on *Underground* magazine with 'Give My Love To Kevin' on it, which transformed my musical life. Unfortunately for myself and my best friend and next door neighbour Paul, also a recent convert to the church of Mr Gedge, The Wedding Present had decided to play at a cheesey Eighties nightclub with a strict over-18s only policy.

We set off on the bus to Derby all dressed in black – natty black roll neck jumper, black cardigan with a couple of Wedding Present badges on, black jeans with a nice turn up and black shoes – in an attempt to appear as old as possible. And not forgetting our forged student union cards. As we approached the venue we could see a steady stream of kids our age walking away shaking their heads. I stopped one and asked, 'What's happening?' He said, 'They are checking everyone's ID and are turning away anyone they don't believe.'

A big gulp of air and we approached the bouncers. They asked for ID, took a quick look at ours and asked us how old we were. '18'. 'Not tonight, boys. Come back when you are old enough.' And that was it – my 'first Wedding Present gig'. A slow trudge back to the train station singing 'Give My Love To Kevin'.

SIR HENRY'S

27 OCTOBER 1988, CORK, IRL

STEVE BARBER

My buddies and I decided to go on the piss early. Somewhere between where we started drinking and the pub we were heading for, my bestie and I stole a cauliflower. We brought it to the pub and decided it would be a good idea to give it to David. So we did. David was a bit bemused but took it in good spirits. We were pretty chuffed with ourselves, having met our hero and all. But not half as chuffed as when, a few weeks later in a music paper interview, David was asked what the most unusual gift a fan had given him. Needless to say, it was our cauliflower.

McGONAGLES

28 OCTOBER 1988, DUBLIN, IRL

NIALL MCGUIRK

I had just started getting used to not having to give all my money over to my parents and was sending away for fanzines, reading music papers and buying records in Dublin's independent record shops. I took a day trip by ferry to Liverpool to go to Probe Records and one of the snags I took home was *George Best*. The cover of that record became iconic for me. It featured a picture of the footballer George Best and the name of the band in white on a green background.

Simplistic but exciting. George Best was the sort of footballer that football fans loved. He didn't always play by the rules and wanted to have a good time but he always had flair. In a sense you could say he was a punk footballer without the politics, anti-establishment and never one to do something he didn't want. Putting him on your album sleeve was captivating.

Of course there was the music. Guitars jangling for ever with a trebly sound that never quite got to screeching but sure did wail and backed by a solid bass and drums and Gedge's voice – much like George Best himself – in a world of its own. The songs weren't about fighting a system that oppressed, they were love songs. Songs that ordinary people could relate to. I quoted 'What Did Your Last Servant Die Of?' so many times. I whispered it under my breath as I struggled with the concept of work.

I never considered them to be love songs – those types of tunes were for people in pop bands, clamouring for stardom. These were tales of everyday life and relationships formed.

They came to Dublin and I proudly wore my 'three balloons' badge; no need for a band name. Their McGonagles gig stands out as a guitar-fuelled blitz in

The Wedding Present

my memory. I travelled to London to see them and remember ringing up David Gedge asking where I would get a ticket. He had sent me a postcard previously and I viewed this act of kindness as an invitation. I didn't think, 'He probably does this for everyone, not expecting them to ring.' Well I did, and will never forget how accommodating he was. Amazingly he was equally magnanimous when I called back asking, 'Could my friend come too?'

CONOR HALL

29 OCTOBER 1988, BELFAST, UK

AMANDA ROBINSON

Brilliant night. *George Best* is a top album. Probably in my top three of all time along with The Smiths' *The Queen Is Dead* and Marillion's *Misplaced Childhood*. I used to live off the Antrim Road many moons ago. I now live in Scotland and own my own bar/live music venue. I just need to get The Wedding Present to gig with us and I'm one happy bunny!

QUEENS HALL

2 NOVEMBER 1988, EDINBURGH, UK

COLIN MALCOLM

The original version of Inspiral Carpets were supporting. At that age I was always looking for a new favourite band and for a while the Inspirals became it, with Tom Hingley at the fore the next time I saw them.

From indie to baggy that night. Maybe David is partly responsible for the indie-dance-baggy crossover. Well, him or whoever booked the Inspirals as a support!

1988: Nobody's Twisting Your Arm

BARROWLAND BALLROOM

5 NOVEMBER 1988, GLASGOW, UK

DAVID MCARTHUR

I remember thinking that the poor guitar tech had their work cut out as David seemed to be breaking strings every song. Given how short The Wedding Present songs are, he or she is to be commended.

FAT SAMS

6 NOVEMBER 1988, DUNDEE, UK

FRASER DAVIDSON

I was blown away when 'Why Are You Being So Reasonable Now?' came on TV. It made the hair on the back of my neck stand up and it still does to this day when I hear them play it – always a good sign. Not long after, my brother said they were playing at Fat Sams. The pace at which they played was breathtaking. It was a Sunday night and I couldn't hear again until the Wednesday morning.

THE RITZ

8 NOVEMBER 1988, MANCHESTER, UK

JOHN HARTLEY

Having a mother who worked in the local library had its advantages. Although the available choice was not usually inspiring, I gained plenty of aural enjoyment from albums for the princely sum of nothing, courtesy of Mum's staff ticket and I could keep hold of them for as long as I wanted. One cassette I borrowed was the *NME* sponsored tribute to The Beatles, featuring a range of alternative bands and entitled *Sgt. Pepper Knew My Father*.

The Wedding Present

One band on the cassette had already come to my attention in the slow evolution of my musical taste away from the mainstream.

I had seen, subversively handed below desks in the middle of an English lesson, a cassette with a striking green cover and a photo of a Manchester United player on it. But I was told I wouldn't like it and I didn't argue. One Sunday evening, immediately after the Sunday play of the Top 40, the first track to be played on Annie Nightingale's request show was a song that sounded interesting. Noisy guitars and a gruff Northern voice, and quite a change from the Top 40. It was by The Wedding Present and was called 'Why Are You Being So Reasonable Now?' I wanted to hear more. I might like it. There was one person to whom I knew I had to turn – Chris, who was the proud owner of that cassette copy of *George Best*.

Chris was surprised at my request to hear more of The Wedding Present but duly obliged with a cassette containing 'Why Are You Being So Reasonable Now?', 'Nobody's Twisting Your Arm' and 'Anyone Can Make A Mistake' on one side and *George Best* on the other. This would not be the first time in my life that the gift of a C90 would make a mockery of the music industry's standard Eighties message that 'home taping is killing music'. Home taping introduced me to many a band, and their back catalogue was subsequently introduced to my record collection. The Wedding Present were probably the first beneficiaries.

It wasn't long before I purchased the single I had heard on Radio 1, not just for the A-side, but for the acoustic version of 'Give My Love To Kevin' and a cover version of The Beatles' 'Getting Better', also featured on the *NME* album *Sgt. Pepper Knew My Father*. The Wedding Present also gave me something new to strive towards in guitar lessons at school. Just how fast could a guitarist play their guitar? I tried my best to emulate it.

In late 1988, Chris, Doz and I got tickets to see The Wedding Present in the flesh. This would have been my first proper gig were it not for my inexplicable decision to take up a friend's spare ticket for T'Pau a couple of weeks prior. I didn't even like T'Pau. They were blander than bland and the support band were just the dregs of Kajagoogoo after Limahl left: Ellis, Beggs and Howard sounded like a firm of solicitors. The Wedding Present were a different kettle of fish. They lay down on their backs and strummed as fast as I'd ever heard whilst the famously sprung dance floor of the venue bounced up and down to the throb of the moshpit. I stood on the periphery, beaded with sweat and drinking illicitly-purchased bitter, and decided twofold: that this should really

1988: Nobody's Twisting Your Arm

be classed as my first gig and that this was the musical way forward.

The Wedding Present were to become the first band since Adam And The Ants to be emblazoned across my torso in the form of a T-shirt, but the garment wasn't purchased at this gig. The only souvenirs I took away, apart from a fuzzy head and a ringing in my ears throughout the next morning's lessons at school, were a badge and a bootleg poster containing the front cover of the band's latest single and images of the four members. The T-shirt was to follow, a gift from Dad one day. This was possibly due to a spot of pleading, but not necessarily, given events that were proceeding with the family at this point: my sister was to undergo major surgery early 1989, around which time I suspect the T-shirt was bought. It was a white T-shirt with three balloons on it and the band's name. I would listen to tapes of The Wedding Present as we travelled back and forth on rainy winter nights to Manchester's Children's Hospital, immersing myself in the ferocious guitars and lyrics of heartbreak.

JASON STEVENS

I joined the Alternative Music Society at Lancaster University's Freshers' Fair. One of their first trips was to see the band I had a huge poster of on my campus bedroom wall – The Wedding Present. The minibus was full of fashionable nonconformists outdoing each other with obscure band and concert references.

I was too ashamed to admit that this was the first concert I had been to since Adam And The Ants as a 13-year-old so I kept schtum, smiling and nodding in all the right places!

When The Wedding Present kicked off, quite a few of the ebullient young men ripped off their shirts and started moshing. I distinctly remember feeling sheer panic – my only experience of young men slamming into each other had been in the Lowfields Road Pens at Elland Road, or in the pubs that lined the mean streets of Bingley. I didn't realise that this was de rigueur gig behaviour.

Half an hour later, I was right in there with the best of them, the blissful wall of noise, frenetic guitars and elastic dancefloor too much fun for an impressionable 18-year-old to miss out on. Many years and many concerts later, this gig will never be bettered.

The Wedding Present

1989: A Big Deal

The Wedding Present's signing to RCA, a major record label, was a big deal in more ways than one. Being an independent band, it was a risky move: the expectations of label, fans and band might well have ended up at odds with each other...

MICK HOUGHTON

Until they signed to RCA, I don't think The Wedding Present ever had a full-time record plugger and certainly the relationship with John Peel was purely between them and him, and David in particular. I think Peel admired their no-nonsense honesty and integrity. That's certainly what I admired and what I always tried to put across to the press, so that even journalists who weren't necessarily great fans of the music would still respect the band for what it stood for.

They were intelligent, unpretentious and not easily flattered, so that by the time it came to signing to RCA they knew it made sense. In the same way that they realised they needed an outside PR, they could see the advantages of signing to a major outweighed clinging onto their independence.

Plus, the deal gave them considerable creative control and Korda Marshall, who signed them, knew how far he or the company could push them. He understood what mattered to them, bringing in Steve Albini, for example, and marketing them as an independent band.

RCA weren't about to try and turn them into something they were not. To some extent, even retaining me was important because I had done a good job and by then had a good relationship with the band. It's quite common for majors to sack PRs at that stage and just hand the artist over to their in-house team. There was never any question of that as far as I knew and if there was the band must have fought to keep me on.

PETER SOLOWKA

Some of the most interesting things that The Wedding Present did were done behind the scenes. They weren't done on the stage. They weren't done even in the studio. When we signed to RCA it was amazing. We actually rewrote contracts and the way contracts are done. Our

1989: A Big Deal

greatest fear was signing to a major label. And we always said we'd never do it.

So we wanted to stay with Red Rhino, another indie. But they ended up going bankrupt – or we'd have stayed with them. We couldn't do anything.

Then RCA records turned up and said, 'Look, we'll give you a contract.' But we were so scared, we didn't really want to do it, because the standard record company contract is bollocks. They control everything. And we got into a process of about three or four months of really hard negotiations. They must have wanted us a lot because we were terrible. We were just arguing all the time about all these clauses that they had in the contract saying that the record needs to be approved by RCA Records before it's released.

We said, 'You can't do that. We make our own records. That clause has got to go. The final record has to be approved by us, not by RCA Records.' And they carried on arguing. We got to the position where, if they wanted to sign us... well, we got there by being independent. We got there by making decisions on how the records sound. 'If you want that unique sound, you can't have the final say on what we're going to sound like. We have to have it.' In the end, they went for it.

And not only that, they had a stupid, stupid system so that they get you into horrible debt and say, 'In the first year, the recording budget is £100,000.' And we said, '£100,000 to make a record?' And they said, 'Yeah. Why? Do you want some more? If you need some more, you can have some more.' 'More? We want a lot less!' They tried to give us £100,000 to make a record, but we would just have got into debt.

'The studio costs: you've got to pay your producers, you've got to pay this bill, that bill…!' We replied, 'Look, you give us control of the budget. What we'll do is – give us £100,000. If we spend less, we get the balance.' 'You'll never spend less.' 'We'll spend less. And we'll get the balance and you're still saving money because most bands don't.' They laughed at us and gave us the contract that gave us that clause. We never spent more than £35–40,000 on a record. And we took the balance for ourselves. It seems quite capitalist now.

But it gave us the control because we weren't getting into enormous debt by letting them control the budget. 'Oh, it's got to be remixed. Another £10,000.' If you get into a horrible debt, you can never pay it back and all the money goes to the record label in the end. We wanted to keep control of it. We made the record that we wanted to make. Within RCA, we were practically an independent band and that was an amazing achievement. I don't know if what we said and the clauses we put in has become the norm with other artists. But I know that we were the first ones that did it with RCA Records. We would not have signed to a major label if we had not been promised

The Wedding Present

that control. We must have had some big fans in the company because it was quite a change to the way they worked. That's one of the things that I always felt was one of our greatest achievements. And it's not because we sold millions of records. We never did. We never made anything that was really commercial. We never got played on the radio. We were always an indie band in that sense. But they signed us on our terms and in a way that didn't get us into stupid debt. And that's something where I think we did really, really well.

THE UKRAINIAN SESSIONS
FEBRUARY 1989

PETER SOLOWKA

My dad was from Ukraine. There's a little Ukrainian club in the middle of my home town of Middleton, and when I was seven or eight I went there on a Saturday morning and they'd teach the language, all the dances and a few songs. I probably went for about a year or so and I hated it.

But when I got into my early twenties I started thinking a bit more about my background. We had band practices where, if I had nothing else to do, I'd just play some of the old Ukrainian songs that I was learning on the guitar and sometimes the rest of the band would play along. And there was one Peel session we did where we had a bit of time at the end and I just started playing a song called 'Hopak' and everyone else played along. And it ended up being on the end of the Peel session. About six months later, John Peel said, 'Could you lads come and do another session?' But we hadn't written any new songs because we'd been on the road for a while. So I said to the rest of the band – it was an off-the-cuff remark, I didn't even think it'd be a serious thing – 'Well, why don't we just do the whole lot of these Ukrainian folk songs that we've got? Let's see how far we can push the boundaries here. Let's see how effective John Peel can be.' And in the end they said, 'Yes'.

To their credit, the rest of The Wedding Present, when you think about how radical we could possibly be, to actually admit to playing Ukrainian folk songs on the radio when you were normally expected to be an indie guitar band – that was truly something. But they went for it and that's great. If they hadn't done

1989: A Big Deal

The Wedding Present, in 'Ukrainian mode', 1989

that, I wouldn't be doing the music I'm doing now. We told John Peel, 'We're going to do a really weird session. Is that all right?' We didn't tell him what it was. And we just went in and played these four songs that we'd been practicing. I had no idea what the response was going to be. I didn't really care. To be honest, we never really cared. We did the things that we wanted to do. It was great that people liked it. And then John Peel asked for another session. So there were two Ukrainian sessions that were done before we went back to ordinary sessions. RCA released the album after they bought up Red Rhino's stock after the latter went bankrupt. Red Rhino Records had distributed the *Ukrainian John Peel Sessions* album, which got to 22 in the album charts. That was the first ever CD made of Ukrainian music. And it became quite an underground thing, before the wall came down even. People had tapes. 'Wow, a band from the West playing the music from here!' And this was at a time when, for years and years, the culture and the music had been suppressed in many ways. You didn't get Ukrainian-language bands. You didn't even get a tiny amount of Ukrainian language on CD out in the old East. And suddenly now you've got [people making Ukrainian music] in a different country.

My father's generation always said, 'There's a country out there and no one knows it's there yet. But it will be one

The Wedding Present

day.' Dads always tell their sons, 'Maybe not in my lifetime but maybe in yours…' That's what the story was for hundreds of years. But it just about was in my dad's life time, and in mine now. The music that we did – it was an eye-opener for many people that there were people that knew about Ukraine in the West, that 'Ukraine isn't just a dead little thing that happened in your grandma's village in the north.' This is almost like contemporary music from a band sponsored by John Peel. That makes a massive difference. When I first went out to Ukraine in 1990, the number of people who knew the group, who had little cassette tapes of the sessions that we'd done, was fantastic. Not The Wedding Present playing *George Best*. The Wedding Present playing that Ukrainian music. It made a difference. It was the first acceptance of Ukrainian culture in the West. Tiny as it is, it made a difference.

The Wedding Present. *Melody Maker*

MICK HOUGHTON

I'm still amazed how readily fans and critics took to that album and the Ukrainian tour that followed. It was a measure of the fan-base's strength; it was fun – it also worked much better live. And I think the fans probably saw it as a bit of an indulgence, but they always knew normal business would soon be resumed.

IAN GITTINS

When *Ukrainski Vistupi V Johna Peela* came out, I interviewed them for *Melody Maker* (published 22 April). The interview was fine. David took a back seat and Pete did most of the talking. Pete's very passionate about the whole Ukrainian thing. He's the one with the Ukrainian heritage and it was very much his idea in the first place. The photographer, a guy called Tom Sheehan and a chatty and larger-than-life, in-your-face Cockney, likes his props in the photo sessions. He turned up to the photo shoot with a fiddle.

He wanted David Gedge at the front of the picture and said, 'Here, Gedgey son, stick this under your chin will you

1989: A Big Deal

and pretend to play it?' And Gedge went 'But I don't play. I can't play the violin. Why would I do that? And this is Pete's project.' And Tom Sheehan was going 'Don't mess about, son. Come on, this is for the cover of *Melody Maker*. Stick it under your chin.' And basically there was a stand-off. Tom Sheehan was saying, 'You're the face of the band. You're the one that everyone knows. Let's get this over with' and Gedge was saying, 'No, I don't play the violin. This isn't a Wedding Present record as such.' In the end, it wasn't on the cover of *Melody Maker* and I think that was partly because Tom Sheehan went back to the office and said, 'He's a bloody herbert, this bloke. He wouldn't play along.' Which is a very Gedge sort of story, this cussed purity he's got going on. Whether it was the right thing to do, I don't know, but he certainly dug his heels in and wouldn't move.

RIVERSIDE

17 APRIL 1989, NEWCASTLE, UK

DAVID ARMSTRONG

This was the first time. An unusual first time at that, what with the tour being based around their infamous *Ukrainian Peel Sessions* album. As a fresh faced 17-year-old, I'd managed to see a number of bands around town in the preceding months, but the band I really wanted to see was The Wedding Present.

Having been introduced to them by my first girlfriend (via a cassette copy of *George Best*), I had quickly fallen in love. The Riverside's monthly listings leaflet had alerted me to the fact they were playing so I quickly obtained a couple of tickets from Volume Records so my mate and I could be there. Riverside tickets at the time, pre-internet and all that, were a hand-written affair, of which I eventually built up an impressive collection of the best alternative bands. But none as good as The Wedding Present to my ears.

A quick pint in The Barley Mow before making our way up to The Riverside and another pint, then desperately try to look cool. A couple of the indie lasses from college were there, smiles of acknowledgement were exchanged. Another group of lasses from Stanley we knew were in – we still see these at every Wedding Present gig now – and after a wave to say hello we made our way to the front of the stage.

It wasn't long to wait before on walked the support band. 'Hello, we're the support band' jokingly said Mr Gedge, leading Peter, Keith and Simon on stage

The Wedding Present

to blast through an unadvertised short set of their 'normal' tunes, primarily consisting of songs from their yet to be released *Bizarro* album. 'That's a bonus' we all thought, giving ourselves a metaphorical pat on the back for getting there in time.

After a short break and another pint the band returned, this time joined by Len Liggins and Roman Remeynes, and pretty soon the whole place was bouncing to a unique mix of folk and alternative music. The fact no one knew the words was neither here nor there. You could pogo to it. You could join in the 'Ois!' that punctuated what seemed like every other song. You could punch the air at all the right parts. It was loud. It was fast. It was mental. With the two guests taking centre stage, the lads stepped back, seemingly enjoying the experience as much as we all were, if their massive grins were anything to go by. The gig flew by, presumably as the songs are short and there's not many of them, but it was long enough to be soaked in sweat, my new Ukrainian T-shirt destined never to be quite as white as it started.

IRISH CENTRE
18 APRIL 1989, BIRMINGHAM, UK

RICHARD ROWSELL

The main talking point in the crowd was 'Do you call them 'The Wedding Present' or 'the Pressies'? My imagination only stretched to 'Is it The Wedding Present' or just 'Wedding Present'? When I got there I was disappointed it was going to be Ukrainian folk songs. Luckily, there was a great support band – The Wedding Present!

BIERKELLER
19 APRIL, 1989 BRISTOL, UK

GUY RUDRUM

'You *do* know it's Ukrainian?' the lady on the ticket counter asked me. I was 15, loved *George Best* and *Tommy* and wasn't going to let the fact I wouldn't be able to understand the songs stop me. The evening finally arrived and I

114 SOMETIMES THESE WORDS JUST DON'T HAVE TO BE SAID

excitedly entered the Bristol Bierkeller. One nervous underage pint of lager later and on stage walked the support band. Nobody particularly paid any attention. 'Hello, we're the support band' came a distinctive voice, before launching into a ferocious guitar intro. The crowd rushed to the front and the pogoing began. That night was also the first time I ever heard 'Kennedy'. The Ukrainian set began with 'Davni Chasy', with its singalong chorus. I had got a place right at the front and more enthusiastic pogoing taught me a valuable lesson about getting too close to the stage when it is only about thigh-height! No Wedding Present gig is complete without a trip to the merchandise stall. I came away with a massive Ukrainian tour dates poster that never stayed up.

TOWN AND COUNTRY CLUB
20 APRIL 1989, LONDON, UK

ANDREW WHITING
Thrilled Skinny

I have a lot of fond memories of The Wedding Present. Some of the loveliest, most generous people and, considering their successes, really modest too. I was a guitarist/singer and we were called Thrilled Skinny. We were a basic noise band – very trashy, not at all like them when we started, but we released records in late 1987 and early 1988 and started gigging widely. We were really young and naive and just all packed in our jobs, bought a van and that was it. We played loads of seriously hardcore punk gigs and benefits and although we sometimes landed gigs with quieter bands such as Television Personalities, CUD, Lush and others, we didn't fit in with that crowd. John Peel got us to do a session and played us loads in those days, and so we started to get lots of gigs. *C86* bands had been a massive influence on us (as well as more punk stuff like Ramones, Wire, Swell Maps, US hardcore, etc.) and our singer and bassist Simon was already a massive Wedding Present fan, as was our drummer Elliot and his brother Tim, who roadied for us. We cheekily wrote to The Wedding Present asking if they wanted to release a record by us! I think they found that amusing and were intrigued.

We played a gig at Leeds Duchess Of York and all The Wedding Present turned up to see us, including Sally and Justine (who were both selling

The Wedding Present

T-shirts for them at that time, as well as being romantically involved with David and Keith, of course).

A few weeks later they phoned our Simon up and asked us to play the Town And Country, Kentish Town with them. It was really short notice so I don't think we were even listed on any gig press releases, tickets or posters etc. It was so nice of them to do that, but they pretty much have done similar favours for small bands their entire career.

The gig itself is a bit of a blur – The Wedding Present went on unannounced and it took a quite a few minutes before people realised it was them playing. I was at the T-shirt stall with Justine and Sally and we kept having to tell people that instead of buying T-shirts they should check out the band on stage! We went on next and were so shambolic and punk we thought we went down pretty badly (our songs were all about one minute long and so odd). But afterwards we completely sold out of T-shirts and sold loads of records too. The Wedding Present went on last and played their Ukrainian set and they were wonderful. Incredibly danceable.

Afterwards we were a bit shell shocked and turned down an invitation to a party with the band as we'd had trouble with our van dying and we had no idea if we were going to get it going again. We didn't. Nine of us slept in the van and it got towed back home to Luton, whilst we caught the train home with all our gear.

Making the papers: a Wedding Present gig review in The Times

ROCK / Roots go east: Marek Kohn on The Wedding Present at the Town and Country

Back in the USSR

THE message has got across. There were no cries of "George Best", or "Why are you being so reasonable now?" For this tour, The Wedding Present have taken a break from sounding like The Smiths without the preciousness, and are performing an evening of traditional Ukrainian music.

Two senior figures stand behind this unusual project. One is John Peel, the focus of the culture in which the Leeds-based band have thrived — they now feature strongly in the upper reaches of the Festive Fifty chosen annually by Peel's listeners, up there with The Smiths and New Order. The other is guitarist Solowka's father, who is Ukrainian.

This was Solowka Junior's night. Frontman Dave Gedge remained on the sidelines, bent gravely over his guitar, while the tousled Slav stood centre stage with a mandolin and a beam of delight that never seemed to leave his face. The rough-hewn four-piece was upgraded by the addition of Len Liggins and Roman Remeynes, instrumentalists who concentrated on accordion and fiddle.

The concerts had their genesis in a session recorded for Peel's show, later released as a mini LP *Ukrainski Vistupi Johna Peela*. Its underlying respectfulness is demonstrated in the accompanying booklet about Ukraine (the definite article, it says, was "a linguistic ploy first used by an 18th-century Tsar in order to lower the status of Ukraine within his empire"). The recording itself does not quite do the idea justice. On the evidence of the show, however, all that was missing was the spirit of live performance.

The songs themselves come in two modes; the poignant, yearning ballad and its exuberant, rollicking antithesis. Both are combined in the Ukrainian song best known here, *Davni Chasy* — recorded some time ago as *Those Were The Days*. In the hands of The Wedding Present, it had a thrash inflection absent from Mary Hopkins's interpretation but that seemed to do it no harm.

It would be easy to dismiss this all as a bit of a joke, like the source of Ruritanian amusement that many Britons find in Albania. But what is actually going on here is, surely, the essence of how a culture renews itself under conditions of migration; the new generation playing the old melodies in its own idiom.

The cultural exchange between Solowka and his fellow musicians was certainly effective; the audience has rather further to go. One crop-headed youth did leap onto the stage and succeed in executing some rudimentary Cossack-style kicks. His achievements paled, however, beside the display put on by the genuine article. At the climax of the show, on strode the men and women of the Reading Ukrainian Dance Troupe. The men wore square-cornered black hats, boots and baggy trousers. They leapt, kicked, and reminded the crowd who really invented break-dancing. The audience gave this magnificent display the applause it deserved. Their own performance was largely limited to individuals climbing on stage and dropping back onto their peers. But it is an infant culture. The Ukrainians showed them what you can manage with a few hundred years' practice.

MIDDLETON CIVIC HALL

30 APRIL 1989, MANCHESTER, UK

ADRIAN WHITE

I really got into The Wedding Present after the release of *C86* in the *NME*. They quickly became my favourite band and still remain that way today. So much so my family are under strict instructions to let 'My Favourite Dress' blast out when I finally leave this planet! To this day no band still gives me that buzz of listening to new stuff as they do.

My mates and I must have seen the band well over 50 times in the late Eighties, saving up every last penny to make long journeys from Stoke-on-Trent to see them all over the UK, often sleeping four sweaty lads to a car! In April 1989 they toured the Ukrainian stuff, playing the songs that no one could ever type up on a cassette sleeve! I was not happy when my mates said they weren't bothering to go and see them on this tour, as it wasn't really The Wedding Present.

That night I returned home from some dodgy part-time job to be called by one of my mates to tell me to dress up as we were going ten-pin bowling. Ten-pin bowling? We were cool indie lads – why were we doing that? 'Dress smart,' they said, so I went for the Eighties staple of white shirt, black shoes and black trousers – attire largely connected with 'lads' that liked Wham! and Dire Straits. When my mates picked me up they were all in jeans and T-shirts, so I took this to be an advantage to me in case we met any girls at the bowling alley. I was looking good!

The car headed towards Manchester. Surely there was a bowling alley closer than that I thought? We eventually ended up in Middleton, just outside Rochdale. As we parked up, nowhere near a bowling alley, it suddenly struck me. My mates' laughter then confirmed

---

THE WEDDING PRESENT release their long-awaited album of Ukrainian folk songs on Monday.

It's called 'Ukrainski Vistupi V Johna Peela', which roughly translates as 'The Ukrainian Sessions Of John Peel', and is available as 10-inch vinyl, cassette or compact disc.

Comprising nine tracks in all, the material is based on original Ukrainian folk songs, and was all previously broadcast on Peelie's late lamented evening show.

The Pressies were joined by two guests for the recordings, singer and Russian graduate Len Liggins and instrumentalist Roman Remains.

All formats will be available at a budget price and The Weddoes are including an explanatory eight-page booklet put together by the band's Ukrainian expert Pete Solowka. The sleeve of the album is based on a colourful Ukrainian tapestry.

Wed Star Gedgski

News of the Ukrainian album in the *NME*

The Wedding Present

everything – we were going to see The Wedding Present doing the Ukrainian stuff! So in we went and took up our usual place in the middle, in David's eye-line, where the hard action was. But my joy was tinged by the embarrassment of my attire and the funny looks I was getting – I looked like some sort of newbie, and when you are a hardened Wedding Present gig-goer that's not a good feeling. My white shirt was ripped to shreds and my posh black work shoes scuffed and crushed beyond repair. Which made it even sweeter in the end.

CHARLIE BRIDGE

The Wedding Present played my – and Gedge's – hometown, and supported themselves with Pete's Ukrainians. David had a brand new guitar that night, still with the price tag on – £115. After the gig, me and my mates, Andy Royle, Chris Pomfret and Dean Heywood, were outside the venue when some guy approached us trying to sell us said guitar. He'd managed to steal it.

We liberated the guitar and took it back into the venue to give it back to David. David came out and thanked us and we had a good chat. We were all a bit pissed and teenagers but – fair play to him – he had a chat nonetheless. I'm certain to this day he thought we'd nicked the guitar and then had a prick of conscience, but I can assure him that wasn't the case.

ACADEMY

8 MAY 1989, PLYMOUTH, UK

FIONA FROM NEWQUAY

I had recently got back with my on/off boyfriend, Mat, but it was clearly the endgame. We were both into The Wedding Present, although he had to wear his T-shirt in secret because his Mum thought the balloons on his T-shirt, floating behind the words 'The Wedding Present', signified condoms. The gig in Plymouth was a big draw, especially as his mate Holman's dad would drive us all up from Newquay to go and watch it. The plan had another thrilling layer for me: I'd recently met a boy called Mark from Plymouth (his nan knew my nan – it was fate) and he was very happy to turn up at the Academy to see me, accepting the requirement of subterfuge. I was very

1989: A Big Deal

happy to let him. I felt like the spider queen in the middle of a big indie web: even Gedge seemed like one of my flies. How kind of him to arrange a gig which facilitated my love life in this way. I remember being a completely moody arsehole on the way up and not wanting to talk to anyone, which suited Holman, who clearly thought I was a complete pain in the arse. I also had terrible sunburn; I think I must have skived off school and spent the day on the beach. I don't remember how I managed to get away with going to Plymouth on a school night either. So I was moody, red-faced and bitchy as hell, which just goes to show how desperate most indie boys were for a girlfriend.

The Academy has two floors: I spent the gig flitting between the two. Mercifully, I think Mat chose to enjoy the gig and forget about his ingrate of a girlfriend. Mark, upstairs, didn't really like The Wedding Present anyway so was just there for the beer and the snog. I remember – or have created a memory – of standing upstairs on the balcony, wearing Mat's favourite dress, looking down on him and Gedge, another boy's hand on my arse, as Gedge woefully sang 'That was my favourite dress.' That was the boy Gedge's great talent: he wrought the lyrics which framed our youth.

Mark and I didn't work out (poor taste in music, for a start). And Mat and I also broke up. I don't know what the hell I was playing at, really: Mat was a truly exceptional young man and changed my life for the better in so many ways. I think I imagined we'd get back together at some point. Tragically, he died nine months later – a drinking binge gone wrong – and I was completely devastated. I still grieve, along with everyone who knew him. And I still play the songs. The Wedding Present formed the soundtrack to our relationship from start to finish. As a postscript: it took me 25 years to find another Wedding Present fan. We knew we were onto something as soon as we compared playlists. Now married – happily.

The boy Gedge and Grapper (Peter Solowka, left) at Plymouth Academy, 1989

SOMETIMES THESE WORDS **JUST DON'T HAVE TO BE SAID**

The Wedding Present

PALÁC KULTURY

24 MAY 1989, PRAHA, CZ

ROBUL CIVOLAB

The first time I saw The Wedding Present was in Prague when our country (Czechoslovakia) was under Communist rule. It was magnificent. As I can remember, the drummer was playing with a broken arm! David had a green T-shirt.

READING FESTIVAL

26 AUGUST 1989, READING, UK

EMMA POLLOCK
The Delgados

The Wedding Present took my ears by storm back in 1989 when I left Castle Douglas to go to University in Glasgow. I'd never really heard of them at all, as my musical exposure at home had sadly been limited to *The Chart Show* and Woolworths, as well as my parents' record collection (a real treasure trove, in fact) but I wasn't aware of this left-of-centre alternative scene until my late teens. Someone let me borrow *George Best* and I loved it. The raw energy, the boldness, the aggression, the direct melodies, and all countered by the knowing and funny lyrics, ever-present sarcasm, nothing saccharine but always bittersweet. That sound became inspirational to me – everything that I wanted to be part of; the rebellion of music, the independent force that they represented in amidst the 'major label/pretend indie label' scene of the

Pete Solowka and Simon Smith at Palác Kultury, Czechoslovkia, May 1989

1989: A Big Deal

Nineties; and always presented with just a little more self awareness than anyone else. They were definitely a force that spurred us on to form our label, Chemikal Underground, and proof that you could make your own voice heard above the din, no matter how different it may sound.

FRASER DAVIDSON

I came down from Scotland to see them. Watching the crowd bounce around to their set was superb. I'd never experienced anything like it before. I started dating my girlfriend Claire, who is now my wife, in 1992 and we've just celebrated 20 years of marriage. *George Best* was the soundtrack to our first night of hoochie coochie. 'My Favourite Dress' was playing and, in the style of a cheesy Radio 2 DJ, it's 'our song'. I now sport a Wedding Present rose logo tattoo on my upper right arm for my wife, a reminder of our first night together.

David and Keith at Palác Kultury, May 1989

SUBTERRANEA
29 AUGUST 1989, LONDON, UK

IAN CUSACK

John Peel was about to turn 50 and his birthday party at Ladbroke Grove's Subterranea would feature a reformed Undertones headlining and The Fall as support. Sadly, the O'Neill brothers lost their father the week before and

The Wedding Present

The Undertones didn't play, with The House Of Love stepping in as openers and The Fall shunted to headliners. House Of Love were dreary and posh, while The Fall made absolutely no concession to the occasion by being as thrillingly contemptuous as ever. However, it was the band in the middle of the bill that utterly blew me away; playing a set that was mainly derived from the unreleased *Bizarro*, I discovered The Wedding Present with fresh ears that night. The songs were longer, the sound more ferocious, innovative and uncompromising. I have subsequently grown to love both original and revisited versions of the band's early back catalogue, but they only became the band I adore when they signed to a major label.

BIZARRO
THE SECOND ALBUM
RELEASED 23 OCTOBER 1989

MICK HOUGHTON

I had started doing PR in 1978 at Warners, where I looked after the Sire roster. When I went independent in 1980 I called my company Brassneck Publicity, so I've always assumed that was in David's mind when he wrote the song. By the time I started working with The Wedding Present I think my forte was for handling indie acts, or perceived indie acts, as most were actually signed to majors. So that included The Teardrop Explodes (and all of Julian Cope's career thereafter), The Jesus And Mary Chain, Creation acts like Felt, Weather Prophets and The Triffids. Over the years I worked with The Wedding Present I was also working with The KLF, Sonic Youth, Spiritualized, Stereolab, Elastica and others. So it was a pretty strong set-up and all very different from each other and from The Wedding Present. What's key to all these groups was that they were all very strong characters or led by very strong characters and The Wedding Present were no exception – although David was markedly different to Julian Cope or Ian McCulloch or Bill Drummond or the Reid Brothers or Jason Pierce. That's what made it so interesting and I guess that's what always inspired and challenged me.

Opposite: David Gedge appears with Ian McCulloch and Guy Chadwick to celebrate John Peel's 50th birthday

1989: A Big Deal

NME
NEW MUSICAL EXPRESS

PAGES

READING Fire and rain: mega report

BOBBY BROWN
Will the Jack of Swing be the next King of Soul?

BARRY WHITE
battles Steven Wells

Plus!
BLUE NILE
CHRISTY MOORE
PHRANC
ROBERT SMITH's solo LP

FESTIVE 50
John Peel's birthday bash
(starring Ian McCulloch, David Gedge, Guy Chadwick and a cast of thousands)

SOMETIMES THESE WORDS **JUST DON'T HAVE TO BE SAID** 123

The Wedding Present

PETER SOLOWKA

It's a learning curve. One of the things that has been said about Chris Allison, who produced *George Best*, is that he got it all wrong and we got rid of him – and then we got him back again. Well, you'd only get him back again if you value what he's done. In the end, whatever discussions we had about making *George Best* built the foundation for a working relationship. There's no doubt about that.

When I was involved in The Wedding Present we did three really, really good albums and two of them were with Chris. It's very hard to turn around and say, 'He wasn't any good at his job'. That's really harsh. The third one we did with Steve Albini – *Seamonsters*. If you do it with Steve Albini it has to be a brilliant album because Steve Albini's done it. You don't even view it objectively any more. It's a Steve Albini album, so it must be brilliant. But we wouldn't even have got to the stage of working with Steve Albini if we hadn't done the two albums we'd done with Chris. They're both really good albums.

They're not radio-friendly albums but they were never meant to be. They were meant to be albums where you stick them on and it feels like you're in a gig. That's what I always thought.

That's what we wanted our records to be like. So it feels like you're down the front and someone's blasting your ears out with a guitar that pierces. That's what we wanted. Radios never do that.

Bizarro's warmer than *George Best*. But I don't think that's because we didn't want to make an exciting, harsh sound. I think when we were younger, with *George Best*, our main thing was fast and furious. And a lot more of the songs on *Bizarro* are actually a little bit more laid back and tuneful and melodious and you can see that path going on to *Seamonsters*.

There are a lot more slower songs on *Seamonsters*. I don't think it's deliberate. I think it's what happens. You can't always make the same record. There's no point. Everybody's got the first record. Why make the second record like the first record? It's got to be a bit different. It's just that path that you're on as a musician. I don't think we deliberately wanted to be slower and quieter.

We were just exploring musically what we could do when we realised not everything had to be like 180 bpm (beats per minute). You can do some songs a bit slower than that. There's some brilliant songs on *Bizarro*. I think that's just from being in a songwriting/playing relationship for four or five years – after that time you get really comfortable with what you're doing with each other. I think that's what happened with *Bizarro*, whereas with *George Best* it was the first two years of fury.

1989: A Big Deal

CHRIS ALLISON

Because *George Best* was pretty successful, they got snapped up by RCA, so there was a bit more of a budget. We had the studio time booked for Jacobs Studios, a residential studio, but Simon Smith (who had replaced Shaun as drummer by this time) injured his arm a few weeks before the album sessions were due to start.

The band was looking at various alternatives, like getting a session drummer for the recording. I can't remember why that was – perhaps they didn't know whether they could get the money back on the studio time or perhaps it was pressure from RCA with regard to a release date for the album. Between the label and myself, we talked to Topper Headon from The Clash and a session drummer called Chris Whitten who used to play for Julian Cope's band and who was then playing in Paul McCartney's band. I went down to Rye, where Paul McCartney has his studio, and I had Chris play against some Wedding Present tracks. Ultimately it was decided by the band that they were going to move everything and wait until Simon's arm was up to the job.

So there were a few little gremlins to iron out before getting started on the *Bizarro* album. We made the recording at Jacobs Studios and mixed at AIR Studios in London, where we mixed the *George Best* album. Coming in as producer of *Bizarro* I knew the band I was dealing with. They called the shots. There's some production jobs you go into where the band really wants you to participate, put in arrangement ideas. The Wedding Present didn't want anyone telling them, 'You could come up with a better guitar riff on that' or 'Why don't you try this arrangement?' There might have been a tiny little thing here and there, but in general they weren't particularly interested in an outsider's ideas. By this time all they really wanted was someone to record them really well, get a great mix on time and on budget. One could see, as an outsider, how they could perhaps consider doing things slightly differently, things which would not diminish their ethic but perhaps add something to it. But they weren't the band to do that with. I definitely got put in my place a few times trying!

The instantly recognisable cover to *Bizarro*, the second Wedding Present album

SOMETIMES THESE WORDS **JUST DON'T HAVE TO BE SAID**

The Wedding Present

STEVE LYON

We went to a residential studio in Farnham to record *Bizarro*. And we recorded that from the bottom up. I love the album and I love their approach. On 'Take Me!' I remember talking to the guys and them asking, 'How long's the tape?' And I said, 'Well, it's 15 minutes.' And they said, 'We've got this song and we want it to last 15 minutes.' So I said, 'I'll put a mark on the end of the tape when there's about a minute to go.'

Basically it was like a white pencil mark on it. And I said, 'When there's a minute to go, you've got to finish the song.' I remember we recorded that and we hit 'go' and they just played for 15 minutes. I was frantically waving through the window saying, 'You've got to knock it on the head!' I got on really well with the band. I really liked them. I can remember there being a few disagreements with Chris. I think that what he wanted wasn't exactly what the band wanted. I was kind of in the middle. And sometimes Chris would say, 'Can you do this…?' and it would be, 'Yeah, sure, but I don't think they're going to like it.' And then the band would come in and say, 'No, we don't like it. We want this.'

But *Bizarro* – great record, great songs and great vibe. I think that was the thing. It was a little bit *more*, fidelity wise. It was a slightly better sounding record, obviously, because it had been recorded differently. Fidelity-wise, it was a richer representation of what they did. And we mixed it there because I wasn't working at AIR by then. I was freelance. I've always followed the band. I've got so much respect for someone that just sticks to their guns and keeps going. My fond memories are of David just reading some of the fan mail that he had. He'd get fan mail from university students asking for help. I thought that was very cool, him feverishly writing back to people. I have very fond memories of the guys, I have to say.

PETER SOLOWKA

In hindsight, it was awkward. When RCA contacted us, some people in the company actually thought that the band was a Ukrainian-language band, because the first record they had was the *Ukrainian John Peel Sessions*. Not the A&R people, they knew us. But the people that signed us up, the legal people, had no idea.

There was this weird 'two bands in one' thing and even when we signed with RCA Records we had it put in the contract that The Wedding Present could do a Ukrainian-language album if we wanted to, if we had the time. As time went on, it got difficult. When we did *Bizarro*, the record label had all the interviews lined up on radio and everything. And you want to talk about the album and three or four questions in they'd say, 'How's the Ukrainian music going? Are you surprised by how many people came to the gigs? They didn't play it on the radio.'

We didn't want to talk about that. We wanted to talk about *Bizarro*. That's what we really wanted to do. It was such a shame because we had this great album, and I absolutely love *Bizarro*, but it was a massive distraction.

JIM BASS

'Brassneck' is not my favourite of theirs but it's a beauty nonetheless. This track has great significance for me and retains a very special place in my heart, psyche and soul. After practically wearing out the album *George Best* on my turntable, I had awaited this second album with an eagerness beyond compare. Shortly after my 21st birthday, on a gloomy October Friday morning in 1989, the moment had come. I knew I had to be one of the first to arrive at Worcester's Magpie Records to get the limited edition version. I had taken the day off work and awoke later than planned, after listening to the John Peel show the previous evening, which of course had played a few tracks from this new album.

Cursing myself, I ran to the bus stop and discovered I had missed my bus and would have to wait another half an hour. Less than five minutes into my fury, a black BMW pulled up alongside, the electric window dropped and a voice called out 'Excuse me mate?' I stooped to peer through the window. It was Jimmy Greaves! *The* Jimmy Greaves. He asked me if I could direct him to Worcester Cricket Club as he was attending a charity event. I said, 'Better still, I will show you' and hopped in. The rather surreal nature of my excitement at meeting Jimmy was yet still masked by my anticipation

The Wedding Present in 1989: David, Peter Solowka, Simon Smith and Keith Gregory, clearly enjoying the Great Outdoors

SOMETIMES THESE WORDS **JUST DON'T HAVE TO BE SAID** 127

The Wedding Present

of the new album, so without thinking I asked him a string of moronic questions culminating with the worst possible: 'How did it feel to not be included in the squad for the World Cup final in 1966?' Conversation dwindled very quickly after that howler, I can tell you! Consequently I arrived at Magpie Records for 8:55am and was the first through the door on opening. Precious cargo in hand, I took two minutes to invest in two packs of JPS Superkings and hot-footed it home. Scrambling through the door and setting up the vinyl to go took a few seconds, performed in the manner of a Formula 1 pit crew. Volume cranked up, the first track exploded on me. I hadn't heard this one before. Adrenaline and nicotine surging through my veins, and tears in my eyes – tears which stayed with me as I repeated this first track several times, before the rest of the album got a look in. Several hours and 40 Superkings later, my eyes were stinging and my ears were ringing. I can relive that day, that moment again and again, by listening to this track.

I didn't like the heavier Albini-produced 'Brassneck' half as much as this album version. Its Olympian blitzkrieg assault in the opening bars and minor series in the final stages still do the same things to me now as they did over 25 years ago. This was a seminal time in my life, an extended childhood soon becoming a voyage of discovery and awareness.

ROADMENDER
28 OCTOBER 1989, NORTHAMPTON, UK

IAN GRICE

Seeing them live in a sweaty Roadmender transformed my view of the band from one in which I had a casual interest to my favourite live band ever. With the gig over, I queued for a T-shirt and asked David to sign the setlist. As he duly obliged I nervously chatted, saying, 'I've not sweated that much in ages.' Without a moment's hesitation he replied, 'You should get out more'.

GAVIN MORGAN

My dad was a long-time listener to Peel, from the beginning of his Radio 1 days, and I always overheard him listening to his shows. Inevitably, curiosity got the better of me and I too became a Peel devotee. One song in particular caught my ear. Hmm, a band called The Wedding

1989: A Big Deal

Present – 'This Boy Can Wait'. Well this boy could only wait until the weekend, dashing into town at the first opportunity to try and source something by The Wedding Present. Fortune smiled on me in my local Our Price. Using some money from my paper round I bought a 12" of 'This Boy Can Wait'. That's where it started, and I played that 12" to death over the next few months. Life was difficult back then – there was no guarantee a record shop would have what you wanted – and trying to get something even slightly alternative wasn't always easy. In a way it made it all the more worthwhile.

That was a bit of a turning point for me. I began reading the weekly music press – *Melody Maker* and the *NME* – and kept listening to Peel and collecting alternative and independent vinyl. I remember being very excited when reading that *George Best* was being released. Again, I saved up to buy it during the week of release, getting a much coveted *George Best* plastic bag with my copy. And I kept buying as much Wedding Present stuff as I could find. 'Nobody's Twisting Your Arm' caused much excitement, my first Wedding Present CD single, and a 'proper' looking video to match. *Tommy* was the next big release, and finally I was able to hear properly some of the earlier Peel sessions and other tracks I'd missed.

The Wedding Present even inspired me to form my own band around that time – we played a few gigs in local pubs, and covered 'Everyone Thinks He Looks Daft'. Alas, fame never came our way. Still, I hadn't yet seen the band play live. In the early days of The Wedding Present I was probably a bit too intimidated to go a gig, but by the time *Bizarro* was released, I was 17 and I just didn't care. They were playing the Roadmender in Northampton – at last! I queued up to get in before the doors were open. Got in, bought a T-shirt, and oh – there's David. That's unusual for a rock star, just wandering around chatting to people. I went and said hello – and he spoke back to me.

I muttered something about that 'This Boy Can Wait' 12" before trying to get as close as I dared to the barrier. The Roadmender was packed, it was a great gig, and the walls and ceiling dripped with sweat that night. Fantastic.

ANDREW WILSON

I stood across from Brennan who addressed me with bright blue eyes, between the rugged CDT tables in Wolfy's class, next to which we stood. The Wedding Present, he told me, were simply brilliant. An ace band and –

The Wedding Present

David Gedge, on the cover of *Melody Maker*, in October 1989

130 SOMETIMES THESE WORDS JUST DON'T HAVE TO BE SAID

1989: A Big Deal

importantly for me – from Leeds, with brilliant tunes; exactly what I needed as I looked to expand my limited wannabe musical knowledge. How could I get hold of some though? So the day came. My mum suggested that I joined her for a visit to Bradford. Bradford! Great. I needed an opportunity, though, and it delivered. As I trudged through the snow in the centre of Bradford, I searched for a half-decent record shop. Then, in the cold, there was my prize – HMV!

It was my first experience of searching through CDs, something which I've done so many times since. So, I found it – a dark cover with red splodges – *Bizarro*. I got it home. I put it in. I turned it up. 'Brassneck' smashed its way out.

I still remember the moment that I first heard The Wedding Present. And, when I heard 'Dalliance' for the first time – well that's another story. Oh, and I saw DLG in town once. I told all my friends…

GUILDHALL

30 OCTOBER 1989, PORTSMOUTH, UK

DUNCAN GREENWOOD

My friend gave me a copy of *George Best* to listen to and I played it so much I must have worn the grooves out. Seeing them for the first time live, the sheer frantic, crazy energy that came from the stage had me hooked for life. I was blown away by how dynamic they were. That feeling has never left me. I even took my cassettes when I went to live in Arizona. 'Dalliance' reminds me of the desert sunsets I used to watch whilst playing it over and over and it still reminds me of a time in my life when I had the time of my life.

LEAS CLIFF HALL

31 OCTOBER 1989, FOLKESTONE, UK

DAN WELLER

I had stopped off at my grandparents' flat in Dover before heading on to Folkestone to see The Wedding Present for the first time. The Elvis tune 'A Fool Such As I' – my nan was a big fan – was spinning around in my head, as was the

The Wedding Present

hangover from trying to explain above the incessant chirping of a budgerigar that The Wedding Present was indeed the name of a band. This was still inhabiting my mind when I came face-to-face with David Gedge for the first time, quite fittingly 'at the edge of the sea'. On a bright but cold afternoon, I noticed our man on a break from the soundcheck, struggling to keep his thick black mop from blowing in his eyes as he savoured the delights of the English Channel. It stretched out before him, shimmering in the sunlight like Elvis' gold lamé suit. Such was the majestic view from the south-facing terrace of the Leas Cliff Hall that I felt a pang of guilt at interrupting this meditation. But I wasn't going to let this opportunity go. After all, we had sent letters, postcards and Christmas cards to one another for several years, our most recent exchange being a debate on the dubious practice of adding wishy-washy colour to old *Laurel And Hardy* films. (David had been looking for videos to show on the tour bus). Like many, I had been alerted to the band via the John Peel show late one night in 1985. I recall those soft Liverpudlian tones confessing that the lead singer had often sent in stuff that didn't quite make the mark, but that

Clearly, Peter Solowka did not get the memo about not wearing white T-shirts to the photo shoot

1989: A Big Deal

he'd now hit the nail firmly on the head. Peel certainly admired the persistence. That enthusiasm was evident the moment the stylus touched the plastic.

For a 22-year-old lamenting the demise of Scotland's exciting Postcard label, the raw energy of those messy opening bars of 'Go Out And Get 'Em, Boy!' were always going to leave an indelible mark. I knew I'd found something precious. Hurtling along on the back of a rhythm guitar, which sounded as though it was being played by George Formby locked in an amphetamine factory, it rang out like an alarm bell. I sat up in bed and fumbled for a pen, in the hope that a contact address would be read out. I had to know where I could get hold of this sparkling delight. These lads were definitely from the same little planet as me. I ended up buying two copies, because I knew one would soon be worn out. And then more joy, for underneath those gorgeous layers of scrap metal and grit there were some sensitive lyrics. At this time, I was part of a team running the art room of a Margate youth club. A few of us had crossed the road that March to see the inspirational Smiths at the town's Winter Gardens. Morrissey had created

Keith liked his denim jacket far too much to take it off with the rest of the boys. He won't feel the benefit when he goes back out

SOMETIMES THESE WORDS **JUST DON'T HAVE TO BE SAID**

The Wedding Present

a culture of abstinence amongst his fans, which countered the greed and indulgence of those who followed Thatcher. So one line of David's would cause my girlfriend much consternation whenever I quoted it in a passable Kenneth Williams whine. Now and then I defended myself from her Hattie Jacques-like advances with 'a little bit of what you fancy doesn't do you any good at all.' 'That's such a shame,' she would sigh. It was. Well, anyone can make a mistake.

The songs' conversational style make them very accessible, but the finer words have not reached the wider audience they deserve. To my mind, Gedge matches Morrissey, Ray Davies and Chris Difford for imagery, poignancy and intelligence. My favourite moment is from 'My Favourite Dress', 'Slowly your beauty is eaten away, by the scent of someone else, in the blanket where we lay.'

I keep many happy memories. The concert at the tiny Penny Theatre in Canterbury, November 1995, when the band was using two drummers and the audience could only see half of each kit. The note sent from a dressing room at the *Top Of The Pops* studios, scribbled as the band awaited their turn, 'In

A Melody Maker review of The Wedding Present's gig at London's Kilburn National Ballroom by Bob Stanley, who was later in Saint Etienne

---

THE WEDDING PRESENT
KILBURN NATIONAL, LONDON

A GIGANTIC contradiction. David Gedge's angst-horror lyrics make The Wedding Present a personal group, one that should be appreciated in a small venue with a small number of similarly inclined lovelorn souls. That's the way it should be. The National Ballroom is huge, full of raucous lads chanting "Weddoes" (God, the power of the press — why didn't they stick to Wed Pres? It was much nicer).

Something's wrong somewhere. On the opening, "Brassneck", Gedge sings, "I know what this means, it means I have to grow up, it means you want to throw up," and a dozen teen terrors, who have frittered away half their grant on five pints of snakebite, duly oblige.

David and the boys don't seem too flustered by all this. Gedge himself — in a fetching red jumper reminiscent of Fire Engines — is rather subdued, barely smiling all evening and only giving us a Jimmy Saville impression for light relief. No matter. This leaves us more time to marvel at his staggeringly fast rhythm guitar work, a technique picked up from the Velvet Underground's "What Goes On" and taken to the max. A string of new songs is unveiled and happily they head in the same direction as the second half of "Bizarro".

"Bewitched" is the touchstone — their most adventurous song to date. It's a beautiful discord, a glorious ebb and flow of acoustic interludes and sheet lightning guitar passages. It could almost be an English interpretation of Bitch Magnet's scary epic, "Americruiser", it's that good, and would be duly praised if only Wed Pres detractors would pull their heads out of their armpits.

Gedge's lyrics remain on the same tragicomic, brokenhearted level, though. The Wedding Present are still the one group that a chap can relate to when his girlfriend wakes up in the night and calls him Nigel — could you relate to The Pixies after an incident like that? I think not. This is why the archetypal Wed Pres song is called "Give My Love To Kevin", one of only two old faves they play tonight. Nobody does it better. Gedge pours his heart out on the brooding "What Have I Said Now" and the evergreen "Everyone Thinks He Looks Daft", but most of the effect is lost in the crowd, the intensity of the performance dispersed by the huge hall. The shy, stuttering Englishness of the lyrics, as tangible as a rainy Sunday in Leeds on record, all but evaporates in this Freshers Ball atmosphere. No wonder David Gedge looks pissed off. "This is the last one," he says after 45 minutes, "You can't complain. That's only 50p a song." The bloke to my left mutters something about an expensive jukebox.

It's taken them four years to undestand fully their own potential, so crystal clear on the first single, but lost somewhere along the way. At last they are extending themselves, the encore of "Take Me" proving that the artistic stalemate which has held a grip since "George Best", is almost certainly over. In the Gents there is sick all over the floor. On the stage, The Wedding Present are beginning to see the light. Next time, let's hope they play a week at the Borderline instead.

BOB STANLEY

1989: A Big Deal

the room next door, Status Quo are warming up. Rock and roll!' And, at that first Folkestone gig, a thoughtful dedication before the group played 'Give My Love To Kevin'. 'There's a bloke out there who has everything by Laurel And Hardy on video. This one's for you.'

KILBURN NATIONAL BALLROOM
1 & 2 NOVEMBER 1989, LONDON, UK

MEIR MOSES

In 1988 a school friend gave me a cassette of *George Best*. He said his sister from Leeds was hanging out with the singer of this band and that he thought I might like it. I took one look at the cover and tracklist – 'Shatner', 'What Did Your Last Servant Die Of?' – and had to listen to it. To say that moment changed my life would be an understatement. I listened to that cassette for months on end; before I went to sleep and when I woke up in the morning. This album was me. I cried to it and I chuckled with it. It covered all of my emotional bases. *Bizarro* later cemented my love, even though to my ears it sounded so fresh and different compared to *George Best*, and I finally scored tickets with my unknowing mates to see the lads at the Kilburn National. Mark Burgess opened with a mellow acoustic set with another guitarist. I only remember this because I caught his chicken shaker! I can only say that I had no idea what was to come for the next hour. And, yes, strictly an hour only, as I was to find out over the next decade or two. But a few things struck me. The crowd was friendly, relaxed and overwhelmingly male. People spoke in hushed tones, pleasantly buzzed. Balloons were being blown and bounced and it seemed more like a gathering of neo-hippies in baggy shirts and extravagant, eye-covering fringes. What a nice bunch!

The lights went down, the boys came on stage, not a word is spoken and – here we go – they kicked off with 'Everyone Thinks He Looks Daft'. The floor literally erupted into scores – hundreds – of flailing and heaving bodies. The sheer physicality (the sweat!) of it was pretty shocking – you were either all-in or banished to the sidelines to observe. I was all-in. I have never stopped being all-in. I remember, two or three songs in, the left flank of the crowd starting to collapse on top

SOMETIMES THESE WORDS **JUST DON'T HAVE TO BE SAID**

The Wedding Present

of each other, many bodies piling up and trying to extricate themselves from being pinned down. Hillsborough had been mere months earlier. It was a scary moment. People momentarily realised what was going on and lifted each other out of their predicament – only to proceed at the same frenetic, insane pace once the pile of shaken kids had recovered. After half an hour, I was begging for it to stop. After an hour I was in a kind of post-climax daze. No encores. 'We don't do encores.' And I got it. It made perfect sense. All This And More. I have seen my favourite band play across decades now. I have always avoided bothering Gedge but we have exchanged a few kind words and knowing glances over the years. I'd like to think he knows who I am – what fan doesn't? He's a bit of a grump as it is and that's just fine. You need some distance from the man, but the music is etched in the heart.

COVENTRY POLYTECHNIC

4 NOVEMBER 1989, COVENTRY, UK

GARY WOODBRIDGE

We were 16, me and Will. We had started going to gigs about six months earlier and were bitten by the bug straight away. The Wedding Present were definitely our favourite to watch and we did so on multiple occasions over the years. On the night in question we got right to the front as always

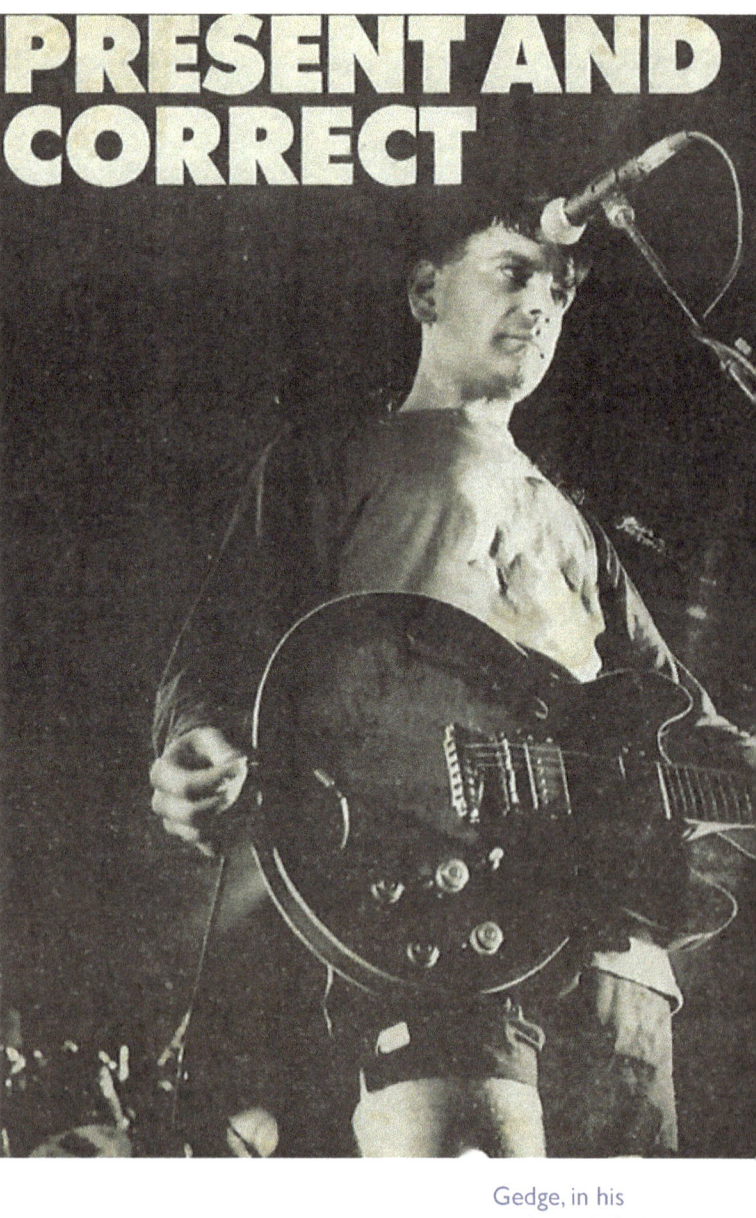

Gedge, in his trademark dinky black shorts, onstage at the Kilburn National Ballroom (Melody Maker)

1989: A Big Deal

and had a good old bounce around, holding our own against all the older lads. At the end of the gig the drummer threw his drumstick into the crowd. Both me and Will got our hands on it simultaneously and began wrestling each other for it, neither of us willing to let the other one have it.

What seemed like ages later, I noticed a big circle had formed around us and we were in the middle with loads of people watching. None of them knew we were best mates! I immediately let go in embarrassment as it looked a lot worse than it was. Will, being over the moon, couldn't help being ecstatic and start taking the piss. He wouldn't have it that I had let go – even years later! One of the roadies must have seen what had happened and us laughing about it after. He called us over and gave me one of David Gedge's plectrums as a runner-up prize! I had it and my ticket stub in a frame on my wall for years. I still have it to this day, although in my memorabilia bag now. Sadly we lost Will a few years ago in a tragic diving accident. Now, whenever I hear or see The Wedding Present, it always brings back great memories of a fantastic live band and growing up with great mates who loved going to watch them.

HUMMINGBIRD

6 NOVEMBER 1989, BIRMINGHAM, UK

PAUL CRESSWELL

I have always liked The Wedding Present but it wasn't until I saw them at Birmingham Hummingbird, just as David sang 'Changing round the posters on your walls' in 'Thanks' that I realised just how much. It was a real 'Fuck, yeah!' moment.

ROCK CITY

7 NOVEMBER 1989, NOTTINGHAM, UK

TIM ABRAHAMS

I've seen The Wedding Present many times. But none more shit than that night at Nottingham Rock City – though it was no fault of the band's. Being on chatting terms with the band and having just moved up to

The Wedding Present

Nottingham Uni, I went down to the venue early to see what was going on and chanced upon them in a local cafe. Apart from a 'hello', I left them with their tea and all-day English breakfast – very rock'n'roll! I had a ticket and so joined the queue to get in. I think The Heart Throbs were supporting in those days and I had quite a crush on Rose, their singer, so decided an early start would be worth it.

As I approached the door one of the Hell's Angels door staff said, 'Oi, you! I've told you already, you're not coming in.' 'On the contrary,' I said, or words to that effect, 'I've never spoken to you before, I have ID and a ticket and in fact I've been inside this dark sticky floored establishment many times before.' He looked at my NUS identity card and dismissed it. I still wasn't getting in, although the reason why was apparently a mystery to both of us. Apart from the fact that he'd told me before, of course. Pissed-off, I sat on the steps, sulking. Then the band appeared. David asked me if I was all right and I told him they wouldn't let me in. He handed me his Access All Areas pass and told me to follow. I did so.

He was able to walk in unchecked but, when I tried for a third time to get in, now with a ticket, ID and a tour pass, I was once again turned away. I gave David his pass back and just shrugged, as did he. Some of my mates appeared and just walked on in, laughing at me. I sold my ticket and went home. To this day I've no clue what happened.

ST GEORGE'S HALL

8 NOVEMBER 1989, BLACKBURN, UK

JAMES TAYLOR & EMMA ROBERTS

The *Bizarro* tour. We were both freshers at nearby Lancashire Poly in Preston and had very recently started dating. What better first date than to see The Wedding Present supported by CUD in rainy Blackburn? How romantic! It was our first Wedding Present gig so we were not sure what to expect and – naturally – too caught up in each other to care. Well, we loved it and have seen The Wedding Present at various venues since. We are still together all these years later and so are The Wedding Present. We will always have that Blackburn gig as our first date to remember. We still love CUD too.

1989: A Big Deal

BARROWLAND BALLROOM

11 NOVEMBER 1989, GLASGOW, UK

ANTHONY HAILSTONES

I went along with a couple of mates who were big followers and who had just bought *Bizarro*. They played stuff mostly from *Bizarro* plus some stuff from their first album. Any concert at the Barrowlands is going to be good. I remember the place jumping, being right down the front and the place going mental! The downside was I lost my watch, which was quite a good one. Telling my mum once I got home, she said, 'Oh, why didn't you look for it or wait behind to find it?' My mum hadn't ever been to a concert, never mind one at the Barrowlands!

SAM GOLDIE

Tickets were rare, precious and highly prized, but not as much to me as my recently acquired girlfriend, who wanted such a ticket. She was (and no doubt still is) beautiful – blonde of bobbed hair and porcelain of skin. I had my own ticket and moved heaven and earth to get her one. Sadly, it was not enough. Her friend from down south was visiting and she pleaded with me to get another. I convinced my

Reaching new heights: the boys shortly after the release of 'Kennedy'

SOMETIMES THESE WORDS **JUST DON'T HAVE TO BE SAID**

The Wedding Present

Nice day for it: The Wedding Present step out of the transit van to enjoy a scenic view

mate at the shop where I worked (Flip – a vintage place of ill repute) to sell me his.

The band were amazing, perfect in every way. As was the manner in which I was dumped for – you have guessed it – the actual boyfriend down south. Kind of sums up my relationship with the band – best enjoyed on your own.

MAYFAIR
12 NOVEMBER 1989, NEWCASTLE-UPON-TYNE, UK

RACHEL SOWDEN

My overriding memory is of Mr Gedge waxing lyrical as to why the band didn't play encores. Apparently, it would be like asking Percy Thrower to add some more plants to what was already a perfect garden – you just wouldn't do it! So here I am, years later, still a massive Wedding Present fan, and I've never contemplated asking for an extra 'plant' since.

1989: A Big Deal

INTERNATIONAL 2
14 NOVEMBER 1989, MANCHESTER, UK

SHAUN KEAVENY
6Music Breakfast Show

In 1989 I was a rabid devotee of The Wedding Present, along with a merry band of vinyl-toting teenaged *C86* fans. I had been introduced to the iconic *George Best* album by my mate Dunny, and soon after picked up *Tommy*, being particularly enamoured with the heart-rending 'Once More', as it perfectly elucidated my feelings for the unattainable Juliet Wood. Juliet wouldn't, as it turned out.

Later that year, I was charged with making a 'project' for my Communication Studies A-level. As I was in a band at the time, and being 17, I decided I was an authority on such matters and began toiling on my *meisterwerk*, a video called, not hubristically, *The Complete Guide to Band Musicianship*. I decided to feature our band (the now-legendary Mosque), a more high-profile local band and another more successful band. I decided to write to David Gedge in the vain hope he would agree to be in the video. 'Fat chance mate, he's a rock star!' scoffed my fairweather sixth form friends, and I concurred.

Fast-forward a couple of months to the summer of 1989. I was, as was befitting of my insurrectionist teenage temperament, watching *Coronation Street* with my mum and dad, enjoying a cup of tea and a Penguin biscuit (I think Alec Gilroy had recently proposed to Bet Lynch) when my nine-year-old brother heard the phone. 'It's for you, Shaun. Someone called David Godge...' I hurled him aside and rushed to the phone. Indeed, it really was. The rock star David Gedge actually had called 21 Beverley Avenue. I noticed he called precisely as the credits of Corrie rolled, and assumed he must also be a fan.

After a minute or two of intensely awkward teen fanboy spluttering and sycophancy, David said he would be happy to provide an interview. We conducted one there and then with me holding a shitty condenser mic up to the receiver and capturing the results on my little tape deck, which were predictably Edison-esque. David invited us as guests backstage to their Manchester International 2 gig later that year and promised us triple-A access and an interview. We could even film it! Fast-forward to November. Myself and my cinematographer/cameraman/

The Wedding Present

best boy grip/Newcastle Brown sherpa Paul Banks were dropped off at the front of the venue. Longsight, Manchester was not then a particularly salubrious place. I imagine it was given the name Longsight as that's what the miscreants relied upon not to get caught by the police when they were turning over shops and houses. Two teenage herberts with a video camera – remember, this is 1989 and so the camera was the size of a holiday suitcase – sheepishly slid up to the front of the queue as instructed. As we did we were met with numerous reactions, from quizzical to mildly aggressive, but sure as Trump's a tit we mentioned who we were and were immediately ushered into the bowels of the brutalist building. Before we knew it, we were in the boys' dressing room. We couldn't bloody believe it! Immediately our offering of a blue bag full of cans seemed naive as it was dwarfed by a young man's fantasy wall of booze from the rider. The place was populated by well-wishers, and we mulled about for a bit. We were first met by Grapper (Pete Solowka), who had his delightful, quite elderly (to us 17-year-olds, at least) Ukrainian parents there. They were so very welcoming and we had a bit of a chat with them. We set up our cumbersome camera and started filming. To our slack-jawed delight, Pete whipped out his SG and started playing the hits for us, unplugged. We

1. CAN'T BE SURE ...... The Sundays (Rough Trade)
2. KENNEDY .... The Wedding Present (RCA)
3. DEBASER .... Pixies (4AD)
4. WFL .... Happy Mondays (Factory)
5. MONKEY GONE TO HEAVEN .... Pixies (4AD)
6. I AM THE RESURRECTION
   The Stone Roses (Silvertone)
7. SHE BANGS THE DRUM
   The Stone Roses (Silvertone)
8. SIT DOWN .... James (Factory)
9. JOE .... Inspiral Carpets (Cow)
10. I DON'T KNOW WHY I LOVE YOU
    The House Of Love (Fontana)
11. SIGHT OF YOU .... Pale Saints (4AD)
12. JUST LIKE HEAVEN .... Dinosaur Jr (Blast First)
13. BLUES FROM A GUN
    The Jesus And Mary Chain (blanco y negro)
14. TAKE ME .... The Wedding Present (RCA)
15. ONLY A PRAWN IN WHITBY ...... Cud (Imaginary)
16. YOU GOT IT (KEEP IT OUTTA MY FACE)
    Mudhoney (Glitterhouse)
17. MADE OF STONE .. The Stone Roses (Silvertone)
18. LAST OF THE FAMOUS INTERNATIONAL
    PLAYBOYS .... Morrissey (HMV)
19. BRASSNECK .... The Wedding Present (RCA)
20. OUIJA BOARD, OUIJA BOARD .. Morrissey (HMV)

1989 was a pretty good year for The Wedding Present, with three top 20 entries in Peel's Festive Fifty (from the *NME*)

1989: A Big Deal

were totally blown away to be given such privileged access. Then David turned up wearing, as I recall, a white hoodie. David was as friendly as we had hoped and not, as we had feared, wondering why the fuck he had invited two tools from Leigh to his sacred space pre-gig. What followed was a good 20-minute chat about the music business and what it was like being in a band. What didn't seem remarkable at the time but which was, looking back, was that the now-legendary producer and Big Black frontman Steve Albini was in attendance. Sitting there, in a stetson and shades, cooler than a choc-ice, already seemingly fully aware of the seismic influence he was to have on the alt-rock scene. In all, it was an unforgettable night which, I have no doubt, had a profound influence on me. I have subsequently spent my entire adult life blagging into gigs and trying to befriend bands. Thanks, boys!

STEVE ALBINI
Engineer

It was definitely a label or manager guy, the first time they approached me for the EP. I saw them once, somewhere in the North – maybe Manchester – before I first went in the studio with them. They were considering having me work on a record and asked me to come see them play the next time I was in the UK.

They had a label rep take me up there, put me up in a nice hotel, the whole nine yards. The kind of thing that happened when the big labels had money to burn. The show was good, their rapport with their audience was great. I remember they either closed the show or opened it with David saying, 'We are The Wedding Present and we do not do encores.' Their music was smaller than a lot of the bands I was into at the time, more consonant and brighter, less noisy, but they had a really clear intent and identity so they sold it well and didn't seem to be trying to wear somebody else's ideas.

MIKE GAYLE
Author

A year after discovering them, and within the parameters I had set myself (owning their entire output), I was not far from being the world's biggest Wedding Present fan. Having started with 'Why Are You Being So Reasonable Now?' on 12". I took up regular residence in Birmingham's

The Wedding Present

premier indie store, Frank's Wild Records, scouting for The Wedding Present's back-catalogue. Slowly, gradually, the discs I longed for fell into my possession, first the mighty *George Best* then 'You Should Always Keep In Touch With Your Friends', 'My Favourite Dress', 'Pourquoi Es Tu Devenue Si Raisonnable?', 'Anyone Can Make a Mistake', 'Nobody's Twisting Your Arm' then finally *Tommy*.

Unlike other bands I'd deemed worthy of the completist route, only to regret having done so by my third purchase, The Wedding Present had yet to ever disappoint. Each and every new song or re-recording I heard only made me love them more and the fact that their first three highly collectable singles eluded me (down to cost, more than anything) caused me the kind of deep all-encompassing pain that only an 18-year-old can feel.

Such was my love for the band that when I arrived at the University Of Salford as a Sociology student in the first week of October 1989 the only thing I was interested in was recruiting mates for the trip to see the band play at Manchester's International 2 the following month. This to me was more important than my degree, comparing A-level results with complete strangers or even the pursuit of unattainable girls in Doc Martens.

Not only was this my chance to see the band I loved live but, more importantly, the album they were promoting at the time was their first since I had become a fully fledged devotee. I was nervous. In interviews in the music press, as the band recorded what would become *Bizarro* in Wool Hall studios in Bath, Gedge was quoted as saying he wanted to take a different direction. Looking back now of course, it's easy to see why they felt a change was due; having honed the sound that they had made their own since their mid-twenties the band were now approaching their thirties and wanted a new sound to match their increasing

'Kennedy', the sole Wedding Present single of 1989, reached 33 in the UK charts in November

maturity. But, to a 19-year-old fan who'd had his fingers crossed tightly for more of the same, this 'different direction' didn't bode well. I simply didn't have it in me to find a new favourite band to who I could show this level of dedication.

Following a Monday morning lecture on ethnomethodology at the beginning of October, I made my way in the pouring rain from Salford Crescent to Manchester's Piccadilly Records to pick up 'Kennedy', The Wedding Present's debut single on major label RCA. I listened to it, as I did to all new music, on the record player in my tiny room in the university's self-catering flats. Thinking about that moment now it's hard to square my initial response with the fact that within weeks I would be belting out the lyrics to 'Kennedy' at the top of my lungs and pogoing like my life depended on it at the front of the gig at the International 2. Because on first listen I felt extreme disappointment. Why do they suddenly need to sound like Sonic Youth? Why isn't Gedge singing about love gone wrong? What's all this about 'apple pie'? I didn't get it. And then one day I just did.

At the time of that first listen it helped matters considerably that the B-side of the 12" contained material more readily acceptable to my Wedding Present attuned ears. The big guitar pop sound of 'Unfaithful', with it's classic put-down of 'I haven't worn a shirt like that since 1974', and the tongue-in-cheek cover of Tom Jones' 'It's Not Unusual' helped to ease the pain but the standout track was 'One Day This Will All Be Yours', a song which helped more than any other to bridge the gap between the two Wedding Presents.

Even though I'd been primed, *Bizarro* still managed to surprise, with the storming album opener 'Brassneck' being an instant Wedding Present classic. This new Wedding Present sound was bigger and more powerful and the lyrical content was beefed up too. This was the sound of a band come of age. Refusing to stand still, they were bolder, brasher and walking tall with a new-found confidence. *Bizarro* was a revitalizing change in direction for the band, a collection of songs which have matured into anthems that can, with a single bar, make the hairs on the back of your neck stand on end.

What The Wedding Present have always been about is articulating the things you felt in your heart but could never find the words to say; taking ordinary lives and everyday moments and projecting them onto the big screen. Not many bands can make you fall in love with them in an instant and fewer still can keep that love going for over twenty years. You grow up, you

The Wedding Present

get a job, you fall in love, you have kids and life gets busy. But then you play an album like this and it transports you to another time, another place and you come to realise without a shadow of doubt that the love's still there.

BATSCHKAPP
3 DECEMBER 1989, FRANKFURT, D

CLAUDIA TUCKER

I made a cake for the band's fifth anniversary. It was my first Weddoes gig and it took ages to convince security to let me backstage to hand it to the band. I didn't get any photos of the occasion but I've still got the picture of the rose I put on top of the cake. When I met David a few years back at a Wolverhampton gig, he couldn't remember it.

1990: All Gigs And No Album

1990 began for The Wedding Present with a handful of European dates, followed by a UK tour and then their debut North American tour, before an appearance at the Reading Festival and then more UK dates - 64 shows in total.

HUDDERSFIELD POLYTECHNIC

27 JANUARY 1990, HUDDERSFIELD, UK

BRUCE ANTELL

I won a competition to spend an evening with the band before a concert and hang out backstage with them. I took my mate Steve along and we got very drunk.

David drove us back from Huddersfield to Leeds and Steve kept sticking his head out of the car window while I was drunkenly negotiating free tickets for the Ipswich date of their tour.

At Ipswich we went up to the merchandise stall to claim our free T-shirts, only to get a slightly frosty welcome as it turned out David and Sally had to clean Steve's puke off the side of their car the next day.

JON PINDER

My friend Doug at college was doing a BTEC in business studies. One of the modules was to run your own business. He decided on running coach trips to gigs and put on a trip to see The Wedding Present at Huddersfield Poly. I had just started seeing Sarah and was desperate to impress her, but as an inexperienced teenager I didn't know that girls wouldn't love The Wedding Present.

Turns out the only new love I got from that gig was for the support band, New Fast Automatic Daffodils. I don't

The Wedding Present

think the girlfriend lasted much longer, although I did bump into her many years later on my stag night. Although nothing really happened, it was a sign that ahead of me was an ill-fated marriage. So really I guess, indirectly, The Wedding Present are to blame for me not being appealing to this girl.

In the very early Nineties my brother's friends were in an up-and-coming band called The Killy Car Thieves. They were great but didn't last and the drummer and singer drafted me and my brother in on guitar and bass. A great idea. Only we were shit. We never made it out of the rehearsal room, but we had our rehearsal space at a place in Horbury which we shared with The Wedding Present. Imagine my surprise as I was struggling up the metal stairs one day with a heavy guitar amp to find David Gedge at the top waiting for me to get out of the way.

STUDIO
30 JANUARY 1990, BRISTOL, UK

DARRELL TAYLOR

The set was short and intense, no more than an hour, but energy-driven and high tempo. I remember Gedge introducing the band by saying that they don't do encores!

CORN EXCHANGE
1 FEBRUARY 1990, IPSWICH, UK

STEVE CLARK

We didn't get many good indie bands come and play live in Ipswich. It wasn't a university town and the main venue was too big for most bands. However, every now and again the Corn Exchange would have a good band on, so imagine my delight when I saw in *NME* that The Wedding Present were coming. I got my

1990: All Gigs And No Album

ticket and waited for the day to come. It finally arrived and, although I was 'Billy No Mates' and going on my own – my friends who weren't already away at Uni had shocking musical taste – I couldn't wait to get there. I decided I was going right down the front in the middle, so I arrived early to take my place. I was stoutly built and was sure I could handle a bit of moshing. As they launched into the first song, the place went wild and the mosh started. I was thrown around and could barely keep my balance, being catapulted into different people and feeling totally out of control.

Eventually, the buffeting was so much that I was forced over to the side of the stage where the view was not so good but there were far fewer people. In fact, I had this section almost entirely to myself. I decided to stay there for the rest of the gig and it then dawned on me that the reason I had so much space to myself was that I was right next to a very large speaker. Never mind; I was thoroughly enjoying myself now that I was no longer being shown up for the physical moshpit lightweight that I clearly was despite my generous proportions!

I went away that night with The Wedding Present's fantastic songs ringing in my ears. Literally. For days. In fact, I didn't think the ringing would ever stop. Friends and family questioned the wisdom of my positioning at the gig and suggested medical help. But I waved them away; it was worth it.

'Brassneck', The Wedding Present's single of January 1990, was a re-recorded version, engineered by Steve Albini

ROB SADLER

Picture the scene. 1987: Chernobyl had exploded, the Cold War was showing no sign of thawing and the UK music charts, in my late teen opinion, were frightful. Holed up in my nuclear family bunker with *Tommy* and *George*, I littered the mixtapes I'd obsessively created with tracks from said vinyl.

Towards the end of side two, sweeping guitars and machine-gun drums swirled like a blizzard of beautiful chaos until a resigned, pining voice exclaimed, 'When I set foot on the bus you laughed and said, 'That's the end for us.'' Our subject matter had been found out! Who was she? Where had he been clandestinely? Why the deception? Then the hopelessness: 'I know that now.' Our composer pleads with her, he hints at previous rows and traits of the outgoing partner: 'Have you taken all you want,

The Wedding Present

is that it, have you really gone?' Many a relationship was mortally irreparable back then especially when, as a politically disaffected youth, we relied upon our *NME* and *Melody Maker* heroes to chronicle the real Eighties. The pleading ends with David's immortal remorse, 'It's so clear to me now.'

The desperate words cease, leading to the self-destructive barb of manic melodic mayhem which overwhelms the listener as the punctured beating and ten-wrists-per-second, broken-string fury swirls and reverberates around my 8' x 8' box room, briefly interrupted by three knocks from the parental lounge below. No one understands me! What of me?

I wed the girl I went to the Weddoes concert at Ipswich Corn Exchange with. I had two sons and divorced in 2006 after coming out. *Tommy* and *George* are still such loyal friends, despite their numerous aural format changes. Mr Gedge, you soundtrack my life and I love you for that.

CIVIC HALL

3 FEBRUARY 1990, WOLVERHAMPTON, UK

'GRAMP'

'Kennedy', 'Give My Love To Kevin' and 'My Favourite Dress' were all stalwart tracks at our Thursday night indie disco, mixed in with The Cure, Pixies and The Smiths. When 'Brassneck' and the accompanying tour came along, I knew I'd be there. Looking at the ad in the *NME*, there it was – Wolverhampton Civic.

It was a Saturday but also my 18th birthday. So... the distinct possibility of a naff family thing with distant aunts all saying, 'I haven't seen you since you were this big' and expecting to kiss you with their hairy lips. Alternatively: get tickets, have my first legal beers and go to a Prezzos gig. I'd been cruising round blasting my *Tommy* cassette out of the 39-speaker system that I'd plumbed into my 1979 three-door Ford Craptina (one of the back doors was welded shut). A 'secondhand' stereo out of the new Volvo 740, a separate graphic equaliser booster and all 39 speakers at their limits. For ages I actually thought Joe Meek or Phil Spector may have produced 'Kennedy', such was the distortion. So it was a no-brainer. Tickets were purchased and my 18th started at 11am, waiting for our local to open. We ended up in there until about 4pm before catching the bus into town. I had a 'power nap' on the way, a quick excursion to McDonalds for tea and then headed round to the Civic to queue.

1990: All Gigs And No Album

Support on the night were The Edsel Auctioneer and, after watching them, I felt the best idea was if we went up on the balcony and found a seat for the main event, as for some reason my legs wouldn't listen to the commands my brain were sending them. So we found some seats stage-right – perfect – and watched the band, led by a certain DLG sporting black shorts, perform a killer set. I will never forget my 18th birthday, although a lot of the day is quite difficult to recall. I still have my 'Brassneck' T-shirt from the gig.

While we slumped in our seats to enjoy the gig, a group of four girls stood behind us, singing, shouting and dancing along and annoying us. A few months later, we started to hang around with a group of girls and it turned out they were the very ones who had done their best to try and annoy us. A couple of weeks later, a friend of theirs joined us who also happened to be there that night. Me and her got together. A perfect story for the book? Perhaps. But we split after five years and she still has some of my Smiths vinyl. It's the reissue albums on 10" vinyl I'm talking about here, not just a 7" of 'Ask'. I've been gutted for over 20 years about that. The girl I can live without, but my vinyl…

When my van at work was broken into circa 1993, they stole the stereo. My *Tommy* cassette was in it. The gaffer was kicking things and swearing. I was more bothered about losing my Prezzos tape.

> "…we split after five years and she still has some of my Smiths vinyl. It's the reissue albums on 10" vinyl I'm talking about here, not just a 7" of 'Ask'! I've been gutted for over 20 years about that…"

KATE SULLIVAN

I remember a letter in the *NME* from somebody whose car was broken into. All their tapes were stolen apart from the Wedding Present ones. A note had been left by the thieves saying, 'We're not students – we don't like The Wedding Present.' I remember thinking, 'That's a lie – they'd take everything.'

I was then burgled three times in quick succession and each time all my CDs were nicked, apart from the ones by The Wedding Present.

KAREY PARSONS

The first time was Wolverhampton Civic on the *Bizarro* tour. I've been looking for my lost *Bizarro* T-shirt for years now, so if anyone has it I'd like it back. It would never fit me now, although to be honest, it didn't really fit me then.

The Wedding Present

RITZ

4 FEBRUARY 1990, MANCHESTER, UK

STUART DAVIDSON

Growing up in West Cumbria in the Eighties, there weren't many opportunities to hear live music. We were still only 15 when The Smiths played Carlisle Sands Centre in 1985 and nobody's parents were prepared to drive the hour or so to get us there, never mind sit and wait for us.

So beyond that, we were pretty much restricted to the 'local lads made good' It Bites or dreadful Cumbrian heavy rock bands.

The Wedding Present were new and exciting, lauded by John Peel. I ordered *George Best* on vinyl from Billy Bowman's record shop in Cockermouth, calling in every few days to see if it had arrived from the distributor as part of their twice-weekly delivery. *Tommy* came mail order from Red Rhino records in York, a signed copy sourced from the classifieds in *NME*. It's still upstairs in the loft, stored away safely.

I started Liverpool University in September 1989, but remember going to Leeds University Open Day before that, and I spotted some huge Wedding Present fly-posters on a derelict building in town. I wanted one, but couldn't peel it off without ripping it.

My first Wedding Present gig was an Ambulance Drivers Benefit. The Edsel Auctioneer supported, the gig was loud and the Ritz sprung dance floor was a bit weird! 'Brassneck' was released the next day.

SUBTERRANEA

19 FEBRUARY 1990, LONDON, UK

KEITH KAHN-HARRIS

A friend and I interviewed David Gedge and Grapper for a fanzine we put together. We were sixth formers at the time. The interview took place

> "I remember that David Gedge – much to my delight – really liked Napalm Death and Extreme Noise Terror"

1990: All Gigs And No Album

Pages from the 1990 diary of Stuart Davidson

before a gig they were playing at Subterranea in Ladbroke Grove. We arrived during the soundcheck, feeling a little overawed. What I remember most about the interview was the incredible generosity with which they gave their time.

We talked for well over an hour. I'm sure our questions must have been pretty inane – for example, I asked whether it hurt that they played so fast. The answer? 'Practice, mate.' But they didn't patronise us and were affable and friendly. I also remember that David Gedge – much to my delight – really liked Napalm Death and Extreme Noise Terror. After the interview, the venue still wasn't open. We couldn't leave, as neither of us actually had tickets, so we just skulked around.

Eventually, through boredom as much as anything else, we snuck into their dressing room. There was no one in there so we stole the crisps from the band's rider.

SOMETIMES THESE WORDS **JUST DON'T HAVE TO BE SAID**

The Wedding Present

LEEDS POLYTECHNIC
23 FEBRUARY 1990, LEEDS, UK

NEIL W

Sometime in the late Eighties/early Nineties, I wrote a fanzine which, although ostensibly about The Smiths, featured other bands too. Naturally I wanted to include The Wedding Present, then said to be a Smiths fan's 'second favourite band'. So I tried to get in touch in the vain hope of an interview. There was an address on the back of *George Best*, so I dutifully sent off a letter or postcard and thought no more of it.

Some weeks later I heard my mother answer the phone and engage in a short and slightly confused conversation, before calling me and passing the phone, 'Hello is that Neil? This is David Gedge. I've got your letter here.'

Once I had picked up my jaw from the floor, I responded and the hospitable Mr G said I was welcome to come and talk to him after the upcoming gig in Leeds. He assured me I would be on the guest list and just told me to come backstage after the gig. I travelled on the train from Grimsby and watched a rollicking performance. I went to my appointed spot to await an entrance backstage. While waiting I got chatting to two girls who it transpired were also there to interview the band for their Wedding Present fanzine, *Something Out Of Nothing*. One of those two girls is now editor-in-chief of *The Guardian* – just shows where good taste in music can get you.

I entered the dressing room and DLG greeted me and found us a quiet corner. He was very accommodating and only slightly sniggered as I took my little sister's Fisher Price tape player out of my bag to record the interview. He answered my puerile and uninteresting questions patiently and I took some photos of him stylishly set in front of the toilet cubicles.

I was welcomed to stay around post interview but I only stayed a short while due to a) being pathetically shy and b) being wary I might miss my last train home. Naturally, I did miss my train, and spent the night sitting in shop doorways and park benches before catching a 6 AM train home.

> "He only slightly sniggered as I took my little sister's Fisher Price tape player out of my bag to record the interview"

The Wedding Present, 1990. Photograph by Andrew Catlin

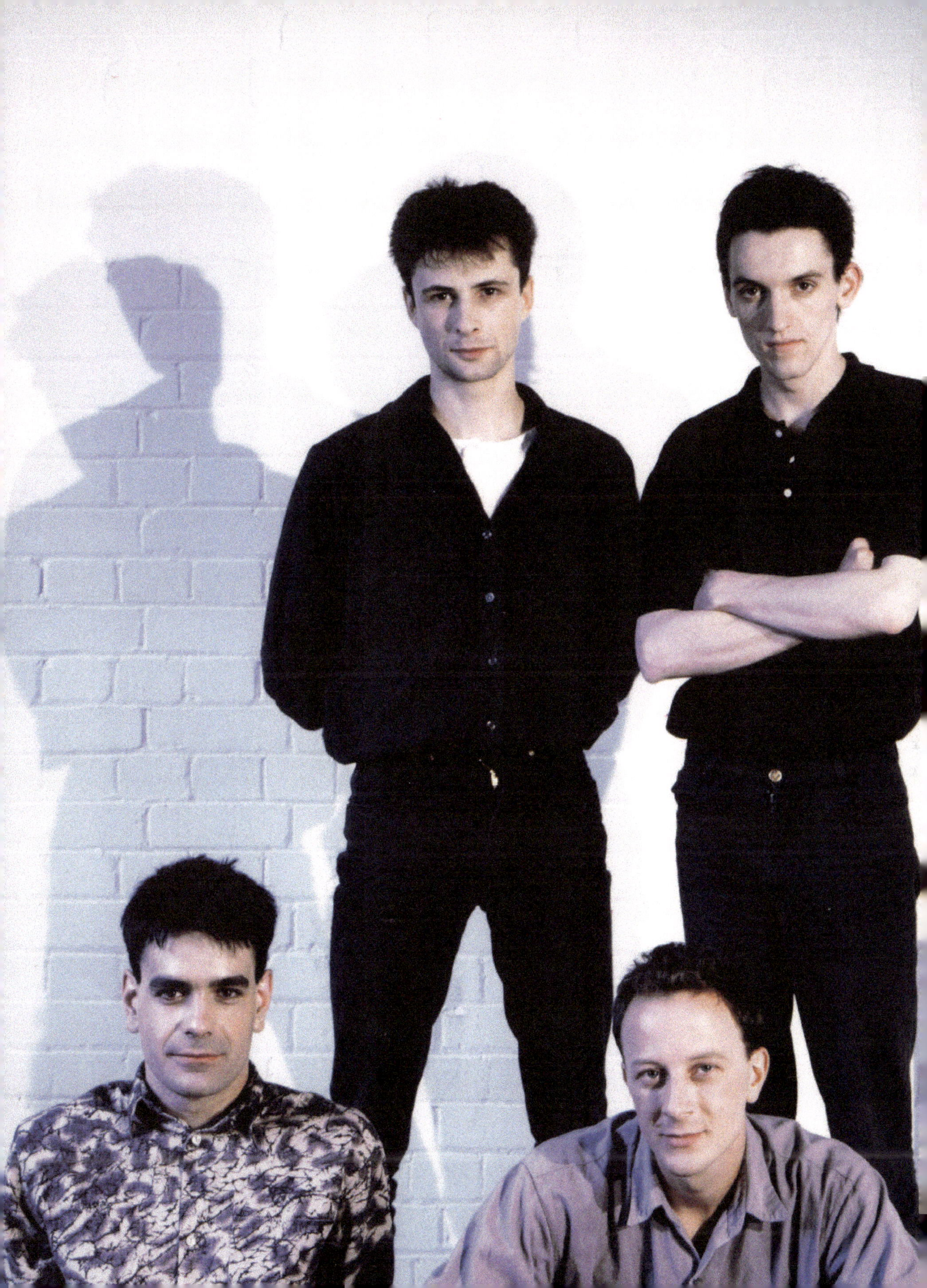

The Wedding Present

LIVERPOOL UNIVERSITY

24 FEBRUARY 1990, LIVERPOOL, UK

JOHN LAMB

I once did the mix when The Wedding Present played at Liverpool Uni. It was a 'secret' gig which, of course, the whole of Liverpool knew about. There was a mechanical wall that rose before the band played a half-hour set and then the wall went down again and the normal club night continued. There were that many people in there that the wall couldn't be raised. Eventually we got it up and then, as the crowd surged forward, the temporary stage was pushed back and all the cables came out of every speaker, all the front of house and stage monitors. It was a mad two minutes but we all got it sorted.

STUART DAVIDSON

The 'secret' band had been widely publicised and the place was heaving! When it was full, the security guards let people sneak in, for a few quid, down a corridor and through the gents toilets from the Mandela Bar in an adjoining building. The gig was fantastic; hot, electrifying, sweaty and loud!

DAVID GEDGE

This was a series of shows where they didn't announce the band who would be playing. There was a screen in front of the stage that was raised just before the concert. So, basically, the band was hidden from view until the very last minute.

CIVIC HALL

11 MAY 1990, MARYPORT, UK

STUART DAVIDSON

I was at Liverpool Uni and received a letter from my mother enclosing a newspaper cutting from the local paper. The Wedding Present were heading to

1990: All Gigs And No Album

Cumbria to play a benefit gig! Not only that, CUD were supporting and I'd not seen them live, although I had *When In Rome, Kill Me* on vinyl. Maryport Civic Hall turned out to be a 600-capacity venue that was more used to bingo and occasional Young Farmers' dances than it was to rock bands.

Four of us travelled up from Liverpool. We arrived early. Maryport was deserted. We headed down the Main Street, calling into the Captain Nelson pub on the quayside. We were the only people in – apart from The Wedding Present and CUD! It turned into a great, if slightly surreal, night. Crap sound, a local heavy metal band opening the gig and a real mixed audience, from local indie kids – pissed on cider they'd drunk in the park before the gig – to townies that seemed to have stumbled into something they really couldn't comprehend. How good it felt, after years of being hindered by distance to gigs, to be just a few miles from home.

BRIXTON FRIDGE

13 MAY 1990, LONDON, UK

PAUL WHITE

I interviewed David at this gig for a friend's fanzine. I wrote to them and he phoned my house to arrange a time. The interview took place after the soundcheck, which I got to watch. The majority of the chat was about how much he loved The Pixies and how he thought Birdland was a great name for a band but that their music was not very good.

COLOSSEUM

17 MAY 1990, LEEDS, UK

JAMES FRYER

Standing right at the front at the Colosseum gig was bound to guarantee me a starring cameo in *punk*, the live video that was being filmed – or so I thought. As it is, my claim to fame is that you see my arm a few times,

The Wedding Present

behind my mate Sam who wasn't even bothered about appearing but who features heavily. But it is definitely my arm – honest. The other video experience was the gig being used for footage for the 'Blue Eyes' video in 1992. As I recall, this took place at Rooftop Gardens in Wakefield. As well as playing 'Blue Eyes' at least twice, they also played a small set. Again, my mates feature heavily in the video and I don't. I was there though, honest.

IAN JONES

Robert and I had been listening to the Weddoes since *George Best*, attending concerts in nearby Liverpool. There, the relative safety of a train home broadened our horizons beyond Chester, a city where, prior to 1990, the visits of My Bloody Valentine, Mudhoney and Mega City Four provided nothing but a false dawn to teenagers looking for local access to new upcoming indie bands.

1990: the music press' news of a filmed concert for a future video release was an attractive prospect for a pair of 17-year-olds. I was in charge of tickets and surprisingly, despite the lack of sophisticated online ticket agencies, managed to secure four – for me, Robert plus fellow fans Sarah and her older brother Sean. On the day we left early, which meant that we had to miss a bit of school (or sixth form or whatever we were meant to be doing at the time). Rob borrowed his mum's trusty Rover Metro and off we went – sunroof cracked open, a tape of *Bizarro*, cigarettes and the occasional McEwans Export for company. On reflection, we either had no concept of how long it would take to drive to Leeds or we didn't fancy our chances of making it in the Metro. We were there by lunchtime. Leeds was warm and sunny, like all halcyon days. A quick recce – car park, venue, pub and we were all set, except for one thing. For some reason I brought with me a pair of bright yellow ski goggles. To this day I'm never certain why.

The band took to the stage, Gedge sporting his usual black shorts and, after a brief introduction, they launched into the first number, 'Don't Talk, Just Kiss'. I decided to dispense with the ski goggles, launching them towards the stage.

They landed safely between Gedge and Solowka, maybe preserved on film forever. The concert was excellent and with the added rarity of a Wedding Present encore, although they never left the stage so I don't think it counted! And then it happened. Pete found the ski goggles and, following all of the logic of why they were there in the first place, decided to wear them. Cue 'Brassneck' – and surely the only version recorded with a band member sporting ski wear. The good-humoured side of the band captured on film forever – and it's all down to my ski goggles! A few months later and with great expectation, I

1990: All Gigs And No Album

purchased the VHS cassette of *punk. A quick scan of the running order and 'Brassneck' was second up. Not quite how I remembered it, but I put it down to artistic licence.

First song, 'Don't Talk, Just Kiss', just like the gig – perfect. Next up, the small-screen debut of the ski goggles. With a feeling of disbelief not too dissimilar to Charlton Heston in the final scene of *Planet Of The Apes*, sadly the live version of 'Brassneck' had been left on the cutting-room floor, replaced by the promotional video, the tale of Leeds preserved only to memory!

Fast-forward to 14 February 1992 and Planet X, Liverpool. I manage to steal a few words with Gedge before the sweat-fest of the opening night on what turned out to be an epic tour of small venues.

'So, David, what happened to my goggles?' With a glint in his eye he retorted, 'One of the road crew had them. Sex games...'

LEE'S PALACE

19 JUNE 1990, TORONTO, CAN

ANDRE GELINAS

The first time I saw them was also the first and only time in my life that I tried body-surfing. I was up in the air and when I touched ground I noticed I was on the stage, standing right in front of my idol David Gedge. Out of the corner of my eye I saw a security guard dashing towards me so I dove back into the crowd and surfed some more until I safely landed back to the ground. Just before the gig I also played pool with the bassist. Very approachable lads indeed. I saw them twice more in Vancouver, the last show about three years ago when they were touring with The Pinky Piglets, now Toquiwa. I talked to them before the gig – those girls from Japan were pretty cool.

Lee's Palace, Toronto, where Andre Gelinas lost his body-surfing cherry

MELODY · MAKER

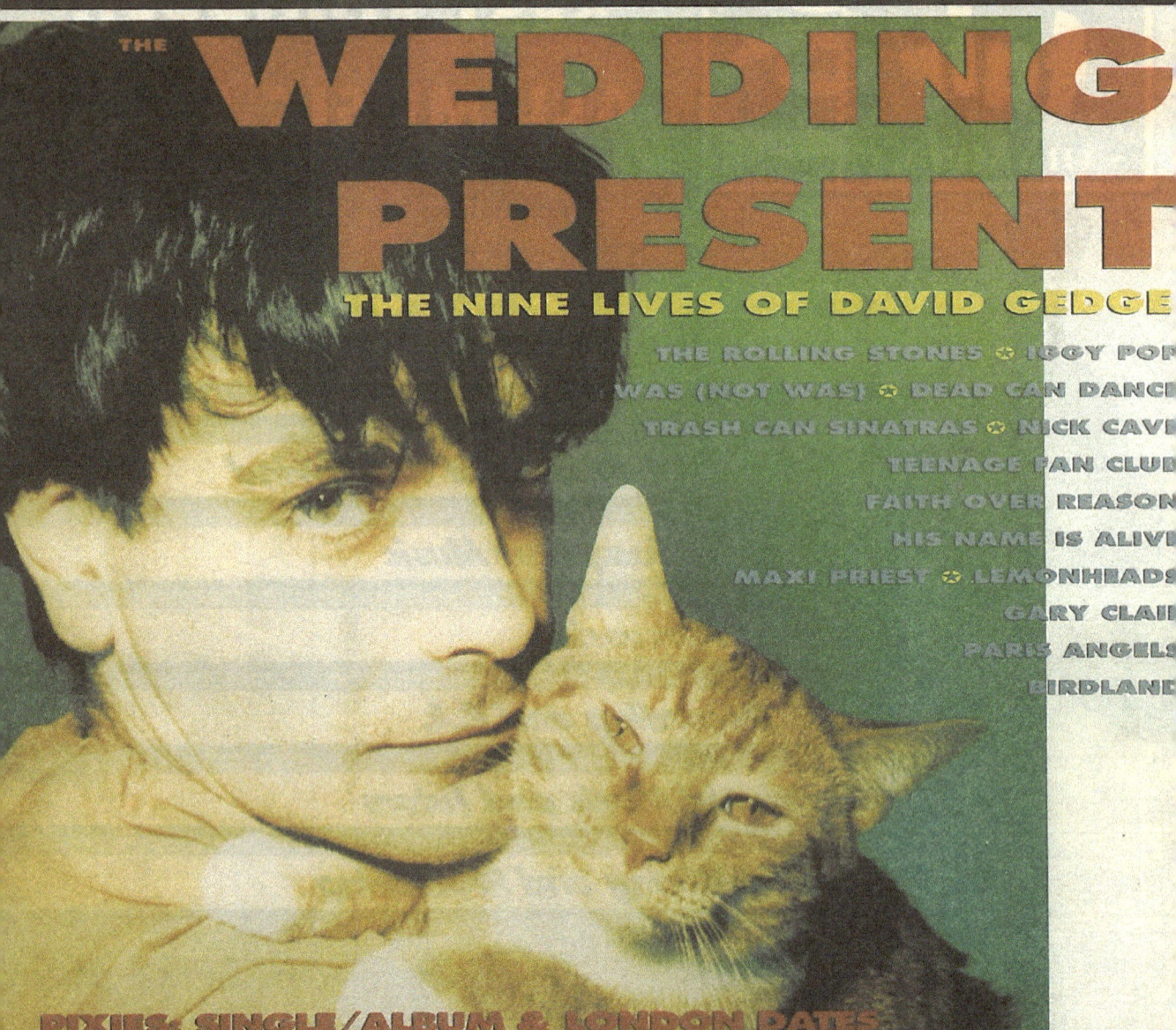

THE WEDDING PRESENT
THE NINE LIVES OF DAVID GEDGE

THE ROLLING STONES • IGGY POP
WAS (NOT WAS) • DEAD CAN DANCE
TRASH CAN SINATRAS • NICK CAVE
TEENAGE FAN CLUB
FAITH OVER REASON
HIS NAME IS ALIVE
MAXI PRIEST • LEMONHEADS
GARY CLAIL
PARIS ANGELS
BIRDLAND

PIXIES: SINGLE/ALBUM & LONDON DATES

SUMMER RAVES
FIGHTING FOR THE RIGHT TO PARTY

Gigantic!
EXCLUSIVE CASSETTE/CD OFFER
FEATURING: THE BREEDERS • COCTEAUS
LIVE! • MARC ALMOND • BIRDLAND

Gedge and furry friend, feline groovy on *Melody Maker*'s cover in July 1990

1990: All Gigs And No Album

BACCHANAL

29 JUNE 1990, SAN DIEGO, CA, USA

MARCO BELTRAN

My friend made me a tape of The Wedding Present in 1987 and I've been a fan ever since. They were playing in a strip-mall in a loser club. I was thinking, 'Wow, this place does not deserve The Wedding Present.' I was thinking Casbah or Iguana's Tijuana. There were, like, ten people there and I brought six! I was at their feet watching and talking but they refused to play 'What Did Your Last Servant Die Of?' How dare they? Just joking! My daughter is a Ramones and Wedding Present fan and loves and requests 'those two songs in a row': 'Don't Talk, Just Kiss' and 'Gone'. Lyrically I love 'Every time somebody laughs I think it's you/every time a car drives by I think it's you/you changed your number and my phone book is such a mess.' They got the 22-year-old me through the worst breakup of my entire life.

READING FESTIVAL

25 AUGUST 1990, READING, UK

CHRIS BOUNDS

They were second on the bill to Inspiral Carpets. I'd worked my way right down to the front. While waiting for them to come on it was, for a shortarse like me, hard to stay on my feet at times. I remember them opening with a cover of the theme from *Cheers*. But the next thing I knew I was lying on the floor near the back of the arena with the concerned face of a total stranger looking down on me. I'd blacked out about two songs in and been carried to safety by a helpful Goth.

RALPH WHITE

Late 1987: every record-shop employee in Peterborough falls in love with *George Best*. Reading 1990: Genesis P Orridge (from Psychic TV) calls me 'Kennedy' because of my T-shirt. Sometime in 1991: first major love ends painfully. I go to most dates on the *Seamonsters* tour. Savage.

STEVEN KING

1988 and the 17-year-old me is waiting for my mates. Whilst I'm waiting, a girl

The Wedding Present

who most of us agreed was the best-looking among all the girls we knew, walked up to me and asked me out. This didn't happen to me. It wasn't right. I assumed I was being set up – that it must be some kind of joke. She was way out of my league but I found myself saying yes. She seemed happy with the answer and walked away. I was in shock and didn't actually believe we were now an item but told all my friends anyway.

A couple of days passed and I had not seen or heard from her. Then, completely out of the blue, she turned up at my house. My parents were out and I invited her in. I made her a coffee and she asked if she could listen to a cassette that she had brought with her. I plugged in my dad's midi system, inserted the tape and pressed play. I expected the Top 40, taped and recorded off the radio from the previous Sunday. But this was stuff that sounded different to anything I was used to. My musical tastes up until this point did not venture any further than stadium rock, with Simple Minds holding the number-one spot. I couldn't work out if I liked this new stuff but I was drawn to it. It sounded exciting. It seemed cool. It was different.

I was only half-listening as I was more interested in the beautiful girl sitting next to me on the settee, but just as I thought we were getting along she got up and announced she had to go. She left the cassette in the stereo and disappeared. Despite her quick exit, I was now head over heels in love and the tape became the most important possession I had. I wish I could remember all the songs on that long-gone tape but the three tracks that I can still remember were 'Ya Ho' by James, 'Unbearable' by The Wonder Stuff and – the best one of all – 'Everyone Thinks He Looks Daft' by The Wedding Present.

There was something special about this. I related to the words. It was plain English. I wasn't having to try and decipher the message like I had to with the lyrics of Simple Minds or U2. It was there, spelt out for me. I understood what the point of the song was. More than that, I could relate to it. I could picture the scene. The guitars, fast and frantic, were like a place I could lose myself in and, despite the energy, I found it calming. It wasn't long before I bought a copy of *George Best*.

A few days later I found out the girl had gone back to her boyfriend, who was older and better-looking than me. I also found out she had asked another boy out at the same time as me and realised the tape she was listening to at my house had, more than likely, been given to her by him. Although I wasn't too upset, I allowed myself to be miserable for a few days. My new album sounded even better! Every song could have been written about me and my predicament. This bloke knew exactly what it was like to lose the girl, but somehow offered a light at the end of the tunnel. It was

1990: All Gigs And No Album

another two years before I first saw them live at the Reading Festival. I've no idea whatever happened to the girl. I just stopped seeing her around. But I will always remember her fondly because, even though she wasn't the love of my life, she introduced me to it.

PAUL HUDSON

I remember it being a scorching weekend. I went with my new girlfriend – now my wife – and my mate and his girlfriend. We broke down on the motorway and got towed to Reading. I was a massive Wedding Present, Inspirals and Buzzcocks fan so Saturday was perfect for me. These were the days before smart phones so I spent Saturday afternoon frantically trying to find out the score of the Leeds game. My missus almost fainted at the sight of David in his short black shorts. She loved him!

DAVID GEDGE

I don't know what I was thinking, really, with those shorts! Well... I do, to be honest. The reason why I started wearing them was because, I think, we played some festival where it was really hot... in Italy or Spain or somewhere... and I did the soundcheck in my little shorts. In those days I think men's shorts were shorter than they are now. All my shorts were like that. So we did the soundcheck and I thought, 'It's really nice that I'm not sweating profusely here. Maybe I'll wear them for the gig.' So I wore them that night and thought, 'Hmmm, I quite like this!' And so I did it all the time after that. For a couple of years, anyway. But now I look back and see photographs and videos and I think, 'Yeah... I'm not sure that was such a good look really.' And I'm far too old nowadays...

CRAIG HUGHES

I met David at the Reading Festival. We were watching The Fall and he was standing next to us. At the end I plucked up courage to speak to David and sounded like an over-excited schoolboy – I was 38! He took the time to humour us and have photos taken. By sheer coincidence, one of my friends was wearing a Ukraine football top with Gedge on the back.

David Gedge at Reading Festival, 1990

INVASION

AUTUMN 1990.   NO: 7.   LOTS OF SPUNK!

OF THE WEDDING PRESENT

WEDDING PRESENT 10" FOUND ON MOON

INVASION EXCLUSIVE

PETE SOLOWKA SAYS: "I'M POSSESSED BY ELVIS."

THE POP WORLD was stunned into silence today when Wedding Present guitarist Peter Solowka announced that his life was being guided by the spirit of Elvis Presley.

The 30 year old half-Ukrainian musician claimed that the ghost of the late icon often visits his Leeds home to "teach" him new playing techniques and songs.

Now Solowka, described by fellow band members as "eccentric" wants the world to know how the Memphis superstar has helped his career.

"I owe so much of my talent to the King of Rock'N'Roll", he said.

REPORTS are coming in of a scientific discovery that has baffled boffins and could change our perception of the universe.

New satellite pictures published in Britain for the first time today reveal that Apollo 19 astronauts may have found a 10" British pop record on the surface of the moon.

Staggered space experts are calling for a top level international conference to discover how the disc, by Yorkshire band "The Wedding Present" ended up in a lunar crater.

"The strangest thing is that it's a limited edition and quite hard to get even on Earth" claimed a Government spokesman.

More details inside.

STUNNING PRIZES TO BE WON IN OUR EXCITING WEDDING PRESENT SIBLING COMPETITION!!

1990: All Gigs And No Album

QUEEN'S HALL
3 NOVEMBER 1990, BRADFORD, UK

ZOE WALKER

Chapterhouse supported. They invited us backstage but we declined. Probably best, being only 15. I remember showing him my Weddoes rose on the back of my parka. He laughed – probably thought it looked daft. Ah, the stories we could tell if only we could remember! And again, in Glasgow, circa 2005 – Gedge sipping Lemsip on stage. Classic.

GEL MCGARTH

That Chapterhouse gig! Oh the irony of stage diving at a shoegazing band's gig. I was rather inebriated at the time. Did they really invite us backstage?

JANE HORRELL

I stole a plastic beer glass David Gedge left on a table at a gig and I still have it. I was a big, sad fan as a student in Wakefield at the time. I've also got a reply to a fan letter David wrote me in 1988 or 1989. I sent him a set of postcards of Bedford and detailed where I'd thrown up a pineapple fritter. He wrote a very sweet reply.

ADELPHI
4 NOVEMBER 1990, HULL, UK

KARL KUTHURIA

I went to see Thrilled Skinny play in Hull, where I had just started studying. The venue was a tiny place but the queue to get in was huge. I was impressed by that, having only really known Thrilled Skinny as a support band for The Wedding Present, but I figured maybe they were more popular up North, despite them being from Luton, very close to my home

Opposite: *Invasion Of The Wedding Present* fanzine

The Wedding Present

in Bedford. As it turned out, I was about the only one who didn't know in advance that it was a secret Wedding Present gig. That was an amazing performance. Just seven songs as a tour warm-up but it was the first time I'd heard songs from the soon-to-be-recorded *Seamonsters*.

JOHN CLAYTON

I saw The Wedding Present at a secret gig. It was a special night. There was a rumour circulating. We turned up. It happened. It was loud and intimate. They came back to Hull a week later and played the Tower.

BARROWLAND BALLROOM
10 NOVEMBER 1990, GLASGOW, UK

CAROLINE MCKENZIE

I had been slow to come to The Wedding Present. *George Best* and the surrounding material hadn't caught my ear, despite Peel's persistence, but 'Nobody's Twisting Your Arm' did and their releases began to make their way to my bedroom cabinet in an array of formats; 12"s, 10"s, cassettes, 7"s in gatefold sleeves, and so on. I almost became a fan without having really noticed; they glided their way into my life with a mixture of mutant guitar sounds, single-mindedness, wry humour and unpredictability. And, now that I was just about a grown-up (cough), I could go and see them.

My first gig was also my first visit to Glasgow's Barrowland Ballroom, which borders on a rite of passage in this city. I was 17 and, to add to the list of firsts, I was wearing contact lenses outside the house for the first time. My mum bought them for me. Apparently I looked 'nicer' without my glasses. 26 years later, I finally agree with her. Thanks Mum.

Keith was on the T-shirt stall. It hadn't occurred to me that people who had been on *Top Of The Pops* might sell their own T-shirts. We were young and foolish. They were previewing *Seamonsters* and I'm pretty sure they opened with 'Dalliance' and closed with 'Niagara'. Even at the time, that felt brave. The place went particulary bananas during 'Don't Talk, Just Kiss' and 'Everyone Thinks He Looks Daft'. But it was

The boys make the cover of Sounds, September 1990

SOUNDS

SEPTEMBER 8, 1990 — 60p

READING '90
A SPECIAL PULL-OUT REVIEW
PLUS all the vibes from our men down the front

NOT QUITE FAMOUS YET!

THE WEDDING PRESENT:
STILL ON THE D.I.Y. ROUTE TO STARDOM

FULL INSTRUCTIONS PAGE 16

FOOTIE FRENZY
ST ETIENNE
BOCCA JUNIORS
EUSEBIO
Kick off the season
PLUS: *Soccer style through the ages*

JESUS & MARY CHAIN

The Wedding Present

'Dalliance' that stunned me – the sheer force of the performance was doubtless enhanced by the occasion and the volume but I can still feel that moment after the second chorus, when the guitars suddenly burst free.

STUART MCMENAMIN

This was my first time seeing or even hearing The Wedding Present. I had stopped listening to music for some unknown reason and a friend suggested we go to a concert and I agreed.

I headed to Glasgow and met up with my pal and we went for deep-pan pizza for dinner. I had my usual 'all you can eat' buffet and we shared two bottles of wine and then headed off to the Barrowlands. When we got there I headed to the merchandise stall and bought a *Bizarro* T-shirt and one of the live tapes – Frankfurt, I think. We then headed up to the hall to watch the support and have a few beers. Then The Wedding Present came on.

It was the best gig I have ever been to at the Barrowlands and I have been hooked on The Wedding Present ever since.

SUNDERLAND POLYTECHNIC

12 NOVEMBER 1990, SUNDERLAND, UK

TIM KING

I'd started a new job in Newcastle upon Tyne. I was in a rented house and one of the female housemates said, 'You like indie. You might like this.' I was given two tapes. I can't remember the first, but the other one was The Wedding Present – *George Best*. There's a good reason why I can't remember the other one. I was just blown away by *George Best*. I must've played that album a thousand times by now. I loved it, and I wasn't sure why I hadn't spotted them at university. I had graduated the year before, in 1987, but what I quickly realised was that something had switched on in my head that wasn't going off. About the same time I was going out with Julie. She lived in Newcastle, and by then I had moved away but I can still remember those cross-country drives to see her a year later to the grinding anthems on *Bizarro*. Julie is long gone, but *Bizarro* remains. I went to my first Wedding Present gig on my own in Sunderland. I loved the sound that much. In the early days they were the band that defined the moshpit,

168 SOMETIMES THESE WORDS JUST DON'T HAVE TO BE SAID

1990: All Gigs And No Album

as it would later become known. These days proper moshing can be a bit hit and miss. Sometimes things are all a bit too cordial and I come away feeling decidedly frustrated, from not being able to influence things enough – when things just don't kick off in the centre. But when you're lucky, you can still make a lot of love in the centre happen – and a lot of friends. I must listen to The Wedding Present most weeks.

I have my favourites, but any Wedding Present song on shuffle is a bonus. I drum to it, especially 'Box Elder', and cycle to it more. Many other bands I have loved and lost, but The Wedding Present have been the constant through the last 36 years. Them and The Pixies.

LANCASHIRE POLYTECHNIC

17 NOVEMBER 1990, PRESTON, UK

MARTIN EAVES

My first glimpse of the group came whilst watching *The Chart Show* in 1988. The video for 'Nobody's Twisting Your Arm' appeared and I was immediately hooked. Back then they came across as 'The Happy Smiths': plenty of angst but with a down-to-earth feel. That was it.

Twenty-odd years later I can recall Grapper telling my brother off for wiping his face on my T-shirt at Preston Poly, and a 360 mile round day trip from the Isle of Sheppey, Kent to Bristol Uni on 11 December 1992.

I still proudly boast a letter and hot-off-the-press *Bizarro* lyrics, with amendments, I received from David in 1989. I know he asked me to keep them to myself – which I have for 28 years.

ACADEMY

18 NOVEMBER 1990, MANCHESTER, UK

PAUL LYON-HAYES

The first time I saw them, I'd been to loads of gigs in a short period of time – Charlatans, The Fall, Happy Mondays, The Man From Delmonte to name a few – but this stood out a mile. The vibe when you walked in was hard to describe. It was

SOMETIMES THESE WORDS **JUST DON'T HAVE TO BE SAID** 169

The Wedding Present

excitement coupled with the familiarity of having a pint with mates. When they came on stage, it was a 'wow' moment – hairs on the back of your neck stuff. It reminded me of my first game at Old Trafford when I was 11. I saw them again in November 2015 at the Academy and still felt the same vibe. I also met David again on the merchandise stall (surprise, surprise!) and he was his usual enthusiastic self!

KILBURN NATIONAL BALLROOM

20 & 21 NOVEMBER 1990, LONDON, UK

STEVE ALISON

David is one of the best songwriters ever. That night, the support was The Boo Radleys. I took the wife, who is not into music. She disappeared and I looked up and she was in the band's lounge, getting my ticket stub signed by Mr Gedge himself.

MAXWELL HALL

27 NOVEMBER 1990, AYLESBURY, UK

RICHARD OLDFIELD

My first exposure to The Wedding Present would have been 'Brassneck', either on *Top Of The Pops* or the John Peel show. I'd been to lots of gigs in the punk/post-punk days from the late Seventies to the early Eighties but, after getting married and not being enthused by much of the music, I hadn't been to one for a while. 'Brassneck' inspired me to go and see The Wedding Present at what was a regular local venue for me.

I went on my own and was a bit apprehensive, but I was soon carried away by the music and joined in the mosh at the front. I remember 'Brassneck' being played towards the end, or maybe even the last song, and the crowd going crazy. My ticket from that night is tatty due to my having it in my trouser pocket and the sweat dripping off me turning it to mush.

CHRIS PORTON

A university friend managed to book two tickets to see The Wedding

1990: All Gigs And No Album

Present at Aylesbury Civic Hall and, having played me *Bizarro* the day before (I was instantly hooked), she worked out the bus required from Oxford to Aylesbury and off we went. She was so impressed at herself for getting us there nice and early that we ended up right at the front.

A girl I ended up never speaking to held my hand for most of the concert and, after no encore, we left the venue hot, sweaty and on cloud nine after a quite incredible experience.

She then took me back to the bus stop to await our bus home to Oxford.

However, after much waiting, I noticed a bus leave from the other side of the bus station and asked her whether she'd checked which bus stop we should be at. 'Ah, not exactly,' she replied. A couple of hours of wandering around Aylesbury followed, wearing our sweaty T-shirts in November, meaning it was getting chilly.

Eventually, finding another couple who'd also made a similar mistake after the concert, the four of us shared a cab back to Oxford at what was – for students – great expense. She never did pay me back for that cab!

ASSEMBLY ROOMS

28 NOVEMBER 1990, DERBY, UK

DAMON PARKIN

David Gedge wants to duet with Madonna. At least that's what he told this journalist that evening. My first Wedding Present gig coincided with a close encounter. Why Gedge granted an audience with a 19-year-old cub reporter on the *Matlock Mercury* – whose rural readers were more interested in tending to their flock than attending a rock gig – remains a mystery to me.

It wasn't a pre-concert interview to promote the band's Derby gig. Support act The Boo Radleys were already rattling through their set on the Assembly Rooms stage as Gedge ushered me into his dressing room.

Besides, the venue was almost sold-out on the back of John Peel's persistent vocal advocacy and Mark Goodier's support for 'Make Me Smile (Come Up And See Me)'. He was playing it regularly on Radio 1's Evening Session and it had become The Wedding Present's biggest hit.

'He's only playing it because it's a cover,' sniffed Gedge, gruffly. For a young reporter on his first

The Wedding Present

celebrity assignment, Gedge was an intimidating proposition.

I told him I was getting married and that my fiancée and I had bonded over our love of The Wedding Present. 'Gedge is the only other man I'd marry,' she revealed to me. You could call it a *Bizarro* love triangle. I told him we planned to walk down the aisle to 'Loveslave' and that 'Gazebo' was to be our first song on the dance floor.

Our dream was that he'd turn up on the day, guitar case in hand and serenade us at the ceremony. That would have been the perfect, ahem, marriage gift. Recollections and revelations from my Derby Assembly Rooms interview included his love of Mad-chester – I think he'd even recently moved to the city from Leeds to soak up the scene – and being bewitched by Madonna.

'I think she's a great artist,' he told me. 'A duet would be interesting. I'm not sure what song we'd record, though.' (Perhaps 'Vogue, Man,

Beside the sea at Blackpool: The Wedding Present, 1991
Photo: Andrew Catlin

172 SOMETIMES THESE WORDS JUST DON'T HAVE TO BE SAID

1990: All Gigs And No Album

Vogue'?). He told me that The Wedding Present name had been inspired by Nick Cave's band The Birthday Party. The Boo Radleys' encore was my cue to scarper. I asked if Gedge would autograph a rather tatty black-and-white press photo of the band. 'A competition prize,' I explained, hoping there'd be no call for Wedding Present memorabilia among middle-aged *Matlock Mercury* readers and that I could keep hold of it as a memento of this momentous meeting. 'Really? That's a crap prize.' He signed it anyway. Then he disappeared, and returned 30 seconds later carrying half-a-dozen Wedding Present hooded sweatshirts. 'Give these away instead.' I imagine there are still Derbyshire Dales farmers wearing white Wedding Present hoodies under their Barbour jackets herding sheep across the hills above Matlock.

SHEFFIELD UNIVERSITY
1 DECEMBER 1990, SHEFFIELD, UK

DAVID POYTON

I lost a brand new pair of specs at Sheffield Refectory when they did some of the Ukrainian stuff. I searched for ages after and they never turned up. I think that was the last time I got 'over lively'. I had to hitch a ride back from Sheffield as I missed my last train and couldn't see a thing without my specs.

WAREHOUSE
17 DECEMBER 1990, LEEDS, UK

MARTIN BOWN

A gang of us drove over from Keighley on a really foggy night in typical December weather. We were queuing outside for absolutely ages, and way past the time the doors should've opened, and the gig started. There wasn't any support on that night. The gig was superb but it wasn't packed. No normal moshpit down front and a low stage. Best of all, to apologise to everyone for keeping us waiting outside, the band came back on for an encore. Yes, an encore! David told

The Wedding Present

the crowd that it was a limited edition, and not to get used to it, but it was an encore all the same. On the way back home, the fog was that thick heading back over the tops to Keighley that my mate Jon got out of the car and walked in front. A real pea souper!

DAMON BROWN

In 1988 I went to Bradford Uni and was able to see The Wedding Present several times around Leeds and Bradford. I recall a special Christmas gig in a Leeds club which included a raffle! The band members had each donated items to be given away and everyone was given a ticket as they entered. Tickets were drawn at the end of the night; mine was number nine. As it was quite late on, a few people had left so numbers were re-drawn until a winner came forward. The ticket for David's bag (which included his famous black shorts!) was drawn and it was number 99. There was a bit of a pause so I shouted out that I had nine but just then the holder of ticket number 99 came forward. Gutted!

While at Bradford I worked in the box office selling tickets for gigs and was amazed to see DLG queuing with the punters to buy a ticket for My Bloody Valentine. I asked him if they were doing a Leeds gig that year but they were too busy with *The Hit Parade*.

1991: *Seamonsters* And (Indie) Stardom

Steve Albini's production brought a more abrasive sound to The Wedding Present on the *Seamonsters* album. The band lost their second original member – Peter Solowka – giving rise to line-up number three.

WEMBLEY ARENA

19 JANUARY 1991, LONDON, UK

JON HEDGES

I first saw the band at the British Music Weekend at Wembley Arena. If there is a lyric written that manages to better evoke such a feeling of betrayal than 'That was my favourite dress you know', then I am yet to hear it and I doubt I ever will.

PACHYDERM STUDIO

APRIL 1991, CANNON FALLS, MN, USA

ANDREW COLLINS
NME journalist

I was already a passionate Wedding Present fan in 1988 when I joined the *NME*, a year out of college, to work as a part-time assistant in the layout room. They had me the first time I heard them on John Peel, which I am fairly certain was their cover of 'Felicity', which must have been the version from their first Peel session in 1986, when I was still at college, the year of *C86* and 'This Boy Can Wait'.

I know I sat up by the stereo and taped the songs I didn't already have from

The Wedding Present

Peel's Festive Fifty at the end of that year and counted 'Felicity' (number 36) and 'Once More' (number 16) among other cherishable gems. Next to The Smiths, The Jesus And Mary Chain and New Order, The Wedding Present felt like young, short-trousered pretenders in 1986, though of course they would come to dominate the Fifty. *George Best* became one of my all-time favourite albums almost instantly when it came out in October 1987.

Having insinuated myself into the editorial end of the *NME* office by bothering the section editors, I feel certain that the first time I wrote professionally about The Wedding Present was a review of the first *Ukrainian Peel Sessions* LP in early 1989. I don't have a full archive of my *NME* writings, but I feel sure I made 'Kennedy' Single of the Week in the same year. I still love that song.

I met the band in April 1991, dispatched by the paper to report on the making of what would turn out to be *Seamonsters* with producer Steve Albini in a place called Cannon Falls in Minnesota (30 miles outside of Minneapolis; population at the time 2,685; I note that its current population has soared to 4,083 in the intervening 25 years). I was not well travelled when I joined the *NME* in 1988 – I'd only crossed the channel once to France on a school trip, and to the Channel Islands for family holidays: that was the full extent of my foreign travel, aged 23, and I had to rush-apply for my first passport for my first trip abroad as a journalist to interview New Model Army in France in 1989.

So, in those first years as a writer, I ticked off many far-flung destinations, broadening my mind in the process, and forever imprinting certain artists of the time on destinations (Carter USM with Prague, The Wonder Stuff with Dusseldorf, Aztec Camera with Hamburg, The Cocteau Twins with Brussels, and so it goes).

Most American trips as a music journalist at the time took you to New York or LA, but rarely to Cannon Falls! It's a series of roads off Route 56 and it was snow-carpeted when photographer Martyn Goodacre and I landed there. We'd flown in from New York, where I'd interviewed and he'd photographed Kitchens Of Distinction and seen them play at CBGBs. This was long before mobile phones proliferated, so it was all phone calls in the room and faxes in the hotel lobby, followed by further panicked attempts at a payphone at Minneapolis Airport, when, late at night, we arrived and were not met at Arrivals, as promised.

We ended up pooling our dollars (Martyn didn't have a credit card and mine was 'maxed out', as we now say) and taking a cab to the motel we were booked into. It was all pretty hairy, I must say – in the middle of nowhere, in the dark. But the couple who ran the motel were homely and helpful, sending us over the freeway to an open diner,

1991: *Seamonsters* And (Indie) Stardom

and personally driving us to Pachyderm studios as there was literally no cab service in Cannon Falls.

We arrived, somewhat slightly dazed, and were met with the sight of Steve Albini railing against our nation's poor pool-playing skills: 'English people! I swear to God, not a decent fucking pool-player in the whole fucking continent!' After this ear-bashing, it was a relief when The Wedding Present – David, Simon, Pete and Keith – ambled into the lounge area. David turned out to be the trivia king – a gift to the journalist with his handy facts about the studio and the local area – and Peter turned out to be vaguely bearded, albeit nothing like the beards men grow today!

Loose talk of a local bar, Jake's, fabled to feature female dancers who lactate for the clientele, never amounted to a fratboy trip out, which remains a huge relief to me. The Wedding Present and topless clubs didn't go together.

They were not that kind of band. They were in fact the kind of band who would painstakingly make their own board game while at Pachyderm, a geopolitical affair based on a map of the world, hand-drawn, and with two axes for left- and right-wing, democratic to dictatorial. I never quite gleaned how it was played, but it had coloured counters and everything.

That evening, we drank in a student bar in nearby town Northfields instead, and I noted in my notebook that the band looked like off-duty squaddies in brown or black leather jackets, practical haircuts and faded jeans. I had hoped to impress my devotion upon them and break the journalist-band Cold War, but only David seemed to thaw in my presence. Nobody was unfriendly (apart from Albini), but the other three remained buttoned-up, even after a few beers. A wall was constructed around them, I felt, and only David seemed willing to open the drawbridge occasionally. At one point, he declared that their music 'soars above the skies.' The others kind of took the piss out of me, certainly out of my earnest questions, even though they were delivered by a self-avowed fan.

Simon was so bored he melted the cellophane on his fag packet at the table. Sarcastic, elusive, blunt, slippery, facetious – these are all words that might describe The Wedding Present that April night in Northfields. I blame myself, of course.

Because *Seamonsters* (then still working-titled Cannon Falls according to my notes, but that might have been a wild assumption or a guess) was recorded in one-and-a-half weeks flat – that's the way Albini works, encouraging the boys to play live – the band were booking early flights home on the day we arrived, and may have been distracted. We, the *NME*, basically missed the recording of the album – quite a scoop! It was, however, a rare privilege to have the whole album played back to me over the studio speakers by Gedge himself, at what I remember to be 'speaker-

The Wedding Present

wobbling volume', especially in light of the fact that when I'd bought the previous two Wedding Present LPs it was with my own money and I'd debuted them on my record player to myself in a small flat in South London. I noted in my notebook that the track 'Octopussy' 'is so sad it will tear your heart out.' David confessed to me, 'I wish this was our first LP.' On the subject of that LP, *George Best*, he and I got into a profound conversation in that collegiate bar that has stayed with both of us ever since.

Whenever I've met David in the intervening years, we often bring it up. I didn't even quote it in the *NME* feature, which ran across a colour, double-page spread the week after. He told me how passionately he'd wanted to go back and re-record *George Best*, to sort of make it right, or make it better. But I told him, as a fan, and not as a journalist, that it was perfect in its imperfections, that you couldn't improve it, as it had already done its job. I was passionate about this, and I don't know if I literally changed his opinion, but it certainly stuck in his mind.

For the photo shoot that afternoon, Martyn had led the band outside into the snowy woodland around the studio and they sat, or stood, seemingly unimpressed, near a narrow river, and at a picnic bench, and by a roadside. They did not make shapes. I seem to remember Martyn climbing into a lone hammock, but that none of the band followed suit. If any of this makes the trip sound like it was a disappointment at all, it wasn't. Martyn and I returned the following day to Minneapolis itself, even more snowbound than Cannon Falls, where we met up with The Trashcan Sinatras, most of whom were ill in bed but who managed to play a gig at a club fabled to have belonged to Prince – I wish I could remember its name, but it wasn't very purple. For the two of us, it had been a band-crawl across two states, and an exhausting one. I had met one of my very favourite bands and, I think, sowed a seedling with David Gedge. We've certainly had better conversations, just the two of us, since 1991, and I was thrilled when he asked me to write sleeve notes for a Cinerama box set. They say you should not meet your heroes. Well, they're wrong. I met four of mine in 1991 and even though they refused to meet me halfway, I liked being around a band in the afterglow of their third LP in a foreign place in symbolically chilly weather. I still think *George Best* is perfect.

PETER SOLOWKA

I don't often listen to music from the past, to be honest. When you're involved in a band it's a bit different. If I do listen to an album, it's *Seamonsters*. Every single song on there I just think is amazing. Whereas I think one or two

1991: *Seamonsters* And (Indie) Stardom

of the *George Best* songs just showed how fast we could play. As time went on, that desire that I had to make Ukrainian music and the fact that you couldn't just turn it off from the press once it's been put out there... I think that's one of the biggest factors why I was, shall we say, no longer needed, in the band. I can probably understand it now. Even then, I don't think I'd go back and change anything. I couldn't. It's just the way things are. I was a distraction from what people wanted to do. Did David and I fall out? It's not easy for someone that you've known for nearly twenty years to turn around and say, 'You're not in the band any more.' That wasn't easy for him. It's certainly not easy to take. We don't talk much anyway now. I think our passion was always making music together. But I can still sit and talk to him. There's no problem like that.

You don't sit and bear grudges. Things could always be done in a different way. But the very fact that they felt that that was the right thing to do? I had no problems with that.

MICK HOUGHTON

I certainly think that when Peter left there was some concern that it would change the sound and the dynamic of the group. With most groups, people either identify with the singer or the guitarist. It may have helped the transition that Peter had been the driving force behind the Ukrainian Peel session recordings. When Peter left, there was a sense that he wanted to pursue that direction so it was never seen as a coup to bring in another guitarist.

By then they'd had hits with 'Kennedy' and 'Brassneck' and that sort of exposure pushed David further to the fore. He was certainly the focus for press interviews and that was largely because he was the only one comfortable doing them – and the others definitely all hated doing photo sessions. David naturally grew into the role of being the spokesman for the group. It's not uncommon that the other band members often become resentful when that happens, but it's usually because they are the ones who didn't like doing interviews.

PAUL DORRINGTON
Wedding Present guitarist 1991–1995

Just before joining the The Wedding Present I was in a band called TseTse Fly and was signing on the dole like most people in bands in the late Eighties/early Nineties. I was on one of those government schemes for the unemployed where you work full time for an extra £10 on top of your dole money, working at Meanwood Park Hospital in Leeds, a strange place. It was a home for people with learning disabilities, but there were people who had lived there all their lives and there have been documentaries made about it. Through some mutual friends of Keith and Simon, I heard that The

The Wedding Present

> The third line-up, featuring new boy Paul Dorrington (far right) on guitar

180 SOMETIMES THESE WORDS JUST DON'T HAVE TO BE SAID

1991: *Seamonsters* And (Indie) Stardom

Wedding Present were auditioning for a new guitarist, but it was just people they knew. They weren't advertising. I was one of the last people to have a go. I didn't really know David, but I'd briefly met him at Keith's house once. I remember towards the end of a Henry Rollins gig at The Duchess of York I was sat on the floor a bit the worse for wear after a few pints and having been in the moshpit and David said, 'I hear you've thrown your cap into the ring.' I had no idea what he was talking about (it's a Northern expression and I grew up in Essex) and just looked at him blankly, and afterwards thought I probably didn't come across as a hugely impressive candidate. I was given a tape with two songs on – 'Suck', which they had just recorded, and a version of 'Blue Eyes' without the second guitar part. I had to work out the guitar part for 'Suck' and write a part for 'Blue Eyes'. I had about a week, channelled my inner Joey Santiago and then went to their practice room and played the two songs with the band. It was pretty nerve-wracking, but I thought, 'At least I've played with The Wedding Present even if I don't get the job.' Once they told me I was in I had two weeks to learn a set, which was mainly *Seamonsters*, before going on a UK tour playing venues like Glasgow Barrowlands and Brixton Academy. It was pretty daunting, but it was better than working nine-to-five in a Victorian mental hospital for next to no money.

WINNING POST

9 MAY 1991, YORK, UK

DARREN BUGG

I remember seeing them at a gig in York where they just wanted to practice some new songs. I was with David and Sally that night and David said, 'By the way, you probably don't realise this but we're playing in York tonight.' I said, 'What are you talking about?' And he said, 'Well, we just need to practice a few songs. We've not announced it to anybody.' They'd approached some little local band who were playing a tiny venue and said, 'We just want to practice these songs. Can we come and support you?' And they basically played a gig that nobody knew about. Because it was only a little band, there were literally about 50 people in the room and they'd all come to see this other local York band. All of a sudden The Wedding Present get on stage and do a half-hour set. And at the end it was 'Thanks a lot for letting us support you. We're going home now.' It wasn't even a secret gig. It was like a rehearsal session.

The Wedding Present

PARKWAY

14 MAY 1991, LIMERICK, IRL

TERRY MCCAUL

My older brother would play 'Kennedy' on repeat and I was hooked. The transition from Shakin' Stevens to The Wedding Present was easy. I'm 14 and my two favourite things in the world are horses and The Wedding Present! Myself and my buddy would sit in school, day in, day out, dreaming and practising drawing the rose from the cover of *Tommy*, drawing it on our jeans and etching it into the desks at school alongside the names of the horses we used to look after at the weekend. Her dad paid for her horse riding lessons. I had to shovel horse shite for mine.

All I had was a taped version of *Bizarro* from my brother and some stuff I taped from the radio – John Peel and Dave Fanning. Finally, sifting through a bargain bin in our local record store, I find a copy of *Tommy* on cassette. Someone had robbed the cover so they were selling it for £1. I was elated! It was white. I never saw a white tape before and I thought it was the coolest thing ever! I hand-made my own cover and secured the slots on the top of the cassette with Sellotape so no one could remove them and record over it and off I went. My biggest fear was that my Walkman would tangle the tape so bad I would have to cut it out. Thankfully that never happened. Eventually I got my hands on *George Best* and the *John Peel Ukrainian Sessions*. I had every *NME* article cut out, and probably still have somewhere. I was obsessed by the music. Being so young, the relationship stuff David sang about didn't resonate – I daydreamed about it. I was living in Limerick when The Wedding Present were due to play a college gig in the Parkway bar near the university. I was 15 with no way of blagging my way in. It was a college gig and they used to be really strict on the whole college ID

Terry McCaul with her hero. Whatever happened to Midway Still?

182 **SOMETIMES THESE WORDS** JUST DON'T HAVE TO BE SAID

1991: Seamonsters And (Indie) Stardom

piece, so I didn't even try. My brother would have killed me. He went and he had a feed of liquor. I was devastated the next day because he couldn't remember what they played or who was there.

MARCUS GARVEY CENTRE
21 MAY 1991, NOTTINGHAM, UK

JUSTIN MCGOWAN

I didn't really know them much but my friend Mike was a massive fan. I had moved to England from Edmonton, Canada, to live with my grandparents after high school. I didn't really know anyone at all. I bought a poster and sat down and started writing Mike a letter on the back of it to send to him. Needless to say they were incredible that night and I was an instant convert. A few years after that, when I was living back home in Edmonton, Mike and I flew to Vancouver to see them play a small club called The Town Pump. Bringing it all back home.

CHRIS WIDDOWSON

The venue was a large cavernous building, high ceilinged with a bar at one end and the stage at the other. Originally built in the Thirties as the head office for Raleigh Bicycles, it is now an 800-capacity concert venue with many original features, so an interesting choice for The Wedding Present. On this particular night the crowd were really up for it. The band seemed to feed off the audience and delivered a blistering set in searing heat. With Steve Albini at the helm The Wedding Present offered a much harder, darker prospect, especially evident on the *Seamonsters* LP that they were touring here. A highlight for me was 'Take Me!' from *Bizarro* played at full speed. There was a surge forward as the song began, arms flailing, heads bobbing in unison. David Gedge confirmed that the song wouldn't run for the full nine minutes due to the heat. The song crashed away, Gedge head-down, thrashing his guitar. The crowd going berserk, the whole room moving in time to the beat, a guy down the front in a wheelchair absolutely going for it, backwards and forwards. To me this just about summed it up – everyone having a great time witnessing a truly great live band. One of my mates purchased a bootleg *Seamonsters* long-sleeved top

The Wedding Present

from outside the gig on the way out and I wished that I had, only to hear that the print came off a month later. I did have an official 'Number 4' long-sleeved top that I wore religiously for five-a-side for years until the cuffs fell off but this seemed far better than the original Grapper & Sons 'Kennedy' T-shirt that to this day is the only see-through white T-shirt that I have ever seen that had a shape all of its own – and is now long since lost.

ACADEMY
23 MAY 1991, MANCHESTER, UK

ANDY BLACK

I was dumped by my girlfriend after the *Seamonsters* tour gig. I was at the front getting tinnitus and she was having a heart to heart. It all seemed appropriate though, given Gedge's lyrics. Still, we stayed mates and got back together again much later. On the way, my mate, who'd never heard The Wedding Present and who was driving us to the gig, was playing a cassette we'd compiled. On hearing The Wedding Present's version of 'Getting Better,' he started shouting, 'What's this crap?'

KATE SULLIVAN

I was a huge Wedding Present fan, had seen them a few times and listened to them continually. Ian Tilton, a well-known music photographer, was a friend of mine and knew the band. He offered to take me as his 'plus one' to the Academy gig and said that he'd take me backstage afterwards. I was beside myself. Ian invited me round to his for dinner before the gig and we agreed to go straight from his to the Academy. I was wearing a black and white striped polo shirt, navy blue shorts with tights underneath and my black Doc Marten shoes. Don't judge me – it was 1991! Just as we were about to leave, Ian went to get changed and came back down wearing a black and white striped polo shirt, navy blue trousers and black Doc Marten shoes. I didn't feel I could make an issue of it as he was taking me to the gig and thought that no one would notice anyway. Before the gig, we were stood having a drink when we saw DLG walking around the crowd. He stopped to speak to Ian. I was crippled with

184 SOMETIMES THESE WORDS JUST DON'T HAVE TO BE SAID

1991: *Seamonsters* And (Indie) Stardom

shyness. After a minute Ian said, 'This is my mate Kate.' David took one look at me and said, 'You're dressed the same.' I wanted to die!

DANI MONK

A friend and I thought we would be bold and invite David around for tea, so we sent him an invite on a pair of very large, very unsexy ladies' knickers rolled up in a small container and launched it at his feet between songs. Two days later David rang us in our student flat in Whitworth Park and invited us to see them play in Leeds, and to the backstage party! You can imagine the noise in our flat that night! Not only did we get to go to Leeds, see them live and meet David, we ended up staying over in his spare room as we hadn't thought about a place to stay amongst all the craziness!

IAN TILTON

I remember I did photographs with them. I wanted to do a book called *Backstage*, because I had plenty of backstage pictures, which I always found the most interesting, rather than the set-up ones. The set-up ones you'd often need for a cover shot or a double-page spread, something that was controlled, so you could put the type above the name of the magazine, or a little bit of writing to say who was going to be inside.

So those pictures invariably were set-ups done in the studio. I approached them and said, 'I'm doing this project and I'd like to photograph you backstage' and they said, 'What do you want to photograph us for? We're the most boring band in the world and nobody is interested in us. We don't do anything at all. We're not rock'n'roll.' And they're right. They're the most un-rock'n'roll rock band ever. Even other indie bands – at least you've got stories about them that they knew would make good stories. But The Wedding Present would never ever play the press. I got a picture backstage once of David stretching a pair of knickers. That was the only moment. A fan had sent in this pair of knickers or thrown them onstage. I said, 'This is what I want to do. I'll photograph you live but as soon as you're off I want to just follow you and take things as they happen, like a fly on the wall.' And the first thing I saw was he had these knickers. He was really kind of awkward but he was laughing and it was a really nice picture and the best shot of that evening.

They were hard to cajole. They wouldn't be anything but themselves. They just wanted to be true to who they were as people. They were shy people.

The Wedding Present

And they just wanted to be honest to themselves. And if it came out boring then so be it, because they had confidence that the music was everything.

Whenever The Wedding Present were interviewed up north after that, I'd go over to Leeds and say, 'Hi again. So what are we going to do this time?' I invariably came up with the ideas. They went along with them. I think they enjoyed that. They were game for being quite boyish. I did covers for *Sounds* and *Siren* magazines. For a band to be given a full-page photograph really meant something, even if you weren't on the cover. A fan came up to me once, and he didn't mean musically, because he was a fan, but he said, 'I've just seen your picture in *Sounds* and I couldn't stop looking at it. Because how did you make such a boring band look so interesting?' They always were a band of the people. They were on the same level. They never were above. They always mixed in. You always looked at them and thought, 'Well, if they can do it... They're us – we could do it if we wanted to be in a band.' They would have been taken down a peg or two if they had been aloof in any way because of the roots they came from.

BRIXTON ACADEMY

25 MAY 1991, LONDON, UK

NICK SPENCE

They had fine-tuned a fabulous 'wall of sound', which really filled the venue and impressed the large adoring crowd. The songs had also matured, which might have had something to do with producer Steve Albini, and the band was at a creative peak. I remember thinking, 'It couldn't get better than this.' It really was a special time for the band and fans, a great time to see The Wedding Present, a time I remember fondly – especially as the band seemed totally unaffected by the relative fame of being on *Top Of The Pops*, having hits and the like.

RICHARD FARNELL

In late 1989 or early 1990 I was playing in a band called The Eunuchs and our singer Marcus and guitarist Matt spotted David Gedge at a gig. They eagerly pressed a copy of our demo into Gedge's hand and he was

When David Gedge removes his glasses, does he become an indie Superman? Melody Maker, May 25, 1991

MELODY MAKER

LIVING COLOUR

Albums
ELECTRONIC
SEAL · NWA

FREE GIG LISTINGS

DE LA SOUL

THE WEDDING PRESENT

the new rage of **DAVID GEDGE**

Live · CURVE · LENNY KRAVITZ · DREAM WARRIORS

The Wedding Present

really encouraging and positive, saying he'd give it a listen, but he quite rightly said, 'You might want to think about changing that band name, lads!'

We changed our name to The Suncharms the very next day and went on to have our own minor success in the indie world. When we played a gig at Norwich Arts Centre in 1991, we had some time to roam around town. It didn't take long, as Norwich is bloody tiny! There was a little record shop which was closed but in the window, totally filling the display, were about twelve copies of *Seamonsters* which was being released the next morning. It was so frustrating to not to be able to buy it there and then but I remember my main impression was the artwork seemed so gloomy and minimal compared to other Wedding Present sleeves.

SEAMONSTERS
THE THIRD ALBUM
RELEASED 27 MAY 1991

STEVE ALBINI
Engineer, *Seamonsters*

I had done an EP with them the year prior to *Seamonsters*. Everybody got along and they approached me about doing the album. I don't recall if the band contacted me directly or somebody at the label. The band had a pretty clear idea for the sound of

> "David's a no-nonsense guy... 'Here's the list of songs, here's what's going on each of them, here's how I like my tea'"
>
> — Steve Albini

188   SOMETIMES THESE WORDS JUST DON'T HAVE TO BE SAID

1991: *Seamonsters* And (Indie) Stardom

each song, whether it was going to be atmospheric or driving, moody or frantic, that sort of thing. That always makes my job easier. It wasn't a case of fucking around with the sounds until somebody heard magic. I recall there was a small amplifier called a Gibsonette at the studio that was used for some guitar parts and it had a sort of resting tone, where the tubes grumbled a bit on their own with no input, and the band were charmed by that and decided to use that as a part of a sound bridge or interlude between two songs.

I haven't heard the album in a while so I forget which two but there was a kind of cross-fade bridge where the Gibsonette sound was revealed as a character, then the next song kicked in. (DLG: 'It was in the long fade of 'Lovenest' before 'Corduroy' comes in.') I was pleased that they were into little accidental charm like that and they definitely made the record to suit themselves, not somebody back at headquarters.

David's a no-nonsense guy, rare for an Englishman, and he's great to work for. He typically has a thing he wants to execute, and if you can satisfy his brief he's content. You always know where you are in the project, he does great planning beforehand and you always know whether he's gotten results he likes or not. There's a kind of equivocation or belaying that's common in a lot of interaction in the music business, where you never know if the deal is on or not, never know if the record's finished or not, that sort of thing. Generally speaking the bigger the label the more of that bullshit there is, but even when The Wedding Present were on a big label there was none of that. I appreciate that he takes it seriously as work, that it isn't a magical experience where the muse has to alight on his shoulder before he can do anything. 'Here's the list of songs, here's what's going on each of them, here's the studio schedule, here's the budget, here's the text of the lyric, here's how I like my tea.'

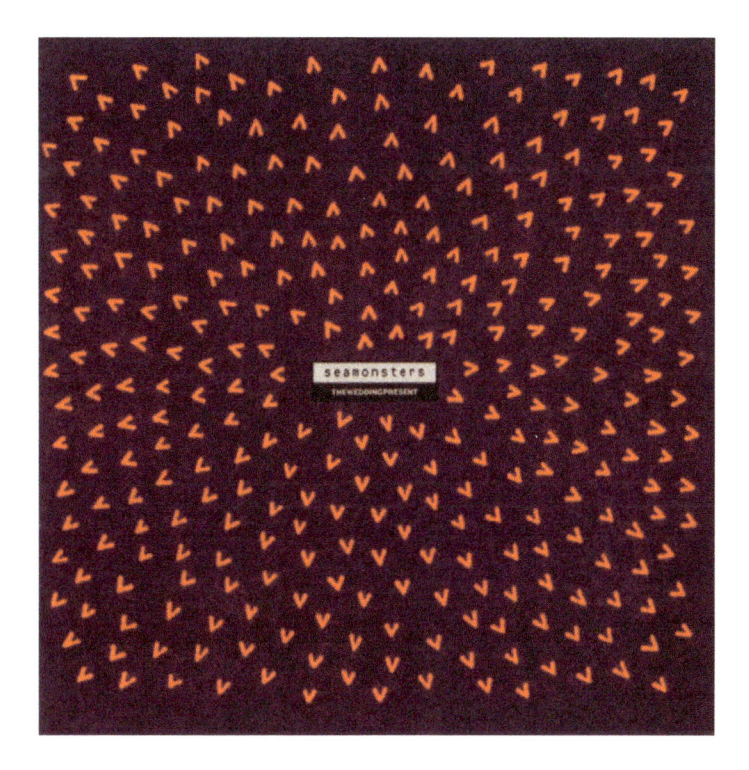

The Wedding Present

LEEDS POLYTECHNIC

27 & 28 MAY 1991, LEEDS, UK

ANDY COLLINSON

The first Cinerama album is dedicated to my older brother Ian. Ian's musical tastes tended to be what I used to describe as 'weird' and basically stuff most people hadn't heard of at the time – The Pixies, REM, even The Plastic Ono Band.

One such band that Ian was keen for me to hear was The Wedding Present. He'd just bought *George Best* and played it to me. 'What a racket,' I thought, 'You can keep that, mate. I'll stick to Prince.'

In 1991, Ian was going to watch The Wedding Present in Leeds with some of his mates. One of them pulled out at the last minute and so Ian asked if I wanted to go. Had I remembered the racket I'd heard three years earlier I would probably have said, 'No.' As it happens, I had forgotten who The Wedding Present were and, on the basis that Ian said, 'They're a bit like a British Nirvana,' I decided I would go.

Well, what a show. I'd never been to anything like it. Loud. Exciting. Moshing. I nearly had a heart attack doing that! There was no going back. I was hooked, bought the back catalogue – my musical tastes had matured by now, so I loved the lot – every song they'd released. I now officially liked 'weird' music. Ian moved to Nottingham after completing a few college courses (art type things) but eventually completed a degree in civil engineering in 1995, which he had chosen as his career path. A few weeks before Ian's 30th birthday in 1997, I travelled to our home town of Selby to get him a card and also visit my mum and dad.

They were out so I let myself in and waited for them to come back. There was a knock at the door – a policeman. He asked if my parents were in. I said they'd just gone shopping and wouldn't be long. Then he told me – straight out with it – my brother had been found dead by his roommate.

It was left with me to tell my mum and dad when they returned. I thought about asking the lady next door if she would tell them, as I didn't know how to, but in the end decided it's something I was going to have to do and it was without exception the hardest thing to do. I felt completely alienated after that, as I almost felt like I had caused it all.

He'd been out drinking the night before, but toxicology tests only showed trace elements of alcohol. Ian was

1991: Seamonsters And (Indie) Stardom

renowned for leaving half of his pint when they moved onto the next pub – so he never actually drank that much. After the post mortem it was concluded that he'd died of Adult Cot Death Syndrome. As you can imagine, the effect on the family was devastating. The importance of music in mine and Ian's lives led me to write to The Wedding Present fan club in 1998 to ask if they would dedicate their next LP to Ian. David's girlfriend Sally responded, saying that there wouldn't be a Wedding Present LP but that David was working on a solo LP and they would like to dedicate that to Ian.

MAYFAIR

29 MAY 1991, NEWCASTLE, UK

DAVID BRUCE

I think it was my first ever copy of the *NME*. It had a review of *Bizarro*. Six out of ten they gave it. 'Treading water,' they said. Hang on a minute. I heard 'Brassneck' on the radio last night and it was immense! Hairs on the back of the neck job. The Saturday after it came out, I was record shopping in Sunderland with some mates. I had a stash of sixteenth birthday money burning a hole in my stonewash jeans.

I raced home and played my brand new *Bizarro* cassette over and over again. What kind of cloth-eared fool would give this incredible album six out of ten? Since then it's been a beautiful romance. Yeah I could talk about girls, unrequited love, nights alone listening to strangers' hands on favourite dresses and how that bloke with the white hi-tops, denim jacket and stupid accent really does look daft, so why aren't you going out with me?

My first Wedding Present gig was a stunner at Newcastle Mayfair, supported by the excellent Buffalo Tom. I bought a red 'Dalliance' T-shirt that never left my back. *Seamonsters*. Gigs. The *Hit Parade* singles? I pre-ordered every one of them. More gigs. *Watusi*. The superb, under-rated *Saturnalia*. Then nothing for nearly a decade until the majestic career highlight of *Take Fountain*. Followed by yet more gigs. Each and every one a joy to witness. David playing till his hands bled and singing like every single word was an exorcism. What a magical band.

No matter how I'm feeling, banging The Wedding Present on the stereo will always make me feel better than I did before. And if they don't? Well, there's always the 'Loveslave' video on YouTube...

The Wedding Present

GUILDHALL
31 MAY 1991, PORTSMOUTH, UK

MARTIN FOOTE

Seamonsters had just come out and Paul Dorrington had joined. Before the gig, my friends and I spotted David at the booking office.

I was 17 and somewhat in awe but went to speak to him and was asking dull-but-sensible questions about the new album. My friend Phil, who had drunk a bottle of Strongbow on the train journey, unhelpfully bounded up and asked David why so many of his lyrics were about break-ups and if he had really bad luck with women.

I don't remember David's reaction – I was too busy feeling mortified! I do remember that they came on to the theme from the *A-Team* and played a blinding set.

PENYRHEOL THEATRE
1 JUNE 1991, SWANSEA, UK

ANN-MARIE LAWSON

Forever grateful to John Peel, I discovered them back in 1988 and saw them in Bristol, Cardiff and Newport in the early year. I went to uni in Swansea. While the town had beautiful scenery and beaches, sadly not many bands ever came to play there.

One day, while ordering my copy of *Invasion Of The Wedding Present* fanzine, I politely requested (or begged) that the boys play Swansea. I'd like to think the photo I sent of the dog our student house used to feed may have helped. He was photographed wearing my 'Kennedy' T-shirt. I will never forget the moment I read that they were coming. I persuaded various people on my course to get tickets. It was sometimes a chore – modern foreign language students have terrible taste in music.

As for my housemates, well I just bullied and threatened them. Everybody agreed to go. There were a mixed bunch – even the gay Madonna fans went along – and, as expected,

1991: Seamonsters And (Indie) Stardom

a great time was had by all. Some of the eleven people in my student house are still big fans to this day. 'Kennedy' and 'Brassneck' were *the* songs of my uni years. In the autumn of 1991 I had to spend a year in Germany as part of my course. My poor mam had to post the *Hit Parade* 7" singles to Germany for me every month. I am still in Germany. The Munich gigs are intimate and, as always, The Wedding Present never ever disappoint.

IOAN HUMPHREYS

The Wedding Present were playing just outside Swansea city centre. For my friends in school who were into indie bands in the early Nineties this was a big deal, as hardly any bands ever came further than Cardiff to play. I was 17. It was a Saturday night and my friend and I had a lift from my sister. I think some booze was sneaked in or drunk before. I really can't remember, but what I do remember is Buffalo Tom were a more than capable support band and got the capacity crowd moving nicely.

The Wedding Present were on top form that night. *Bizarro* was on constant rotation on my record player and they had just released the Steve Albini re-recorded CD of 'Brassneck', backed by the gorgeous 'Don't Talk, Just Kiss' and a cover of 'Box Elder' by Pavement. We knew all the words to this release and were well up on the stuff from *George Best*.

The gig is a bit of a blur, but I distinctly remember an incendiary version of 'Bewitched' that got the whole place jumping and a sizeable moshpit ensuing. We waited outside the venue for the band and David very kindly signed a postcard for us. We then piled into my sister's car, slightly drunk and with a friend hanger-on who was chopsy to my sister and very nearly didn't get home. A blurry, yet very happy, memory.

ROB SHIRLOW

Three of us tripped down to Swansea from Cwmbran – 60 miles – at the age of 18, in my Dad's crappy old car. I bought a T-shirt, left it on the car roof by mistake and someone nicked it.

I saw David inside looking thoughtfully at a book. He was quite abrupt at first, and then kind, and signed the cassette cover. I didn't go over – my mates had to ask for me! The show was only my second ever proper gig and was brutal. Battered and bruised, but beaming from ear to ear. *Seamonsters* is still one of the greatest LPs ever!

The Wedding Present

CORN EXCHANGE
2 JUNE 1991, CAMBRIDGE, UK

MARC ANDREW HEIGHTON

None of my friends were into them. So I went to Cambridge Corn Exchange, aged 15, on my own. I'd seen 'Brassneck' on *Top Of The Pops* and loved them ever since. The pain and melancholy of the failed love songs just spoke to me.

1-IN-12 CLUB
3 JUNE 1991, BRADFORD, UK

IAN RICKARD

The Wedding Present have always held a special place in my heart. I saw the *Bizarro* tour and it's still my fave Wedding Present album. Two of my school friends wanted me to go see The Wonder Stuff the following Thursday at the same venue – St George's Hall – but I'd made up my mind to see The Wedding Present. No debate really, they were the ones for me, and it was an excellent gig that gave me the buzz to see bands regularly. My second Wedding Present concert was the **punk* filming at Leeds Colosseum and, if you look closely, the camera flashes past me during 'Granadaland'. My third Weddoes gig was Bradford Queens Hall, where I scuffed my brand new Doc Martens doing my first ever stage-dive. But my favourite memory is from the 1-in-12 Club. I'd been banging on about how great The Wedding Present were live and convinced three or four of my work colleagues to come along. I was on day release at college studying for my electrical qualifications and, in the afternoon break, I wandered up to the venue only to find the gods of indie rock'n'roll doing a sound check. I hung around and, as luck would have it, got the chance to speak to DLG. I told him how great his band were, that some of my workmates were coming tonight and could he do a dedication my workmates? 'Call me Bully,' I said.

He signed my ticket and I went back for another couple of lessons until the

194 SOMETIMES THESE WORDS JUST DON'T HAVE TO BE SAID

1991: *Seamonsters* And (Indie) Stardom

NEW MUSICAL
Red Gedge

Parole up! Parole up! CRYSTAL WATERS at work in Washington

ROBBIE COLTRANE
THIN WHITE ROPE
BILL PRITCHARD
JOCELYN BROWN
MARY WHITEHOUSE EXPERIENCE
MEXICO 70
SPIKE LEE
REBEL MC
CUBIC 22

DAVE ON!
How The Wedding Present survived dance

Gedge on *NME*'s cover, July 1991

SOMETIMES THESE WORDS **JUST DON'T HAVE TO BE SAID** 195

The Wedding Present

gig that night. After a few songs, DLG said, 'Can you believe this lad Bully's been here all day? He must be mad but anyway – this one's for him.' My workmates hoisted me into the air – no mean feat – and I felt like the winning captain in the cup final, as proud as punch. I looked round. 'Tell everyone that's me! That's me!'

'This one's for Bully' said our hero, and they went straight into... 'Everyone Thinks He Looks Daft'.

ROOFTOP GARDENS

28 AUGUST 1991, WAKEFIELD, UK

LYDIA PAPPAS

It all began with a giro and a dream; a bunch of teenagers living in the small villages of rural west Wales who needed music more than most. But living in the sticks has its problems, one of which is that no band worth its salt ever plays within 100 miles. But these kids are persistent and one of them has a car. And a driving licence.

It was the summer of 1991 and my life was changed forever on the day that I was persuaded to drive to Swansea to see a band called The Wedding Present. I hadn't heard of them at the time but they were soon to become a force in my life and a presence ever after. I hadn't planned on going and was only invited at the last minute as I had a car and could drive to the gig, many miles away. The sheer exuberance that I witnessed on stage that night turned me onto live performance and I have never looked back. This experience made me want more, so when the *Seamonsters* tour continued and I had a few months over the summer to investigate the back catalogue of the band, I determined to follow them.

NME came out that weekend, much awaited by this little gang, and it was duly noted that a date had been added to the *Seamonsters* tour, a one-off gig at the Rooftop Gardens in Wakefield. 'Where's that?' said the kids from west Wales. We didn't know exactly, but we figured 'What the heck, it's time for a road trip'. So plans were made, as we didn't want to miss this opportunity. Plus we were a bunch of bored teenagers on the dole – so what else were we supposed to do?

And the day expectantly arrives and no giros come. Disaster. It's a Wednesday and we all signed on on the Monday, so they should be

1991: *Seamonsters* And (Indie) Stardom

there on the doormat waiting for us. Nooooo! However we were not to be dissuaded from our grand scheme for live music and the persistent spirit prevailed. So between me, James and Matt we managed to rustle up the cash with promises and pleas and by 11am we were on the road. Wakefield is about 322 miles and five or six hours away by car from Fishguard. Back then, in a crappy old repainted Fiat 131, without a GPS and with no roadmap to go by, we were lucky to get there in seven hours.

After driving around Wakefield for a long time we finally asked directions and found the venue. We were early and stopped off at a local hostelry for some refreshments as we obviously had not been drinking on the journey, being responsible and all that. After two hours in the pub we headed to the gig and lined up ready to go in at about quarter to eight. I was so excited that I didn't even notice when David Gedge brushed past me, as I was too busy stealing a flyer off the wall as a souvenir of the big adventure. Missed opportunity number one. My dear companions said, 'Hello' and then teased me mercilessly because I had missed the chance to say 'Hello' myself. Once we were inside we were sat at a table having more drinks and Gedge went past us again but I was far too nervous to say anything. The gig was fantastic, of course. There were two support bands, Moonpump and Tse Tse Fly, the latter being the band that the new guitarist Paul Dorrington had come from. That night he played in both bands. Impressive. The Wedding Present played for over an hour and Gedge was on top form, laughing and chatting with the crowd between songs.

The band played their hearts out, their hands flying all over the strings and feeding off the crowd. The atmosphere was electric and the stomping and bouncing that was going on really made the crowd pulse with exuberance. I danced so hard I thought I would explode and Matt came out of the crowd with a huge lump on his head. But we didn't care. It was the best gig of our lives so far and we were making the most of it; the fact that we had driven so far just to be there only fueled our energy.

I can still remember the venue and the stage and the look and feel of the crowd. These things will be forever emblazoned on my memory even without a video or pictures of the event. We were too busy just being there to take pictures – and who could afford a camera or to process films when you were on the dole?

But my mind's eye captured images that day that can never be erased, like the crowd going mad for 'Kennedy' just from the intro chords, and the music that still echoes in my head,

The Wedding Present

The band model their summer look, July 1991

from 'Corduroy' to 'Crawl' – all my favourite songs sung just for me. Or so I thought at the time.

We hung about after the show as we didn't really have anywhere else to go and it was a bloody long way home. But after about half an hour it was obvious that we had to make that long trek. We were very sweaty and thirsty by this point and thoroughly exhausted from the dancing and the emotion poured out in that gig.

Slowly we left and as we were outside trying to remember where we had parked the car James spotted Gedge walking by and around the back of the place with boxes of gear. I nearly fell off the wall we were sitting on but managed to shout out a quick 'Hey, we came all this way to see you and you were great!'-type statement and got a 'Cheers' in return and I was

198 SOMETIMES THESE WORDS JUST DON'T HAVE TO BE SAID

1991: *Seamonsters* And (Indie) Stardom

happy but my travelling companions thought different. Next thing I know I've been pushed off the wall and go legging it round the corner where Gedge has just disappeared and I chase after him babbling a story of our journey and probably acting like a crazy person. I didn't have a pen to ask for an autograph so gave him a friendship bracelet. They were all the rage at the time and I had been making them for friends when I was bored, so I gave him one of the many on my arm to say thanks for an amazing show.

In return he gave me his 'access all areas' backstage pass which, of course, I have treasured to this very day and he chatted to me before sending me back to the arms of my friends on Cloud Nine and stargazed with joy.

The drive home was all of a daze. We had to stop so many times because we got lost and ended up sleeping in a petrol station when we got about halfway as it was all too much to do in one night. I think we even tried to find 'Granadaland' at one point. Not the most comfortable night, as Matt was six foot tall and three people trying to sleep in a small Fiat 131 is not a good idea at the best of times.

But we were young and tired and drunk so what did we care? We woke early though and needed to get back before we were missed, but the car wouldn't start. After an hour of trying and no jump leads we eventually managed to push-start it and made it home. We were thoroughly cream crackered and exhilarated and guess what? Three weeks later we drove back to the Queens Hall in Bradford to do it all over again! But that's another story.

MARTIN BOWN

I remember the strangest venue for a Wedding Present gig. Picture loads of Yorkshire indie kids turning up to a typical *Hit Man And Her* type nightclub. The venue was packed and, with it being summer, absolutely red hot. The sold out crowd was packed into a relatively small area in front of the stage, but with nightclub-style circular seating booths dotted here and there! I remember most of the gig, having a cracking view of the band from my own booth.

I moved to Wakefield a few years later and had the misfortune to go the club on a 'normal' night. When I told the people I was with that I'd seen The Wedding Present there a few years earlier, their reaction was, 'Here?!' The Wedding Present are a great band that have been there every step of my adolescent and adult life. I got stuck behind David Gedge at a gig at the Cockpit in Leeds once – he's taller than me! I had a

The Wedding Present

good chat with him though. I also remember randomly answering, '18', when he asked on Twitter how many times they'd played at the Leadmill. He asked what I wanted as a prize. I told him I wanted a signed photo of the pictures he'd tweeted of himself stood in front of the Mallard steam locomotive. My grandad was once a fireman on the train.

David, in autumn 1991, remembering an earlier visit to Kulturhuset in Jonkopping in Sweden in 1987

1992: Top Of The Hit Parade

In 1992, The Wedding Present released one single each month. Devoted Wedding Present fans had to rush to the shops to buy them before they were deleted: each single reached the Top 40 and so The Wedding Present matched Elvis Presley in scoring twelve hits in a calendar year.

PAUL DORRINGTON

I played on all the *Hit Parade* singles and it was pretty much non-stop. I remember when we were recording the first batch of singles in Stockport, I got up at 7am one day, got a train to Liverpool to get a passport (in the days when you could just queue up and get one in a day), got the train back, did some recording and then the day after, drove to Germany for a European tour.

I would have been quite happy to write and record an album, but the rest of the band wanted to do something different and I was the new boy. So I was more than happy to go along with whatever they wanted to do. When we weren't touring we rehearsed Monday to Friday, 11am until 7pm, at Riverside Studios in Ossett. Working out the cover versions was harder than writing the original material, because you're figuring out bits that don't necessarily feel natural to you to play. It's always a good exercise though, because you discover things you wouldn't normally do. And although we only recorded twelve covers, we tried out a lot more in the practice room: a lot were abandoned quite early on. We had a go at 'Seven Seas Of Rhye' by Queen, 'Outdoor Miner' by Wire, Michael Jackson's 'Black Or White' – all sorts of things. As well as writing and recording the songs, I was involved in designing the record sleeves. I drew the cartoons for the inner labels too, a lot of which I did on tour. I remember drawing one of them in a hotel room in LA at the last minute and searching for a post office to get it to Hitch, the designer who put together the artwork.

The videos were very limited in budget, and a bit hit and miss really. There's a fine line between lo-fi arty indie and just rubbish – and there were a few that some

The Wedding Present

of us felt were the wrong side of that line at the time, so we re-shot a few at a gig in Doncaster. Looking back, I don't think the ones we rejected were that bad really, but if in doubt, or if one person really didn't like it, they'd ask 'Would Nick Cave or The Fall shoot a video with a traction engine?' Which would normally convince the others to cave in (excuse the pun). I'm glad we filmed the Doncaster gig though, because the footage of 'The Chant Of The Ever Circling Skeletal Family' is a pretty good record of what the gigs were like at the time.

We also did *Top Of The Pops* four times that year, which was a dream come true having grown up watching it every week. We'd just randomly chat to other people who were on that week like Wet Wet Wet or Jason Donovan and see the cast of *Eastenders* in the bar. A surreal moment was driving our van round the set of Albert Square, and Keith and I wrote our names on the door of the cafe. Shameful vandalism! There was already a lot of graffiti so it didn't feel too scandalous, just adding a little authentic texture to the set.

We did the singles in four batches, with four different producers. I sometimes wish that the internet had been around at the time, because I would have researched the studios and who we were working with more. At the time it was just, 'We're going to Stockport to record with someone called Chris who produced Inspiral Carpets.' Then twenty years later, I find out that Chris Nagle engineered *Unknown Pleasures* (Joy Division) and that The Smiths and The Bay City Rollers recorded at Strawberry Studios and that it's where 10cc famously recorded 'I'm Not In Love'. A legendary studio.

All the producers were great, and all really different. I seem to remember Ian Broudie used various gizmos for processing sounds, like amp simulators and effects units, which worked great for 'Falling' and 'Pleasant Valley Sunday'. I loved doing the backwards guitar on that.

Jimmy Miller was such an imposing figure. He was about six-foot-six, with long grey hair, a moustache and I think he wore a cowboy hat – but my memory might be playing tricks on me. We all seemed to click with Chris, Ian and Brian Paulson, but Jimmy Miller seemed to be from another planet. I don't know if it was because we were all a bit in awe of him because we knew he'd made these legendary Rolling Stones albums, or if it was what he was slipping into his

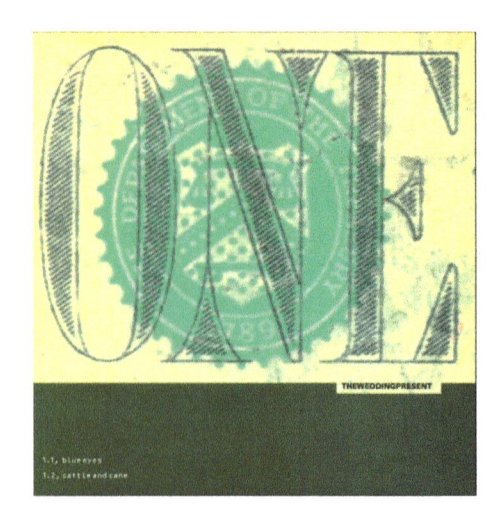

The first single of the marathon year: 'Blue Eyes' backed by 'Cattle And Cane'

1992: Top Of *The Hit Parade*

coffee, but there did seem to be a bit of a communication problem. A year later he went off to hang out with Hunter S. Thompson and then died, so we were probably just too boring for him.

Working with Brian Paulson in Rockfield was really great. We were all massive fans of Slint's *Spiderland* so were excited to work with him. The owner of Rockfield told us stories about Queen recording 'Bohemian Rhapsody' and how, after The Stone Roses recorded there, they kept finding various drugs down the back of the sofa and under the chair cushions. Because we'd been touring so much the band were really tight. I remember there were a couple of songs where we did the backing track on the first or second take with no overdubs. Brian loved it because the place had loads of vintage compressors and various gadgets he could play with, and I think his production was amazing. It was a hot week in summer and we played cricket on the lawn one afternoon. I was quite sad when it was over.

DAVID GEDGE

Paul contributed some very cool American-sounding guitar riffs to the *Hit Parade* recordings. He brought a very different dynamic to the band, along with an impressive knowledge of rock and pop culture.

Using a different producer for each of the singles in the *Hit Parade* would have been brilliant, but it would've been far too expensive and logistically very difficult. We compromised on the number of producers and recorded it over four different sessions. Choosing which cover versions to do was challenging. We'd be asking ourselves the question 'How do you improve on a great song?' because, obviously, we hadn't picked rubbish ones to cover!

PAGODA

5 FEBRUARY 1992, CARLISLE, UK

BOB FROM BARROW-IN-FURNESS

I come from a place where no bands played during my formative years in the early Nineties. Me and my mates were into The Wedding Present and got tickets to see them at a nightclub called the Pagoda. We were 18 or 19 years old. We were to get a coach with other Barrow fans, who had organised

The Wedding Present

it. It was either a Friday, and an early finish in the shipyard, or we had holidays. My mate was going round picking us up in his MG Maestro, and he managed to take out a bus stop on a straight road, writing it off and nearly making us late for the bus. He was fine.

We got the bus at the local cinema. We were to meet my mate's dad and uncle in a pub called The Cranemakers. They were contracting up there. We had a few beers with them and it must have looked like a scene from *Trainspotting* – talking garbage at an increased rate.

From what I remember, the gig was great! The usual meeting the band beforehand, T-shirts signed (I had the 'Ask The Eight Ball' one, and wish I still did). I think they played either 'Brassneck' or 'Kennedy' early in the set and the reaction was much jumping. But my mate got over-enthused and was turfed out for crowd crawling. The set was good – mainly *Hit Parade* stuff. I recall watching the band in awe. Gig over, we headed downstairs to congregate and work out where to get the bus from. I think a bar was open. The band came in the bar. Someone rolled a joint and the bouncers showed us the door, or the person was kicked out and for some reason we all went: that's what I think happened. Anyway, great gig.

The bus broke down somewhere near Shap on the way back and we had to wait for a replacement. No toilet, and tempers fraying in the usual drunken way. Fortunately, the replacement bus turned up and we got home safe and sound.

PLANET X

14 FEBRUARY 1992, LIVERPOOL, UK

DAVID MCNALLY

I grew up in Litherland, part of Liverpool. I got home from college and my dad answered the door to let me in. 'Someone from that band The Wedding Tackle that you like has rang for you' he said, doing his best to get the name wrong. 'Oh aye, as if,' I said. 'Yer mother took the call, not me.' Then he shouted 'Doreen' at the top of his voice up the stairs. My ma came down and he said, 'Tell him who's rang for him.'

'Oh, a woman called Sally from The Wedding Present. She said she'll ring back later.' 'As if. What did she want?' I was getting excited by now, thinking, 'What does she want and how does she

1992: Top Of *The Hit Parade*

even know my number?' I still thought my Dad was winding me up. That's what he was like.

'Probably ringing to see if you've bought the new single – it's only you and your mate who buys them, isn't it? You won't have even heard of them next year, let alone in 20 years' time. That's the problem with today's bands. They only last ten minutes.' 'Yer, alright dad,' I said, before going upstairs. 'And take that bag upstairs with yer,' he said.

I remember not putting music on for possibly the first time ever in case I didn't hear the phone. About ten minutes later, the phone went and I legged it down the stairs. 'Hello.' It was a woman's voice. 'Hello, is that David?' 'Yes, hello.' 'Hi, it's Sally, David's girlfriend from The Wedding Present.' 'Oh, hiya.' 'It's just to let you know that they are playing a secret gig in Liverpool tonight at Planet X, under the name Christmas. And it's free to get in.' 'Thanks, yes – I'll definitely be there!' I said.

I rang my mates and we arranged to meet to get into Liverpool town centre on the bus – the L3, bus fans! We were all buzzing, as if we were the only ones invited. We arrived at Planet X and there was a massive queue. 'Thought it was a fucking secret?' my mate said. I was starting to panic in case we never got in. We got near the front and we were told it was full. The venue closed the door.

We overheard some lad telling the people he was with that his mate had got in and was going to open the fire door to let him in. We decided to follow them around the side of the building. When we got there, the door opened and a bouncer came out. 'It's full, so yous can fuck off' he said. 'Come on, mate, surely you can get a few more in?' some lad said.

'Yes, come on mate' I added. 'I'm not yer fucking mate. Now piss off before you get your head kicked in.' It all went a bit quiet. 'Come on, let's get off' my mate said. No chance, I thought, I'm not missing this. 'Come on lad, we were queuing up for ages. I got a phone call off the band to turn up' I said. He looked over his shoulder. 'Alright, but it's a fucking fiver each.' I couldn't get the fiver out quick enough and we all paid him and walked through the side door. The other group were all shaking my hand. 'Nice one, mate' etc.

At the end of the gig, we were waiting around and I saw the band hanging around by the car park as the gear was being loaded up. I remember the sweat pouring off me and my Edsel Auctioneer T-shirt was wringing wet. After some deliberation, we approached. 'Alright, The Wedding Present' I said, stupidly. 'Hi.' 'Superb gig that, by the way.' We got chatting and I said that Sally had rang me to let me know of the gig. 'Ah, are you David? I think I spoke to your mum.' We had a brief chat and I was a bit starstruck.

David Gedge thanked me for coming and gave me the plectrum that he had used for the gig. I was absolutely made up

The Wedding Present

as I was in a band and just starting on the guitar. I got home and put *George Best* on.

'Lower that down, will yer?' shouted my dad. 'Yer mother's in bed.'

WATERFRONT

16 FEBRUARY 1992, NORWICH, UK

JANE WARNES

My abiding memories of The Wedding Present are of being uncharacteristically transformed, Belieber-style, into a groupie. A Gedgette? Take the time that I went to see them with my then-boyfriend and a group of friends, including Richard, the author of this book.

Memories of the gig itself are hazy, the usual pulsating songs belted out in David's inimitable style, the cider, the atmosphere, the special bond that has united diehard Wedding Present fans for decades. Even then, arguably at the height of the band's fame – it was the era when songs from *The Hit Parade* featured on *Top Of The Pops* – there was a feeling that we were part of something special, an enigma that somehow escaped the majority of the population. To their loss.

But afterwards, more excitement thanks to a friend of my boyfriend's. Conveniently working at the venue, Walter became my second hero of the evening by negotiating for us to go backstage. I can still remember the excitement of talking to David and planting an innocently chaste kiss on his cheek. The look of horror from him as I did so, and disapproval too, as I was with my boyfriend. And we all know what he thinks of girls who betray; not that I was. Perhaps it was the cider I had drunk.

Then, in 2005, David was again performing in Norwich, this time at the Arts Centre. Smaller venue, all of us older, the fickler fans of the dizzy heights of the *Top Of The Pops* era weeded out to leave a hardcore of loyal Wedding Present faithfuls. An impromptu reunion with long-lost friends, nostalgia, fading youth and my second Gedgette moment. Pre-gig, my friend Julie and I were stumbling around the venue recalling the even longer ago days when I'd been part of a theatre group there. A narrow flight of stairs and a familiar looking man courteously stepping aside to let us pass. At the bottom of the stairs, a dawning realisation and a hiss to Julie, '*That* was David Gedge.'

1992: Top Of *The Hit Parade*

Straight back upstairs we went, and there was David, having chill time before the start. Did he remember Norwich in 1992, and my sweet kiss? A blank look and a polite shrug. No he didn't, but he would be doing signed T-shirts later. The bathos. But guess what? Reader, I bought one.

ROGER DENTON

Dear Jane,
It was early 1988, we were still mourning the end of The Smiths, spending an alcoholic afternoon in the room of the Boy Wylie. Well it was the early hours really, but if you can't romanticise your own memories, who can? Throbbing, venomous guitar awoke me from my semi-slumber. The opening bars of 'Give My Love To Kevin' blasted my auditory cortex and settled in my cerebrum. 'Anyone Can Make A Mistake' sealed the deal. Would my life ever be sane again? I wonder to myself... but really I knew then that I had entered a completely different world.

First there was my history, then there was our history... and The Wedding Present provided the soundtrack to our history. For our gang – you, me, Mandy, Ian and the Boy Wylie – four skinny indie kids (well five, if you want to split hairs) – Gedgey was our leader, our bombers, our high. Like a modern day Mao, we hung on his every word. And what words. Do you remember the first time? UEA: the Ukrainian tour. I've still got the T-shirt. The Wedding Present would be supporting The Wedding Present. This guy's got a sense of humour and an arrogance, we like that – for who could ever follow The Wedding Present?

A question that was no doubt troubling Inspiral Carpets at Reading 1990. We were working for the Workers Beer Company, raising money for the Derbyshire Sacked Miners and Norwich Anti-Poll Tax Union, but we'd secured our slot off to see the main event – Saturday night, The Wedding Present. Wow – what if I never come down? Of course, how do you follow The Wedding Present? Well the Inspirals spent all their fee on fireworks. The fireworks were bloody good but though the fireworks have faded now, memories of The Wedding Present live on.

Of course we always liked it, at the Norwich gigs, when Gedge would tell his story about the origins of the name Gedge – 'Did I tell you that already?' – and the tea shoppe on Elm Hill. Then there was Brixton Academy, the *Seamonsters* tour. I've still got the yellow carrier bag. There was an extra edge, probably with being up 'that London' and The Wedding Present at the peak of their powers. How could an encore follow

The Wedding Present

the perfect performance? The next month we went to Zakynthos and I kept playing *Seamonsters* on the beach through a pretty lo-fi cassette player. It probably annoyed quite a few people but I think I just wanted to let others know what they were missing. Of course, we both got sunburnt one day and, when sunstroke set in that evening, we ended up running out of the restaurant and both throwing up right outside.

The Waterfront and *The Hit Parade*... Well it was February 1992 so some *Hit Parade* numbers, but at UEA at the end of the year we were treated to many more, possibly all of them. I bought a stylish 'Go-Go Dancer' T-shirt. We drank a lot – though that perhaps goes without saying.

As luck would have it, a comrade, Walter, was working that night at The Waterfront, so at the end of the gig he got us backstage. Ian had bought a T-shirt for Mandy (who wasn't there) and asked Gedge to sign it in indelible ink. I was so struck by this idea that I got Gedge to do the same thing to mine. And do you remember? I was really keen that Gedge kissed you, so some of the magic might rub off on me? So that I could say that Gedge kissed my girlfriend? Gedge coyly remarked that most boyfriends don't like other men kissing their girlfriends. He then duly obliged. It was only in the morning that I realised that

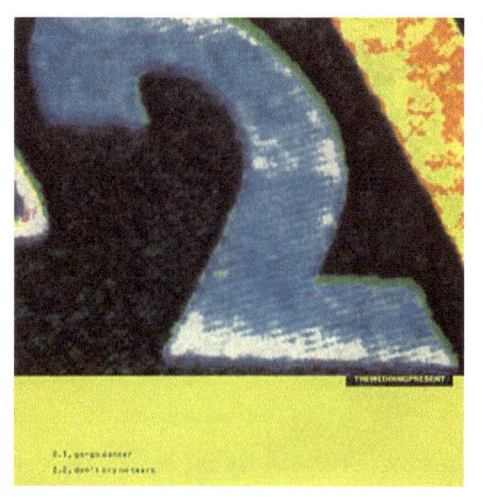

Two down, ten to go: 'Go-Go Dancer'/'Don't Cry No Tears'

I had soiled goods – I was not keen on walking around in public with a T-shirt with 'To Jane & Roger, Love David L Gedge' scrawled over the back. Fortunately though, what self-respecting indie kid would be seen in public without a cardigan anyway. It was a very stylish T-shirt. I don't have it anymore.

The following year you started to like that bloke in the pub. That was my favourite pub y'know. You thought he looked like David Gedge. Is that it? Have you really gone? Love and pain. The Wedding Present. The rest, as they say, is history. Afterword: Norwich Arts Centre, March 2005. The Wedding Present are re-formed. For one night only, Jane and Roger are back together. Well, they're in the same building. Roger drinks beer and leaps on people. Jane chases after Gedge. The fireworks have faded now but The Wedding Present live on.

1992: Top Of *The Hit Parade*

SIOBHAN PLATTEN

I was 14 years old. When the gig was over, my friend and I asked the security guard if the band would sign the T-shirts we'd just bought. To our amazement, David appeared a few minutes later and signed our stuff. He stayed to chat for a while too. We'd just started mucking around with guitars so we asked him if he had any good names for our band. He christened the band 'Think Bike' (like the public information films). We continued playing under this moniker for a few months. We were terrible. Soon after that gig I wrote a fan letter to David. I can't remember what I wrote, probably an earnest question about bar chords. Not only did he reply, we corresponded for a few months (including a postcard from Berlin) and he remembered me when I met him again at the Cambridge Corn Exchange. Things like this matter to teenagers.

Over the years I must've been to a thousand concerts from small bars to massive stadiums. Nothing matches the excitement of waiting for The Wedding Present to come on stage.

JERICHO TAVERN
17 FEBRUARY 1992, OXFORD, UK

BEN LAMBERT
Carter USM

It was the year of the twelve *Hit Parade* singles, and it was a massive deal getting permission from my parents to go to the gig as, at 16, I was judged too young to be exposed to the live evils of indie music. They eventually relented by extracting several promises from my older brother that he couldn't possibly keep and promptly broke (thank God) the moment we ascended the stairs of the Jericho. At the time he was a student at Oxford and was doing a bit of writing for a magazine called *Spiral Scratch*. He had been asked to review the gig and interview David in the afternoon before the show. I was the official photographer.

We turned up at the Jericho and met David in the afternoon, me being very meek and star-struck and not having a clue how any of this worked. I kept my gob shut whilst my brother failed to find a pub that was open (those were the days, eh?) to conduct the interview, so we ended up in the band minibus,

The Wedding Present

my brother professionally conducting the interview and me being utterly in awe of David and marvelling at the slabs of beer and cider stacked up in the bus. I think the only thing I managed to say to David was mentioning at the end of the interview that I had a CD copy of *Bizarro* that was misprinted and had a load of classical music on it. The gig was fantastic. I got some decent pics which I believe did get used in *Spiral Scratch* – not that I ever saw it – and to boot the band played my all-time favourite Wedding Present song, 'Crawl'. What a first gig! Whether that planted the seed for my future life is anyone's guess – but four years later I was playing in Carter USM and gallivanting round the country on our own tour bus. I then went on to work in the live music industry, doing bits of playing, but mainly earning my bread and butter working for many different artists, the best ones being the indie bands – naturally.

GAZ COOMBES
Supergrass

The Wedding Present were a big part of our early band adventures. We had a band at school called The Jennifers. I was 14, so this was around 1989 or 1990. After school we'd go and rehearse round each other's houses, wherever the folks were out, or didn't give a shit about us getting stoned and making noise. We'd play for a bit then just put records on for ages. I remember listening to *Bizarro* and *George Best* a lot around that time. They were different to the other bands we listened to. I always liked their raw kind of double-speed energy, the lyrics and the cool throwaway vibe to David's vocals, which I always tried to get but never could. That's the kind of shit we wanted to do. Myself and Danny Goffey managed to blag into their gig at the Jericho Tavern in 1992. I think it was January, maybe February... I just remember walking in from the freezing cold into the famous Tavern sweat box. It was great to finally hear songs like 'Kennedy', 'Something And Nothing' and 'Corduroy' live. It's one of my earliest live music memories... and still easily one of the best. For us, The Wedding Present were the perfect antidote to the shiny stadium snares and chorus guitars of the mid-Eighties. And I still hear their influence on bands today.

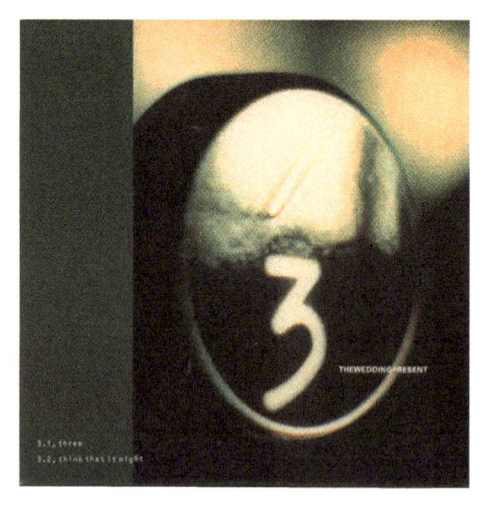

'Three' had a better time than the first two *Hit Parade* singles, reaching 14 in the UK charts

1992: Top Of *The Hit Parade*

Captain Gedge mans the cockpit, 1992

TIVOLI BALLROOMS

26 FEBRUARY 1992, BUCKLEY, UK

SIÔN WILLIAMS

A packed house. I was there with my girlfriend, mates and sister. I managed to get my brand new Wedding Present T-shirt signed. My sister and girlfriend didn't have new T-shirts, so David signed their midriffs. He then dedicated 'My Favourite Dress' to the 'girls with the midriff.' I have been married to my midriff girlfriend now for 20 years.

Our first dance was to 'Flying Saucer'. Great gig. Great memories. I saw them again in 2012 when they returned to the Tivoli. I tried to get a support slot for our band Ian Rush but failed. We are a Welsh language band from the Nineties and we have been described on occasion as the Welsh Wedding Present – and many other things!

The Wedding Present

LEADMILL
1 MARCH 1992, SHEFFIELD, UK

STEVE BARNES

I took my girlfriend, who insisted on wearing silver shorts. Short shorts. She felt ill and stood to one side of the floor. As soon as Gedge got on stage she leapt forward, fully recovered and right to the front. Ah, silver shorts…

HI POINTE
14 APRIL 1992, ST LOUIS, MO, USA

ADAM HARTZELL

I was attending Washington University in St Louis, Missouri when I was introduced to The Wedding Present at the campus radio station, KWUR, where I was a DJ. This radio station had such low wattage we used to joke that your hair-dryer probably had more. When I pulled *Bizarro* from our stacks of albums and put the needle to that particular record, 'Brassneck' hit me hard with that opening riff. It would be years before I saw the music video on YouTube but I probably was unknowingly imitating those modern dancers that bounce around Gedge and the gang in the video for 'Brassneck'.

And if I were to become a professional baseball player, the beginning of 'Brassneck' would be the music I'd have them play as I walked-up to home plate to bat. I was hooked on The Wedding Present immediately. I bought myself my own copy of *Bizarro* at Vintage Vinyl on the Delmar Loop near campus soon after that first listen.

My first live venue experience with The Wedding Present was at the Hi-Pointe bar above the Hi-Pointe movie theater across from the world's biggest Amoco sign. The Wedding Present was touring to promote *Bizarro* and I arrived to find the show not that well attended.

But I, a growing die-hard fan, was there and was enthralled in the moment. Singing – more likely wailing – along and flailing to the driving guitar licks of 'Crushed' and 'Kennedy', I was in complete bliss. 'Take Me!' totally took me. When it was all over, I was spent, sweaty, and delighted. On my face was

1992: Top Of *The Hit Parade*

David Gedge says it with flowers, in the video for 'Silver Shorts', single number four of the *Hit Parade* year

likely that special sheepish grin that appears after happily confirming your favourite band's live show can match the music production levels that made you hop around your room ebulliently when listening to it on your sound system at home.

Just after they finished their final song, a perfect opportunity arose. Gedge and company all walked over to the counter at the Hi-Pointe bar for a drink. With a fairly sparse crowd, I could easily have joined them. I could have either let my fan boy freak-flag fly so high they might have recoiled before calling the bouncer, or I could have mustered my best fake casual to strike up a conversation. I had that rare chance to tell my favourite band how much their music meant to me, how they helped me through romantic rejections, how they helped get me hyped for a night out, or how they made the monotony of long drives tolerable. In the end, I let the moment pass. I left the venue with the friend I brought along without sauntering up to the band at the bar. As for why I was willing to give up on this chance to meet the biggest star in my rock constellation, I told my friend something along the lines of, 'I idolize these guys. I don't want to learn that they are assholes and have that ruin how important their music is to me.' It's one of the decisions I made in my youth that I don't regret. The Wedding Present will stay with me as great music, keeping their personalities under wraps.

The Wedding Present

IMPERIAL

5 JULY 1992, NOTTINGHAM, UK

ADAM CURTIS

We saw Gedge in the foyer. Being slightly oiled we asked, 'Have you been laid lately, David? Your lyrics suggest you haven't.' 'You haven't been listening to the lyrics correctly,' he said, awkwardly. Spoke to him since many times since. Top guy.

CHRIS WIDDOWSON

Mr Gedge was sat inside the door selling T-shirts. There was a giant rotating fan hanging from the ceiling. I spent the evening with one eye on the band and the other on the crowd jumping up and down, furiously wondering how high you would need to go to lose an arm!

ASTORIA

7 & 8 JULY 1992, LONDON, UK

LESLEY O'NEILL

I fell over and, as I hit the floor, I heard the opening to 'Kennedy' and the moshpit started to jump on my legs. Massive thanks to whoever dragged me up. Apart from that, it was a fantastic gig! One of those where everything comes right. It was hot as anything. My now-best-mate Rob – who I'd not even met at the time – was also there. He should have been at home revising for his philosophy final exam the following day but he went to see The Wedding Present instead. He still passed with honours!

CHRIS BOUNDS

I don't remember much other than we somehow ended up with upstairs tickets and spent a lot of the gig trying to find a way to get downstairs. It wasn't loud enough upstairs. The Wedding Present need to be listened to at high volume.

214 SOMETIMES THESE WORDS JUST DON'T HAVE TO BE SAID

1992: Top Of *The Hit Parade*

DUCHESS OF YORK

10 OCTOBER 1992, LEEDS, UK

MATTHEW CHILDE

I was at the counter of HMV in Leeds when I overheard a girl, who I assume was a friend of the band, saying that The Wedding Present were playing a surprise gig at the Duchess Of York that night and would they help to publicise it. I went over to her and said that I'd get some friends together if she put me on the guest list. Later on, I brought along two people but my name wasn't down – not that I minded, I was chuffed to be seeing the band in such an intimate venue.

As you might expect from a hometown gig, the crowd was friendly and knowledgeable. The band were mainly playing the *Hit Parade* singles of that year but people kept shouting for 'My Favourite Dress', 'Once More', 'Shatner' and the like. For some reason I was irritated by this and – just as the room went quiet – shouted, 'Stop shouting for old stuff, the new stuff is all right!' It was a case of damning with faint praise. Everyone laughed, someone patted me on the back and David said, 'We'll have to let him in free next time' before adding, 'Well, this is a fairly old one' and launching into 'Lovenest'. I remember feeling embarrassed but pleased that I'd got a mention. Looking back I think it was an example of how the closeness that Wedding Present fans feel to the band means that they tend not to be overwhelming in their praise, just as they might be towards members of their own family. Or at least that's my excuse!

Left: backstage at a French festival in Belfort, July 1992

MICK INGLESON

My favourite of all the many times I've seen them was at my favourite venue, the Duchess in Leeds. It was also a secret gig. I was on the mailing list, and got a letter a day or so before telling us that the gig was happening.

SOMETIMES THESE WORDS **JUST DON'T HAVE TO BE SAID**

The Wedding Present

So not only did I get to see my favourite band in my home town in my best venue, it was only about a fiver to get in, and we got to witness a band at the top of their game enjoying the low-key surroundings with just a half full Duchess fan club-style crowd.

RITZY

12 OCTOBER 1992, DONCASTER, UK

BOBBY OVEN

They filmed the 'Blue Eyes' video for the *Dick York's Wardrobe* collection and I'm in it. I'm one of the people sat on the stage. The stage was really low, just above knee height, and we were down at the front and getting crushed – a standard gig hazard back then. We had to clamber up and out of the bouncing crowd and spill over onto the stage. I had an eight-inch line of bruising on both legs from where the edge of the stage had been. The Wedding Present just kept on playing. All good fun!

STUART LINDSAY

I was introduced to The Wedding Present by my elder brother. I was 13 years old, quite a young age to enter a world of lost love, heartache and angst. My first gig was at the Ritzy nightclub and I was 15. I had my brother's friend's driving licence as ID and was desperately trying to remember the date of birth in case I got challenged at the door. I wasn't missing this one. I'm still convinced you can see me in the footage on *Dick York's Wardrobe*. I will always remember going to watch Boyracer and shocked to see David Gedge and John Peel, sat together deep in conversation, sharing chips on a wall opposite the venue.

NATALIE DOIG

I don't remember when exactly I first heard The Wedding Present, but it was probably on John Peel's show, which I started listening to when I was 16. What I do remember is my friend Lorraine giving me a TDK tape with *Bizarro*, *Tommy* and a few other tracks on it – a D120 nonetheless,

1992: Top Of *The Hit Parade*

which to this day has never snapped! Lorraine had drawn a swirling pattern of greens, purples and pinks on a makeshift card sleeve. The track listings were written inside the fiery speech bubble of a dragon she had also drawn. For us, The Wedding Present inspired creativity.

We needed inspiration, we needed creativity; growing up in a dreary northern town where we could get yelled at in the street for wearing 'the wrong clothes', which was anything verging on the Goth or the hippy, or anything that made us look like students. Our escape pod was the Ritzy on a Thursday night: 'alternative night'. A ragbag bunch of kids in army surplus gear, ripped jeans, flowery dresses, oversized jumpers and shirts or long black cloaks were joined by the ageing punks, metalheads and rockers for a night that was just ours. For me at 16 or 17, Ritzy on a Thursday night was both a place to belong but also a place of danger and wonder, full of dry ice and dark corners. We were swimming through sound thick as molasses as we stomped our Docs on the sticky dance floor, drinking snakebite and black. It was here that The Wedding Present made their indelible mark.

We had particular dances to certain songs or styles of music, but not like the co-ordinated dances of the Sixties. These were more like primordial shape-shifting movements we made to different beats. When 'Brassneck' was played, for example, we would start with a half-strut, half-pace about the dance floor with our hands clasped behind our backs. When the guitars got really wild and fast, we would flail our arms about and shake our heads like demented rag dolls, then return to the restrained shoe-gazing strut. For songs like 'Kennedy', we would be the demented rag dolls for the whole song. The DJ, Dave DD, always played at least two songs by The Wedding Present, usually around the time he played a few tracks by CUD. The dance floor would just go mental.

Then one night The Wedding Present came to play our Ritzy! I remember the buzz amongst my friends in sixth form who were into them. And anyone who was anyone in the alternative scene was going. I remember we were very excited when we got there because we heard that the gig was being filmed. Three of the videos from the night made it on to *Dick York's Wardrobe* collection. At the time, I think we only saw the video of 'Blue Eyes' on the TV afterwards. I remember all the tall lads we knew pushed to the front to shake their hair about! There were also a lot more people there who we didn't know from our usual Thursday nights.

Some of the lads were being a nuisance, as my friend Lorraine

The Wedding Present

remembers the funniest sight being David Gedge propelling another stage invader off the front of the stage with the sole of his boot with vicious gusto. He did seem quite grumpy and we didn't blame him. We pushed our way to the front of the stage for a short while but the big drunk lads were elbowing us so we retreated.

I was disappointed that David Gedge didn't have his baby blue guitar with him. I loved that baby blue guitar. I was learning to play at the time and had my eye on a similar guitar in the local music shop. After the gig, there were some girls getting their boobs signed by David and other band members, but Lorraine and I thought this was a ridiculous thing to do. We were too cool to behave like that.

Although Lorraine has reminded me that before the gig started we were talking to a friend, Andy, at the bar and I was pontificating about how the support act, The Bridewell Taxis, got their name, making a right prat of myself, only to be told that David had been standing behind me the whole time. I was mortified!

One of the reasons The Wedding Present resonated with me and my friends was that they were ordinary but their music was extraordinary. Other bands we liked appeared ethereal or as if they had never been anything other than famous. But The Wedding Present were from just up the road in Leeds, they sang about ordinary things – arguments, unrequited love, the frustrations of being young. We also knew people who said they'd seen The Wedding Present in the really early days and they'd bought David Gedge a pint.

I particularly loved how the downbeat delivery of David Gedge contrasted with the frenetic guitars but also how he could imbue his words with so much seething frustration or anger or exhilaration, or how he could just be down right sinister without ever sounding theatrical or contrived. I loved the snippets of everyday life in their songs, name checking streets and places, ordinary lives transferred into extraordinary music.

After Lorraine had introduced me to The Wedding Present with that tape – in exchange I'd recorded some of my dad's Bob Dylan collection for her – I went out and bought what I could. I remember being deliriously excited the first time I heard 'Dalliance' and rushed to buy it on single. I used to play it over and over again whilst standing on my head. I said the blood rushing to my head really made listening to 'Dalliance' so much more intense! As if it needed any help. I was a strange teenager! I also remember rushing out to Track Records to buy *Seamonsters* when it was released and listening to it when I was babysitting one evening, once the children were in bed.

1992: Top Of *The Hit Parade*

The boy Gedge onstage and in the zone, 1992

But *Bizarro* must be the album I have listened to most, more than any other album by any other band, including my beloved James albums, or REM or Tori Amos, The Cure, Kate Bush, David Bowie, or Nirvana – any of them.

The reason why is simple. I used to put *Bizarro* on every Saturday morning without fail and clean the house to it. At first I would be cleaning my bedroom at home, then it was my rooms at university and eventually my first flat in London when I moved there. For a decade my 'cleaning whilst listening to *Bizarro*' ritual took place every week. It only stopped when I moved in with someone and cleaning became a shared responsibility and not mine alone. Even 26 years later, if I am at home cleaning, I will put on *Bizarro* and it makes the mundane task go by so much more pleasurably. I think this really mundane fact is in someway fitting for The Wedding Present, who seem to have managed to remain completely down to earth whilst creating amazing music.

DAVID POYTON

It was a night club on Silver Street in Doncaster and one of my least favourite memories. The band came on so late and the crowd were way too rowdy. I had got bored waiting and ended up having far too much to drink. I was slumped in a dark corner somewhere when the band came on and all I can

The Wedding Present

remember is David shouting, telling people off as they kept climbing on the raised stage area. Not the best night. I can't remember getting home either! Is that the latest they were ever on stage? I couldn't tell what time it was to be honest – I didn't know my own name by then!

OLD TROUT
25 OCTOBER 1992, WINDSOR, UK

STEVE ALDERSLEY

I discovered The Wedding Present through listening to the John Peel show in the late Eighties. I remember hearing some of the songs from *George Best*, so I picked up the vinyl of that and *Tommy*. The Windsor Old Trout was a tiny venue and David Gedge had to have one of the fastest strumming hands I had ever seen. There was something immense about that jangly guitar when it was played live. It was bigger, louder, fuller and more rewarding than anything I had heard from the band's recordings. They were the first act I ever saw after moving to Toronto. The locals seemed a bit confused about the 'no encores' policy, but it has always made perfect sense to me. So – nothing astounding. I've tried to introduce the band's music to any of my friends who care about music. A few of them loved what they heard. *Seamonsters* has become my favourite Wedding Present album over the years, with 'Dalliance' being my favourite song. That wall of sound is always appealing; 'Dalliance' is superb in every way, slowly building and telling a story before exploding into action two-and-a-half minutes into the track.

L'AERONEF
7 NOVEMBER 1992, LILLE, F

FREDERIC BOUVEUR

In Lille in the Nineties, I went with three friends who did not want to come but who went out of the gig enchanted. I was so satisfied to have them discover The Wedding Present. One of my best wishes for the concert. Pure energy. The song 'Brassneck' for the guitars at the beginning. Always the same shiver now!

1992: Top Of *The Hit Parade*

KROGEN
18 NOVEMBER 1992, UMEÅ, S

JIMMY SJOLUND

I was attending a music school way up north in Sweden. Among the classes we got to play in different band line-ups. My favourite was the band where we played covers by The Wedding Present, Sonic Youth, The Stone Roses and other great indie bands of that time. One day a band mate said that The Wedding Present was going to play in Umeå, a trip of 400 km south. We had to go, even though it was in November and on a Wednesday, a school night.

That might sound like no big deal, but let me tell you about Haparanda. In November it is cold. I mean minus thirty degrees cold. Any long adventures in the crappy cars we could afford as students always posed a risk. It is also dark outside that time of year. All the time. So all travelling was to be done in pitch dark, no matter when we started. Then there are reindeers roaming the roads where we were to travel. Reindeers are very much a hazard. Three of us decided to go and we embarked on our first leg, to Luleå, a modest trip of 130 km, in the guitarist's old Volvo. We were meeting up with friends, part of the then-popular Swedish band Bear Quartet. For some reason, still unknown to me, we were then to change cars and cram the now seven of us into an even older and smaller SAAB. This car is normally a bit tight for four people. We solved this by letting two people share the second front seat and one of us had to sit in the laps of the others in the back seat. We were young and stupid. In hindsight, it was not only quite dangerous but also illegal. The remainder of the drive was then almost 300 km. Contrary to the odds we arrived well in time for the concert to begin. The venue at Krogen was really small. There was a bar and a small dance floor and, in front of the dance floor, a small stage. Exactly to my liking. When the show was about to start the band had to squeeze themselves through the crowd with their instruments to reach the stage.

This was only my second Wedding Present show. I'd been to a show earlier the same year at the Hultsfred Festival. There I'd had to stand outside where they were playing because there were too many people to fit into the small area. So really I had only *heard* them live once before – I didn't see anything.

The Wedding Present

This time I would be within a few metres no matter where I positioned myself in the venue.

Besides the gig being fantastic (as always), I do remember that after the show (no encores) we were having a beer at the bar and I found myself standing beside David Gedge himself. I was so surprised. I had never been to a concert where the band actually spent time in the venue other than playing on stage or in the backroom. Not only were they spending time there, they were talking to the audience and fans. I was gobsmacked. I figured I had to say something. Finally I managed to stutter, 'Great show!' to which David nodded and replied, 'Thanks.' We then left immediately before I could make a fool of myself trying to think of anything else to say.

The drive back shouldn't have been much different than the drive down. However, destiny thought it would be a great idea to throw some snow into the mix. Yay. I didn't envy the poor driver who had to drive all the way himself in the middle of the night with his somewhat drunk friends chatting away or falling asleep. The car was still overcrowded which made the windows foggy. Thinking back, I can't believe we didn't have an accident. I can only thank our fabulous driver for his heroic achievement. At least when we reached Luleå more than half of the passengers left and we changed car to the Volvo. Our bass player fell asleep in the back. I was in the front seat scanning the road and nearby woods for wild animals and our guitarist focused on keeping the car on the road. We made it back and stumbled into bed to get a few hours of sleep before getting up to another day at school. I woke up the next morning tired but happy, sporting my new '8-ball' T-shirt. I didn't know this was the beginning of many years of Wedding Present gigs in several countries. Or that I eventually would own one of the amps used on my favourite record. The '8-ball' T-shirt was my favourite for years until it eventually literally fell apart.

MUSIC HALL
26 NOVEMBER 1992, ABERDEEN, UK

ANDREW YOUNG

I'd have been 18 when I saw them for the first time with my then-girlfriend Elaine. I was nipping to the loo during the support act, only to spot

1992: Top Of The Hit Parade

Mr Gedge at the merchandising stall. I immediately forgot my urge to pee, shrieked like a four-year-old and ran back into the arena to get Elaine, grab her by the hand and frogmarch her back out to the stall where she made me summon up the courage to go speak to him. Which I did, and we chatted about the *Hit Parade* singles and how difficult it was to find a copy of 'Blue Eyes' – four years, as it turned out!

November's sci-fi themed single: 'The Queen Of Outer Space'/'U.F.O.'

BARROWLAND BALLROOM

27 NOVEMBER 1992, GLASGOW, UK

MARK LANDELLS

At the time of the gig I'd heard a few Wedding Present songs and found them decent enough, but I didn't consider myself a fan. In those days I viewed indie music with a large amount of suspicion – the domain of people who thought they were far cooler than they actually were. My listening hours were mostly consumed by Lou Reed, Neil Young and Pink Floyd. If you hadn't made music in the Sixties you didn't really matter – not a particularly healthy viewpoint from a person who was only 19-years-old! But I was beginning to open up: PJ Harvey's debut album, released in the summer of 1992, was getting regular plays and I had recently fallen in love with Julian Cope's *Peggy Suicide*. Things were changing. The previous year I'd attended my first gig: Dinosaur Jr supported by The Boo Radleys at the Barrowlands. I only went because I had a huge crush on the girl who offered me the ticket. I didn't especially enjoy the music but I loved the buzz of people having a good time and I was keen to experience more gigs. So a couple of months later I went back to the Barrowlands to see The Ramones. Eleven months and a few gigs later I was there for The Wedding Present. It was a defining moment in my musical

The Wedding Present

education. The place was a riot and it was impossible not to be sucked in by the insanity that was engulfing the venue. At the previous gigs I'd attended, I'd occupied a spot roughly in the middle of the hall. I'd tapped my foot. I'd bopped my head. And on a couple of occasions I'd even sung along. But I'd always remained in control. During that Wedding Present gig, control was abandoned. After the first song I looked at my mate. We both nodded silently and then flung ourselves into the pit and danced and jumped around like a couple of indie rock veterans. We ended up soaked in sweat and battered and bruised but – oh, so blissfully happy!

CAROLINE MCKENZIE

I had kept up with the *Hit Parade* singles with only a minor hiccup on a nervous morning in July when 'Flying Saucer' proved unusually elusive. It cost more than the other singles for some reason. Anyway, there was only December to go by the time they hit Glasgow and the tour felt like a victory lap. Moonshake were the support band and they pretty much blew me away with their incredibly intense post-PiL, sample-infused noisescaping. Suddenly, The Wedding Present actually had a job to do. They opened with 'Come Play With Me'. Job done; the crowd exploded with the song. They didn't play 'Boing!' though. I had to wait until 2013 to hear that live. I bought the '8-ball' T-shirt out of solidarity with poor neglected 'Boing!' The venue was packed and, even by Barrowlands standards, very hot and sweaty but this was perfect for an upbeat, singles-heavy celebration. For some reason, I remember thinking that the group looked really happy as they piled through the set. I hope they were.

HMV STORE
DECEMBER 1992, CENTRAL LONDON, UK

ANDY PRESTON

In the early Nineties, I moved to London from the North West of England. I was a junior-grade civil servant and got a transfer of jobs so that I could chance my arm in 'that London'. Pretty soon, my admin-level

1992: Top Of *The Hit Parade*

pay packet wasn't stretching too far in covering my living expenses, so I looked around for a part-time job. HMV Records was advertising for part-time counter staff at one of their central London branches.

One Sunday morning, the manager waved me down and said, 'Job for you today. Video department cash register.' That was the extent of my training. I wandered off to that section of the store. The guy restocking this part of the store grunted his hellos, explained the in-house player was below the counter and that I should help myself to some videos to play on the extensive bank of screens that decorated the video sections of music chain stores in those days. Like a kid at Christmas, I hurriedly grabbed a bunch of my favourite VHS tapes, including *Dick York's Wardrobe*. I could share my passion for The Wedding Present with the Sunday lunchtime browsers in HMV that day! After loading up the tape, I set about the business of the day, pleased to be getting paid to watch The Wedding Present on dozens of ceiling mounted monitors across my section of the store. The in-store security guy was less than impressed as the opening scenes of 'Love Slave' bounced across every screen in the department. The bright colours and naked flesh (and the spaghetti, I guess) were clearly too much for a couple of the children innocently browsing the shelves with their parents at that moment. The security guard hurried over, hit stop on the player behind the counter and began a sequence of events that culminated in me sitting in the manager's office and being told that it was probably best if I found myself a job somewhere else. I don't know whether sales of *Dick York's Wardrobe* benefitted from my avid promotion or whether kids in the store that day have been able to eat spaghetti since. But every time I watch the video for 'Love Slave' I'm warmed by the memory.

EVENT

7 DECEMBER 1992, BRIGHTON, UK

STEPHANIE COATES

The Wedding Present were the very first band that I saw when I went to Brighton Uni. I studied Library and Info Studies and was very, very shy. I somehow plucked up the courage to ask one of my housemates to come

The Wedding Present

1992: Top Of *The Hit Parade*

with me. The gig was great, and I felt so independent and grown up! A few months later I got together with Jeff in my home town of Colchester. On our second date I was introduced to his fantastic vinyl collection and I remember listening to *George Best*, which just blew me away. Travelling back to Brighton I wore the *George Best* T-shirt he had given me. The next time we got to see The Wedding Present was in 2008 in Brighton. They were fantastic, of course, but I was newly pregnant with twins and I had to keep running off to be sick! It's a story that I like to tell the twins when I hear The Wedding Present on the radio or play their music in the car.

Opposite: NME celebrates the band's record-breaking year

PYRAMID CENTRE
9 DECEMBER 1992, PORTSMOUTH, UK

JAMES WOODWARD

I got into The Wedding Present when my older brother bought 'Dalliance' on 7" from Woolworths in Ringwood, Hampshire. I think I bought a record by The Cult at the same time and remember lamenting him for buying something where the guitars were drowning the vocals and there wasn't a guitar solo. After repeated listens, 'Dalliance' started to get under my skin, and my brother took me to see The Wedding Present at Portsmouth Pyramids, Salisbury Arts Centre and Portsmouth Wedgewood Rooms. I also saw them at Reading Festival a couple of times, and Phoenix Festival at least twice, one of which was notable for them playing to not many people, with two drummers, in absolutely brutal cold rain. That last show is actually on one of the box sets and you can clearly hear me whistling several times between songs, yet I still haven't received a royalty cheque. Fast-forward a few decades and I'm in a band called Falling Stacks. We were asked by our label to contribute to a Record Store Day compilation in which all acts were to cover a band or song that had a particular relevance to their younger experiences of record shops. I pushed for something off *Seamonsters* and 'Dare' was deemed easiest, which it was. Easy to make terrible, anyway. We weren't sure we liked it, but at that point hadn't released a hard copy of anything, so the lure of it being pressed on purple vinyl meant that when it went to the band vote as to whether to pull it or not, 'release it' won two votes to one. So it exists. It's a bit shit.

The Wedding Present

LEMON GROVE
10 DECEMBER 1992, EXETER, UK

BECKY WELLS

I was about 15. I remember going backstage and David and the band signing a poster for me which I still have framed in my bedroom. I'm now a bit older and have seen them several times since, each time better than the last, but that first gig will always stay in my mind.

NICKY VIGNOLI

I was 15 and I had my mock GCSE maths exam the next day. I went with my then boyfriend, Will, and our friends Tim and Paul who were all a few years older than me and had been to see them play live many times before. Paul was wearing a shirt that had previously belonged to David Gedge and which he'd recently won in a fanzine competition. I was stood next to Paul and he knew the words to every single song and was singing along, seemingly word-perfect. I'd already bought the *3 Songs* EP from Woolworths when it first came out. I can remember playing it for hours, and 'Corduroy' is probably still my favourite track. And the 'Dalliance' 10". Of course, my friends and I were all desperately hunting down the *Hit Parade* singles around Exeter. And we were also buying the live cassettes when available. For a French A-level assignment, I had to record a role-play in a restaurant. My boyfriend had the French version of 'Why Are You Being So Reasonable Now?' so we recorded my role play with 'Pourquoi Es Tu Devenue Si Raisonnable?' playing in the background for that authentic French restaurant effect.

BRIXTON ACADEMY
12 DECEMBER 1992, LONDON, UK

PATRICK DUNPHY

It wasn't packed, just the right sized crowd. The Wedding Present opened with 'Dalliance' and 'Dare', no speaking between songs and no encore.

Dark but not gloomy, it left me buzzing for days after. My other favourite memory is for personal reasons. On 4 November 1994 I was married to my wonderful wife Hayley. Living in Guildford at the time I popped into town and was browsing in a record shop when I saw *Watusi* and thought, 'Great, The Wedding Present as a wedding present!' Twenty years on, we were delighted to discover that The Wedding Present were playing *Watusi* on 4 November 2014 at the Wedgewood Rooms, Southsea. We loved the idea of celebrating our 20th anniversary on the 20th anniversary tour of the album I bought on our wedding day. We even got Mr Gedge to sign happy anniversary on the remastered copy we bought at the gig.

UNIVERSITY OF CENTRAL LANCASHIRE

16 DECEMBER 1992, PRESTON, UK

ANDY BARTON

I was wearing my new burgundy 'Number 11' *Hit Parade* top. Before the gig, David very kindly signed my top with a great big marker pen. After much jumping about, 90 minutes later, my top was absolutely drenched in sweat with no sign of the autograph left either. David very kindly tried to re-sign it after the show, asking 'Have I not signed this already?'

LEEDS POLYTECHNIC

17 DECEMBER 1992, LEEDS, UK

MARK WOFF

Friends gave me tapes. I had *Bizarro* on one. The only tape I can find has *Seamonsters* plus the single version of 'Brassneck' and the *3 Songs* EP on the other side. I was pretty much a metal kid but the guitars swung it for me. I remember being taken immensely by them and then 'Dalliance' fried my little brains. It was the sound of the galaxy ending. *The Hit Parade* started coming out. I was now committed to following them, and had a pre-order in for the

The Wedding Present

singles to make sure I got them. First time I saw them was at Leeds Met. I still have an 'Ask The 8 Ball' poster for the tour somewhere. While we were queuing up for coats after, I was admiring some guy's Bobby Charlton T-shirt. He said, 'Here, have it!' It was very sweaty, but I took it in the intended spirit and (after washing it) wore it until it fell off. This heralded the start of the T-shirt era. I had a 'Number 11' long-sleeve top which also disintegrated eventually. I was wearing it two nights in a row in November 1993, when I saw them in Glasgow the night after seeing them in Galashiels, which was the best night ever.

IAN FLETCHER

My plans for 1992 would have already included a quest to hunt down a copy of each one of those essential 7" singles, of course. My plans for 1992 definitely did not include hobbling around to get them with one leg plastered literally from toe to mid thigh. In February I turned 20, having by that stage already been laid up with a double fracture of my right tibia for almost three months. I should really have been away at university in 1992. I had been to college; I had offers from two universities and plenty of my mates were already seeking out places to stay in their chosen campus cities. I however got slightly cold feet at the wrong moment and a strange sense of monetary neediness that I really shouldn't have cared about. I deferred for a year and instead took a job in my chosen career of information technology in an office about 30 minutes away.

Less than two months into this job, a huge crunching sliding tackle in a local Sunday morning eleven-a-side pub footie match from someone far larger than me ruled me out of almost all action that life could offer a 19-year-old for over six months. Or at least that's how it felt for a football- and music-mad lad brought up and then still living in a small crappy North East town. This was some time before the internet as we know it now, before IT workers could connect up and then type away from the sofa and a huge leap from the social whirlwind that university promised. Instead, stuck at home with mum and dad, it was six months wondering what the hell I'd done.

As soon as each one was released on the first Monday of every month – broken leg, shite town with no record shop, long before anything approaching a music shop website

1992: Top Of The Hit Parade

existed, whatever – I was out there in some way to get myself a copy. That might consist of conning my dad (who himself always seemed to hate all forms of music) to give me a lift to Durham City on some pretence so that I could slowly sneak off to Volume Records. It may involve begging my mum (who could drive but barely actually ever did) to go shopping to Newcastle, with my destination again being a branch of Volume Records, where those walls always seemed to be filled with vivid Gallon Drunk tees for some reason. Or it could be that I would convince a friend to give me a lift to more nearby Darlington in the hope (but not exactly expectation) of a record shop there stocking anything by a band like The Wedding Present. In March, I somehow hobbled all the way to the bus and around Newcastle for a precious copy of Three.

Even now, years later, few sets of songs mean more to me. It was about the time, that place, my own seemingly semi-disastrous situation; it was that great band from (not so far away) Leeds who I loved and it was those twelve lumps of small circular plastic which meant so much. I did eventually turn myself around that year and, towards the back end of 1992, I finally made it to university. Even my badly broken leg eventually made it back into something like the shape that it was in before all of this happened and I did play football again. In many ways, I was much wiser and more determined for the experience also – in no small part due to that set of superb singles which made me want to tell you this story.

And then there were 12: the final, seasonal single of 1992

SOMETIMES THESE WORDS **JUST DON'T HAVE TO BE SAID** 231

The Wedding Present

1993-94: Island And Watusi

The band spent most of 1993 taking time off, occasionally playing gigs. A compilation of archive radio sessions, *Peel Sessions 1987-1990*, was released by Strange Fruit. They re-emerged in early 1994 with the news that they had signed to Island Records, For their next album, The Wedding Present again left for the US and enlisted Steve Fisk (Screaming Trees, Nirvana). The result was *Watusi*.

TOWN AND COUNTRY CLUB

6 FEBRUARY 1993, LONDON, UK

IAN NESBITT

They were playing my favourite venue, the Town And Country Club in Kentish Town. Chris, my best gigging buddy, wasn't going to pass off a chance to chat up some indie girls and my brother, Rob – a Wedding Present nut – was bringing his new squeeze, a flame-haired beauty by the name of Jo, to her first ever gig. Living out in rural Buckinghamshire, we got the train into town and entered the Bull And Gate pub in Kentish Town at 6pm.

Usually we'd have a couple of drinks before moving on to the main venue but tonight the gig was taking place after a seminar arranged by *NME* called Lost In Music. This meant that the doors wouldn't open until 9pm and, by the time we got in, we were suitably oiled. There were three support acts – Sugarblast, Flower Sermon and Molly Half Head – and, by the time they had all performed, the crowd was getting restless. We warned Jo that The Wedding Present were no ordinary live band and she should prepare herself for an onslaught of the senses. Perhaps we were overdoing the hype but she giggled nervously and said she couldn't wait. When the lights finally went down, we had manoeuvred ourselves to a point just on the edge of the massed knot of people by the stage, all waiting eagerly for the pogoing fun to begin.

1993–1994: Island And *Watusi*

Finally, at midnight, the band shuffled on and David Gedge stood centre stage. The memory is hazy as to what he said to the crowd, but what happened next is still as bright as day in my memory. The long wait meant the crowd was chomping at the bit anyway. The Wedding Present opened with the unmistakable descending chords of 'Kennedy' and the bass and drums kicked in, smashing us with a wave of sound. The crowd went completely bonkers. The *NME* said, "'Kennedy' prompted mass ecstasy.' It was all too much for Jo. She instantly fainted. All around, arms flailed and beer and sweat mingled in the smoke dense air. Rob and I somehow managed to help Jo to the sanctuary of a small room at the back of the venue where she slowly recovered. Much to Rob's disappointment, he had to content himself with watching the rest of the gig from the back whilst I made my excuses and got back near the front. It was an awesome gig. Whether Jo would agree with me is another matter!

SHIBUYA ON AIR

17 MARCH 1993, TOKYO, J

YOSHIAKI NONAKA

It was my first ever Wedding Present gig and is still my best gig ever. That gig made me a die-hard Wedding Present fan and that's why I've been operating my own Japanese website dedicated to The Wedding Present and Cinerama (twpcinerama.com) ever since.

LEADMILL

5 APRIL 1993, SHEFFIELD, UK

BOBBY OVEN

There were no tickets left in Leeds for the Sound City event. I had to drive to Sheffield and traipse all over to get the last three tickets from the last outlet that had them: I got the last tickets in the world for the Leadmill. I ended up in a drunken conversation with Gedge himself. Well, I was drunk. I don't think he was.

The Wedding Present

In 1993, Keith Gregory announced he was leaving The Wedding Present. This left David Gedge as the sole original member in the line-up. Gregory was replaced on bass by Darren Belk.

DAVID GEDGE

Keith leaving the band was very difficult for me. He'd actually tried to leave a couple of times before and I'd talked him out of it. I saw him as my main ally in the group and someone who'd shared the original vision I'd had for The Wedding Present. I went home and burst into tears!

PHOENIX FESTIVAL
18 JULY 1993, STRATFORD-UPON-AVON, UK

JAMIE JONES

I had vague thoughts about being gay without every really believing that I was. In the pages of the *NME*, I was reading about ambiguous or bisexual indie popsters like Brett Anderson, without having a clue what either phrase meant in reality. That July, something happened which showed me with definitive certainty that I was not gay. It occurred during a raucous and particularly sweaty set by The Wedding Present at the Phoenix Festival. The crowd was tightly packed together as the band blasted through their set and I was throwing myself around with the best of them. About halfway through 'Blue Eyes', I noticed a hand pressed against the front of my jeans, on my crotch.

At first I thought it was just an accident, someone inadvertently trying to find somewhere to put their hand in the packed crowd. I did my best to ignore it and jumped around as Gedge and Co. banged out another tune. I started to change my opinion as, during the intro to 'Silver Shorts', this errant hand began to force its way inside the front of my jeans. I froze, not so much out of terror but more out of a sense of, 'What the hell is happening here?' After a few seconds of this unwelcome

1993–1994: Island And *Watusi*

The Wedding Present, fourth line-up: Darren Belk, David Gedge, Paul Dorrington and Simon Smith
Photo: Jayne Lockey

foreplay, I turned my head to see who had their hand perilously close to my two day old festival pants. I came face to face with a lad with a Suede 'Drowners' T-shirt on, who was probably in his early 20s.

Me: 'What the hell are you doing mate?'
'Drowner': 'You've been grinding your arse against me for the last half-hour, thrusting against me and brushing your arm against mine.'
Me: 'Fuck off. I wasn't doing anything, just dancing. I'm straight!'
'Drowner': 'I'm bisexual...'
Me: 'Well not with me you're not.'

At this point the world went dark. 'The Drowner' had headbutted me and made good contact with the bridge of my nose. Thankfully, I had taken off my glasses and stored them in their case, in my shorts pocket. With the help of a kind young lady in a James 'Sit Down' T-shirt, I made my way out of the crush and flopped down in a sweaty, bloody heap at the back of the crowd. As the ringing in my ears slowly receded, I went back over what had just happened and happily concluded that I didn't deserve the 'prick-tease' title that

The Wedding Present

the Drowner had foisted upon me. I shook my head clear and showed an adolescent's ability to get on with life by running back to my tent to get a clean T-shirt. I didn't want my mates to find out what had happened, so wiped the worst of the blood away with my now ruined Wedding Present '4' T-shirt. Miraculously, the mark on my nose was tiny and was covered almost entirely when I put my glasses back on. I pulled on my own Suede 'Drowners' T-shirt and jogged unsteadily back to the arena. I got back just in time to see The Wedding Present leave the stage. My friend Maff bounded over, wreathed in sweat, and exclaimed, 'Bloody quality gig mate, weren't it?' I nodded my agreement and off we went to the bar to get a pint. I never discussed the incident with anyone and it didn't make me angry or vengeful. It was all just a bit odd.

JOINER'S ARMS

30 OCTOBER 1993, SOUTHAMPTON, UK

EDWARD KOMOCKI

I was admonished by David Gedge, when I was at the front of the moshpit for shouting a request for 'Crawl' and not "Crawl', please!' And delighted when they went ahead and played it anyway.

VOLUNTEER HALL

28TH NOVEMBER 1993, GALASHIELS, UK

MARK WOFF

Two hours drive there. A bit chemical. This bonkers band from Carlisle called Cosmic Cat supporting. A deadpan Gedge drawing a tombola before the gig, guitar on and looking totally unfazed by proceedings. The absence of a barrier in front of the stage and being in the front row who – to a man and woman – were doing a linked arms leg kick dance throughout the verses of 'So Long, Baby', breaking into twisting for the chorus.

1993-1994: Island And *Watusi*

UNIVERSITY OF STRATHCLYDE UNION
29 NOVEMBER 1993, GLASGOW, UK

PETE KIRKWOOD

Standing up the back watching the support act and having a chat with a nice bloke about the band on stage.

Only realising later on when he took to the stage to headline that it was Mr Gedge I'd been talking to. D'oh!

LIMERICK UNIVERSITY
1 DECEMBER 1993, LIMERICK, IRL

TERRY McCAUL

In my eyes they were the coolest band on the planet. I absolutely loved them. Myself and a girl I knew shared a love for The Wedding Present's music. There was one downfall. We disliked each other immensely. I'm not sure why. I think it was because we were so alike. We never really talked – actually, that's probably why I don't know why we didn't get on. Of course I was going – ticket bought, the whole lot. I met a friend in town two days before the gig. The girl I disliked was in her class in school and had come up with an idea to get to meet David Gedge and had written me a note. In the note she asked me to join her in a fake interview for a fake fanzine she was creating for school in order to get to meet David.

She wanted to know, 'Did I want to join her?' It didn't mean we would be friends afterwards but she guessed we shared a love for the band so much that I was bold enough to do it. So we did. I got together a few questions. I was freaking out – the sweat was pumping out of me. I thought I would make a fool of myself and/or get busted. David would know our fanzine was fake, he would cop that we were 16, and laugh at us. We got through the questions. I guess we stuck out like a sore thumb – big nervous heads on us! He did laugh, but only when I asked him if he could send me some Lost Pandas tapes. Best night of my life! We were too nervous to ask him the one question the both of us wanted to know: what did his

The Wedding Present

'Favourite Dress' look like and could he describe it for us? The gig was amazing and afterwards I met David at the T-shirt stand. I asked him about 'My Favourite Dress'. He told me it was black, fitted not too short – just above the knee – and it had a square neckline. I can't remember if it had sleeves or not. I remember being disgusted at the description. My friend and I agreed we didn't think we liked the dress but we went on the search to buy something similar. When we met through mutual friends, we would only talk about all things Wedding Present related and considered getting the dress made and trying to convince ourselves we would look good in it, even though it sounded like it was completely not our style. We never did find the dress.

> "Black, fitted not too short – just above the knee – and it had a square neckline"
>
> Gedge's description of his favourite dress

TIVOLI
3 DECEMBER 1993, DUBLIN, IRL

DIARMAID DOHERTY

Ever find yourself heading straight for the W section when you happen to be in a record shop? Did you used to tune in to a John Peel show in the hope that he might just happen to play a tune from your favourite band? Did you count down the days back in 1992 to when a certain band's new single for that month would be on sale? And, at the end of it all, were you the proud owner of a collection of twelve singles that in years to come would be worth a small fortune? Mind you, they'd never be put up for sale. We didn't have any big record stores in my part of the world. In Letterkenny in Co. Donegal, we had a nice wee record shop in the town's Market Square which my big brother reckoned once stocked the *George Best* album for a couple of years without anyone taking a chance on it.

By the time I first heard of The Wedding Present there was no *George Best* album there for me to get my hands on. It was either bought by then or, more likely, returned. I think the first song I heard from the band was '(Make Me Smile) Come Up And See Me'. I was hooked. The song was off the 'All The Songs Sound The Same' EP which also included 'Corduroy'. Once I heard

1993–1994: Island And *Watusi*

Gedge, Smith, Dorrington and Belk, 1994

'Corduroy', suddenly 'Come Up And See Me' was no longer my favourite Wedding Present track. A year or two later, I got chatting to a girl about music and when I mentioned The Wedding Present, she replied, 'Yeah, I know them. All their songs sound the same...' Let's just say, I was impressed. My big brother was by this stage living in Glasgow where the record stores sold more than just the *George Best* albums in the W section. I'd been over to him a few times and had added to my new collection of Wedding Present material. I got singles, 12" records and albums. I'd bought a couple of T-shirts from the *Hit Parade* collection – quality stuff that nobody back home would have. Well that's what I thought. On a night out in our local disco, I ordered a pint from the barman who just happened to be sporting a 'Dalliance' T-shirt. Peter Curran was friends with my other big brother and I knew that he was into his music. There and then, we'd found we'd something else in common – a love and passion for a band that we still share today. When The Wedding Present are in town, Peter and me will put life's problems and struggles to one side. We'll lose ourselves on the dance floor and in the music that has been part of my life for the best part of 25 years. A bit more than just a dalliance...

The Wedding Present

SLIM'S

23 MAY 1994, SAN FRANCISCO, CA, USA

CESAR VIRAMONTES

I discovered The Wedding Present at a thrift shop in Berkeley in 1990. I don't recall buying anything but I was stopped in my tracks by a song that was playing over the shop's hi-fi system. The guitars were unbelievably fast and the singer's accent was thick! I asked the clerk if he knew what was playing and he said *Bizarro* by The Wedding Present. I left the shop and, instead of heading off to campus, headed over to Amoeba Records and bought *Bizarro*. By the time *Seamonsters* came out I was a fully fledged Wedding Present fan.

One day I read that The Wedding Present were going to play The I Beam in San Francisco in support of *Seamonsters*. I was 20 at the time and the venue was 21+ but I was sure that they would let me in. They didn't, and I was devastated. I pleaded with the bouncer to let me in – put two giant Xs on my hands. I didn't care about drinking alcohol; all I cared about was seeing The Wedding Present. I went back home to Berkeley with a broken heart and tears running down my cheeks, knowing I might never have a chance to see them again.

At the Garage, London, in April 1994

1993–1994: Island And *Watusi*

One day, about three years later, I was flipping through the SF Weekly and saw that The Wedding Present would be playing Slim's in support of *Watusi*. I was reading this while my girlfriend and a couple of friends were sitting next to me. I dropped the newspaper and started to cry tears of joy even as my friends looked on incredulously. They didn't understand I was crying because I finally had a chance to see The Wedding Present!

HEINEKEN FESTIVAL

7 JULY 1994, LEEDS, UK

JASON STEVENS

The only concert I've ever seen that reached the same heights of shamanic ecstasy as the Ritz in Manchester in 1988 was The Wedding Present at the Leeds Free Festival at Roundhay Park. Fuelled on cheap beer and some local produce from Chapeltown, I made my way into an enormous marquee and slipped through the crowd and into position.

The concert itself was a bit of a blur but there was one unforgettable moment when they played 'What Have I Said Now?' and the strobe light was flashing and they just played and played and played, on and on, faster and faster. It was one of those transcendental communal moments – everyone in the tent seemed hypnotised, bouncing in unison, faces chiselled in euphoria and the steam of sweat and beer lit by the oscillating light. A heady cocktail of Leeds, weed and breakneck guitar speed!

NICKY VIGNOLI

I suffered really badly with travel sickness when I was younger, so the only way I could go was if I was able to be the one who drove up there. It was a long way from Exeter, and I was still taking driving lessons when the trip was planned. If I hadn't taken it yet, or failed it, I would be driving up the A roads. If I passed it would be a straightforward drive up the motorway. Thankfully I passed in time, and it was my first really long trip driving my friend's car.

The Wedding Present

WALPOLE PARK FESTIVAL
30 JULY 1994, GOSPORT, UK

EDWARD KOMOCKI

I remember that initial epiphany during a John Peel session when The Wedding Present play 'Softly Softly' and the grand obsession begins and the comedown when, before my very eyes at my first ever Wedding Present gig at the Gosport Big Top Festival, the majestic 'Softly Softly' is transformed into the still-great-but-not-as-good-as-the-original 'Yeah, Yeah, Yeah, Yeah, Yeah'.

ESQUIRES
25 AUGUST 1994, BEDFORD, UK

KARL KATHURIA

After leaving university, I moved back to Bedford, having got a job fairly nearby. That summer The Wedding Present played there. For them, this was a Reading Festival warm-up gig. For me it was a major event.

I went with a friend who I'd been to many gigs with but who was due to go to the airport at midnight to go on holiday. Most concerts I was going to at the time finished at 11pm, so we figured it would all be OK. For some reason, this one didn't start until something like 11.30pm, by which time panic about having to miss it had made way to resignation. It didn't help that the opening 15 minutes seemed to be taken up by the introduction to 'Corduroy', being played for possibly the first time by Darren Belk, who we had played pool with earlier in the evening. I stayed for the whole thing, even getting a half-price T-shirt at the end of it all.

Thinking back now, I don't know how much of that evening in Bedford is actually real. I know it happened, and I know my friend had to leave to get to the airport. I also have some very badly taken photos of The Wedding Present in action. The rest of it somehow doesn't seem entirely real – but that's my memory of it.

1993–1994: Island And *Watusi*

Come on in, the water's lovely: David Gedge models the shorts that appealed to and appalled fans in equal measure

READING FESTIVAL

26 AUGUST 1994, READING, UK

IAN GITTINS

A lot of people in bands are very snotty when they get a bit of fame. It goes to their heads. But David was always incredibly nice to deal with. *Melody Maker* used to have this thing called the autograph signing tent at festivals, where you'd get some of the biggest bands that were playing to do autographs for fans for an hour. And all the fans would queue up and get photos signed. David did that a couple of times. It was the year Kurt Cobain died. Hole were playing at Reading. I bumped into David backstage and he said, 'Oh, I think I'm doing your tent later.' I said, 'Yeah, you are. You're down for doing it at four o'clock.' And he said, 'Oh no, that's the same time as Courtney. I wanted to see Hole.' And I said, 'Oh god, I'm really sorry but I can't really move it.'

A lot of bands would just go, 'Oh, fuck it. I'm not doing it then.' But he

The Wedding Present

The line-up for the Melody Maker Stage at Reading Festival 1994

went, 'OK, fair enough.' He did the signing session, although occasionally he'd crane his head to try and see a bit of Courtney Love on the main stage out of the corner of the tent.

Another time, I did an interview up north with a band, I forget who, and we started talking about bands. And the PR girl said she absolutely idolised David Gedge and The Wedding Present. This was a Saturday. So I called Gedge up – by this time I'd got quite friendly with him – and said, 'I'm in York. Do you want to have lunch tomorrow?' And he said, 'OK' and told me a pub in Otley or Batley or somewhere. So I said to the PR girl, 'We're going to meet this friend of mine for lunch. Do you mind?'

So the next day we drove over, me and the photographer and this PR girl, and I only told her it was David Gedge when we got there. And the look on her face. She couldn't believe what she was seeing!

1993–1994: Island And *Watusi*

STEVE THOMPSON

I recall as a 17 year old being lent a copy of *George Best* by some of the cool indie girls in the Sixth Form Common Room at school. At the time I'd just discovered Shoegaze and was all about Ride, Chapterhouse, Slowdive, Lush, etc. I was also partial to some Neds, Stuffies, Charlatans and the Inspirals though, so I was excited about being presented with this record with the coolest sleeve I'd ever seen.

I got home and put it on on the record player and – I just didn't get it. I liked the jangle, but Gedgy's harsh Leeds voice was just a step too far for an innocent, spotty 17 year old from Reading who was into Slowdive. I gave the record back with a full debrief, much to the ridicule of the cool indie girls, who promptly sent me back to the darkest depths of shoegaze (which has finally become cool, now I'm married and fat).

Fast forward to Friday night in the Evening Session tent at Reading Festival 1994. I've just watched Lush but shoegaze is all but dead, grunge is dying, Britpop is about to get very big and Suede and The Boo Radleys are my current kings. But a song called 'Kennedy' is still being played in every decent indie disco in the land and I love it. I can't dance to it – it's too damn fast and it gives me a stitch – but at volume it is just an unbeatable tune and it consequently makes it onto every indie mixtape I ever made. (Apparently it's not ideal on a Valentine's mix). At the time I still don't own a Wedding Present record though – that voice still scares me.

So, I'm in the session tent. I'm pissed, I'm with a girl I'm trying to impress and on come The Wedding Present. What happened next is all a very loud and intense blur. But I've sobered up, I'm sweaty, I'm fuckin' knackered, the girl I was with has disappeared – and I'm completely hooked. That voice! I totally got it – the energy, the jangle, the crowd. It was simply amazing.

Fast forward again to 2013. By sheer coincidence, I'm in a pub in Auckland and I'm about to see The Wedding Present again. Apparently it's the band's first ever gig in New Zealand and I'm surrounded by big scary-looking middle aged New Zealanders. I'm fortunate. I've seen the band numerous times and I've been lucky enough to speak to David over the years, so I'm trying to be the cool Englishman near the back. The gig is great. I'm nodding my head and tapping my foot (remember, I'm being cool). Then the first chords of 'Kennedy' are struck, the big burly Kiwis go mad and I get a pint thrown over me. I'm pissed off, really pissed off. Then I remember – this is their Reading Festival 1994, only they've been waiting 20-plus years for this. They've every right to go mad and enjoy themselves!

The Wedding Present

WATUSI
THE FOURTH ALBUM
RELEASED 12 SEPTEMBER 1994

STEVE FISK, SEATTLE
Producer, Watusi

I loved The Wedding Present but I didn't realise how much of a departure *Watusi* was going to be from what they traditionally did and I know the band wasn't really ready for it. They kept trying to make sounds like they just did with Steve Albini. It was like, 'Well, why aren't you working with Steve Albini if you want to make those sounds?' We were recording in a small room with close microphones. Probably the opposite of how Steve Albini would have done it in his giant garage when he recorded them back in Minnesota.

David wanted democracy and everybody got a vote in putting the mixes together. The band would come into the control room and they would listen and then they would go back into the band break room and have a giant argument. It was like a cartoon in that they would come in the room dead silent, because David didn't want them talking and telling us what to do with this or that. And they'd go back into the band room. And then there'd be paper plates being thrown and people screaming and yelling in that crazy north England accent. And then they'd come back in dead faced and then, 'Turn the snare down please.' And then they'd walk out of the room and I'd turn the snare drum down. And they would go listen to it again and have another argument and go, 'Turn the background vocals down please...'

If a song was just good enough to be a Wedding Present song but hadn't gone anywhere new, David would chalk up that song and twist it to make it something better. He'd say, 'This is one for the punters – we have to make something better than that.' And that's when he had the idea of having Darren Belk sing the vocal on

1993–1994: Island And *Watusi*

'Shake It'. Darren didn't want to sing the vocal. He had to become pretty inebriated to get in the mood. We set it up so he actually was singing to a blown-up little speaker he had in his headphones, just working with the sound. He had the artificial leg and everything so we set him up in a small room with a chair – and he did great! It was really fun. Once he sang it a couple of times, he started crooning and going for the big notes.

PAUL DORRINGTON

Listening back to *Watusi* now I love it! I think at the time I had a certain idea of what the band should sound like, and definitely what my guitar should sound like. The brief we gave to Steve Fisk was that we wanted to do something different and we wanted to sound like a Sixties band. And Steve pretty much fulfilled that brief, although it might not have matched what was in my head. He got hold of an amazing collection of vintage guitars including a six-string and a twelve-string Mosrite, which was wonderful. I played it on 'Swimming Pools, Movie Stars'. He contributed loads to the album, playing keyboards on a few songs, coming up with the idea of using an Optigan on 'Spangle'. It would have been a completely different record if we'd done it with someone else, and I'm quite sure not as interesting.

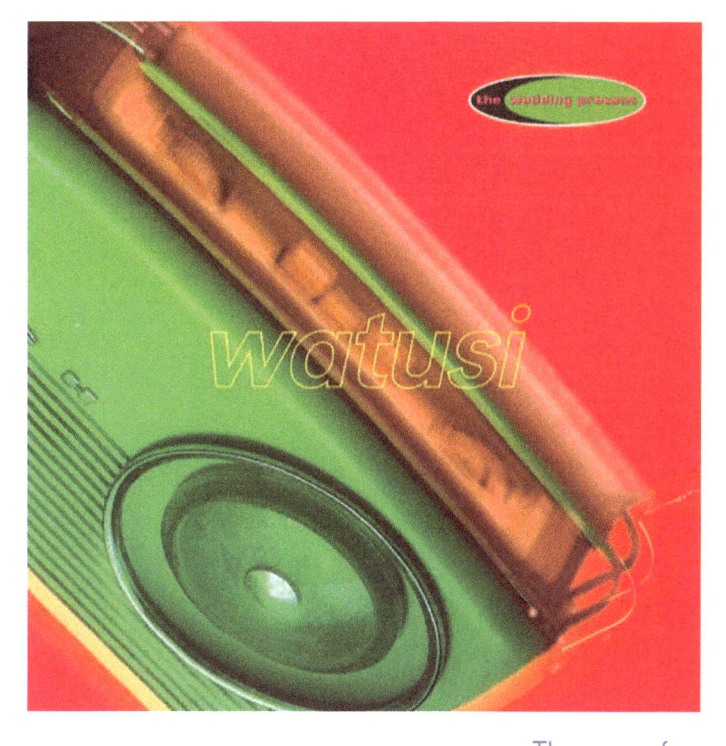

The cover of the Sixties-influenced fourth Wedding Present album, Watusi

STEVE FISK

On the website apparently the big argument is – is 'Spangle' (done with the weird little home organ) the very best song they've ever done or the very worst song they've ever done? Wedding Present fans like to be contrary.

PAUL DORRINGTON

I seem to remember the main disappointment was listening to a tape of it when we got back to England with some friends, who asked Darren something like, 'Are you on this record?' It confirmed what we suspected when we were mixing: the bass was very quiet in the mix.

SOMETIMES THESE WORDS **JUST DON'T HAVE TO BE SAID**

The Wedding Present

STEVE FISK

The *Watusi* record never got promoted properly. The whole thing was set up to happen and they had singles and videos – and the A&R got fired. And because they were English the whole thing fell apart in America. We all had high hopes for that *Watusi* record. I thought it was a great album.

We all were all friends, as much as anybody with that cutting north English sense of humour lets you be a friend! It was fun. It was a lot of me kidding and them saying insulting things about me in a way that I didn't realise they were saying insulting things about me until they were almost through with it. And then, 'Wait a minute, they're talking about me!' It was cool. I had a good time.

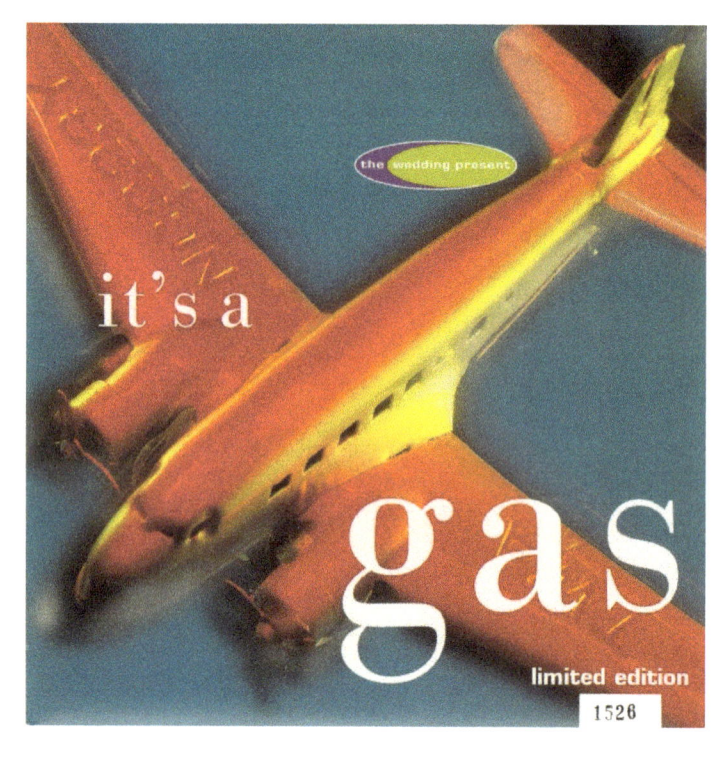

PAUL DORRINGTON

I think we remastered a couple of songs in another studio (my memory is a bit fuzzy about that) but we definitely recorded a different version of 'It's A Gas' with Ian Broudie which ended up sounding like how the band used to sound, rather than how the band sounded on *Watusi*, which probably proves that even though we asked Steve to do what he wanted, subconsciously we didn't want too much to change. Of course, saying we wanted it to sound like a Sixties record wasn't exactly that clear a brief. Although we discussed surf music, garage rock and The Velvet Underground I probably wanted it to sound like *Sgt. Pepper*. And it ended up sounding like The Velvet Underground and surf music for some crazy reason. I actually got on with Steve pretty well at the time. I remember the recording being really enjoyable. And he drove us to Snoqualmie Falls and North Bend, where David Lynch made *Twin Peaks*, so I am forever in his debt for that. It was amazing.

The cover of the 'It's A Gas' single, released in November 1994

1993–1994: Island And *Watusi*

NEWCASTLE UNIVERSITY
4 OCTOBER 1994, NEWCASTLE-UPON-TYNE, UK

CHRIS OLIVER

To say that my brother Stephen (or Steve, as he liked to be called) was a bit of a Wedding Present fan would be an understatement; he lived for the band. Steve had a bad hand dealt to him. He was a haemophiliac and was so ill he was given his last rites within 24 hours of being born.

But he was also a fighter. He was in and out of hospital when he was younger, and he was constantly bullied for his use of walking sticks and wheelchairs. He was also given HIV and Hepatitis C from contaminated blood products when he was about 12. He was told he wouldn't live past 16.

He started to listen to The Wedding Present straight from *Tommy* and he was hooked. It was his way of coping. When he'd had a bad day you could hear the dulcet tones of David Gedge coming out of his bedroom, often competing with my Bruce Dickinson, and much to our parents' annoyance! He and I used to fight like cat and dog. We would wind each other up to the point of physical violence – he once knocked me out with a frying pan and I once kicked him so hard he was hospitalised for six weeks!

When I was 16 or 17 he came up to me and asked if I'd like to come and see The Wedding Present at Leeds University. 'Why would I want to go and see them?' I said, sporting a Megadeth T-shirt. 'Because I know the guy who's doing the lights and I'll get you in for free!' So we went.

That single night transformed our relationship. It brought us closer together, more than anything had before. Whenever there was a Wedding Present gig on he'd ring me up to see if I could come, and more often than not I would. One of the best gigs was Sound City in 1994 at the Leadmill in Sheffield which was broadcast live on Radio 1. It was nice to see Pulp as a support act too.

Steve would spend his time searching out rare Wedding Present records. His collection included: number 003828 of the 'Dalliance' 12" single; another 'Dalliance' 12" single with no number on it; two complete *Hit Parade* box sets (both signed); signed copies of *Tommy*, a white-label pressing of a single (I don't know which); a 'Brassneck' single with the sleeve hand-painted by the band; and several T-shirts all signed by the band and girlfriends.

The Wedding Present

There's also a setlist which I liberated from a gig at the Leadmill, and two of the more unusual items are a CD of *Bizarro* which sounds like one of Mozart's piano concertos and one of Steve's crutches signed by David. David said, 'I've never signed a crutch before, so I'd better sign my full name', and he did.

The last time we saw the band together was in 1994 at Newcastle University. By this time Steve's health had started to really deteriorate. He was pretty much wheelchair-bound but I can remember him saying, 'I'm not going to a Weddoes gig in a fucking wheelchair.' He had a chat with David after the gig. And as we were walking back to my house he had a massive smile on his face, something I hadn't seen on him for a long time.

He died in 2000, aged 29. I wrote to the band after he died just to say thanks for giving Steve so much pleasure in his life. My family and I were so made up when we got a letter back saying that they'd dedicated *Disco Volante* to Steve's memory. OK, I know it's not The Wedding Present but who cares?

It took me a while before I could listen to any Wedding Present as it brought back too many memories but now, when I do listen, it always makes me smile and think about the smile Steve had on his face after that last gig in Newcastle. I'm still predominantly a metal-head but The Wedding Present will always have a special place in my heart. Steve's always with us through the band. My wife and I had one of his favourite songs played at our wedding when we were walking down the aisle, and I'm making sure our son is being indoctrinated into The Wedding Present. He loves the band. He is also autistic so he can't hide his feelings. So when he says he likes something you know he means it.

One last thing. When we were picking Steve's gravestone, we were trying to think of a suitable inscription. We went for 'So long, baby' from *Watusi*. I don't think the vicar understood.

David Gedge with one of the most dedicated Wedding Present fans ever, Stephen Oliver

1993–1994: Island And Watusi

WULFRUN HALL
11 OCTOBER 1994, WOLVERHAMPTON, UK

ANDY BUCKLEY

A lot of my memories of The Wedding Present are attached to cars – brown ones. I had been a Wedding Present fan since 1989, when I heard 'Kennedy' for the first time. A lad I barely knew at college was showing us his 'new' metallic brown Ford Fiesta and he was driving at a much higher speed than he or the car was capable of, ripping around the twisty dry stone walls of Huddersfield. It was also my first introduction to Pixies, as 'Debaser' followed 'Kennedy' on the tape playing in the car. Maybe the near-death experience caused the end of me listening to The Sisters Of Mercy and moved me onto furious guitar pop. My first concert wasn't until the winter of 1994. I'd just graduated and bought a V-reg 1000cc brown Mini. The speedo either flicked wildly around the dial or didn't work at all. The brake master cylinder was on its way out and I lost the brakes several times on the way from Birmingham.

To make it a bit more fun, there were five of us packed in the Mini and you could barely see out of the steamed-up windows. It was the best gig I'd ever been to and still ranks right up there in my top five Wedding Present gigs of all time.

WATERFRONT
13 OCTOBER 1994, NORWICH, UK

MARK WOFF

I travelled to Norwich from Glasgow (where I was at uni) to see them, and then saw them at the Glasgow Garage on the same tour. Any time they played 'Dare' I went home happy. They may have been sick of me coming to see them and getting their autographs. I remember dimly a squiffy conversation with them at the Garage about possible pronunciations of *Watusi* ('you know, like "what you see… is what you get?"'), which I recall was met with bemused yet indulgent chuckles. I still maintain *Watusi* is a masterpiece, however you say it.

The Wedding Present

VICTORIA ROOMS
14 OCTOBER 1994, BRISTOL, UK

NICKY VIGNOLI

I can still remember this gig really well, including what I was wearing (patchwork suede skirt with black and white stripy tights) and us bumping into the band as we were trying to find somewhere to eat before the gig and they were having a walk around. There was some debate between my friends as to whether David had recognised me inside the gig when we saw him again when we arrived at the venue because of my zebra legs – very unlikely. We went to see them play a few other times at other Bristol venues. There was always the same pattern – I liked us to stand a bit near the back so I had some room to dance, and we'd always get very lost trying to find our way back to the M5.

Back in the early Nineties, Nicky Vignoli was really into The Wedding Present... and advertising hoardings with big pictures of dogs on them

MARQUETTE BALLROOM
4 NOVEMBER 1994, MILWAUKEE, WI, USA

THOMAS AUGUSTINE

I was a DJ at college radio station WMSE in Milwaukee and, in addition to doing a weekly show, I helped out in the music department labelling new releases for the library and listening to CDs for objectionable lyrics. I was given *Seamonsters* and really liked it. I also listened to The Ukrainians debut album but didn't make the connection between the two, although I did record

1993–1994: Island And *Watusi*

them both on cassette to listen to while on the job driving a truck. *Seamonsters* would become my second favourite album of the year on my annual 'top ten' list but, over time, it has become my favourite album. It wasn't until spring of 1992 that I would notice The Wedding Present again. While listening to John Peel's BBC World Service show, he played the B-side of the fourth *Hit Parade* single, their version of 'Falling', the love theme from *Twin Peaks*. I was just driving out of range so I actually pulled over to hear the end of the song. I was blown away, having always loved the original. From that moment on, they became one of my favourite bands. I only wish I had tried to catch up on all the early singles back then, when it might have been easier.

In 1994, The Wedding Present played their first show in Milwaukee, or the first one I noticed. I had quit truck driving and was working on the Milwaukee field office staff for the Democratic candidate for Governor of Wisconsin. In the last week of the campaign, things were not looking good for our guy and so they told me I was going to 'volunteer' to help a candidate for state Senate – my boss was in the Senate at the time. The only problem was I would be staying there for a week and it was a three and a half hour drive to Milwaukee. So I drove back for the show on Saturday and saw the show, then drove back Sunday morning to continue. Both campaigns lost, by the way, but the show was great. I was impressed by David's charming and humble presence at the merch table and introduced myself, telling him about how I had to drive so far even though I lived in town. His reply was, 'I hope we don't let you down.' They didn't.

The Wedding Present

1995: Cooking On Vinyl

1995 was a relatively quiet year for The Wedding Present as a touring outfit. In total, they performed only 33 shows.

DAVID GEDGE

People start out thinking that being in The Wedding Present is going to be fantastic – you're on TV and the radio, you make records for a living, you travel around the world. But it can also be quite hard work and there can be a lot of stress involved.

After *Watusi* I think Paul just decided that he'd had enough. The first time you go to the USA, for example, you think it's brilliant. The second time? Yeah, it's great! But by the time of your third or fourth visit to some of these places the novelty starts to wear off and you'd probably prefer to go where the band is possibly never going to tour. And even when you are playing in these exotic locations there isn't always the time to do the fun touristy stuff because of time and economics.

You can also damage your social network at home because you're away so much... or your girlfriend or boyfriend hates you never being there. So it can wear people down after a certain point. That's what happened with Paul and he moved on. Some people last twelve years, some people last twelve months...

PAUL DORRINGTON

I decided to leave the band for a few reasons. Firstly, I didn't like being away from my girlfriend for weeks and weeks at a time. Secondly Keith, Simon and I had been doing another band – Cha Cha Cohen – in whatever spare time we had and I wanted to spend more time doing that band. Nothing against The Wedding Present – it just felt like time for a change. I'd been in a few bands before and Cha Cha Cohen had put out a few records on Chemikal Underground so it seemed like a viable option. But it wasn't really a full-time thing, mainly because the singer lived in New York. So I decided to go to university. Getting a degree seemed like a sensible idea. I am a digital project manager at a design agency now, so being in The Wedding Present isn't directly related really. But it has been a talking point in some interviews – so maybe it has had an influence. These days when people find out I was once a 'rock star', they're keen to find out what band I was in. About 95% of people have never heard of The Wedding Present and the other 5% can't believe it and are massively impressed. There's not much in between.

HUDDERSFIELD UNIVERSITY

21 JUNE 1995, HUDDERSFIELD, UK

MARK STEPHENS

I had just turned 18. I remember walking to the venue with mates in Huddersfield and as we arrived at the university grounds saw some people on roller blades, only to realize it was David Gedge and other band members! I was too nervous to say anything so just carried on walking to the venue. The gig was in a former church and I remember the moshpit being wild. The Wedding Present meant so much to me then; they were expressing real sensitivity and depth of feeling with such emotional response through the guitars and Gedge's voice. Still today I feel a release when listening to their music and, although my teenage angst has gone, I feel great nostalgia.

CITADEL

22 JUNE 1995, ST HELENS, UK

PAUL BOLAN

They played in my home town of St Helens. In my giddiness beforehand, me and my mate got rat-arsed. The concert was going well and I was shouting for 'Brassneck' when David engaged me by saying, 'Stop asking for 'Brassneck' because we are playing the songs that are written down here' and showed me an A4 piece of paper with the setlist on.

The Wedding Present

BENICÀSSIM FESTIVAL
6 JULY 1995, BENICÀSSIM, E

CLAIRE WADD

I might have said, 'Hi' at the Tropic Club in 1986, or another gig in Leeds later, but we basically lost touch until the first Benicàssim festival in 1995. Running Sarah Records didn't involve much rock star backstage glamour – there was a Japanese tour with Heavenly with some quite swank hotels and then Benicàssim, also with Heavenly. We had accommodation for the whole event – again, nice hotel – a backstage pool, a backstage chef and a big dining table for all the bands to eat together. We were reaching Sarah 100 and stopping the label at this point, so it never got any better than that for us. David and I got chatting, got drinking, became friends and stayed friends this time. I'm actually not in touch with anyone I've known longer than David Gedge. And I'm not in touch with anyone else I met by interviewing them back in the day.

HEINEKEN FESTIVAL
22 JULY 1995, LEEDS, UK

STUART BAIRD

When I entered real life I became a journalist for a group of weekly newspapers in west and south Yorkshire. I could get free tickets for most bands but never got green room passes until the Heineken Festival 1995, when Pulp headlined. I didn't realise how easy it was to get served and took my girlfriend (now my wife) along where I had a few too many, too quick. David Gedge was in the green room area but I can't remember them being on the bill. The tale my wife recounts is that I sat at a table and slurred, 'I see Gedge is back then' at the top of my voice as the man walked past, much to her lifelong embarrassment. It's great that we can play Wedding Present stuff in the car in front of our three kids and we're getting told off with, 'What on earth is this?' I am waiting for the, 'All the songs sound the same.' They will come round eventually.

1995: Cooking On Vinyl

In October 1995, Jayne Lockey joined The Wedding Present as bass player, ending their period as a three-piece; Darren Belk had previously been playing both guitar and bass

David Gedge, Jayne Lockey and Darren Belk, at a soundcheck, late 1995

STAGE

15 NOVEMBER 1995, STOKE-ON-TRENT, UK

CLAIRE DUROSE

The Wedding Present first appeared on my musical horizon when they were number two with 'Kennedy' in John Peel's Festive Fifty in 1989. I was aged 16 and that was the year I discovered 'proper' music. I bought the 12", probably from Woolies, but then I didn't really take an awful lot of notice of The Wedding Present. *Seamonsters* and *Hit Parade* somehow passed me by! In 1995 I had a little bit more time on my hands having just finished university and something clicked and I rediscovered The Wedding Present with gusto. They were up to *Watusi* so I bought all the back catalogue, discovered the fanzine *Orange Slices* and heard them play live on the radio at the Phoenix Festival, which really made me want to see them live!

I first saw them live in November 1995. I started as I meant to go on by getting a little tiddly, discovering the dressing room and annoying David – something I still do to this day! Then came *Mini*, *Saturnalia*, a few more gigs, then Cinerama. I didn't think I liked Cinerama at the time. I bought *This Is Cinerama* and I wasn't impressed. They fell out of favour.

The Wedding Present

Jayne, Darren, Simon and David, 1995

1995: Cooking On Vinyl

In July 2002 this email appeared in my mailbox: 'Dear Claire, while idly flicking through the pile of "Go Out and Get on the Database" forms I noticed your rather odd email address. Any significance? Or am I too nosey?! David Gedge.' Imagine! There followed a little email correspondence, but it did re-ignite my interest in Cinerama, by which time they had developed and had released *Disco Volante* and *Torino*, which today are up there with my favourites! In August 2002, after confessing to David my previous lack of interest in Cinerama and then my change of heart, his response was: 'Don't know whether to be sad or happy! I'm obviously pleased that you've finally caught up with me... but it makes me wonder how many old Wedding Present fans there are out there who'd love Cinerama if they give it a chance! I suppose *This Is Cinerama* is the weakest of the albums we've done, so I guess I'm not surprised that you weren't immediately turned on by that one. I think *Torino*'s the best album we've made... x' Needless to say I have felt brave many times over the years and always go and see/pester David after the gig. He's always got time to speak to his fans. I have a collection of photos, signed setlists (getting manhandled by an over zealous bouncer at the Leadmill once but I still got it!) I even got a mention on Twitter when I knocked over, and according to David, broke the lamp on their stall. Oops!

ORANGE SLICES FANZINE
NOVEMBER 1995

DARREN BUGG

It was David's idea for me to do *Orange Slices*. At the time I was doing graphic design work. They used to do a mini newsletter to sell the merchandise and promote the gigs in the days before the Internet, mailing out to between five and ten thousand people, three or four times a year. That's how you'd find out if a gig was coming up. When they started doing it, it was a very amateur photocopied thing that Sally, who was David's girlfriend at the time, used to do herself. Because I

The Wedding Present

knew Sally, I said, 'I'll do it for you.' So I started doing a professional version. And then, rather than photocopying it, I got it printed professionally. I organised all the printing. I did the graphic design. And we did this for many, many years. I used to live quite close to where they had their office, which was a spare bedroom in Simon Smith's house. For many years, The Wedding Present was effectively David and Simon. And Simon had hundreds and hundreds of T-shirts and souvenir items stored at his house. I had a bigger house with a spare bedroom. So I said to David and Sally, 'Why don't you set up the office in my house instead?' Basically, Sally would come every day and get the mail and the fan letters and they'd write handwritten replies to all the fan mail. They used to get three or four hundred letters every week to reply to.

We used to go out for curries on a Sunday night and, on one of the occasions, David just said to me, 'We haven't got a fanzine. Do you fancy doing one, Darren?' And because I was already doing this little merchandise leaflet for them, he talked me into it. I said, 'I'll do it if you can help me sell them.' It became semi-official. It was my fanzine. I was paying for it. But David gave it official status. It was an independent fanzine sold at gigs. I was selling copies outside before the gigs and selling copies outside after them. But they were selling them inside as well. David always checked every issue meticulously. Then a friend who was a better graphic designer than me came on board and there were two of us doing it. He was doing all the design and I was doing the writing. And when we got to issue three I had hundreds and hundreds of people writing to me and saying, 'Can I do an article and photographs?' We had a whole team of people from all over the world sending in articles. It went on for years and years but unfortunately it got to the point where it wasn't selling. People don't want to pay for paper when they can go on the Internet and get the information off the Scopitones website for nothing. The last printed thing I did for them was at the very first At The Edge Of The Sea. David decided to do a programme for At The Edge Of The Sea. It was a lovely souvenir on lovely paper and we only charged a quid for it. But we had 200 printed and we only sold 100. And at that point we thought, 'Is there any point in continuing?'

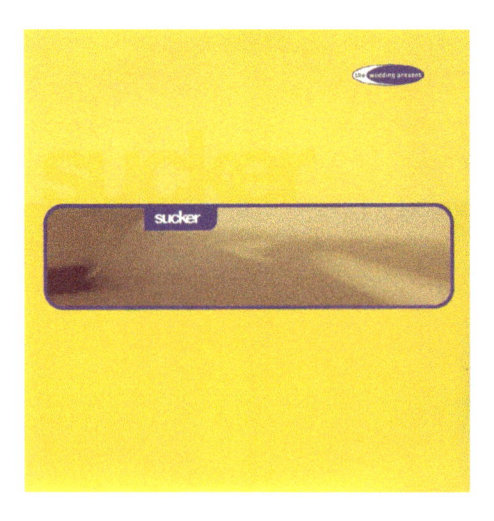

The 'Sucker' single, released in the autumn of 1995

1995: Cooking On Vinyl

AMULET

25 NOVEMBER 1995, SHEPTON MALLET, UK

MATT PARTRIDGE

I sent a letter as I usually did to order merchandise and included my home phone number to Sally, outlining what I would like to do during the Shepton Mallet concert. A couple of weeks later my dad answered the phone and he said it was a 'Sally'. I didn't know any Sallys apart from *that* Sally. No way could she possibly be ringing me! Lo and behold, it was the one and only Sally Murrell on the phone. I remember being incredibly nervous speaking to one of the members of my favourite-ever band. We had a conversation about how we could make this happen at said Amulet concert and Sally agreed they could definitely sort this out for me.

Fast forward a few months and there I am at The Amulet with my (hopefully) soon to be fiancée and two of my best mates. They were roped in for camera duties, although both were big Wedding Present fans. I haven't seen them in years so I can't be sure that they still are.

I approached Sally and, out of sight of the others, introduced myself. She took me into the main stage area to meet the band, who were sound checking. David then suggested a song that he would stop after, and he would then make a little speech and introduce me on to the stage. The plan was all in place and I felt very nervous but excited at the same time.

The Wedding Present duly arrived on stage. As the songs came and went, me not knowing if I should jump around to them or stay completely still due to my impending date with destiny, the moment suddenly arrived. I was at the front looking up and David started his introduction. I am now shitting myself. I'm about to go on stage at a concert being performed by my favourite ever band and propose to my favourite ever person. David's introduction ended and I remember freezing for a second and David stepping back from the microphone and shrugging. It was now or never, so I hauled myself up onto the stage. Imagine a secondary school stage – it was about the height of my chest as I stood. I approached the microphone and started talking. I cannot remember anything I said apart from, 'The Wedding Present has been a massive part of my life and now I want to make you a massive part of it too.' She said, 'Yes.' Cue rapturous applause from the audience. She got a kiss from David. I didn't. I asked, but only got a handshake. They dedicated the next song, 'The Queen Of Outer Space', to us as we left

The Wedding Present

the stage to join the crowd again. Then it was back to the T-shirt stand for pictures and drinks. I seem to remember David or Darren drinking from a bottle of wine at some stage of the proceedings. I can't be sure as by then I was drunk on a) the euphoria of meeting my heroes, b) the euphoria of proposing to my girlfriend and c) drink.

Fast forward to 1998 and we moved in together. In March 1999 Harry was born, in April 2000 we were finally married and by June 2000 she had left me! Bearing in mind we had been together for six years prior to the marriage, that came as a bit of a shock. Her name was Becky, my name is Matt and I'm very much still single, despite a few attempts. So ladies – form an orderly queue!

I now have the Reception Records rose tattooed on my upper arm, such is my love for this band. I know David hates tattoos but I had to get it. I showed it to him at a later concert in Bristol. He seemed impressed, but also unsure about a man removing his shirt in front of him…

Matt Partridge and his fiancée, just after he had popped the question, backstage with The Wedding Present

SIMON COX

I've wondered what possessed the band to play at the Amulet. A bit of a trek for those of us in Bristol and from memory not the best attended gig of all time. The Wedding Present not being in the Bristol area all year, I jumped at the chance to see them at Shepton. It was a chilly November night with my friend Geraldine, heading across the countryside. We got there massively early and sat in the cafe for what seemed like ages. I was expecting something a bit new age with a name like the Amulet but it was a Sixties or Seventies art centre which seemed an oddity for a town of the size of Shepton. The hall was a bit cavernous. The gig was great but seemed less than well attended. At one point we wondered if we might be on our own. Looking back I find it bizarre that we didn't go and see them at the legendary TJs in Newport as, given the motorway, that would have been less of a trek and much closer. A very Bristolian approach to not crossing

1995: Cooking On Vinyl

the Severn. As for the Amulet I'm pretty certain it is viewed as a white elephant in Shepton and is quite possibly closed. I always assumed there might have been a Glastonbury statement give the proximity of Shepton to Pilton and The Wedding Present never appearing at the festival. It still strikes me as an odd place to play.

MARKET TAVERN
30 NOVEMBER 1995, KIDDERMINSTER, UK

KEITH EVANS

Somewhat surprised the legendary Wedding Present would be appearing in my near vicinity of Kidderminster, I rang the venue about a week prior to the gig to find out how I could get a ticket. I was told by some probably Dolly Parton-loving barmaid, 'Don't worry, just turn up and get in on the night.' Fair enough, I thought, the countryside bordering town surely wouldn't be a hotbed of indie guitar fandom.

The day came and I swung into the bar area to find a calamitous scene that included an old work colleague and his girlfriend frantically trying to ascertain if there were any tickets left. A cold sweat crossed my brow followed by mild panic. Next thing I know the last ticket got snapped up by some lucky so-and-so! There was a small corridor area to the side of the bar, which contained the merch table and the smoked glass narrow doors through to the actual venue. Two burly security guys stood the other side of it as fully paid up patrons began to straggle through into its cramped confines. Me and my friend and his girl and about ten others entrenched ourselves here. David suddenly appeared behind the merch stall, so I thought I'd try my luck, first

Jayne Lockey at Rockfield recording studio, late 1995

The Wedding Present

off talking our shared love of comics to break the ice. It quickly degenerated into me trying to see if he could get us in to the gig. Unfortunately his hands were tied as the capacity was filled and, to be fair, it did look rather heaving. David told us there was nothing he could do. Fortunately the flimsy doors to the venue offered little soundproofing and people coming in and out afforded us the occasional glimpse of the band doing what they do best, making the place jump. The stage was only about 20 yards away tops. So we kind of settled down, jigged up and down, clapped and enjoyed it anyway. The best bit was when David dedicated a song to the fans, 'Just in the hallway who couldn't get in' so that delighted us no end! Heaven knows what song it was but, you know, it was a great song anyway!

On 14 December 1995, John Peel appeared on the TV show *This Is Your Life*, hosted by Michael Aspel, who surprised Peel as he finished presenting an episode of *Top Of The Pops*. In the studio, David Gedge was one of the guests.

DAVID GEDGE

ITV rang me up and said, 'We're doing John Peel's *This Is Your Life* and we've been given your number by Sheila, his wife, as being somebody who might like to contribute to the programme.' I said, 'Yes, of course... thank you very much. I'd love to.' And they said, 'OK, great... we'll be in touch.' And that was it! I didn't hear from them again for months and months and I thought, 'So... is that how they do it? Do they just ask a load of people to see who's up for it and then come back to you if they've got space?!' So I kind of forgot about it. And then, finally, one day, they rang me up again and said, 'Right, we're on. Can you still come? We're sending a car to pick you up on Monday at three o'clock!' So I was ill prepared, really. It was going to be in a couple of days' time and I so started frantically trying to think of something fascinating to say.

I turned up at the television studio and, obviously, it's a big surprise to the 'victim'. So you're in this secret dressing

1995: Cooking On Vinyl

room with all the other guests. So there I was... sat next to Tony Blackburn and Alan Freeman! It was surreal. As a child I'd listened to them ardently on Radio 1. Anyway, because the show progresses chronologically, my bit was towards the end. All the other guests were leaving the room one by one and going out there telling stories, from the Fifties and Sixties and so on. But they also have a very special guest for right at the end. 'You've not seen him for twenty five years and, now, here he is... all the way from America!' – that kind of thing. So it was eventually just me and him in this room: me and this American bloke.

I was getting more and more nervous. You can see on video how nervous I am. Finally, this woman approached me and said, 'Right David, it's you.' My heart was beating so fast that I was sure they'd be able hear it through the microphone. It was ridiculous. I had some things I'd prepared but then, at the last minute, I thought, 'No one's saying that he's actually a really nice bloke. It's all about his contribution to the recording industry and how he's the BBC's greatest presenter, blah de blah.'

So I decided that I'd just tell the story about how he'd gone out of his way to give me and Keith a lift. That had really surprised me. I'd met him a couple of times because I'd taken demo tapes to the BBC. But when I went to watch him DJ in Ilkley he asked, 'How are you getting home?' I said, 'I don't know. We hadn't really thought about that.' Ilkley is about 15 miles from Leeds and so I suppose we'd just thought that we'd find a way of getting back, even if it meant walking.' And he said, 'I'll give you a lift!' This is John Peel. From BBC Radio 1. And he's going to give me – me! – a lift home! He doesn't know me from Adam. And I thought, 'How many people would do that?' Even 'normal' people would be saying, 'Oh, you can probably get a bus.' So, yes, that really affected me. I thought it'd be a nice story to tell.

I remember chatting to Tony Blackburn about The Wedding Present. He obviously didn't know who we were but he impressed me because you think of him as this 'Smashie and Nicey' kind of character but he's actually an authority on soul music. I remember we were talking about that a lot and the depth of his knowledge stunned me. I thought, 'You're obviously not just 'Mr Celebrity', are you?!' He seemed like a genuine music fan. I think Peel said that about him as well. In some ways he was the anti-Peel on Radio 1. But if one thing could connect them it was a love of music, which a lot of DJs, surprisingly, often don't have.

The Wedding Present

1996–1997: Cars And Planets

The Wedding Present gave away a Mini to promote the release of their mini-album, entitled *Mini*. The prize draw took place live on the John Peel Show on Radio 1.

TRAMPS

15 MARCH 1996, NEW YORK CITY, USA

DEZ JONES

In 1996, the newsletter arrived on my doormat with details of tour dates and I got over excited when I found out they were playing New York on the night me and the then girlfriend were due to arrive for a holiday. I wrote to David to find out details and, returning to my shared house following a night out, a housemate casually tells me some bloke called David Gedge phoned to say you're on the guest list for some gig in New York! It was a fantastic night. There was a long line of youngsters queuing outside the gig and some very big, aggressive bouncers on the door but as soon as they found our names on the guest list they were incredibly polite and invited us into the bar. Some band called Prolapse supported and then the mighty band themselves came on and were wonderful as ever! My T-shirt told everyone that 'All The Songs Sound The Same'. I'm middle-aged now but managed to bop around down the front the last time they were in Manchester. They are still the soundtrack to my life!

1996–1997: Cars And Planets

SOUND CITY FESTIVAL
12 APRIL 1996, LEEDS, UK

SIMON ROBERTS

I wasn't present at the Sound City gig in Leeds when the prize draw for the Mini took place, as the gig had sold out. I was, however, in Leeds watching other bands take part in the BBC-sponsored event. It wasn't until I arrived home on the Sunday evening that my housemate greeted me with, 'You lucky bastard.' As I had not heard John Peel that evening, I had no idea what he was talking about. I had won the Mini! I remember David

The mini LP Mini gave Wedding Present fans a chance to win — yes — a Mini!

SOMETIMES THESE WORDS **JUST DON'T HAVE TO BE SAID**

The Wedding Present

> "*Mini* is the Darren Belk Wedding Present album. He wrote the bass lines and some great guitar parts. He inspired me to write a load of car-themed lyrics"
>
> David Gedge

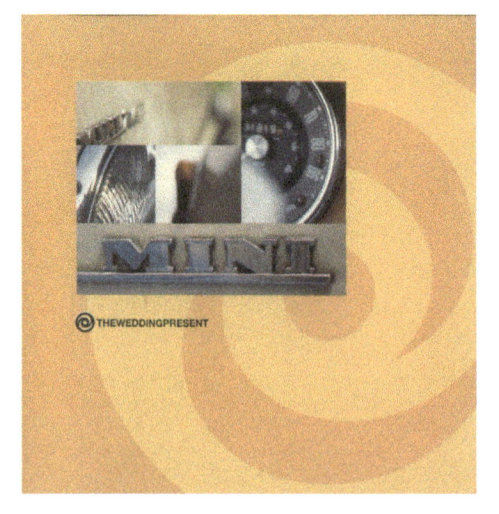

Another *Mini*: this one won't get you from A to B, but it's a lot more fun to listen to

calling me on the phone to discuss delivering the car and me being a bit nervous and telling him what a great album *Seamonsters* was, and still is. It's not often David Gedge comes to your house with a car for you, is it? Not only was this delivered by David himself, but the grand announcement was made on John Peel's show. This broadcast has since appeared on the *Peel Sessions* CD which in itself is a pretty amazing thing. Regretfully, I had to sell the car. At the time, I didn't have the money or the know how to restore it. It was a great little motor and I made many memorable trips to the coast in it. It was sold to a couple near Telford in Shropshire. It was given a complete re-spray – red, I believe – and went on to take part in a London to Paris trip. Not bad for a 1968 Mini.

SIDNEY SUSSEX COLLEGE

18 JUNE 1996, CAMBRIDGE, UK

JON RITCHIE

Cambridge is an interesting place to go to university but a combination of being a skint student and the town not being on the main concert circuit meant that I didn't see that many bands in my three years there. From memory I think I saw The Wedding Present a couple of times at the Corn Exchange,

268 **SOMETIMES THESE WORDS** JUST DON'T HAVE TO BE SAID

1996–1997: Cars And Planets

Gedge and Peel,
Sound City,
1996

but I mostly relied on trips home to see live music. The university is organised around twenty or so colleges – I went to a small place in the centre of town and not much happened there. They certainly didn't go in for annual balls like some of the larger colleges did. However, 1996 was its 400th anniversary – the Queen even came for tea that year – so they decided to host one. I didn't think it would be that exciting – drunken posh students in black tie and ball gowns was my immediate thought – but much to my delight the lad booking the bands secured The Wedding Present and needed someone to sort the rider, cook them tea and generally look after them.

I'd love to say that I was key to their wellbeing that night, but the reality is that I walked around in an awestruck daze all afternoon and evening. Den, my then girlfriend and now my wife, was down for the ball and did all the graft, cooking a veggie lasagne as well as getting her hair and make up done. I tried to act cool and not babble about random things and we watched England beat Holland 4–1 in Euro 96. For some reason I tried to convince them that Terry Venables had co-written 'Save All Your Kisses For Me'.

Even before they played, it was a great night. I'm not sure what they made of the crowd – see my earlier reference to black tie and ball gowns – but it was one of their best performances that I've seen. Singing 'Corduroy' in a marquee wearing an ill-fitting dinner jacket is something I didn't ever expect to do, and I doubt that I'll get the chance again, but the memory will stay with me forever.

The Wedding Present

Den saw them later that year at the Riverside in Newcastle and talked to David at the merchandise stall before the gig – he said he remembered the lasagne and said it was nice, or was polite enough to pretend to remember it. Along with playing a giant keyboard with my feet on the Radio 1 roadshow, that night is my best showbiz claim to fame. I'm not quite on the after dinner speaking circuit off the back of it, but many a Wedding Present fan has been jealous of the hours I spent with the band.

SIMON CLEAVE
Wedding Present guitarist 1996–2005 (incl. Cinerama)

I've got very rosy memories of everything. At that time, just about everyone was in an indie rock band. I was an art student and we were in a little band. Every cellar in Leeds 6 had a band in it. But The Wedding Present were the ones that had got somewhere with it. It was the time of John Peel, where you didn't need much musicality. You could just make a record, send it to him and he would actually listen to it and potentially play it. It was a nice time to be – not musicians, but in bands. That's what I was. Of course, we knew them. They weren't friends at that time. They were people you'd see in the pub. And you'd not be jealous but admire them because they'd done it, they were actually making a living out of doing it. For the rest of us it was just a hobby, but a nice one.

Me and Jayne (Lockey) were good friends. We'd been in our band for years but that came to just a natural end. People stopped being students and then we were on Job Seeker's Allowance. That was at the time when the government would actually let you play in a band on it. I think it was to massage the unemployment numbers. But it was good for us. We were just four friends. But my indie band split up. Jayne had joined The Wedding Present as the bass player, taking over from Darren Belk, who moved from bass to guitar. And when he left, they had to come to me, or they had to at least ask. And I was really flattered to be asked. I can't remember if I auditioned or anything. I think they said, 'You might as well do it.' The Wedding Present were professionals so they asked me. Me and Jayne went back to art school during the first two years we were in the band to do our Masters because we could do MAs part-time. The art school said, 'Well, you're off on tour but, when you come back, come and apply yourselves' and we had to do it part-time so it took two years rather than one.

The Wedding Present, 1996 model: Simon Smith, Jayne Lockey, Simon Cleave and David Gedge

1996–1997: Cars And Planets

The Wedding Present

LOUTH FESTIVAL

27TH JULY 1996, LOUTH, UK

NICK PEACOCK

Nothing ever happens in Lincolnshire. Nothing. It is bleak and, except for a tiny hilly patch in the north of the county, flat and featureless. My maternal family comes from Louth, which has a fantastic church and not much else to commend it.

Most people assumed that the Louth Festival would be a chance to compare tales from the front line of the latest potato crop and, if things went really well, win some booze in a raffle. Clearly the ads which suggested The Wedding Present were playing were some kind of joke, possibly aimed at the band themselves. So, arriving in a marquee one evening I really didn't expect that the boy Gedge would actually be there. Never meet your heroes, they say. This is largely because you will turn into a gibbering wreck and lose the power of speech – that's what happened to me anyway when I shook David's hand. In Louth. Louth, FFS!

I can't remember the setlist, but I've seen The Wedding Present more times than I can remember anyway and, with one exception (London circa 1990, when they seemed a bit bored), they are magnificent. They were the soundtrack to my late teens, 20s and 30s. May they live forever.

> "We were our own roadies and our touring party was six people"
> Simon Cleave

SIMON CLEAVE

Luckily, The Wedding Present had done the two *Hit Parade* albums and my band, TseTse Fly, was the support band on that tour – so we had an idea of what it's all about.

Although we were first on when the doors opened, I had stood on a stage that big before. And even though there weren't that many people there it wasn't a huge shock. It was more of a shock to other people. They couldn't believe that we did everything ourselves. That we were our own roadies and our touring party was six people, with one roadie to change strings when we broke them and one sound engineer. That was the thing most people got shocked about.

But to me that was like, 'Well, this is what we've always done. It's what they've always done.' So it isn't that shocking.

1996–1997: Cars And Planets

READING FESTIVAL

25 AUGUST 1996, READING, UK

STUART SMITH

I dropped my hash on my first festival and spent the rest of the weekend sponging joints off my mates. I don't remember much – it's all a bit hazy. I had to survive off my mates' joints and the odd blim when we wanted to see different bands for the rest of the festival. They all went to see some other band when The Wedding Present were on. All I remember is rolling a couple of joints and watching the band. I can't remember what songs they played but every time I saw them I was disappointed that they didn't play 'Kennedy'. I'm just looking at the line-up for Reading 1996 to see if I can work out what my mates went to see during The Wedding Present and asking myself – why the hell I didn't go to see Sonic Youth?

SIMON CLEAVE

I think the fourth gig I did was the Reading Festival, so that was very nerve wracking. We were on in the afternoon on the main stage but it still felt huge. I'd done nothing like that before. But the band were very relaxed about it. Jayne had been in The Wedding Present a year, two years more than I had. She'd done the Reading Festival as well, two years before. People were kind of used to it. 'Don't worry about it.' I don't have many memories of it to be quite honest. I have heard it, because it got recorded. I thought, 'Wow, it's definitely me!' Not too many mistakes.

POWERHAUS

12-14 SEPTEMBER 1996, LONDON, UK

CRAIG SCROGIE

I went on Friday night and thought the gig was superb, particularly 'Snake Eyes', 'Kansas', 'Bewitched', 'Come Play With Me' and 'Crawl'. It was good to be able to move after the somewhat unreal experience of the

The Wedding Present

Virgin Megastore show at lunchtime. All very good to be able to see the band for free during the daytime but I wonder who had the idea for these record shop appearances? Was it David or someone from Cooking Vinyl? Presumably it was done for promotion, as David joked during the set, but judging by the amount of Weddoes shirts present, I imagine that most of the audience would have purchased the album anyway.

GAVIN THOMPSON

In 1996, I was a young Australian just moved to London and on my first overseas trip to boot. I had many plans to be at the heart of the music I had painstakingly listened to from half a world away, and I was desperate to finally see The Wedding Present live after thinking about it for ten years. A friend had set me up with a place to live, the couch in the living room of a one bedroom flat in Finsbury Park. My co-tenant was Felicity, a gentle, sweet and cheeky Maori girl from a small town in New Zealand. She had unadventurous MOR leanings in music and she was four feet ten inches and built as solid as a brick.

When The Wedding Present announced three nights on the *Saturnalia* tour at the Powerhaus just down the road I was beside myself. I decided to take Felicity along, despite her hesitations. We moved up near the front and just to the left, beers in hand, and the boys came on. David Gedge stepped up to the mic and said, 'There's one more thing...' and then the guitars exploded into life as 'Dare' swung into top gear. What I wasn't expecting was that, when the guitars detonated, so would the crowd. In a flash, we were pushed upwards with the crowd surge, struggling to keep our drinks level as the heaving mass ended up swirling us to the other side of the room. When I caught my breath I turned to find Felicity, hoping she had not fared too badly in the chaos. Her eyes were wide and blazing. She had assumed the position – a balanced, semi-crouching fighter stance. She was beaming and full of intensity.

The show was a knockout. I was rapt to be fulfilling a long-term dream. Felicity had a riot. After the show I approached David Gedge, breathless with the tale of travelling across the world to see him. To be kind, I'll just say he was disinterested. However, Felicity went to say hello a little later and they chatted and laughed for ages. About what, I never found out.

1996–1997: Cars And Planets

SATURNALIA
THE FIFTH ALBUM
RELEASED 24 SEPTEMBER 1996

DAVID GEDGE

Jayne Lockey and Simon Cleave joined the band after Darren Belk left and they influenced the sound of the *Saturnalia* album. Jayne was the first permanent female member of The Wedding Present and it was great to have a woman in the group because, up until that point, we'd only ever added female backing vocals in the studio. So Jayne's presence introduced me to a new way of working on the singing during the song writing process. They also both brought a certain experimental feel to the arrangements. Simon's guitar style is very inventive; I've often compared it to Michael Nyman. *Watusi* might have confused a few Wedding Present fans but then *Saturnalia* wasn't really a particularly 'typical' sounding Wedding Present album either! It had innovative vocal ideas and some peculiar arrangements. I think that's partly because Simon and Jayne came from a more avant-garde background in terms of the music they'd been playing before.

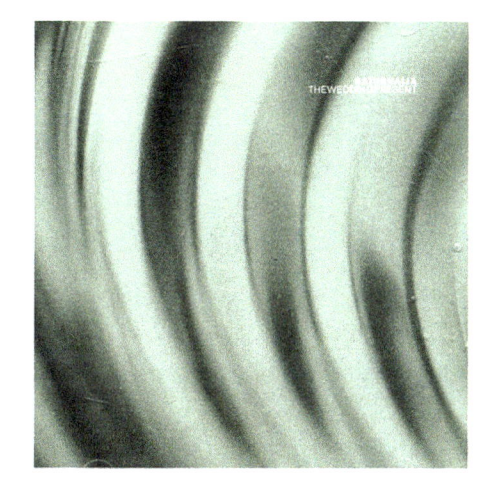

Cenzo Townsend co-produced *Saturnalia*, as he had done with *Mini*, but we wanted to refresh the sound of the band between those two releases. Unlike many of The Wedding Present's other albums, I don't think you can describe *Saturnalia* as having a particular 'mood'. But I think it's a decent album and often underrated by Wedding Present fans.

SIMON CLEAVE

Saturnalia was my first time professionally in a big studio. Up to then, the records I'd done, you'd thrash them out in a

The Wedding Present

day. This was the first time you could do constant overdubs and you could really take it apart and think about it. And David and Simon Smith, the drummer, they'd been in bands for ages and knew exactly what was possible. And Cenzo, the engineer, could throw in a load of ideas as well. He was great.

MARK BEAUMONT
Journalist

I've always wondered, in my more red-pill moments, if I was unwittingly chosen as the guinea pig in a cruel and cynical experiment to find out if it was possible to artificially construct a Wedding Present fan. My introduction to them, you see, came late, and through suspicious methods. In 1991, a girl I was besotted with in my second year of university handed me a lovingly-compiled compilation tape, designed to make me think she was equally besotted with me; the first song on the tape was 'Dalliance'.

Two months later, just long enough for me to virtually wear out the tape and lose myself wholeheartedly in the dank depths of *Seamonsters*, she dumped me, mere weeks before the accompanying tour tore through the London Astoria. In the moshpit I bawled and thrashed and wept and bounced to these songs clearly written specifically about my detestable life – this filthy frenzy of melody and monstrous noise sounded like The Wedding Present were merely an amplifier for my anguish.

Time passes, wounds heal, more gruesome wounds open and eventually (kind of) heal too, but that visceral, cathartic rush of David Gedge's songs still energises me more than any other band, sends me into the same teenage paroxysms and drives me far out of town to catch them, like some giddy tour-chasing stalker-fan. Friends come to watch The Wedding Present just to watch me watching The Wedding Present!

Their gigs are a blur of anticipation, euphoric empathy and snatched memories; drunk as hell at At The Edge Of The Sea, missing most of Festival No.6 waiting for David to play a couple of acoustic numbers in Portmeirion town square, hanging from the Koko balcony on the *Seamonsters* full album tour. At one *Hit Parade* tour show, I almost ran into the worm an ex-fiancée had cheated on me with, an experience that felt like living in a Wedding Present song in which The Wedding Present were actually playing. Countless gigs, but perhaps my proudest Wedding Present moment was the one I made happen; as a cub writer at the *NME* when *Saturnalia* landed, at the first spin of '2, 3, Go' I started my own personal indie disco by the office stereo and bagged the – obviously glowing – review. There's little as satisfying as overturning engrained critical opinion on something you truly believe in, or giving something back to a band that have given you such lifelong succour. If all this was a callous plot, it backfired like hell.

1996–1997: Cars And Planets

SIMON CLEAVE

The first album I worked on was *Saturnalia*. And that was good because there were so many guitarists involved in that. I'd given some riffs in. I think two or three got made into songs. But there were also riffs by Darren Belk and Paul Dorrington. So that was really good for me. And such a weird record, guitar wise, because how do you play these? I don't play like Paul and I don't play like Darren. And it was odd. It was two ten inches, I think, as it came out. In our heads it was going to be a four sided thing. It was on Cooking Vinyl and they wanted to do a lovely box set thing. But I think it was a very odd record because Keith still had something to do with the writing. So there were lots of people involved in it although there were four people playing it. When I got credits, it sounds as though we wrote them together. I used to just give David riffs and he'd use them as a springboard. That's always been a strength of The Wedding Present, having lots of people submitting riffs and then he does his take on them. It was always inventive. Technically, the vocal melody and the chord progression are what the PRS counts as an actual song. But David's always been really, really fair about that. If he says, 'I wouldn't have come up with that without this riff,' he'll credit you. Most of the time it was just me giving David a cassette, or recording things into his four track and then he would just go away and work on them later.

WEDGEWOOD ROOMS

16 JANUARY 1997, PORTSMOUTH, UK

IAN THOMAS

Myself and Jamie Sheppard had been in the pub all afternoon. Suffice to say we were both in the party mood and ready for the gig after a particular hot and sweaty couple of hours. It was always red hot in the Wedge back then. The band finished and the crowd began to disperse. As I was in a little bit of a confused state, I was adamant that the band hadn't played 'Kennedy'. Jamie was adamant they had and that it was the last song of the set. I wouldn't be persuaded until, walking out past the merch stall fresh from the stage, David Gedge tapped me on the shoulder and said, 'Erm, mate. I've just played 'Kennedy'.'

The Wedding Present

ULU
17 JANUARY 1997, LONDON, UK

CRAIG SCROGIE

It was my umpteenth Wedding Present concert. The atmosphere was the best I can remember in London for a few years. For a band who spent much of the previous year touring, there was still a vitality to the performance, although David's voice sometimes dropped into that Mark E Smith-style of grunting heard on Montreal's live B-sides. David said that it had been ten years since he last played at the venue, and joked to the heavy student contingent that many of them were not even born then! The set started with 'Rotterdam' followed by 'Crawl', and ended with a blistering 'Kennedy' and an epic version of 'What Have I Said Now?' They also played 'Montreal' ('our new single, which I'm sure you've been hearing on Radio 1 all week') and 'Dalliance', which was my highlight of the set and very well received. It was top stuff, even after all these years. After living with it for a few months, I rated *Saturnalia* as my second favourite Wedding Present album after *Seamonsters*.

LOMAX
18 JANUARY 1997, LIVERPOOL, UK

STEVE GIBSON

After university I stayed in Liverpool, having met my wife and married there. I got to meet David at the brilliant Lomax. I was missing my wife's birthday meal to go and see this concert. David was stood by the merch stall after the gig and I plucked up the courage to go and get my ticket signed. As I left my mates in the bar, they all called for me to stop and not go! I wasn't missing this chance though. It was only as I asked David to sign my sweaty ticket that I realised he already had done! My mate had already had it signed for me as 'a surprise'! It meant my first meeting with my hero ended with him just staring at me and saying, 'Er, I've already signed it for you!' Panicking, I said, 'Yeah, I know. Could you write happy birthday to my wife on the stub, please?' Becky, my wife, has nearly forgiven me.

The Cinerama Years

The Cinerama Years

The Wedding Present stopped touring in 1997. Instead, David turned his energies towards a new project, Cinerama, which eschewed his previous band's traditional guitar sound.

DAVID GEDGE

I felt like I needed a break from The Wedding Present after *Saturnalia*. We'd been touring a huge amount and I definitely wanted a rest from that. But also I was beginning to fancy doing some writing completely on my own for a change. Cinerama came out of that period, of course. I started learning how to use sequencers and samplers alongside other recording techniques that were becoming more accessible to someone like me, who's not a studio engineer. By the mid-Nineties computers had become a lot more user-friendly and cheaper. I never intended for there be an eight-year hiatus for The Wedding Present. I thought I'd just do Cinerama for a few months, to be honest! But it took me a while to learn a different way of writing music and I was really enjoying the freedom and the opportunity to work within a totally different field. Simon Smith wasn't happy about me concentrating on Cinerama at the expense of The Wedding Present and who could blame him? I think he'd also perceived *Saturnalia* to be the beginning of a move into a more experimental area. But I wasn't ready to pursue that, at that point.

CENTRE
9 FEBRUARY 1999, BRIGHTON, UK

MIKE BAKER

I'm the bloke who gets Wedding Present tickets for his wedding present. I'm the bloke who names his business after a Wedding Present album. I'm the bloke who nearly named his dog Gedge (wife said no). It's fair to say I quite like The

The Wedding Present

Wedding Present. It all started for me in 1998 when a good mate lent me a cassette of *George Best* and I was immediately hooked. The fast guitars, the pounding drums, the energy! I wanted more. I borrowed another cassette with *Bizarro* on one side and *Seamonsters* on the other. I was blown away. Still the same band but somehow different, more polished. Their sound had grown, almost literally, into the eponymous 'seamonster' itself.

Within weeks I had collected almost everything they had released. *Hit Parade* showed their ability to create more 'radio friendly' songs without losing any of their credibility (songs like 'Blue Eyes', 'Come Play With Me' and 'Boing!' stay with you forever). Even though *Watusi* and *Saturnalia* were less of a commercial success, I found them to be among some of the best albums they had done. February 1999 I found myself at the Brighton Centre

The first Cinerama line-up: David Gedge and Sally Murrell
Photo: Julia Hember

to see The Beautiful South and while queuing for beer the unmistakeable voice of David Gedge came pouring out of the auditorium. Cinerama were the main support act. Very different but somehow the same. I went to several Cinerama shows over the years and was elated when they played Wedding Present songs. I hadn't been lucky enough to catch The Wedding Present first time round. I could really sense the love for this band but you couldn't miss the grin on David Gedge's face at the crowd's response to classic songs.

RAISON D'ETRE

2 JULY 1999, HARROGATE, UK

JAMES FRYER

A carload of us drove up the road to Harrogate for a gig at a place new to all of us – which is why it took us ages to find it! This small bar-like venue had a low stage and this bijou gig was surely one of the best Cinerama ever played – and had one of the biggest and best looking tickets too.

GLOBE

8 NOVEMBER 2000, MILWAUKEE, MN, USA

THOMAS AUGUSTINE

Cinerama played in Milwaukee and I was thrilled to interview David live on the radio station, where he also performed. Because David doesn't tour with an acoustic guitar, the radio station arranged to borrow one from a store in town. When I went to pick it up, they said they would be happy to donate it for the fundraising drive. It was auctioned on air but nobody made an opening bid of $400, the actual retail value of the guitar and case. So I abused my credit card balance a little more and picked it up for myself. It hasn't been played since then, partly because I don't play guitar and even if I did, I wouldn't want to mess up the signature. It seems a shame to let such a fine instrument sit idle, and I beg forgiveness of the guitar gods. But the interview itself was something I still

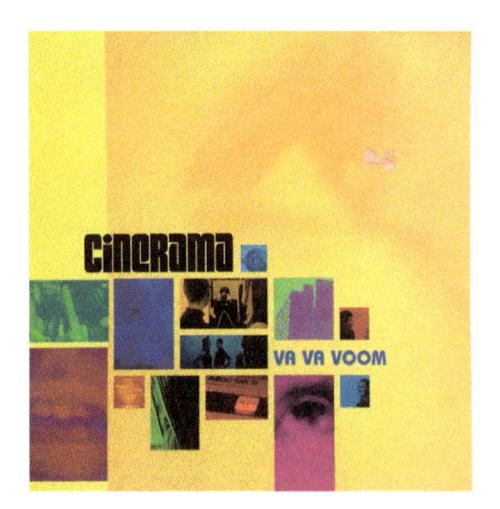

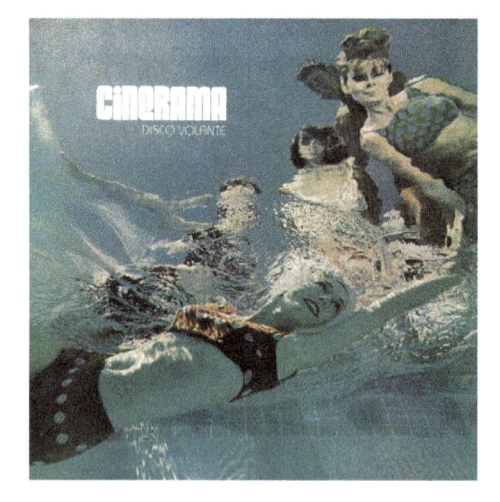

The Wedding Present

Va Va Voom (1998) and *Disco Volante* (2000): the first two Cinerama albums

have many regrets about. The night he was there it was also our pledge drive and so, during his performance, I was distracted by dealing with phone calls and the like. I did win the bid for the autographed guitar he played that night, but the amount I paid for it doubled the amount I raised in total pledges.

I attribute the low amount of calls to the fact that it was the day after the Bush/Gore election and no one knew who our next president would be. Also unfortunate was the turnout at the club for the show. They have not returned to play Milwaukee since. But I still try to catch them when I can.

STARFISH ROOM

6 JUNE 2001, VANCOUVER, CAN

RYAN BOGGS

The first time was Cinerama, during a solitary journey of trains and Greyhounds out west from Toronto to visit family and friends, the mountains and the ocean, stopping in every province along the way. I had seen an advertisement for the show in a local music magazine while staying at the downtown hostel, and purchased a ticket at a record shop. From the hostel, I walked down to Pacific Street and across to Homer. I went in and sat hunched in a booth at the back of the eerily vacant circular venue during what I would later realize was a version of 'Superman'. Previously, my only

The Cinerama Years

exposure to Cinerama had been through the B-side compilation, *This Is Cinerama*, but these unfamiliar new songs resonated emphatically, as the journey I had been on for the past few weeks had resulted in personal turbulence and tragic traffic, which had left me feeling uncertain of any previous identity. A new sense of self felt imminent. I felt an unprecedented surge of youth and innocence when the opening chords of 'Bewitched' began and the ending slide of 'Suck' concluded.

David and Sally: 'What do you mean, my black shorts don't go with this shirt and jacket?!'

SIMON CLEAVE

My fondest memory? It's going on tour in America. America's huge. So you're driving all day long, every day, and then doing a concert. And touring parties only work if you play practically every day because otherwise you're bleeding money. You need to generate the cash. In America, we found it very hard to play between Seattle and, I think, Minneapolis. Or sometimes Seattle and

The Wedding Present

David channels his inner lothario with a teasingly unbuttoned shirt. Sally thinks: 'Not again!'
Photo: Julia Hember

Chicago. That's miles. And I remember what I really liked was being in the van for that drive. That's funny because Kari, Cinerama's drummer at the time, hated it and he used to fly. But I liked that, because America's got such fascinating scenery and it really felt like you're doing something unusual. We were just driving from one place to another. In most states you had to drive about 60 miles an hour on roads that were straight as anything. So it would take even longer. But I loved it because we just talked so much banal rubbish. We just talked shite the whole time. But it was really funny. And every now and again David got into recording it on his little video recorder and he played it back to us one time and it was amazing just how much banal rubbish you say. But how good a time we had, the tedium juxtaposed with this fantastic landscape, and yet we had to do it because we were due to play a concert. It sounds a bit strange but I've got very fond memories of that. We were friends, all of us, but you put any six people in a van and you're going to get on each other's nerves. And so you develop a camaraderie. But there's

284 SOMETIMES THESE WORDS JUST DON'T HAVE TO BE SAID

The Cinerama Years

also the little peaks. It's a very unique experience. I hadn't had anything like that before. You're in such a bubble and yet you're going through this amazing landscape and you have a reason to do it. It's not like you're a tourist. And Americans are very, very interested in you. You stop at this petrol station, they hear your accent, they want to know what you're doing there. Because people don't stop at these places. Those huge drives and these little towns... I have very good memories of that. Even the Americans in our touring party, Terry de Castro and Jessica McMillan, hadn't done it. They hadn't actually done that themselves. A lot of people haven't even if they live in that country. There's nothing like the States. I'm living in Europe. I've done European tours. But it's nothing like that. Even in Europe you have some long drives but you wouldn't be completely cut off in a bubble. It's of a scale that, if you come from the UK, you just don't comprehend.

Taking flight: Cinerama's third album, *Torino*, released on 1 July 2002

SUGARMILL
21 OCTOBER 2001, STOKE, UK

EDWARD KOMOCKI

I secretly recorded the Cinerama gig at the Sugarmill in Stoke with a Dictaphone borrowed from work up my sleeve, only to mix up the tapes afterwards and record a whole outpatient clinic's worth of letters over the top before having even heard it.

SIMON CLEAVE

I think 'Starry Eyed' is my favourite Cinerama song because what you can't hear on the record is my favourite riff. I wrote it on a guitar, gave it to David and he gave it back to me on a glockenspiel! And I liked that, because I'd never thought of it done that way. All the noisy guitar on 'Starry Eyed' is David playing with a bottleneck. I do play the main riff but there's that one [glockenspiel] riff that I came up with just by chance: so it's on there but not on there, if you know what I mean?

The Wedding Present

NEW ROSCOE
3 JULY 2002, LEEDS, UK

DAVID POYTON

I was on my way to see Cinerama at the Leadmill when my wife went into labour with our first child. It took some time before I actually got to see Cinerama again. The next time was at the New Roscoe in Leeds, when I dragged along my wife who was due to give birth to our second any day. We sat at the back by the merch desk. It must have worked as my second-born has got an impeccable taste in music. We got loads of funny looks.

DINGWALLS
10 JULY 2002, LONDON, UK

PETER KENNEDY

Maybe the best gig I've seen, a completely mental summer evening. The crowd started unexpectedly moshing during a quiet opener and never really stopped; I rudely nabbed a setlist before they'd actually finished (sorry), and I got to chat to Kari and Simon as well as David. One of those odd nights where everyone just seemed to be up for a big mad party.

HALF MOON
6 SEPTEMBER 2002, CORK, IRL

TONY TAYLOR

The official reason given for Cinerama changing their name back to The Wedding Present in 2005 was that, as the guitar sound had morphed back into the one associated with The Wedding Present, there was no point continuing with the Cinerama moniker. Whilst the statement

The Cinerama Years

was undeniably true in itself, the frustratingly small audiences Cinerama played to in some towns and cities must surely have played a part. Possibly the smallest audience the band ever played to was at the Half Moon.

The crowd size notwithstanding, the gig holds special memories for me as a) my wife Erika and I were celebrating our wedding anniversary and b) it was our last weekend of 'freedom' before our adopted children arrived. After a short flight from Manchester on the Friday evening in question, we headed straight for the venue which turned out to be unlike anywhere I have watched a band before or since.

The room was liberally dotted with circular tables and high stools, which presumably we were supposed to sit at or dance around – I'm not quite sure. As the band took to the stage and the familiar strains of 'Bewitched' started up (Gedge had long since abandoned his policy of answering requests for Wedding Present favourites with 'You're at the wrong gig!') it became apparent that many of the crowd – we counted 39 including ourselves – were unfamiliar with the band's material and intent on choosing the 'Sit on high stools' option! Ever the professional, Gedge continued undeterred and tried to engage the audience. He announced that he'd been to Giant's Causeway the previous day and joked about being disappointed that, 'It wasn't, well – very big!'

The Cinerama band: Simon Cleave, Terry de Castro, David Gedge and Kari Paavola
Photo:
Tim Middlewick

SOMETIMES THESE WORDS **JUST DON'T HAVE TO BE SAID** 287

The Wedding Present

Later, when the time came for the final song, he answered Erika's shouted request for 'Health And Efficiency' with, 'I can do that for you, love!' Of course, we'd seen the set in Manchester a few weeks earlier and knew full well what the final song was going to be. Gedge brought the evening to a close in amusing fashion: 'We've been Cinerama, next time bring a friend!'

It wouldn't be long before The Wedding Present were once more and that sort of quip would be rendered redundant forever.

DOLAN'S WAREHOUSE
7 SEPTEMBER 2002, LIMERICK, IRL

TERRY McCAUL

Throughout the years I've seen The Wedding Present in almost every place they've played in Ireland and have different memories for each gig. I was obsessed with the music and emotionally connected to it on a few different levels for lots of different reasons. We had so much fun over the years. The one thing that really used to annoy us was at the gigs when the crowd would look for something from *Tommy* or *Bizarro*. David would almost get cranky and say, 'We've moved on from that era,' etc. Some of my friends weren't too fond of the newer stuff and that, combined with the lack of their fave songs being played and David's arrogance, meant they drifted away from The Wedding Present. I didn't.

I wasn't that fond of Cinerama. I tried but they just didn't do it for me, unfortunately. They were due to play Limerick. I can't remember the date or year but went along as it was David Gedge. I remember we went for dinner beforehand. I had the usual apprehension I have before a Wedding Present gig, especially in this case as it wasn't The Wedding Present but had the ingredients to be. I drank some wine. We went to the gig. I drank some more wine. Cinerama played Cinerama songs. Then they played Wedding Present songs – a lot of them. I started crying. I couldn't stop crying.

I met David afterwards and gave out to him. It ended up in an argument. I couldn't believe that he had advertised the gig as a Cinerama gig and played loads of The Wedding Present songs, even songs that he refused to play at The Wedding Present gigs we had

The Cinerama Years

been at. To me he was going against everything. I remember saying if he had advertised it as The Wedding Present the venue would have been sold out. At that point, he told me to leave him alone. The Wedding Present was his band and he could do what he liked with the band. I was so upset. Of course, my boyfriend and friends thought this was hilarious. None of them even tried to stop me. They were happy for me to make a fool of myself. To this day, I still get slagged off about it and it happened years ago. When The Wedding Present came back as The Wedding Present and played Dublin, we went and my brother asked him did he remember me? And he did – I was so embarrassed. I apologised, but he did agree I made some valid points amid the blubber. He signed a poster 'Apology accepted – David' and it's framed on the wall in my house today. I'm still a huge fan. I still go see them when they play Ireland. When I meet him he refers to me embarrassingly as 'the girl who cries'. I haven't got to The Edge Of The Sea yet as it's the weekend before my kids start back to school. Maybe I will make it someday.

DAVID GEDGE

Ah, 'the girl who cries'. She knows we call her that – ha, ha! She's a really lovely woman actually and we've met her loads since that first encounter. But it did make us laugh... because she was *so* upset. It was a Cinerama concert but we'd played quite a few Wedding Present songs. The thing is that she's actually a big Wedding Present fan so you'd have thought she'd have been pleased with that! But, in-between the tears, she was sobbing, 'I'm Cinerama's biggest fan and I can't believe you didn't play all Cinerama songs.' I asked her what Cinerama albums she had and she said, 'I've got *This Is Cinerama*.' I said, 'Is that it?! You've not even got a proper album; you've only got a compilation. You can't be Cinerama's biggest fan.' But her point was that it had been advertised as a Cinerama concert and so we should have played all Cinerama songs. Fair enough, I guess.

At the beginning we only played Cinerama songs at Cinerama concerts. But then we started filtering in the odd Wedding Present song. Simon and I missed playing some of the old material. So we thought, 'OK, let's slip in 'Spangle', let's try 'Bewitched'...' Ones that would fit comfortably into a Cinerama set, I suppose. As time moved on, though, we started to include more and more.

The Wedding Present

CASBAH
26 SEPTEMBER 2002, SAN DIEGO, CA, USA

SHARON BOLAND

Early Nineties: I met and fell in love with Neil. He introduced me to The Wedding Present by means of a mixtape for my car. We were a perfect couple. He loved the loud guitars and I was smitten by the lyrics of lust, love and longing. We went to gigs. We sang. We danced.

Fast forward to February 2002. We got married. A perfect day with all our family and friends and of course The Wedding Present (although it was a Cinerama song – 'Barefoot In The Park') for our first dance. We delayed our honeymoon and set off for the West Coast USA. Planned or coincidence I'm not sure, but Cinerama happened to be playing the Casbah in San Diego and the Troubadour in LA whilst we were there. We met David at the merchandise stall, had a chat and bought him a drink – a bottle of water. Top night, ace gig. We drove to LA the following morning and caught up with David again at the gig that night. He remembered us. Not hard I guess when you hear two Lancashire voices in a sea of American accents. Neil exchanged emails addresses with him and so began years of messaging. Fast forward again to February 2006. We had our little boy Finn Alexander. We sang Finn Wedding Present songs instead of nursery rhymes. Life was wonderful. And so it continued until July 2008, when Neil became sick. Lymphoma. But he was young, fit and strong. At 37, he'd beat it – surely? Rounds of chemo followed but he lost his battle in January 2009.

We carried on with life. Just me and Finn. We'd listen to music in the car. Proud mum moment when Finn could pretty much sing along

Sharon and Finn Boland, with David Gedge

to The Wedding Present's back-catalogue. I'd booked tickets to see The Wedding Present on their *Seamonsters* Anniversary Tour at The Ritz in Manchester in November 2012. First time I felt strong enough to go to a gig on my own. Wished Finn was old enough to come with me but he was six at the time, so I did what Neil would have done and messaged David. Not sure of what to say or do – just wanted him to know what we were up to. A few messages later we were invited to the sound check. Such a kind gesture. We met David, drank tea and talked about Lego! In Finn's words, 'It was ace!' They say never meet your heroes but we did – and I'm so glad we did. So this is for you: Neil and Finn. xxx

TROUBADOUR
27 SEPTEMBER 2002, LOS ANGELES, CA, USA

BERNADETTE GILBEY

In the late Nineties I was co-host on a very early internet radio show out of Long Beach – The Indieshop. I was working and living in Los Angeles and would make the drive down to Long Beach every Wednesday night in rush hour to get to the station to broadcast out to our legions of fans which some nights nearly hit double digits! We actually did have a tiny but loyal base and internet radio wasn't really a thing yet, but we did manage to crash the server one evening by having too many tuning in to hear the Sweet And Tender Hooligans. The Indieshop's main host was unemployed (naturally) and had a lot of time on his hands to look up new bands and pester tour managers for interviews of bands that were touring.

One evening I came in all excited because he had secured an interview at the Troubadour the following week with this little Scottish band I was really into at the time – Ballboy – and they added in time with David Gedge as well. I had always read in the import music mags that David was a notoriously difficult interview but I was assured that my co-host had everything in hand and that he would come up with an amazing list of questions for the interview and I didn't have to do a thing. The day of the interview, I took the afternoon off from work and waited at my place for him to come pick me up.

Co-host shows up with a young woman in tow (he was in his mid-30s and she had to have been 22) whom

The Wedding Present

I believe he was trying to date. We decided to toss some headphones on her and pass her off as our audio tech for the day. We had lunch before the interviews and I got along really well with this girl, which really annoyed him for some reason. We sat down with Gordon from Ballboy and had a lovely chat as I was a frequent traveller to Scotland at the time.

He gave me some tips on good places to visit on my next trip. I dominated that interview and our special 'audio tech' also joined in with some questions. The host was just getting increasingly annoyed. We had a few minutes to wait around in the bar before David came down and I asked to see the questions that he had prepared. He blew up at me about how it was clear I didn't need him at all and that I could just do the interviews all on my own since the bands liked me so much. With that, he stormed out.

The tour manager came down and told us David would be a little late because he was awaiting the return of someone who had gone out to fetch some cold medicine and he wasn't feeling very well. I thought, 'Great, let's back out of this so I don't have to worry about being woefully unprepared.' Tour manager said no, David still very much wanted to conduct the interview (I'm not sure what was told to them about the size of our audience!) and he would be down shortly. Small waves of panic had started to spread in me as I had minimal intel about the band and the man that was about to sit down next to us other than he was supposed to be super cranky and I'm sure illness wasn't going to help the situation.

David sat down and I just froze. Complete panic had taken hold and it took a minute of me just standing there, like a deer in the headlights, before composing myself and getting him set up with the mic. The other band was sound checking so it was quite noisy in there and I had our 'audio tech' take notes as I started in. Thankfully he was in a good mood even with the illness setting in. He put up with my silly questions like had he ever been to Welwyn Garden City and what was better about Brighton Pier – the hot donuts or the arcade game where you try to nudge all those 2p coins over the ledge? He seemed amused and put up with me for more than half an hour before someone came to fetch him. It was one of the more interesting afternoons I had with the radio show and a band. I left the radio show later that year but the interview with Gedge will always be my favourite one we ever did! The co-host came sulking by a bar down the street we had settled in to after we left the Troubadour, completely unapologetic. I decided to catch a lift home with a different friend and he left before The Wedding Present even came on stage!

VOID

27 APRIL 2003, STOKE-ON-TRENT, UK

VICKI BRETAGNE

I bought a Cinerama top from David. I got a little starstruck and blurted out, 'I've got a cat named after you and he's got black hair too.' He gave me a very despairing look and said, 'A cat, oh well that's, erm, great – thanks.' I ran off, burning with embarrassment!

ATOMIC CAFÉ

8 APRIL 2004, MUNCHEN, D

STEPHAN DIETRICH

I drove 200 miles with my girlfriend for the Cinerama gig in Munich. We weren't as skint as usual so decided, rather than driving back after the glorious show, we'd book a nice small boutique hotel not too far from the venue. On the next morning, no less a figure than DLG himself was in the breakfast room of our hotel. He explained that he had his car parked outside and the meter had run out and would anyone have some spare change for him? So my gracious donation of coins saved him from having his car towed off.

DAVID GEDGE

It would have been the band's van, not my car!

The Wedding Present

2005: Return Of The Wedding Present

After eight years as Cinerama, The Wedding Present came back into being in a very seamless and organic way. 2005 was to see a new Wedding Present album, *Take Fountain*. It was produced by Steve Fisk, the man who had been at the controls for *Watusi*.

TAKE FOUNTAIN
THE SIXTH ALBUM
RELEASED 14 FEBRUARY 2005

STEVE FISK
Producer, *Take Fountain*

When we recorded *Take Fountain*, it was much lower key. David had been living in Seattle for a while. There really wasn't a record label. There was Scopitones. We didn't have the huge budget. We didn't have half the time we spent on *Watusi*. We probably didn't have a third of the time we spent on *Watusi*. It was put together in a real studio at Robert Lang Studios, which was much more like the giant big drum sound and all that hugeness that people associate with The Wedding Present. And we took it back to my home studio and did the vocals and the majority of the guitar overdubs and all the strings – they're all done in a small room in my house. That's how a lot of the records I've done over the last twenty years are put together. Spending the majority of your budget getting the basic feel in the real studio and then doing the overdubs at home. It was a laugh. It was a good time.

When I started recording *Take Fountain* it was supposed to be a Cinerama record.

2005: Return Of The Wedding Present

But they realised that they were turning back into The Wedding Present even before they started recording that record.

David's an upright guy. He didn't want all The Wedding Present fans to come out and say, 'Hey, that's The Wedding Present!' They had to own up to the fact that Cinerama, as great as it was, was impractical to tour with and so the last two Cinerama records ended up featuring guitar, bass and drums even though they had other instruments on them as well. They realised, like it or not, they were The Wedding Present. They were playing with Simon Cleave, for God's sake, and Simon was certainly part of The Wedding Present!

We recorded 'Snapshots', which has the chorus line 'beautiful forever'. David said he wanted to put a Mellotron on it. And he wasn't specific about what he wanted. And I have a way of wandering around on organs and Mellotrons where one hand goes left, one hand goes right, very simple stuff. And basically we tried to sound like the organ solo from 'Your Time Is Gonna Come', the Led Zeppelin tune.

As a child I learned how to wander around aimlessly on the white keys. And after I'd done it three times, David said, 'Wow. You're done. That's perfect. You're the first person I ever let jam on a Wedding Present song!' I think he was upset but he was realising this was the first time he'd ever let someone wander into a Wedding Present song without telling them what to do specifically. He was

Terry de Castro, Simon Cleave, Kari Paavola, David Gedge: Cinerama becomes The Wedding Present. Photo: Tim Middlewick

The Wedding Present

happy with it as well. It's a beautiful song. That was a breakthrough moment.

Another thing David said is that he loved recording at the house. He thought he sang better and was more relaxed. It seemed like a smoother thing because he wasn't spending $1,000 a day to have the band watch him through the glass. People have said that about working in a home studio. You're alone. When you're recording in a studio, the rest of the band is bored to death. Their job is done so they're just staring at you through the glass the whole time you're singing, which nobody likes doing. So he sang better and quicker and was more relaxed in that environment than on any other record he'd worked on up until then.

My dog got in on the record in a couple of places. I had a little noisy pug which would wander in and start snoring and barking. And they made me keep all of that. They thought that was great. 'Interstate 5' was used in a TV commercial. It got used on a General Motors TV commercial. I never received any royalties off the first record because nothing from *Watusi* ever made any money. That's OK – record producers are used to that. But when this thing got used in this ad it was right after the economic crash. GM had been bailed out by the Obama administration with something called TARP money, which was the Troubled Asset Relief Program. And David gave me a big chunk of the royalty. He paid me pretty much like I was in the band. He gave me a band share for that, which I think was 1,200 or maybe 1,300 bucks. And everybody in the band got paid too. And I had the privilege of telling all my American friends that I was getting paid TARP money because that's what GM was paying for their ad with. And that it was being paid to me by a proper Socialist from England. Further outrage! TARP money shouldn't be going for TV ads!

The Wedding Present album which begin as a Cinerama album: *Take Fountain*

SIMON CLEAVE

David and I only ever sat down and wrote one song together and that was 'Interstate 5'. It's a very simple song. I said, 'Can we do something that kind of 'drones'?' Because I wanted to do a 'driving' song. He came up with the title and the vocal melody and that was pretty much it. It was the only time we ever sat down in the same room together and ended up with a finished song after an hour. We did it all

2005: Return Of The Wedding Present

from scratch. I think I played the floor of the main riff and then we both added bits. By the time we'd reached the end of it, it was a case of 'We're probably done now! We'll have to polish it a bit but it'll be fine.'

My favourite Wedding Present songs are 'Bewitched' and 'Interstate 5'. 'Interstate 5' because I was really involved with that... and 'Bewitched' because I had nothing to do with it. But I always enjoyed playing 'Bewitched' live. I think David's lyrics are really good - and also the way he sings them. In a way, it reminds me 'Interstate 5' because it has a similar dynamic. The songs aren't really anything like each other but it's the kind of long, droning track that reminds me of driving across America.

'Interstate 5' was recorded with Steve Fisk. He's a really good bloke. He had lots of ideas to throw at it. Kari Paavola was our drummer at the time and he said, 'Shall we do it like the Red Hot Chili Peppers?' I said, 'No! It's a driving song. We've even called it 'Interstate 5' now... it's like calling it the M1 or something!' I don't think he quite got it. While we were recording it I was telling him 'It's got to drive along' but he was saying 'No, no, it's a slow rocker.' It's because he had his own take on it. But we got there in the end. Then, when we went to master it, I sped it up a bit... but he didn't notice. I asked the engineer to physically speed up the master tape. That means that people probably won't be able to play along with it because it's in the wrong key or something but these are just the little tricks that you can do. Kari hadn't played it incorrectly or anything... I just felt, in my head, that it was slightly too slow. You have to be careful when you speed up the tape because, obviously, the voice will go up in pitch as well. And, if you do it too much, David's singing is not going to sound right. These days you can speed something up on the computer and the pitch stays the same. But in those days you couldn't. I'm really happy with the way that one turned out.

DAVID GEDGE

When we returned with *Take Fountain* as The Wedding Present, I didn't have any expectations. But then I don't really ever have any expectations, to be fair! It was just the way the music was going, the way that album came together. It just didn't really feel like Cinerama any more. Even though *Take Fountain* has strings on it and certain other cinematic touches to it, it just felt more like a Wedding Present record: a Wedding Present album that had been influenced by Cinerama. It just didn't feel right to be calling it a Cinerama LP, so I said, 'Well, let's call it a Wedding Present LP then!' And there was also a time when we were recording a Peel Session as Cinerama, of songs that were destined to be on *Take Fountain*. On previous Cinerama sessions we'd had a string quartet and a flute player and a trumpet player or whatever... all the usual

The Wedding Present

Cinerama instrumentation. But this time it was essentially just guitars, bass and drums. So the engineers, who know me quite well because I've been going there for years, were saying, 'David, this is The Wedding Present! You come in here, calling it Cinerama... but it's obviously The Wedding Present.' And that set us thinking. We still carried on as Cinerama after that but a seed had been firmly planted in my mind.

As we were finishing *Take Fountain* we talked about releasing it under the name of The Wedding Present. We had little band chats about it. Kari, the drummer, was adamant, 'No, no, it should definitely be Cinerama! Calling it The Wedding Present would feel like a backward step.' And I thought, 'Yes, that's a good point.' So I was listening to all these different arguments and then I woke up one day with my mind made up. It was just me, Jessica and Simon sat in the van outside Steve Fisk's studio in Seattle when I broke the news. '*Take Fountain* is going to be the next Wedding Present record.'

It did bring back a lot of fans. I underestimated the brand name of The Wedding Present, even when we started Cinerama. Because we did The Wedding Present and it was fine, and then I signed to Cooking Vinyl. And they said, 'Oh yeah, we'll put a big sticker on the front saying new album featuring David Gedge from The Wedding Present. Solo album or whatever.' And I said, 'Absolutely not. That sounds horrendous to me. This is a new band. It's my new project. It's Cinerama and nothing to do with The Wedding Present.' And they were like, 'Are you sure?' And I said, 'Yes, definitely.' That was one of the biggest mistakes I've ever made in terms of marketing. Because obviously people didn't know who Cinerama were. It got loads of press, probably more press than a lot of Wedding Present records, but because it was a new band and didn't say David Gedge or David Gedge's Cinerama or whatever, it got buried a bit. Even now

Pop art: David's influences include the Andy Warhol-managed Velvet Underground

2005: Return Of The Wedding Present

I'm meeting people who know The Wedding Present and they go 'Oh, you have another band called Cinerama? I've just found this out and it's brilliant and I really like it.' Even now, I meet people of a certain age who didn't even like The Wedding Present's music or that type of music, but they know the name of the band because it was on *Top Of The Pops*, it was on the *NME*, it was on John Peel. So there's all these references. Like the painter outside. He said, 'Oh yeah, The Wedding Present. I've heard of The Wedding Present.' All the time, people know the name. It doesn't always mean they're fans but there's that recognition. And it was more popular than Cinerama. So from a marketing point of view it was a good idea as well. But that wasn't the reason I did it.

SIMON CLEAVE

Joining the band was a really nice opportunity and then I never really left until over ten years later. I think I'd been with them a year or two when David decided to do Cinerama. I was the guitarist he asked to continue, even though he did the first record practically on his own with session musicians. I was definitely in the first touring incarnation of Cinerama. And that just led into a revamp of The Wedding Present when we started getting more and more rocky, because that was more my taste. In the original Cinerama there were strings and a flute and a kind of standing around playing little riffs. Like proper musicians. But we started touring as a four-piece again and that made us more guitary and more rocky until David pointed out that it was actually... The Wedding Present. So it wasn't really rebranding. It was just that we called *Take Fountain* The Wedding Present and not Cinerama.

ACADEMY 2
21 FEBRUARY 2005, MANCHESTER, UK

DAVID LINGERAK
Persil

Persil have been fans and following The Wedding Present since their early days. So for us it was quite natural to try our own version of one of their most poppy

The Wedding Present

bouncy songs, 'Kennedy'. Gedge must have heard our rather primitive version on the Peel show, and apparently he liked it, as one day we received an email asking if we'd like to support The Wedding Present on a part of their new UK tour. Nine gigs, many sold out – clearly this email was a prank from one of our friend's bands? At the risk of making fools out of ourselves we replied and, lo and behold, it was David Gedge – the real one! For us it was an amazing experience to join them, and to see so many dedicated fans showing up at the gigs. They had quite a few diehard ones that even we recognised after a few evenings. And quite a few started enjoying our tunes as well. The Wedding Present always had a strong fan connection.

So looking back at it, it makes sense why we often saw Gedge checking routes shortly before a gig. What's the fastest way to the merch desk? Straight through the venue or through a backstage path? Because, surely and miraculously, after each gig and with the guitars still ringing with feedback and audience in awe, Gedge could be spotted at the merchandise stall before even the first visitor turned their back to the stage to get to the exit. Which is a warm and direct way to be in touch with the audience, who in turn, of course, reward the band by buying tons of merch! They are known for not doing encores and now you know why – Gedge is already at the merch desk!

Another warm memory is when David Gedge and Simon Cleave brightened up our album release party at Paradiso in Amsterdam. We were too nervous to remember much of that. The day after we drove some extra rounds through the centre of Amsterdam so Gedge could make a nice panning shot from the car of the neon lights of the Cinerama cinema, now long gone.

CONCORDE 2

24 FEBRUARY 2005, BRIGHTON, UK

PETER KENNEDY

I drove down with a couple of mates through some fairly heavy snow and parked right by Concorde 2. We saw a madly energetic gig. During 'Kennedy', David knocked so many strings off his guitar he had to stop to replace it. So we carried on singing while he did so. Magic.

2005: Return Of The Wedding Present

The first time I ever heard of The Wedding Present was someone at school in 1987 telling me they were the cool new thing to like now that The Smiths had sold out. Being a bloody-minded contrarian, that was my cue to finally start listening to The Smiths, having studiously ignored them up to that point. I didn't hear anything of The Wedding Present until *Bizarro* because I didn't listen to John Peel at all either.

The first Wedding Present album I got was a tape of *Bizarro* in WH Smith in late 1989. I was so disappointed at having spent £5 of my hard earned cash on it that it made me cry with frustration. I nearly took it back, but then tried it again, and again and again. By the end of the following day it was on constantly and remained so for most of the rest of that year. And it remains my favourite. 'Bewitched' and 'Take Me!' are all you need in life, and 'Take Me!' is the sound of being overjoyed. It's like a perfect football match or being head over heels in love.

I once fell asleep in a hotel room in New York in late 2001 listening to my newly acquired single of Cinerama's 'Health And Efficiency'. When I woke up the next morning, it was still playing as it was on repeat. When I listen to it now it still vividly reminds me of New York then, with its heart breaking floral tributes outside 9/11 fire stations and desperate photos of missing people. There's a yearning for lost innocence there that chimed perfectly with the time. I once talked to David when *Take Fountain* had just come out and he asked me where I was from, and I entirely missed the opportunity to answer, 'I'm from further north than you.' It still annoys me now. I got married in Las Vegas

'You Should Always Keep In Touch With Your Friends': David checks his messages. It used to be postcards to fans, now it's tweets

The Wedding Present

Playing an 'in-store' in Galway

and the first thing we listened to after was 'Perfect Blue' – my wife's favourite. We got married on New Year's Eve 2014 having known each other since early 1987, following a series of misunderstandings, mishaps, failed attempts at romance, spiteful jealousy and general crapness that are nicely captured in many Wedding Present songs. I was jealous and mean, she was fragrant and flirty...

I have a Wedding Present clock on my wall at home made from the *Hit Parade* singles – The Wedding Present shared it on their Facebook page in 2015 and it was startlingly popular. We saw David at the merch stall at the brilliant Cinerama gig the next day and he was politely impressed.

What does it all mean to me? I like lots of different types of music ranging from Italian operas to Paramore gigs with my daughter, but nothing has ever got under my skin like The Wedding Present and Cinerama. Even now there are lines which suddenly jump out at me unexpectedly and make me catch my breath, in songs I've heard hundreds of times before, that perfectly capture a complex mood or memory, as well as that glorious wordless music which somehow captures the wildest mixes of elation, anger, tenderness, bitterness and joy.

2005: Return Of The Wedding Present

ACADEMY

28 FEBRUARY 2005, BIRMINGHAM, UK

EDWARD KOMOCKI

I remember seeing Simon Cleave trash his guitar, in a rock-star style, during the final squalling moments of 'Wow' as Cinerama effectively morphed back into The Wedding Present during a performance that was almost terrifying in its volume, passion and forcefulness.

READING ROOMS

3 MARCH 2005, DUNDEE, UK

PAUL ADAM

My friend Kelly got up on stage and danced in front of David and the band whilst they performed 'Perfect Blue'. David still remembers it – we mention it every gig when I catch him at the merch stall!

QMU

4 MARCH 2005, GLASGOW, UK

SALLY HAMILTON

My Wedding Present memories start in 1988, so I must have been 14 or 15. I question whether I really was this young, but given that 'Nobody's Twisting Your Arm' was released in February 1988, I guess I must have been! My memory is notoriously bad but I remember this particular moment so clearly that it feels – in every clichéd sense – just like yesterday. I was sitting cross-legged on the floor one evening after school next to my friend Louise, in her small narrow bedroom in her parents' house in West London. In front of us, also on the floor, was her record player and we'd been rummaging through a selection of

The Wedding Present

instantly forgettable discs until she took out a recently purchased 12": 'I'm Not Always So Stupid' by a band intriguingly entitled The Wedding Present. She thought I might like it. As soon as the needle went down and the crackling first notes started to play, I was absolutely transfixed. There was something about those songs which called out to my shy, teenaged self, something about the angst and the humour and the absolute realism of the lyrics. We played and replayed 'Nobody's Twisting Your Arm' and 'I'm Not Always So Stupid' for what seemed like hours, and those songs pushed their way so deeply into my psyche that to this day, several decades and a world away later, they are still two of my favourite Wedding Present songs. I will never tire of hearing them and of being transported back to a teenaged me, sitting on my friend's bedroom floor and just starting out on what would end up being a life-changing musical journey. 17 years later, I attended my – and their! – first Wedding Present gig for many years on the *Take Fountain* tour at the QMU. It is equally a night that remains at the front of my memory for various reasons, and was the first time that I met Jessica. I guess it was this night and our subsequent friendship that started the second phase of my Wedding Present journey...

METROPOLITAN UNIVERSITY

6 MARCH 2005, LEEDS, UK

SHONA GILBERT

The life of a Wedding Present fan can be lonely. I feel like I am part of a secret club, but I cannot understand why it remains so undiscovered. As a teenager, music united you. We were the 'alternatives' in a small town Yorkshire high school. From the day I found *Tommy* in the basement of a patchouli smelling shop near Leeds railway station, I was classified as the Wedding Present fan. Josephine and Jules were the CUD-ettes, Lou and Ali were the metalheads and the boys were 'straight edge', with diverse tastes from punk to rap. We all appreciated each other's music choices and went to their gigs when in Leeds. We dutifully learned the lyrics of each other's favourite songs. All my friends could do a cracking, growly, 'Oh why do you catch my eye and turn away?' Me, I often surprise myself by knowing the words to 'Fuck Tha Police' or 'Master Of Puppets'.

In the interests of having a true soul mate, I'd long decided I didn't think

2005: Return Of The Wedding Present

I could love anyone who didn't love The Wedding Present. In retrospect, this was probably far more restrictive than the usual wish-list of handsome, rich and good sense of humour. Teenage loves gave way to my first long relationship and there was no chance. Too posh, his music taste wasn't overly disastrous, but middle of the road was probably the most favourable description. No chance of a conversion. Not to worry, the music came in very handy when we broke up, leaving me alone in an attic flat in Didsbury while he went to sail around the world (yes, seriously). There is only one cure for a break up and that is the entire back catalogue, played very loud in a quite unneighbourly fashion and accompanied by many bottles of £2.99 wine.

A year later and a few red-herrings en route, I was allocated a new team member at work. I saw his name on an A4 list and a distant chord struck. I dismissed it. I moaned to my boss that my team was too big: couldn't he be placed somewhere else? It was a very Wedding Present-esque courtship. Five months and pretty much nothing but glances and finding excuses to talk to each other. Music came up in conversation. He said he had spent his teenage years in an attic room in a house by the edge of the sea in Kent listening to Metallica, Queen and The Wedding Present. You might think that was it, that was when fireworks lit the sky and we both declared undying love for each other. On the contrary, the flirtation merely stepped up a small notch, indiscernible to our colleagues.

We were both dating other people, not unhappily really, but we all knew it wasn't for keeps. A few months in, I had a sudden realisation that I would have to do something at some point or I would never know if this was love or just a persistent gnawing ache in my stomach. Rubbish at flirting, one move was – classily – squirting desk cleaner down his back. We just so happened to go for lunch at the same time. We both agreed to go the Christmas party. I wore the most daring dress I've ever worn. In fact, I blush to think of it. It was now or never. It was now.

In 2005, we cemented our relationship dancing like mad things

Before Doris, David once had a soft spot for a different canine Photo: Jessica McMillan

SOMETIMES THESE WORDS **JUST DON'T HAVE TO BE SAID**

The Wedding Present

together at the reformed Wedding Present gigs at Leeds Met, Sheffield Leadmill and the Leeds festival. As we wrung out our original sweaty tour T-shirts in the car park outside the Met, I knew for sure he hadn't said it just to woo me. We married and we now have a very beautiful and smart daughter. This is a very good thing as, much as he is a fan, I don't think he would have been too convinced on Gedge as a middle name for the boy I thought we were having until the 20-week scan.

The Wedding Present have been the soundtrack to my life for the past 20-something years. I could maybe get it to a top five songs or gigs, but only if you put a gun to my head. My obsession with the band lives on with vigour. The Wedding Present aren't all about broken hearts and/or falling in love. The Wedding Present is for those of us who wrote letters and caught buses and walked past people's doors, rather than stalked their Twitter feed. For people who have their 'tea' not 'dinner', and call each other 'love'. They are the band for romantic realists everywhere. But most of all, The Wedding Present are for people who love their music live, their singers gruff and their guitars played very, very, very, loud.

ROADMENDERS

8 MARCH 2005, NORTHAMPTON, UK

GAVIN MORGAN

It was when David began using the Wedding Present name again that things stepped up even more for me. That first tour back as The Wedding Present in 2005 I was determined to get to as many gigs as I could, and from then on I've tried where I can to get to each and every gig. This too was around the time that I joined the Scopitones Forum – somewhere where like-minded Wedding Present fans can chat to each other. Perfect.

During this time, I've met some great people who have become wonderful friends. Going to a gig becomes a bit like going to an away football match, travelling and meeting up with people in some often very weird towns scattered across the country.

The Wedding Present has also directly led to me meeting the love of my life, during a Wedding Present forum meet up. Attractive, and a Wedding Present fan – can life get any better?

2005: Return Of The Wedding Present

ROTOWN
2 APRIL 2005, ROTTERDAM, NL

ANDREW LAMBLEY

In 2005 my mate Simon Clark and I decided to venture into Europe to see The Wedding Present as we had seen them many times all over the UK but not overseas. I wrote to the band enquiring how I could buy tickets for their Dutch dates of the tour. I got a reply saying if I could guarantee that I would be attending then the band would place us on their guest list! I was delighted with this and couldn't wait to go. The Rotown in Rotterdam was the venue for the first gig played in The Netherlands. Simon and I met up with another English traveller, Peter Mark Craig, who was a regular member of the band's fans forum. The venue was like a wine bar and it seemed a strange venue until the evening when they transformed the place into a set up that we were a lot more used to. I thanked David for our guest list inclusion on arrival, to which he thanked us for coming. The show itself was fabulous as usual as the band promoted their *Take Fountain* album and mixed it up with some old favourites and a couple from the Cinerama era.

At the end of the show I remember having to run to the railway station to catch our train back to Amsterdam, as that's where we were staying and The Wedding Present were playing the Paradiso there two nights later. We attended the Amsterdam gig too, which made it ten gigs on that tour which we had been to.

DOUBLE DOOR
23 & 24 APRIL 2005, CHICAGO, IL, USA

TIM MORTON

I'd not seen The Wedding Present for several years but they were showing at the Double Door, two nights in a row. I dragged along a good work friend to one of the days. He loved it and bought me a T-shirt. I then followed up going along on the second day alone. Bliss!

The Wedding Present

LEE'S PALACE
26 APRIL 2005, TORONTO, CAN

RYAN BOGGS

My introduction to The Wedding Present had been via the video for 'Kennedy' on a midnight program called City Limits when I was 14 years old and living in Niagara. It was a weekly highlight to stay up that late to listen and watch the show of strange and weirdly wonderful sounds from around the world. What was even stranger was my parents' encouragement, until I realized one night upon heading to bed before the duration of the show what the assurance of my preoccupation with obscure television and noisy music allowed my parents some time to do.

On a shopping trip Stateside, I found a cassette copy of *Bizarro*. I became an instant fan. Though I sought out each new release, I never saw the band play live until the reunion responsible for *Take Fountain* and a show at Lee's Palace in Toronto. I had moved there to work. Tickets had been purchased months in advance. I studied until the last moment and then headed to the subway, where I met my brother and cousin. Lee's Palace was packed. I saw my friend Joe whom I had been in a band with in high school and who now operated Yummy Records and a recording studio. We had held a similar fascination with *Bizarro*.

The band stepped onto the stage, plugged in and the entrancing resonance of 'On Ramp' drew us all in, until the opening notes of 'Interstate 5' focussed and dared us into a driving ride through to the closer of 'What Have I Said Now?'

After, cognizant of the time and the ensuing examination, I went frantically looking for my brother who had ambled off during the exiting feedback. Walking towards the back of the venue, I heard, 'Catch!' and turned towards the direction of the intonation to receive a flying T-shirt in the face. My brother then approached, having hit his target and, noticing that no one was at present at the merchandise table where Mr Gedge stood patiently, urged me to, 'Go talk to him.' I baulked and refused but my brother wouldn't let me walk away and said, 'We're not leaving until you go and talk to him.'

I tentatively approached. I was expecting every possible dismissal. When I reached the table, I muttered my name and something about having listened to his music since I was young and wanting to let him know my appreciation. He listened and, tactfully, given my first introduction to his music, and rather conclusively rejoined, 'Thanks.'

2005: Return Of The Wedding Present

MIDDLE EAST
28 APRIL 2005, CAMBRIDGE, MA, USA

JULIEN BUDYNEK

To see The Wedding Present again – I did not think it would happen. When David Gedge decided to focus on Cinerama, and to let violins play louder, I really thought we were done with those roaring guitars that I like so much. But in 2005 Gedge is once again on the road with The Wedding Present, touring a new LP: *Take Fountain*. I got it from the shop on the day it was released, and this hardly happens any more. The album features pop gems and a few completely awesome western tunes. Hence, I am looking forward to meeting them again on stage. And it is an uninterrupted sonic flood of an hour and half. An incredible setlist revisiting 20 years, from the early songs of 1986 ('Once More', 'What Have I Said Now?') to the latest LP (a terrific 'Queen Anne'), not forgetting the glorious 1992 *Hit Parade* ('Go-Go Dancer', 'The Queen Of Outer Space'), *Seamonsters* (a breathtaking 'Dalliance'), and the classic 'Kennedy'. During that song, I remember thinking, 'They could not possibly play louder' and at this moment Gedge hits a pedal that brings the volume up another notch. Besides Mogwai, I don't think I ever heard another band that loud. It is physically strange, like I am losing my balance. David Gedge seems like the nicest guy, his old black Fender patched with duct tape, his making faces, his screaming and his unstoppable songs, this unique rough sound. I see myself back in 1992, hooked to the radio every first Monday of the month, waiting for the new single of The Wedding Present. I can see now that nothing was more important.

David tops up his tan

SOMETIMES THESE WORDS **JUST DON'T HAVE TO BE SAID**

The Wedding Present

A scenic stop-off in Wisconsin, USA, with John Maiden (second right)
Photo: Jessica McMillan

PETER CRAIG

The plane was delayed by nearly two hours due to the bog pipe being blocked (apparently by the cap of a toothpaste tube) and there was a further half-hour delay in Boston before we were let off the plane. As a result, I only found the venue with a couple of hours hotel-searching time to spare and ended up paying $189 plus tax for a room and that was after I haggled it down by $50. Ouch! It was very close to the venue which was some compensation.

The Middle East Club was the venue where they sold more than acceptable draught Guinness, which I consumed enthusiastically. When in America, drink what you always do! Although not sold out it was pretty packed. Jessica looked surprised and a little

2005: Return Of The Wedding Present

worried when she saw me and David looked positively scared, but I got a peck on the cheek from Terry which made the 'plus tax' all worthwhile. Simon didn't know I was there until he came on stage and he looked suitably gobsmacked but highly amused.

By the time the gig started I had been on the go for 24 hours and was beginning to feel it but the second 'Interstate 5' began all my physical and emotional fatigue slipped away and I found myself leaping about enthusiastically (alone of course) as ever. For the first time ever on this tour I had to take a toilet break and ended up singing a duet of 'I'm From Further North Than You' with an American guy at the bar. It was really funny and he seemed impressed with my knowledge of the lyrics. A fantastic gig as ever, with all the usual banter from David, my favourite being, 'Yes, you're right of course. I am the man' in reply to the rather predictable shout from the crowd.

BOWERY BALLROOM

29 APRIL 2005, NEW YORK CITY, USA

PETER CRAIG

The Bowery is on Delancey Street, but I surfaced from the subway to find that there is an actual station called Delancey Street but it's not on Delancey Street. After two ten-minute walks in the wrong direction I eventually found the Bowery.

When I walked past the venue at about 7pm, David was stood outside and when I returned to the venue after something to eat I found him in the middle of the road with his arms outstretched, Gene Kelly-style, and Jessica videoing him. The venue had a large horseshoe-shaped bar as you entered with the merchandise stall at the bottom of the stairs leading to the gig room.

The doors were wide open and the merchandise was all laid out but no one was there so I spent 20 minutes guarding it until David and Jessica got back from their film location. All DLG's banter was a variation on the same theme, and he kept glancing down at me during his patter as if to say, 'I know you've heard this all before, but this lot haven't.'

The Wedding Present

MAXWELL'S
30 APRIL 2005, HOBOKEN, NJ, USA

PETER CRAIG

The venue was tiny and access to the stage was only via the dance floor. This may explain why they started with 'Bewitched' rather than 'Interstate 5', as David couldn't do his delayed entrance stage door bit after 'On Ramp'. Luge turned up hoping to get in on spec and complaining that he had got so drunk the night before that he couldn't remember any of the gig! After discussing the best and most plausible sob story, he presented his sorry case to the doorman who gave him a stamp on his skin for $20. Then Steve from Warrington introduced himself – he was over here coaching soccer with his best mate who was from Chorley. Then Andrew from Leeds – a banker working in New York – introduced himself, or rather, I accosted him to congratulate him on his choice of a *Tommy* Reception rose T-shirt.

When he introduced 'Health And Efficiency', my facial expression prompted David to ask me if I was going to cry. I replied, 'No, that would be at the end of 'Perfect Blue'' and I very nearly did cry then. 'Perfect Blue' was the highlight of every one of the 17 gigs I went to on this tour. It was 17 gigs, five countries, two continents, over 11,000 miles travelled and in the region of £2,500 spent. I enjoyed every moment. The best thing of all was meeting so many wonderful, friendly, interesting and interested people all with the same passion for the finest producer and performer (after Dr Feelgood) of music one could ever wish to hear and see.

ROXY
14 MAY 2005, LOS ANGELES, CA, USA

CLAIRE DEAKIN

Whilst on honeymoon, we had the opportunity to see one of my husband's favourite bands at the Roxy Theatre in Los Angeles. We had a chat with David before the show and he dedicated 'I'm From Further North Than You' to 'the honeymoon couple from Leeds'. A fantastic 'Wedding Present' and a truly unforgettable experience.

2005: Return Of The Wedding Present

STEVE HILL

I've been watching The Wedding Present in the UK since the Eighties. Nevertheless, I was still immensely excited to learn that they were due to play LA mere hours after my plane landed for a business trip. Swerving the corporate meal, I bowled down Sunset Strip and casually took a place at the front, where I was eventually joined by a fellow devotee from a later flight. Apart from the displaced thrill of seeing a favourite group away from home, and the close proximity to the stage, by far the best thing was the waitress service, even in the thick of the non-moshpit. It was a refreshing change to have an attractive woman deliver a steady stream of Coronas, as opposed to being elbowed in the temple by a man in a black T-shirt. The crowd were more curious than frenzied, and it's fair to say that most of the action was on the stage, with Gedge's right arm becoming the trademark blur. I don't particularly recall what they played, although I do remember intently watching the bass player's shirt become entirely drenched in sweat over the course of the evening. At one point an enthused American bellowed 'I've been waiting 18 years for this!' To which Gedge deadpanned, 'We played here last month.'

SÉDIÈRES FESTIVAL
23 JULY 2005, CLERGOUX, F

CHARLES LAYTON
Wedding Present drummer
2005-2006 & 2009-

I've experienced many wonderful things since first joining up with The Wedding Present in the summer of 2005. I was living and gigging in London when I received the call asking if I would like to play a one-off show at a festival in the south of France. With only five days between accepting the offer and the show, I had just one day to learn the 15-song set. I was soon in a car with Simon Cleave – whom I had just met – en route to Brighton to meet the rest of band. On first meeting David, he just said, 'Hiya. Alright?' I couldn't tell what he thought of me! It was a fun evening; we chatted and we drank (due to my nervousness I drank a little too much). En route to rehearsal the next day, Simon said, 'Oh yeah, forgot to say… don't worry about David. He's always like that!' The rehearsal flew by and we were ready for the show. That night,

The Wedding Present

back at Casa Gedge, I overheard Terry on the phone to her boyfriend, 'Yeah it went well. Nice chap and played well.' That eased my mind a little. I later found out that, had it not worked out, David was ready to pull the show. It was a 12-hour journey to Clergoux. Soundcheck was the following morning at 11am; the show was at 1am, and then it was back in the van for the 12-hour journey home. Three days for an hour's set! Being in a band is a lot less rock'n'roll than one might think, but I bloody loved every minute and that's why I'm still here 11 years later. Other memories from that weekend: I had a tick in my stomach; The National went on before us and we had no idea who they were; and I fell off my chair backstage after the gig, through sheer elation that I'd made it through.

Terry de Castro on bass, in Valencia, 2005

DAVID GEDGE

Charles Layton's joining was quite a last minute thing. Simon Pearson was drumming for us at the time but he'd just found out that he couldn't do a one-off festival in France. Terry's friend, Dan, knew Charlie and so the deal was 'OK, let's meet and try a rehearsal and see how it goes.' Obviously... if it hadn't've worked out in the rehearsal I would've just cancelled the concert. But he's still in the band ten years later so I guess it went OK...

GRAEME RAMSAY
Wedding Present drummer 2006-2009

I think Terry was writing the setlists when I was drumming. Maybe, when I was new to the guitar, I probably had a bit of input in order to be comfortable and then Charlie took it over long-term. You can't please everyone, though, as we quickly learned! Charlie's a latter-day pillar of the band. I replaced Charlie as drummer. I laugh about it now, but I used to get nervous when I

2005: Return Of The Wedding Present

knew he was at the gig and we wouldn't speak at all for a while. And then we became as thick as thieves when we were touring together. So I still keep up with Charlie. I'm sure he's keeping smiles on faces in the band.

LA ROUTE DU ROCK FESTIVAL

12 AUGUST 2005, ST MALO, F

PETER KENNEDY

2005 was generally a big Wedding Present year, with the daftest bit being to break off from my summer holiday in Brittany to attend the La Route Du Rock festival in St Malo. So I ended up buying a whole festival ticket just to see The Wedding Present, then driving back again and missing The Cure! David sang 'Mars Sparkles Down On Me' with Mars indeed sparkling down on him, which was wonderful.

SHEPHERD'S BUSH EMPIRE

20 NOVEMBER 2005, LONDON, UK

PAUL HANNAM

I was in a London band called The Colony and we were fortunate to support The Wedding Present. The main support band was The Organ, who were an amazing Canadian band that split up well before they could have been big. My main memory from this gig is the fact the soundcheck was running behind schedule and our band's soundcheck was quite close to the doors opening. David Gedge told the venue staff, 'Do not open the doors until The Colony has had their soundcheck!' It was a lovely gesture as he knew we were a very new band who were lucky to get the gig. It was literally our 15 minutes of fame as our singer decided to end our set early – possibly due to nerves – even though the rest of the band wanted to continue.

The Wedding Present

The eighth Wedding Present line-up: David Gedge, John Maiden, Terry de Castro and Simon Cleave

CHRIS WEBB

I was emigrating to New Zealand two weeks later, so it was a fitting goodbye to all my UK friends. A brilliant set naturally, followed by a quick chat with David at the T-shirt stand. I crashed at a mate's house in Crouch End. Next morning, he went to work and inadvertently locked me in. I had to break out of his house and then try and scale the garden wall. I ended up losing a shoe and a toenail in the process. I had to take the train back to Southampton with my new Wedding Present T-shirt wrapped round my bare and bleeding foot.

SIMON CLEAVE

I got a bit despondent towards the end of touring *Take Fountain*. I was having a really good time but I was burning the candle at both ends.

2005: Return Of The Wedding Present

So David asked me to take a break, because he cared. And in that break I said, 'No, I think it's time for me to go back to what I wanted to do originally and do the art.' And then it was kind of like a reward – because we were always friends, we never fell out or anything – 'Do you want to do Japan?' Because they'd fallen out with Chris, my replacement, or he'd left or whatever. I said, 'Yeah, that'd be great.' So that was me going back in again. When I got back from Japan, I really liked the idea of that being my last concert. David was always 'You can do more if you want' and I was like, 'Well, this is a really good time to jump off.' I think he'd have been keen for me to keep writing, just submitting riffs every now and again, and I thought, 'Well if I do that maybe I should do my own band.'

And I did one concert with a bunch of friends here (in Cologne) just to see what it was like and it was just like an after life. And I thought, 'No, that's it for me really.' We played one concert and it went down all right. It was completely old-school indie rock, really noisy like Jesus And Mary Chain. And I thought, 'OK, I've done it.'

I'm left-handed but I learnt to play guitar right-handed. But people never realised that about me. So I was never going to get much better. I wasn't going to be like Matt Bellamy from Muse, a virtuoso. Halfway through my career I should have swapped back over to being left handed again but I never got round to it. But it was really good for me because it made me inventive and it made me do stuff or come up with things that suited a left-handed person playing right-handed guitar. Most of the time in The Wedding Present it was a professional job, but it was still a labour of love. It had to be really. If you sat down and worked out the maths of what you earn for the effort you put in, because the job on tour is 24/7, of course it doesn't make financial sense. But I have absolutely no regrets about spending years on the road. The Wedding Present is basically David plus whoever he'd like to have along to do it. When the band come through, I end up talking to a lot of the fans. It doesn't disturb me to talk to them. When you're in the band, your head's somewhere else. You've played the concert, you're thinking about driving to the hotel, blah blah blah, and so often concerts are the worst place to talk to people, just because your head's not there, not with any intention to snub the fans. When I go to see them now, I get to talk to some of the people I didn't talk to enough back in the day.

The Wedding Present

2006-2007: *Take Fountain* On Tour

The Wedding Present continued to tour the *Take Fountain* album through 2006 and 2007, taking in over 100 shows with the re-invigorated band.

RICHARD'S ON RICHARDS

22 FEBRUARY 2006, VANCOUVER, CAN

SAMANTHA ROBERTS

I lived in Vancouver for ten years. Seeing them at Richard's on Richards with maybe just a few hundred people was so different to the gigs in the UK. It was the *Take Fountain* tour and I remember being level with the stage and having lots of room to dance – weird compared to the Wedding Present gigs I was used to.

LEE'S PALACE

10 MARCH 2006, TORONTO, CAN

SIMON HINCHCLIFFE

I always used to do my runs and exercise to *Bizarro*. I loved the fast-paced jangly guitars. When I went to university it remained one of my favourite albums. I was lucky enough to be around when the *Hit Parade* singles were released, and used to go to HMV on the release day to buy them. Anyway, life carried on and I started my career, moved around but always loved *Bizarro*. It's remained in

2006–2007: *Take Fountain* On Tour

The North American tour, 2006: the gang play pool (left); backline technician Jessica tunes up (bottom left); setlist for the New York date (bottom right)

CORDROY
SUCKER
BLUE EYES
ALWAYS THE QUIET ONE
APRES SKI
GO OUT AND GET EM BOY
DONT TALK JUST KISS
LOVESLAVE
A MILLION MILES
SUCK
FURTHER NORTH
COME PLAY W/ME
ITS NOT YOU ITS ME
CRUSHED
FALLING
2,3, GO
CLICK CLICK
RINGWAY TO SEATAC
BRASSNECK
NOBODYS TWISTING YR ARM
HEATHER

Charlie
Sam
Bot wiles Chris x
Cheers! NYC
Tony St 06

SOMETIMES THESE WORDS **JUST DON'T HAVE TO BE SAID**

The Wedding Present

Another stateside snap: The Wedding Present (left to right: Charles Layton, Chris McConville, Terry de Castro and David Gedge) with Jessica McMillan

my top albums of all time. When *Take Fountain* came out, I was blown away. Now, sadly, in 2006 I'd still never seen The Wedding Present despite them being one of my favourite bands for over 20 years. By this time I was living in Canada and had got used to seeing my favourite UK bands in small venues. When I saw that The Wedding Present were coming I rushed home, told my wife and promptly got two tickets.

When we got there I saw David Gedge over by the merchandise desk. I couldn't believe it – one of my musical heroes was stood right there. I didn't know at that point that this is common behaviour for Mr Gedge. Egging each other on, my wife and I walked over to David to chat with him. I wasn't sure what to expect and must admit I was surprised at first by how difficult it was to get him chatting. It wasn't really a flowing conversation – but then again I can't imagine how he must feel with complete strangers coming up to him, often in awe, and trying to strike up a conversation. Anyway my lasting memory, which my wife and I still joke and laugh about, was this part of the conversation. My wife: 'So David, how's it going?' DG: 'Well you know... it's touring.' At the time, there was no witty retort or easy response. But now, still years afterwards, my wife and I always laugh to ourselves, 'No David, we don't know! We don't tour!'

2006–2007: *Take Fountain* On Tour

SOUTHPOP FESTIVAL

8 APRIL 2006, SEVILLA, E

GRAEME RAMSAY

In my teens, doing a rubbish job, I met a guy who was into music and had a few good stories handy. I was heavily into My Bloody Valentine's *Loveless* at the time and was drumming in three bands, while also trying to do my own indie/electronic hybrid things. Anyway, this guy, whose name was William Moody, gave me his copy of *Bizarro*, so that he could be confident I'd listen to it. 'Brassneck', 'Crushed' and 'Take Me!' grabbed me immediately, while the rest would burn in a bit more slowly – but burn they did. Later I remember listening to the intro of 'Take Me!' over and over as I walked to lectures. I'd think, 'I'd love to be the guy playing that second guitar!' I still have that cassette.

In late 2004 or early 2005 I went to a studio in Fife to record a few songs with my friend Alexander, and Chris McConville was working there. He had done live sound for Gorky's and others, which impressed us hugely, but hadn't been touring lately. Chris's name had been put forward to mix The Wedding Present in Europe and, while I think he had some reservations about going on the road, we were telling him he should do it – it was very prestigious in our minds. A while later Chris had started playing guitar in the band, and before long David was asking him if he knew a suitable drummer. In March of 2006 David rang me and the following month I played my first two gigs: Seville and Reykjavik. As drummer in the band I went on to experience just about everything I could hope to, after which the balance of pros and cons was starting to change slightly.

It was a very big deal to join the group and I remember the first gigs very well. Because I started in Europe, it was a while into the tour before I saw, from the stage,

Making a splash: Graeme Ramsay, Terry de Castro, David Gedge and Chris McConville

The Wedding Present

a British-style crowd response to the band: that heaving soup of limbs, sweat and lager that you'd see when Leeds or Glasgow would sell out and really react to the old favourites. I always felt on a bit of a tightrope while playing live, but there would be euphoric moments. I do remember a particular French festival. Some flavour-of-the-month UK band had cancelled and we went straight into their slot – between The Hives and The Kooks. There was a captive audience of between 10 and 20,000 people, which was paralysing, and I could see myself on a giant screen 400 yards away. I didn't look cool taking a photo of the crowd as we left the stage, but now that I live a normal life I'm glad that I did.

David, giving it his all and singing his heart out

KOKO

8 JUNE 2006, LONDON, UK

ADAM TAYLOR
Victorian English Gentlemens Club

We met David and The Wedding Present whilst supporting them before the release of our first record. Playing to a small crowd of 100 people was a big deal to us, so to suddenly find ourselves playing to a crowd of 1,000–2,000 people per show was hugely daunting. For a band with an incredibly loyal fan base, The Wedding Present's audience took to us well and it was a very important step for our band. One of the biggest shows we did for them was Koko in London, a three-tiered Victorian theatre, and by far the biggest crowd we had ever played to. During the load in, we were ticketed by a petty traffic warden and threatened with a hefty fine. David happened to witness

322 SOMETIMES THESE WORDS JUST DON'T HAVE TO BE SAID

2006–2007: *Take Fountain* On Tour

this and stepped in to our defence. He virtually chased the guy down and managed to argue us out of the fine! Later that night, I suffered what can only be described as a nasty bout of stage fright. I literally couldn't get myself off the toilet seat! Outside the toilet door, the promoter was screaming furiously at me – claiming she would cut our set short if I didn't get myself on stage pronto. Obviously this didn't help the situation! As I sheepishly stepped out of the bathroom having recovered slightly, I was embarrassed to find David there filming the incident, apparently trying to capture my 'pure fear' for a documentary he was making. I would love to see that footage.

Roughly a year later, we played South by Southwest festival in Austin, Texas, and were shocked to see David and the band show up to one of our sets. It was the first of a series of gigs that day and we had flown in at 3am the previous night before getting up far too early for a 10am set. The audience was thin on the ground at that time of day – just a sound guy and a handful of people who were all drinking soft drinks. Needless to say, it wasn't exactly the most raucous of gigs and we hadn't got much of a response from the audience – disheartening at the beginning of an important festival appearance. When David and band showed up, the room filled and we immediately felt a surge of confidence. His gesture of support to a young band spurred us on to a successful SXSW.

We did two great tours with The Wedding Present along with a festival in Brighton. We've always been incredibly grateful for the support that they gave us and consider it our first leg up. David even requested our song to be played on 6Music during an interview with Marc Riley. That was a proud moment.

FIBBERS

9 JULY 2006, YORK, UK

ANDREW WILSON

We'd managed to get to the front and might have had a few shandies. When they came on I was rather excited when I saw David's new guitar – the black Sheraton – as I have one. I shouted to my friends, 'He's got my guitar!' David heard this and replied, 'No, this is mine.' I also remember someone shouting, 'Sing one about relationships!'

The Wedding Present

STEVE BARNES

It was during the World Cup Final. I remember David asked who was winning. I went to the merchandise stall to get something signed. Me: 'Last time I bought a shirt for the missus she said it was on the small side.' David: 'That's surely a good thing?'

ROB'S 40TH

13 JULY 2006, CHESHIRE, UK

TONY TAYLOR

For most people, the idea of their favourite band playing at their birthday party is a fantasy, a distant dream. Yet this is precisely the dream that came true for a close friend of mine when the mighty Wedding Present played a staggering set in a marquee erected in his own back garden.

To set the scene, back in the late Eighties, this particular friend (let's call him 'Rob'), had already formed his own manufacturing company and embarked upon the road to becoming a bona fide captain of industry – despite being only in his early 20s with no qualifications to speak of. Wary of the cultural abyss this particular route could potentially lead him into, I felt it was incumbent upon me to keep him on the straight and narrow regarding music and books. Consequently we shared a love of – amongst others – Morrissey, The Pixies, James and of course Cinerama and The Wedding Present. We would get to gigs as often as possible and by the time 2006 came around we had seen the band in both guises an almost embarrassing number of times.

It was at the start of the year when Rob first floated the idea of the band playing at his 40th birthday party. I can't remember my exact reaction but I almost certainly scoffed at the thought, reminding him that The Wedding Present were serious players who 'didn't do that type of thing'. Rob (now Rob CBE) had become very successful by this point though and was used to getting his own way. He duly made contact with Gedge's girlfriend Jessica and, although I wasn't party to the conversation or negotiations, it was agreed (to my astonishment) that the band would provisionally add the date to the end of a very conveniently

2006-2007: Take Fountain On Tour

planned UK summer tour. And so it came to pass.

Rob described to me the almost surreal experience of watching through his security cameras as the tour van rolled up to his gates and one of the band members getting out to announce 'It's The Wedding Present!' through the intercom. The birthday party itself was a very extravagant affair on a glorious evening, akin to something from *The Great Gatsby*, and so by the time the band took to the stage, launching straight into 'Sticky', it was already turning into one of the most memorable nights ever. Rob had invited several of my friends to boost The Wedding Present fans' ranks and lend an air of authenticity at the front. This helped to counter the somewhat bewildered reaction displayed by some of his business associates further back. The band was on great form, in particular Mr Gedge, who joked that a gig at the Cheshire village concerned 'Could become an annual event on the national music calendar. Or maybe not!'

The set itself was phenomenal, containing personal favourites such as Cinerama's 'Wow', the aforementioned 'Sticky' and the entrancing 'Click Click'. The band stayed behind afterwards to mingle and partake in a glass or two, as you would expect. No encore though, even at a private party. Some things have to remain sacred, after all.

Terry, Chris, David and Graeme

The Wedding Present

Taking in the view; not the view of Doncaster. Photo: Elaine McConville

DONCASTER LIVE 2007

21 JULY 2007, DONCASTER, UK

JON PINDER

I'd taken up photography as an excuse to get out of the house and away from the then wife. I could combine my two loves – cameras and music. This was at a time before every Tom, Dick and Harry had a DSLR: standing about with a half-decent camera made everyone think you were with the *NME* and you could get into places you probably shouldn't have. I took advantage of this and got to the front for The Wedding Present.

2006-2007: *Take Fountain* On Tour

MARK LECH DALOWSKY

I've had many memorable times following the band. The gig at the Kentish Town Forum, when The Wedding Present effectively supported themselves playing Ukrainian music, was a standout moment as, for me, it was completely unexpected. Then there was when the band headlined a town-centre festival in Doncaster where David was kind enough to have a photo with my kids Alex and Joe. They were aged about five and eight then. I have no idea what came over him but he was smiling – it might have been wind.

One other thought. The strange choices of support acts over the years. A few years back we had Decoration, and it was wonderful. Indeed, a few supports I have stuck with – The Pains Of Being Pure At Heart, for example. But a few years ago, Mr G himself strongly advised me to get down early to catch The Victorian English Gentlemens Club.

So I told all the guys we had to be early, as I had it on the top authority that the support were awesome. And well, each to his own and all that – I'm never one for pulling any kind of music to bits – but suffice to say, I was not popular.

ACADEMY
26 OCTOBER 2007, MANCHESTER, UK

EDWARD BOWEN

The Wedding Present are doing the *George Best* 20th anniversary tour. Sadly, I'm flat broke and haven't got a ticket. I'm sat in my home office when I get a message from my good friend who works with BBC 6Music as a producer on Marc Riley's show. Did I know that The Wedding Present were on the show that day? No. Did I know they were playing in Manchester that night? Yes. Was I going? No. Unless... there's a chance they'll put me on the guest list?

Eventually, the message comes back. David will try to remember to put my name down. So now I've got a bit of a dilemma. Doors open at 7.30pm and it's already 7.15pm. I'm on t'other side of the Pennines near Holmfirth. I have literally £5 to my name. But the car has half a tank of fuel, the roads are quiet and it is The Wedding Present after all. I'm off!

I managed to find a parking space near the Whitworth Art Gallery, just

The Wedding Present

The band were none too pleased about missing breakfast for an early morning photo shoot
Photo: Elaine McConville

328 SOMETIMES THESE WORDS JUST DON'T HAVE TO BE SAID

2006–2007: Take Fountain On Tour

across the park from where I'd been living 20 years earlier, and virtually sprinted to the Academy. I then had to find a friendly-looking security guard and keep my fingers crossed that my name would in fact be on the list. It was! There was just enough time to get my one drink and take up position at the back of the crowd before the band took to the stage. After the white rabbit counted down to 'Everyone Thinks He Looks Daft', I could have been back in the West Indian Centre all those years ago! As an added bonus, on one of the Wedding Present DVDs there is some behind-the-scenes footage from that tour with a short shot of a guest list and what do you know, there's 'Ed Bowen +1'. If only I'd known, I could have taken the wife!

MALCOLM WYATT

As all true Wedding Present fans understand, David and Co. were never remote: the inter-song banter and general feel from the band always ensured, however large the gig, an intimate feel, something that continues to this day. The band made those early songs sound as fresh as ever on the *George Best* 20th anniversary tour, in my case at Manchester Academy the day before my 40th in 2007. Tears welled up for this punter as the giant bunny with the album cover counted down, then the band launched into that life-affirming opener. It was a triumphal concept, repeated for the *Bizarro* album 21 years on – this time witnessed on a snowy night in late 2010 at Preston's 53 Degrees.

PARADISO
16 NOVEMBER 2007, AMSTERDAM, NL

DEAN BARTLE

I'd discovered The Wedding Present around 1988 thanks to BFM, the local student radio station. It's funny how the music of a band sometimes fits you like a missing jigsaw piece. I had to hunt around Auckland to find *Bizarro* and *George Best* and anything else related. I loved the music – I still recall the first time I heard 'Take Me!' and how amazing it felt – but living in New Zealand meant I'd have little chance of seeing The Wedding Present live.

Fast forward to 2007 and now living in Australia – I'd just come into some

The Wedding Present

money and at the same time found out that The Wedding Present were going to do the *George Best* album tour, so I made the bookings and flew from Sydney to Amsterdam for the weekend to see The Wedding Present. I arrived at the venue to see DLG at the front selling T-shirts. I explained I'd flown over from Australia just for the concert, got a photo and a T-shirt and then piled into the hall to bask in the glow of seeing The Wedding Present play live. At the end of the concert, someone yelled out for an encore saying they'd come all the way from England for this. DLG laughed and said, 'That's nothing, there's a bloke here who's flown all the way from Australia!'

Malcolm Wyatt, Wedding Present fan and dedicated indie kid, in his bedroom, early Nineties (top); Dean Bartle, who travelled from Australia to The Netherlands to see The Wedding Present (with David Gedge, bottom)

SOMETIMES THESE WORDS JUST DON'T HAVE TO BE SAID

2008: *El Rey* And A *George Best* Reboot

Gedge, de Castro, McConville and Ramsay visited legendary engineer Steve Albini in early 2008, at his Electrical Audio Studio in Chicago. By the end of the sessions, they had not only recorded their new album, *El Rey*, but they had also re-recorded an old classic...

TERRY de CASTRO
Wedding Present bassist
1998-2010

It was the January of 2008 and The Wedding Present were finishing off another session at Steve Albini's Electrical Audio Studio in Chicago. We'd just recorded the collection of songs that was to become *El Rey* and we had time to spare at the end. Electrical Audio had always been one of our favourite studios and David thought it might be a good opportunity to squeeze in another recording project. We had recently come off a twentieth anniversary tour of *George Best* and, having played the entire album dozens of times, it was fresh under our fingers. So David suggested we record a 'live' version of it in the studio. Steve wasn't too keen on the idea because he likes to keep sessions focused for simplicity's sake. But David assured him it would be quick and easy, so Steve reluctantly caved. David was right; it was quick. If you're expecting a recreation of the original album, this is not it... we played these songs fast! But that's often the way with a live album.

DAVID GEDGE

I didn't have a burning desire to re-record *George Best* because of the flaws I saw in the original. It was purely and simply because we had a couple of hours spare in the studio and, since we all knew it so well, I thought, 'Why not?' And then I promptly forgot about it for nine years. Well, it's more that other projects took priority. I'm involved with so many things that there would need to be three of me to do everything on my 'to do' list. But I was inspired to release it in 2017 because that was the 30th anniversary of the original album and when I mentioned it to Andrew Scheps he said he'd be interested in mixing it.

The Wedding Present

EL REY
THE SEVENTH ALBUM
RELEASED 26 MAY 2008

GRAEME RAMSAY

One of the more atmospheric songs we recorded in my time was 'The Trouble With Men' from *El Rey*. It was a tune I had brought to the group – although the people playing always shape the end product – and the sounds we got up with Steve Albini still impress me. It was used in a BBC documentary and earned me about £6, since I didn't write the words.

SIMON CLEAVE

I think I'm on the record, even though I wasn't in the band anymore, simply because David found some riffs. And he didn't have to tell me but he credited me as being a writer, which is nice.

Steve Albini could be quite disparaging when there was something he didn't like. He never felt that it was his job to offer an opinion. He said he was a recording engineer, not a producer. He thinks that it's our job to come up with whatever producers do. He just wants to give you a hard copy of whatever you get up to in his studio. But there are a lot of things that are his sound. Those drum sounds come from him. It's what we wanted. That's why David employed him. But he will stand back and say, 'No, I had nothing to do with the writing of this record. I'm just recording, I'm nothing to do with the sound.' Even the parts that are his sounds.

I think the one record he's down as a producer on is *Surfer Rosa*, by The Pixies, and he was annoyed about that. He says, 'No, I didn't produce this record – I recorded it.' And they say, 'Well, those sounds are what you came up with. We didn't sound like that before.' So it's six of one and half a dozen of the other about what he does. But I can usually recognise an Albini recording because of the drum sound.

2008: El Rey And A George Best Reboot

BUTTERMARKET
27 MAY 2008, SHREWSBURY, UK

NICK WOOD

When *El Rey* came out, I went to Shrewsbury to see the band and they played my favourite song, 'I'm Not Always So Stupid'.

A couple of days later I went to Brighton to see them again and stood with the girl I've always been in love with but alas can never be with, and I stupidly held her hand when they played that song. I still think of that now, and I still can't be with her! So I guess I am always that stupid!

WATERFRONT
29 MAY 2008, NORWICH, UK

MARTIN POND

I arrived early at the comparatively small venue and secured a spot right by the stage and, pint of Summer Lightning in hand, settled in for a good night. That night they were excellent beyond even my fan boy expectations. Frontman David Gedge, the only ever-present member of the band's line up, was in good form, bantering with the crowd and informing us that his surname came from the area, though he's from Leeds, and that he's probably the most famous Gedge ever. As such, didn't he deserve a statue here, he mused? They didn't overdose the set with too much new, inherently unfamiliar, material but crossed the span of the band's 20-plus-year career

El Rey, the seventh Wedding Present album

SOMETIMES THESE WORDS **JUST DON'T HAVE TO BE SAID**

The Wedding Present

fairly evenly. The setlist, as chosen by bassist Terry de Castro, even contained 'You Should Always Keep In Touch With Your Friends', which Gedge described as 'Eighties indie pop'. He then introduced 'Santa Ana Winds' as 'modern indie pop' and, with barely a trace of irony, offered the observation that the two songs sounded much the same. As the final song, 'Dare', tailed off into a whine of guitar feedback, guitarist Chris McConville threw his setlist into the crowd and straight into my hand. I didn't even have to move my arm to catch it! And, better still, Gedge appeared at the merchandise stall after the show and signed it for me. Ever the fan, I was embarrassed to find myself informing Mr Gedge that he was a 'top man' for doing so.

12 BAR

25 JULY 2008, SWINDON, UK

ANDY SHEARER

I wondered if I had come to the right place as it just looked like a pub. I knew that they played more intimate places these days but I was unsure until I walked through the door and saw David Gedge stood by the merchandise table. I have to give presentations to hundreds of people but I still get tongue-tied when I see The Wedding Present's lead singer. This man helped to shape my life in a small way and it's weird to meet your heroes, particularly when they seem to be wearing a shirt that I am pretty sure he had on in Brixton in 1988.

That night in London in 1988 at the Fridge was my first Wedding Present gig. Sure, I had been to see people like Prince at Wembley but this was different – standing only, an audience dominated by sweaty men and not a programme in sight. I really felt like I had discovered something and it influenced my musical taste right to this day. I can remember fighting to get the setlist after the gig and then treasuring it for weeks afterwards (and to think I wonder why I didn't have a lot of girlfriends back then). I wish I had got hold of the setlist in Swindon as I'd be able to talk more about which songs they played but it doesn't really matter – they were all great, with my personal highlights being 'Wow' (a Cinerama song) and 'Palisades' from the new album, *El Rey*. The Wedding Present's songs have always been about falling in and out of love so it is only appropriate that I do just that during the gig. Terry de Castro, the bassist

2008: El Rey And A George Best Reboot

that joined David during his time in Cinerama, looked fantastic in her little black dress. She also looked like a woman who would chew you up and spit you out. She had that whole really cool American thing going on, which I find a little scary. However there was a moment, during 'The Thing I Like Best About Him Is His Girlfriend', where Gedge's voice and the music faded and she sang, 'He'd be completely devastated', that my heart melted. Sadly, by the time 'Brassneck' had finished I remembered that I am married with two kids, and the moment's gone.

LIQUID ROOMS
16 AUGUST 2008, EDINBURGH, UK

CAROLINE MCKENZIE

My sister is visiting Glasgow. She has a week off between a hen night and the wedding itself, doesn't feel like schlepping back to her home in London and fancies a day at the Edinburgh Festival. With conceptual purity in mind, she buys us tickets for The Wedding Present's T On The Fringe show.

I had to admit to her that I was only vaguely aware that the group had reformed and that I wasn't quite sure who was actually involved. Things had changed a bit; I was mostly devouring experimental and electronic music – my favourite band around this time were Nurse With Wound. Songwriting, melody and so on had become a bit alien to me.

Promisingly, the gig was packed out and my sister's outstanding ability to negotiate a crowded bar meant we were in good spirits when they arrived. They opened with 'On Ramp' and 'Interstate 5'. The effect was very similar to the first time I heard 'Dalliance' fifteen years earlier – the song and the performance absolutely thrilled me. To this day, 'Interstate 5' is probably my Wedding Present desert island disc – and what a first contact with it.

It was quite a long set but didn't feel like it, as they reminded the crowd of the greatness of their back catalogue ('Venus' was particularly wild) and played around half of *Take Fountain* with only one sly remark from Gedge before 'Queen Anne' to give the impression that he'd detected a lesser degree of audience enthusiasm for the newer songs, 'This is from the new album... ah, that shut you up, didn't it?'

Well, they worked on me; as much as it sounds like a romantic cliché, I bought *Take Fountain* the next day. And our brother asked us to phone him if they played 'Brassneck'. They didn't.

The Wedding Present

ALAN SHEARER

I work in Edinburgh as a bus driver and was coming home after a backshift just after midnight in January 2005, listening to Bob Harris's show on Radio 2. Without introduction, he played the album version of 'Interstate 5'. At the sound of the first chords I was hooked. As the song progressed I just had to find out who it was by and which album it was on. Needless to say, he played another tune afterwards and so I had to sit in the car for a while to hear him back-announce it. I ordered *Take Fountain* for delivery as soon as it was released and played it as much as possible over the next few months. The band came to the Edinburgh Festival Fringe that year and I saw them in concert for the first time at the Liquid Rooms with my 17-year-old niece Kezia. I still have 'Interstate 5' as my phone ringtone.

JOINER'S ARMS

3 SEPTEMBER 2008, SOUTHAMPTON, UK

PAUL TYACK

My brother drove all the way from Pool in Cornwall for the gig and it was ace. Afterwards we went back to my flat. The guy from the flat opposite was unconscious in the car park. We managed to get him into an ambulance but ended up locked out of my flat. The night in the car was colder than you can imagine. But still a top night. And the neighbour was OK. Turns out the guy was an alcoholic but he recovered just fine.

BESTIVAL

5 SEPTEMBER 2008, ISLE OF WIGHT, UK

DARREN BUGG

I went to see them down at the Isle of Wight. It must have taken 15 hours to get there, for various reasons. I got stuck in traffic jams. I was picking

2008: El Rey And A George Best Reboot

up my best friend in Luton and I got lost. I spent three hours driving around trying to get out of Luton. We eventually got to Southampton just as the boat was pulling out. I just put my foot down and drove onto the ferry at fifty miles an hour as the ferry was pulling away. It was like something from a Hollywood movie.

We got to the Isle of Wight and it was absolutely pissing down with rain. It was one of the worst festivals I've ever been to. The weather was so bad we couldn't even put our tents up. We went out with David that night for a curry, me and my friend and the whole band. We went to this curry place and we were just covered in mud. We had to sleep in the car covered in mud. And the next day The Wedding Present were the first band on at the entire festival. At the end of the first song they played, David said, 'Hello Isle of Wight and hello Darren.' Because we'd had such hassle to get down there. And after we'd seen them, it poured down again with rain and we said, 'We've had enough – we're going home.' So I drove for 15 hours from Leeds to the Isle of Wight, saw The Wedding Present and just left.

TROUBADOUR

19 SEPTEMBER 2008, LOS ANGELES, CA, USA

ANDY GILLESPIE

My girlfriend Kellie, myself and nine other Wedding Present enthusiasts from the UK decided to rent a van and follow our favourite band from San Diego to Vancouver BC for a total of seven gigs. David graciously put us all on the guest lists for these dates and in return I was the Scopitones Barmy Army tour bus driver and West Coast merchandise guy. Oh well, a fine time was had by all and it was the least I could do.

The second date was at the world famous Troubadour. I took up my spot at the merchandise table before the gig, sold a couple of shirts and tried to strongarm the locals into buying some CDs. When The Wedding Present took to the stage, the lovely support band Earlimart came and took over at the table to allow me to watch the show. I tracked Kellie down on the balcony and sat down next to her. The

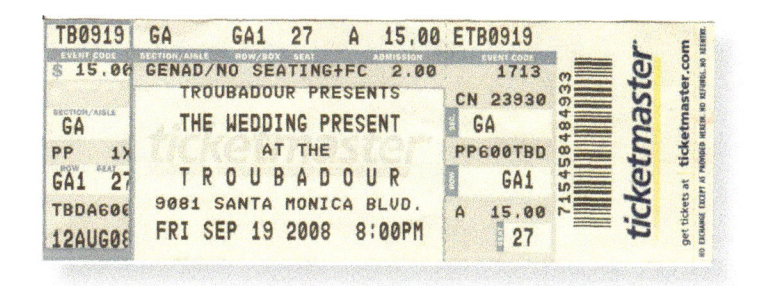

The Wedding Present

bloke sitting to her right looked pretty familiar so I did a double take. Now I've seen *The Matrix*, *Point Break* and a few other dodgy movies. 'Kellie, is that...?' 'Yeah, it's Keanu Reeves.'

I was a bit starstruck and spent almost as much time watching him as I did the gig. Although he did seem to be quite a fan and really into the gig, strangely enough he didn't seem familiar with obvious material such as 'Brassneck', but seemed to know more obscure songs like 'Flying Saucer' and 'Lovenest'. Maybe he had only listened to *The Hit Parade*. As the Wedding Present performance was winding down, I took my cue to return to the merchandise table and, as I was passing Keanu, said, 'I'm selling merchandise for the band. If you come and see us in the bar, I'll sort you out with a few CDs.' 'Oh thanks,' he replied. 'I'll be there.'

I then saw Keanu outside the venue being stalked by the paparazzi. While this was going on, David walked into the bar and over to the merch table. 'Keanu Reeves is at the gig. I said I'd give him a couple of CDs. Is that alright?' I asked. 'Sure,' replied David. Soon enough, Keanu tired of the cameras in his face and approached the table.

'Hi, Keanu' I said, impressing myself that I was now on first-name terms with a movie star. The fact that he was ignorant to my name didn't really come into it. 'Hey,' he replied, scanning the table, 'So which ones do you recommend?' 'Well they're all good,' I answered, while

Songs, bands and compromise

At the outset of The Wedding Present, everyone in the band knew what they were doing. You hardly needed to talk about anything because we were all so unified. But, before long, people started to move in different directions and have dissimilar views on the way the band was heading and so compromises had to be made. Obviously band-members are never always going to agree on everything and that can really affect you as the main songwriter.

There have been times when I've left rehearsals thinking, 'I hate what that person's done to my song... they've ruined it!' But, after a good night's sleep, you often wake up with a different perspective on things. You realise that it's possibly not what you'd have done with the song and perhaps that's why you don't like it. But maybe you wouldn't have thought of doing it in that particular way and so they've added something innovative to it and made it different. So... encouraging those kinds of contributions, even if I haven't always enjoyed the procedure, has been an artistically rewarding process.

David Gedge

2008: El Rey And A George Best Reboot

handing over various CDs, clearly proud of my embarrassing attempts at humour. 'Cool, so how much do I owe you?' 'They're on the house mate. Enjoy.' 'Oh no, I couldn't possibly do that. I must pay.' Sensing that he'd be offended if I insisted on palming them off on him for free, I came to a compromise. 'All right then, I'll charge you half. Twenty bucks for the lot.' 'Are you sure?' With that, he dug his hand into his jeans pockets and pulled out a crumpled up wad of assorted bills. He handed over the cash and seemed really happy with his purchase.

David came over to the merchandise table, I introduced them and they had a little chat. I have no idea what they said as I was busy hawking Wedding Present T-shirts and CDs, but I'm pretty sure it involved Keanu telling David how much he loved the gig, what a great band The Wedding Present are and what a helpful, pleasant and handsome guy he had on the merchandise table. Afterwards, David said, 'I thought you were going to give him those CDs?' 'I was, but he seemed a bit embarrassed to get them for free so I charged him half.' And, I added, 'Let me ask you this – did he give you any of his DVDs?'

KERRY SAUNDERS

I was in LA on business and it coincided with a Wedding Present gig in West Hollywood. I changed hotel for the weekend so I was 20 minutes walk away and went along on my own with just some cash in my pocket, which meant I failed to get the right colour band at the door to allow me (mid-30s at the time) to buy alcohol. America's attitude to alcohol is ridiculous – but that's a whole other topic!

The Troubadour is a nice cozy venue for a few hundred people and was full up. At the end I was hanging around to see Jessica and pick up a T-shirt I had been emailing about and, as she was busy clearing the stage, I went and stood at the bar chatting to a couple of ladies. Then I noticed that Keanu Reeves was there and everyone was around him getting photos. I hadn't noticed that he was up on a balcony as I had been focused on the stage. Anyhow, he came to the bar and I introduced myself and said I didn't have a camera or phone so I had to make do with a handshake. We spoke about the show. 'Boo Boo' was the final song which, though we both liked it, seemed an odd choice to finish with. His girlfriend had introduced him to The Wedding Present (darn, he had a girlfriend!). As he was buying drinks he asked if I wanted something so we had the discussion about me not having ID but I said he could see if he could get me a G&T. He tried, but the bartender clocked it was for me and refused to serve him. So a claim to fame is that Keanu Reeves almost bought me a drink at a Wedding Present gig.

The Wedding Present

JOHN HENRY'S
23 SEPTEMBER 2008, EUGENE, OR, USA

JESSICA McMILLAN
Assistant Tour Manager

We kind of agreed, reluctantly, to do that show. The fee was about $600. Not a huge amount but we went, 'Well, alright – it's on the way from San Francisco up to Seattle so we'll do it.' And then it turned out, when we did the settlement, that the $600 fee included a $250 payment to the support band! So our fee was $350, which wasn't even going to cover our expenses! Nowhere near! And it was really not a nice place. It was a dive bar. A scuzzy bar. It was probably an OK place to go for a drink and play some pool but it wasn't a great place for a concert. But we had our friend Andy Gillespie and a load of British people in the audience. They were probably a third of the crowd and their enthusiasm and support really transformed it into an event.

DAVID GEDGE

We do have a reputation for turning up in places like Stourbridge or Salt Lake City. 'The Wedding Present – you're playing in my town! Normally I have to travel for hours to see you. What are you doing here?!' But that's one of the benefits of our job. We can travel and actually get paid to see places we wouldn't normally have visited. We're fortunate to have journeyed all around the world, really. We've been to pretty much every country in Europe.

When you play a smaller venue, like the lovely Brudenell Social Club in Leeds, which is probably going to sell out, they'll offer you a guaranteed fee based on them selling all the tickets. 'Here's what we're going to pay you.' But there are also what are called 'versus' deals.

In that instance, they give you either a guaranteed fee or you take a percentage of the night's profits – usually 80 percent – whichever's the highest. You have the 'guarantee' to cover your costs, basically… but, if the show does well, you get the percentage split. That's the basis for most concert deals, really. There are certainly times where the guarantee is so low that we know we're going to make a loss on the night. However, we would accept it if, for example, we were playing in Berlin, where we know we're going to get a good

2008: El Rey And A George Best Reboot

fee, and then we were playing in Dresden, where we know we're also going to get a good fee, but there's a day off in between.

If we are offered a show for that day which is a low paid one, it might still be worth doing. Because otherwise we've still got the same expenses – van hire, musicians, crew, hotel, food, fuel, whatever. So even if it's an outrageously low fee it still might be worth doing

That happens a lot in the US, actually. We do OK on the coasts... and Austin and Chicago... the bigger cities. But in somewhere like Salt Lake City, there'll be 30 people there. So we definitely wouldn't make any money... but it's probably on the route between Denver and Seattle or something, so it just makes sense not to be sat in a hotel twiddling your thumbs for that night.

MEDIA CLUB
26 SEPTEMBER 2008, VANCOUVER, CAN

SAMANTHA ROBERTS

It was the *El Rey* tour. The Media Club was jam-packed. I was going to say that a good proportion of the audience were Brits but it just felt that way. In reality it was ten or so following the West Coast tour, but they filled the room with their enthusiasm, energy and sweaty moshing.

GARE DE LION
20 NOVEMBER 2008, WIL, CH

MIKE HARRIS

I was living in Switzerland. No one ever plays in Switzerland; it is a music vacuum. But The Wedding Present did, especially with a Swiss member (Pepe le Moko was on bass). So we went to a tiny village just outside of Basel to see them. When we got there it became immediately obvious that the venue was tiny, no bigger than a living room. I asked at the bar, 'How many tickets are sold?' and was told, 'None yet – you two are the first!' so straight away we booked a room at a nearby hotel and parked the car up for the night and

The Wedding Present

started to celebrate. In total there were twelve people in the 'crowd' that night, including myself and my wife. It was amazing, really amazing. After the gig we hung around and stood chatting to Mr Gedge and his partner Jessica for hours. They were great fun. A year later, I went alone to see them play in a different town in Switzerland and David and the merch lady both recognised me and came to speak to me – because I was one of the twelve! Fame at last.

CHARLOTTE
5 DECEMBER 2008, LEICESTER, UK

DAVID GEDGE

I like a venue that's clean, safe, well lit. Not too warm, not too cold. So it'll have air conditioning or heating, depending on the temperature... and nice staff! I always think art centres are good places to play. They tend to be subsidised by the council so there'll be loads of employees, it's well run and we always get well looked after. For me to do my job to the best of my abilities, that's perfect.

However, people who come to see us often don't like those kinds of venues because they want to see us in a dark, dingy, little club. One that springs to mind is The Charlotte in Leicester, which, if I'm honest, as a venue I never really liked because it was just a bit too much of a dive. The equipment was always breaking down and there were so many other things wrong with it that I could give you a list. But the point is that people loved concerts there because they were so rock 'n' roll... they were edgy and exciting and the atmosphere was great. And, once you're on stage, of course you tend to forget about all the terrible things and think, 'Yeah, actually, it's really great here.' Then the next day you'll play another venue where everything's perfect; it's a fantastic PA and lights but the atmosphere's really just not there. It's a balance.

There've been loads of times where we've arrived at a venue and thought, 'Eurgh, we're trapped here in this dirty, freezing, horrible club for the next eight hours!' But then, by the end of the night we're saying, 'Wow, we should definitely play here again because that was one of the best gigs of the tour!'

2008: El Rey And A George Best Reboot

ACADEMY 2
6 DECEMBER 2008, MANCHESTER, UK

MARTIN DUNN

I came home on leave not long after joining the military and my younger brother said to me, 'Listen to this' and pressed play on the old cassette player to be greeted by, 'Oh why do you catch my eye then turn away...?' It was of course 'Everyone Thinks He Looks Daft' from the album *George Best*. I had never heard anything like it and I was immediately hooked. Did my brother get his cassette back? Er, sorry Jon! I never got the chance to see The Wedding Present live as I spent the next 17 years being shoved from pillar to post round the world but in 2008 I found myself in my 40s and at the Academy with my friend and fellow Wedding Present fan Matt. We're out in the foyer and Matt says, 'Look, there's David Gedge at the merch table!' We had purchased the obligatory T-shirts earlier on and Matt says, 'I wonder if he'll sign my shirt?' 'Go and ask him,' I reply. 'No, you go.' 'No – you go!' Eventually, after about ten minutes, Matt wanders up and says, 'David, can you possibly sign my shirt?' 'Of course.' Well that was it. We asked if he would mind having a photo taken, and Matt later got said picture blown up and signed by David, which I received for Christmas 2008. After the picture was taken I thought I'd chance my arm and asked, 'David, are you doing 'Crawl' tonight?' It's one of my favourite Wedding Present songs as the lyrics mean a lot to me personally: 'I stole and of course I lied, yes to you but you must see why you couldn't just be told, there were some things I had to do.' He looks at me with the faintest hint of a grin and says, 'Don't know – we'll have to see.' It was halfway through the show that he said, 'This is a song called 'Crawl''.

PAVILION
8 DECEMBER 2008, CORK, IRL

STUART MCMENAMIN

My pal and me flew into Cork in the afternoon and got something to eat in the restaurant below the venue. We then headed up to the venue and when I got

The Wedding Present

to the merchandise stall David Gedge was standing beside it.

I bought my usual T-shirt and headed to the bar. As we did, my pal asked me if I had said anything to David Gedge and I said there was more chance of pigs flying than me saying anything.

As I was watching The Pains Of Being Pure At Heart, who were the support that night, my pal disappeared. I saw he was talking to David Gedge and getting something signed. When he came back over, my pal handed me the advertising poster I had seen in the stairwell. Written on it was 'Stuart – don't be shy' and it was signed by David Gedge.

That poster now sits in my hallway, framed, for everyone that comes into my home to see. This gig was also very funny as it is the only gig I have ever been to where a guitarist has needed a toilet break halfway through the set. David Gedge was heard to say, 'Unbelievable!' I never built up the courage to talk to him.

MOSHULU

13 DECEMBER 2008, ABERDEEN, UK

SUZANNE CLARK

I've seen The Wedding Present in Aberdeen a couple of times but my most memorable is when I went to buy my gig T-shirt. I've bought band T-shirts at every gig I've ever been to over 30 years, from the age of 14. My collection now runs to over a thousand!

I walked up and asked the guy for my size and didn't realise until I went to pay that I was being served by my hero – David Gedge! I ended up having a chat and getting an autograph which is framed at home.

It was an awesome gig and chatting to him totally made my night and gave me a special memory.

Babylon's burning: David in Istanbul

2008: *El Rey And A George Best Reboot*

BABYLON
22 DECEMBER 2008, ISTANBUL, T

KIRK OLLASON

Exeter in May was the first date of a mini-tour to support the release of *El Rey* and The Hub was rammed full. 'Santa Ana Winds' and 'Palisades' were played for the first time but the highlight was the triple salvo of 'I'm Not Always So Stupid', 'Don't Talk, Just Kiss' and 'Never Said'. Add 'Gone' a few songs later and it was a fantastic night for us fans of the band who love to hear B-sides in the set. I did the rest of the week too – Shrewsbury the next night followed by a night off (after Blackpool was postponed, I recall) then Norwich and Brighton to finish – and what a finish that was.

Two months later and I was back down south again for three dates revolving around the band's headlining slot at Indietracks. First up was Swindon, with the brilliant Container Drivers in support, and then off to the Midlands. Indietracks was ace, the band attracting a large crowd into one of the big halls, and it's always good to see how they go down in that sort of environment with the doubters at the back being more and more won over as the set progresses. The weekend finished off in Blackpool and then it was a matter of looking forward to the big one – seven dates up the West Coast of America and into Canada with the rest of David Gedge's Barmy Army.

This was certainly the trip of a lifetime, San Diego, LA, San Francisco, Eugene, Seattle, Portland and Vancouver. Seven gigs in nine nights with a lot of driving in between. Highlights included: the unique Casbah venue in San Diego, where it felt like you could reach out and touch the landing planes; an amazing night at the Troubadour in LA including drinking with Keanu Reeves at the bar while his girlfriend shopped at the merch desk; and a sweaty bouncy finale in Vancouver with a crowd that could have easily been Leeds or Manchester.

It was back to UK dates in December so I took in the first two dates, in Oxford and Leicester, as well the three Scottish dates in my home town of Edinburgh, Aberdeen and Glasgow. That wasn't quite the end though as 21 December saw me on a plane to Istanbul for the final date of the year. My sister was living in Turkey at the time so this seemed too good an opportunity to kill two birds with one stone! A great way to end the year and I ended up accompanying Graeme and Chris on the flights back to Heathrow and onwards to Edinburgh. Sadly, little did I know that this was to be the last gig with the 'two Scotsmen' line-up which had been responsible for the 20 fantastic 2008 gigs I had attended.

The Wedding Present

2009-2011: At The Edge Of The Sea

2009 was a quiet year for The Wedding Present, with a short Japanese tour. But David was busy as ever, planning his first festival close to home in Brighton.

GRAEME RAMSAY
Wedding Present guitarist 2009-2012

When the guitar vacancy came up I didn't want to replace Chris but, after Simon Cleave was unable to continue, I let David talk me into it. Switching instrument made things novel again. There was a lower turnover of band members at that time and the guitar was quite a lieutenant-type role; David needed to have someone he knew well and trusted, I think.

In the different roles I had in the band I saw it from different sides. The first thing I saw of writing with the group was as drummer, so most of my input was when the four of us would be in the room. It would be someone else who would bring the original idea and David would always be very happy for someone else to do that. It would make a structure of some bones that he could put the David Gedge sauce on. For me, at the time, writing a song seemed all about a great guitar line or something catchy that's not necessarily verbal, but I came to see it differently from the years working with them. David is a *songwriter*, which is a different thing from a composer of music in the sense that he was so much more interested in melody and a story than I was. I don't think his songs are vague. They may not be completely truthful or factual but they're specific, and always very up close to the people and the emotions in the story. David doesn't get too hung up on the particulars of the guitar parts, or whatever, in more recent times. He's more interested in the story, the atmosphere and melody. For all that David can seem like an unorthodox guitarist, he really does have a keen sense of melody and I think melody is really his focus when he's writing a song. I had more responsibility for bringing the initial music to the group after I changed to guitar. And I could be

2009-2011: At The Edge Of The Sea

quite fond of a guitar line here or there or a rhythm or something and David would say, 'Why don't we change the key of that?' and it would seem like quite an ordeal to me. 'Oh, I'll have to play that on different strings or maybe I'll have to tune differently.' But everything serves the song. The story that you might find in the song and the melody is what's key for David.

I'm sure that he had many little pieces of lyrics here and there, at various stages of completion, but he would keep that to himself. And lyrics especially would be something that would come at the very end, to the rest of the band, no matter how they were bubbling away in the background for David. The band would arrange the music first. Maybe, once the words were introduced, sections would get pushed around to serve the song, but he'd have the backbone of the band instrumental before anybody else knew about the words. So no one else was ever really involved in or invited to be involved in that sort of thing. That was very much David's preserve.

Grame Ramsay

In August 2009, David Gedge curated the first of his At The Edge Of The Sea festivals, which has gone on to become an annual event held in Brighton.

The Wedding Present

DAVID GEDGE

We were in a Little Chef near Wakefield after a concert. Terry de Castro was still in the group at that point and we were just chatting over breakfast about how one of the great things about being in this line of business is that you meet a lot of lovely people. But we were also saying how it's a shame that, sometimes, you might have a support band for a week... or meet somebody at a festival you're playing... and you really hit it off with them but then you never see them again! And we thought wouldn't it be great if we could invite them all back and see them again for a day? And so I had this idea of doing a little festival. It was one of these ideas where you knew it was going to be great straight away because everyone was enthusiastically pitching in, 'Oh, we should do this,' 'Oh, we should do that' and, 'So and so would be a great band to invite.' Within fifteen minutes it was all sorted. 'OK, we'll do a festival every year in Brighton and invite people that we like.' When I say, 'we'... I mean me really. Because when people say, 'We should get whatshername to do it' it's inevitably me who does all the work! I'll contact her. I'll sort it out. I'll negotiate with her agent. I'll explain what the event is and what facilities are available. And when she pulls out because her drummer's ill, I'll find a replacement.

I'm padding my part a little bit here... but it does involve a fair amount of effort. But it is great and I do enjoy it. It's almost like my Christmas. It's a stressful day but it's a lovely thing to do.

AT THE EDGE OF THE SEA FESTIVAL

22 AUGUST 2009, BRIGHTON, UK

SIMON PARKER
Villareal

Villareal were lucky enough to support The Wedding Present at the very first At The Edge Of The Sea festival and also on a date on the *Take Fountain* tour. Having been a fan since the mid to late Eighties this was a big deal for me. I loved *Take Fountain* and mentioned this to David just before our soundcheck.

2009-2011: At The Edge Of The Sea

At Cultura Quente in Caldas de Reis, Spain, July 2009

I also remember loving his leather jacket, but didn't feel the need to mention this at the time. But what I recall the most is that, whilst we performed, he helped man our merch table. As we threw ourselves enthusiastically around the stage there was Mr Gedge patiently searching for change. What an absolute legend!

TROUBADOUR
2 APRIL 2010, LOS ANGELES, CA, USA

RUDOLPH CARRERA

My brother had let me know that they were playing and, as it had been at least a decade since I saw them perform, I jumped at the chance. Mind you, I was pretty sauced once the band was halfway through their set, but I remember how great Gedge's voice was. He was in fine form and the band sounded like they were playing so hard that the instruments were going to break apart.

The Wedding Present

BOWERY BALLROOM
11 APRIL 2010, NEW YORK CITY, USA

GRAEME RAMSAY

Touring the US in 2010 we played *Bizarro* in full, but the line-up of the band was still new and hadn't completely clicked. That was until the Bowery Ballroom in New York City. Everything was falling into place, and by the time we came to 'Take Me!' the energy felt great, both on stage and from the crowd. Playing the best song at the best gig – it felt good. Even David rated it as one of the best ever. I watched a video of it online and someone had commented that he'd remember a certain part of the song for the rest of his life. It was a great moment.

HORSESHOE TAVERN
14 APRIL 2010, TORONTO, CAN

DANNY D

It was the *Bizarro* anniversary tour. A pretty full house and I was pretty pumped. There was a group of guys who had a blown up inflatable lady doll with them. Within three songs these idiots were shirtless and moshing and crowd surfing this inflatable doll on top of them. It was quite a scene!

PIKE ROOM AT THE CROFOOT
15 APRIL 2010, PONTIAC, MI, USA

RICHARD SHIMMIN

It was a small venue. A few songs in David said, 'Everyone to the edge of the stage.' It went from watching the band to joining the band! I was two feet from the guitar player. David was five feet to my right. What a blast! The Wedding Present are the real deal, no matter what the line-up.

2009-2011: At The Edge Of The Sea

MAXWELL'S
10 JUNE 2010, HOBOKEN, NJ, USA

ED HALL

I landed at Gatwick early December 1986. I quickly found out about *C86*, bought the LP and while everyone was fawning over others, I immediately freaked out when I heard 'This Boy Can Wait'. What was this I was hearing? Coming from rural NE Ohio this was like music from another planet. It struck me hard and I played it over and over and over on my Walkman cassette player to and from my work as a temp for City Girl Temp Agency.

I could type and it made me a boatload of money over my pub/bookstore working flatmates. I remember standing on an open veranda on the top floor of a house in Blackheath where I was staying for a while in the fall of 1988 and on a gorgeous evening listening to your beloved John Peel when, out of the blue, he announced a new single from his man Gedge and then 'Why Are You Being So Reasonable Now?' kicked in.

I jumped up and down, yelling over the balcony, and felt such joy, such warmth and excitement at hearing another gem from the gods. I can see it in my mind to this day. I went to plenty of shows on the East Coast in the Nineties while living in Washington DC, including The Wedding Present's first gig in the US at Maxwell's, then NYC the next night, then Philly the next night, then drove back to DC at 4am and arrived at my work at USA Today advertising just in time to change clothes and walk into the office. I was backstage in the dressing room for their first DC show at the old 9:30 club the next night, and on and on. Saw a number of Cinerama shows too and just loved it all.

Then in 2005, I threw on a small rucksack and followed them around for a half dozen shows in Germany and The Netherlands, on the *Take Fountain* tour. The last time I saw them was in Harrisburg, PA in 2010 for a one-off at some brewery – not part of a tour. A young poser crowd. But there I was with my wild, greying hair as *Bizarro* washed over around and through me. The beer was strong, but I remember just before 'Take Me!' I said out loud 'Tek!' and David asked me if that had something to do with the next song. And of course, it did. Ohio ain't the hippest state in the world and it's been cut out of subsequent tours. I get it partly, as the shows were not full. I noticed they started doing the Detroit to Toronto route, going north

The Wedding Present

Barcelona, 10 July, 2010

of Lake Erie instead of south. I am green with envy every time a UK tour is announced. I regret I'll never attend David's own festival. I am envious of every Brit Wedding Present fan who can see them multiple times every couple of years and in the company of his countrymen and women.

I could go on and on and on about how I became a one-man Wedding Present American promotions office after I got back to the US in 1988. I spread the word because I had to. I had no choice. And people responded. I have a handwritten letter somewhere from Sally Murrell during that time in response to my letter where I specifically asked what I could do to promote the band in America. I felt like I'd stumbled onto the Next Big Thing and I had to do my part to bring converts into the fold. I remember getting my copy of *Seamonsters* and playing it with so much anticipation I could barely stand it. What would he do after *Bizarro*? How would it change and be the same like he had done so far? I bought *Watusi*, Frank Black's *Teenager Of The Year* and Jesus And Mary Chain's *Stoned And Dethroned* together but it was obvious which one I'd start with. 'Click Click' floored me and I am pretty certain I cried the first time I heard 'Spangle'. It was always, always about the music. The stuff left off the albums, covers and the gems that run deep: how does a track like 'Don't Talk, Just Kiss' not make a final cut? Gedge is that good, that's

2009-2011: At The Edge Of The Sea

why. I remember him wearing shorts in concerts and he did – sometimes – do encores. I collected live tapes from the get go; some are lost, many are looking ragged, played to death. I bought their mag at every show in the late Eighties and Nineties – they are all packed away somewhere around here.

I lived this band. Anyone who knew me knew where The Wedding Present stood and how far down everyone else was. His music just hit me. I was his target audience, in the right place, by happenstance, in a random connection that has stayed with me to this day. I love the man and his music.

SLADE ROOMS

16 JULY 2010, WOLVERHAMPTON, UK

NEIL OAKLEY

Over the years, I have had many, many hours of pleasure listening to David's clever and touching lyrics and musical prowess. It was in Nottingham when I first got to see them. I had recently finished with my first proper long term girlfriend and David's lyrics were really hitting home and ringing true. I was unaware of David's approach to gigs and his love of mingling with fans and helping to sell the band's merchandise before gigs. This was all too much for me to handle. Over the years I have been lucky enough to meet some of my favourite artists and always given a good account and not embarrassed myself too much, but on that night in Nottingham I was unable to present myself in the best light. I was star struck (that's my excuse and I'm sticking to it). I strolled over to the merch stall and, whilst thinking of the best way to tell Mr Gedge of my love of his music and how his beautiful and heartfelt lyrics have touched and brought comfort and happiness to me, I picked up a couple of stickers and asked him if he'd sign them for me. This was my moment. But nerves got the better of me and all my carefully constructed words of appreciation and love came down to this phrase, which haunts me to this day. When he handed me back my signed stickers, I said, 'Cheers, Dave. I think you're shit hot!' David looked back at me and said, 'Cheers mate' with a baffled look and – in my mind – a slight bit of contempt. I was gutted. I had so much to say and this was not my most poetic or complimentary moment. As the years have passed, I've been lucky to see the band more times. Even though I'm older and wiser now – I'm in my 40s – I still get

The Wedding Present

starstruck and I'm convinced that when I've tried to do that cool 'alright' head nod if I catch David's eye he still thinks 'knobhead' from that moment he won't remember from years before. Yes, I've learnt over the years that David is a David not a Dave. Yes, I'm sure I could tell him now in a more constructive and heartfelt way how much I love his music and lyrics. But I still feel the angst of that encounter to this day. When we went to see the band a few years ago in Wolverhampton at the Slade Rooms for the *Bizarro* album tour with my best friend, I was convinced that, if the opportunity came my way to put it to bed and a passing of words were to happen, I could confidently just say, 'Thank you' to David for all the pleasure and joy the band had given me. But it was not meant to be. My friend left me standing next to the merch stall and his last words were, 'Don't go speaking to him whilst I'm gone!' which was a tongue in cheek swipe at me. But I couldn't resist. As soon as he left I seized my moment, strolling confidently over to where David was chatting with fans. As I got closer I began to overthink it all again and before I knew it, it was too late. I was in the 'chat' zone. Awkwardly, I did the first thing that came to mind, produced my ticket and said, 'Excuse me, David, could you sign this please?' (At least, I used the right name this time!). I had to break the cycle. 'Thank you, and thank you for the music.' I avoided eye contact. David smiled back at me as I mumbled and I scurried off. My friend returned and knew straight away I had broken ranks and approached David again like a mumbling, nervous stalker.

AT THE EDGE OF THE PEAKS FESTIVAL

26 AUGUST 2010, HOLMFIRTH, UK

CHRIS BOUNDS

I was having a party for my 40th birthday and I managed to persuade a couple of my oldest mates, Mike and Rich, to come over to mine a couple of days early and drive over the Pennines to take in a gig at the Holmfirth Picturedrome for the 21st anniversary *Bizarro* tour. The three of us were all 40 within a few weeks of each other and we had all seen the *Bizarro* tour in Kilburn back in 1989. So this was a great opportunity for us to laugh in the face of the aging process and jump around down the front pretending we were 19 again! By the time the band got into the middle of side two, Mike and Rich had decided they couldn't take the

2009-2011: At The Edge Of The Sea

pace and had gone to stand a bit further back. As the band finished the relatively gentle paced 'Bewitched', it dawned on all of us in the middle-aged moshpit that next up was the twin guitar onslaught of the nine minute epic of 'Take Me!' The feeling was much like I imagine it was in the World War I trenches just before the order to go 'over the top'. The bloke next to me, a total stranger, gave me a pat on the back and said, 'See you on the other side!' I was joking about the trenches. I'm not really suggesting that spending ten minutes purposely bashing into some sweaty bald blokes to the accompaniment of some manically strummed electric guitars is actually comparable to facing almost certain death.

AT THE EDGE OF THE SEA FESTIVAL

28 AUGUST 2010, BRIGHTON, UK

PAUL DORRINGTON

There were a few years when there was very little contact between David and I but I would still see him every few years if he played nearby, so we never completely lost contact. When I saw that David was going to put on the At The Edge Of The Sea festival in 2009, I asked him if I could play, as I was doing a solo project at the time. He had already booked all the acts but said if it went well he would do another one the following year and I could play then. It was nice to catch up after what seemed like quite a long break and we've stayed in touch. I've been down to At The Edge Of The Sea a few times now.

ASSEMBLY

2 OCTOBER 2010, ROYAL LEAMINGTON SPA, UK

HAIKU SALUT

Having been asked to play At The Edge Of The Sea festival three years running we thought we had better make the effort, finally find a dog sitter and make the four hour trip to Brighton. We hadn't grown up listening to the band but were

SOMETIMES THESE WORDS **JUST DON'T HAVE TO BE SAID**

The Wedding Present

aware of their presence and cult status. The festival had a really nice vibe, there was a real mix of bands performing and the audience was very attentive. This would be the first time we would meet David and become acquainted with David's dog Doris. Doris doesn't mind The Wedding Present but does not like Cinerama. She is very small, her ears are very soft and she has very kind eyes. The second time we would meet Doris would be at the Assembly in Leamington Spa, a building decorated by Laurence Llewelyn-Bowen with an exhibition of curiosities in the green room. Disused fairground rides, Egyptian mummies and the main attraction – Tammy Wynnette's lipstick pink caravan guarded by an actual Dalek from the actual television. Haiku Salut were supporting The Wedding Present that evening who were playing *Bizarro* in its entirety. As The Wedding Present performed, we stood at the side of the stage and watched in awe, with the view of both the band playing their hearts out and the adoring audience as close as they could be to the stage and meaning every word they sang. We soon came to realise the depth of feeling that The Wedding Present have garnered over the years. The purity of people's enthusiasm for them that night was unparalleled and we were very humbled by the unpretentious happiness on show that evening. There was such a collective joy. At the front was our friend's dad, who we had brought with us as a guest; he has loved The Wedding Present for years and it was a pleasure to see him enjoying them so much. We came away having witnessed something special. It was clear that David and the band were absolute heroes to their fans and it was a pleasure to be part of it. We never got to say bye to Doris that night.

KNUST

22 OCTOBER 2010, HAMBURG, D

BARBARA HOEFGEN
Precious Few

In 2005 I was on a German tour with The Wedding Present with my two bands Dorian and Gloria. On the morning after the show in Hamburg we met the band at the venue Knust to load our stuff and say goodbye as they were going to Copenhagen. John Maiden, who was playing drums for The Wedding Present on the tour, was quite upset because he'd forgotten to pick up his clothes from the laundrette and, as it was Sunday, it was closed. I had a couple of spare grey

2009–2011: At The Edge Of The Sea

women's underpants which I offered him and he accepted them very thankfully. According to Terry de Castro, he liked them a lot and wore them for the rest of the tour. Half a year later a grinning Simon Cleave gave them back to me at a gig in Cologne. Years later it was still a running gag when we talked about the tour. In October 2010 I was on tour with The Wedding Present again with my new band Precious Few. The day after the show in Porsgrunn, Norway, Chris and me took the car ferry to Denmark and drove to Hamburg to stay there overnight. Meanwhile David and the band took the overland route and stayed in a motel in Bad Bramstedt, somewhere north of Hamburg. The next day, when we went back to the hotel we passed the laundrette where Johnny had left his clothes and coincidentally saw drummer Charlie and the rest of the band inside. He was just wearing his long underpants and a jumper as the rest of his clothes were in the washing machine. They had decided to go to there since it was the only laundrette they knew in the area. Funnily enough the crew of Carlos Santana were there too and we had a little chat with them. Let´s see what happens with drummers, laundrettes and underpants next time I'm on tour with them…

TUNNELS

1 DECEMBER 2010, ABERDEEN, UK

STEVEN STEWART

I'd been to a couple of Wedding Present gigs at larger venues, and also seen them up very close and personal at the Lemon Tree in Aberdeen. A great gig as always, with the boy Gedge about three feet away from me, but what made the gig for me was the fact that before and after the gig David was mingling with the fans. I'd never been to a gig where this had happened before and I built up the courage to go and speak to my idol. I can't remember exactly what I said but it was along the lines of, 'Your music changed my life.' Then I bought him a glass of red wine before leaving. A great songwriter and a very nice man. Then I was at a Wedding Present gig at the Tunnels in Aberdeen. I had been moshing about at the front. And as soon as the final song finished I made a grab for Pepe le Moko's setlist. She saw this as me trying to steal an effects pedal or some kind of gear and she grabbed my arm. David had seen what was happening and was totally cool, saying, 'It's only the setlist he wants.' I then got a big smile from Pepe that finished off the night beautifully.

The Wedding Present

ACADEMY 2

10 DECEMBER 2010, MANCHESTER, UK

SUZY ROBINSON

I've seen The Wedding Present twice – 20 years apart! First in 1991 at Norwich UEA. I was 16 and my older sister had just left home to live in Manchester and I was feeling quite bereft. We'd hated each other as kids but as we got older we bonded through a shared love of indie music. She was quite a big fan – I was more into The Stone Roses and Happy Mondays but I used to listen to The Wedding Present a lot too as it reminded me of her. It was her best friend who invited me along to the gig. I think she was missing my sister too

Left to right: Charlie, David, Graeme and Pepe wonder whether to upgrade their tour van for something more sumptuous after checking out Tammy Wynette's caravan backstage at Leamington Spa
Photo: Stephanie Colledge

2009-2011: At The Edge Of The Sea

and felt sorry for me so invited me. I don't remember much about the actual gig – I was probably a bit blotto on Newcastle Brown Ale. Fast forward 20 years and I'm now living in Manchester and end up going to see them again at Manchester Academy. I had not planned to see them. In fact it was the day of my works Christmas do and I had no intention of doing anything other than enjoying a good few drinks. It was also a colleague's last day and we had our meal and then ended up in some Northern Quarter bars. At this point I was quite suggestible, and so when my work pal tried to persuade me to go to the gig I was like, 'Yeah – why not?' Despite the fact I was all dressed up in my Christmas do finery (I think heels were involved) I loved it! I was a regular at gigs when I lived in Norwich, but I'd lost interest in live music and hadn't been to a proper gig – the ones where you don't sit down – in years. They played all the classics I remembered from my youth, and I remember everyone going bananas for 'Kennedy'. I wonder if I'll go and see them again in another 20 years?

KOKO

13 DECEMBER 2010, LONDON, UK

RICHARD OWEN

I first saw the band as a student in Manchester in the late Eighties. Having wooed my wife Kate by placing 'Queen Anne' on a Valentine playlist, it became our wedding song. She contacted David who hand-wrote the lyrics for her, which she got framed and gave me as my wedding present. We were married in London on 11 December 2010. Two days later the band played at Koko in Camden, so we delayed our honeymoon for the gig and met David afterwards to say thanks.

FRIENDS OF MINE FESTIVAL

21 MAY 2011, SIDDINGTON, CHESHIRE, UK

MIKE PRIAULX

Apart from it being freezing cold and wet and windy, which is possibly why the festival was never held again and why no-one else runs a festival in May in Cheshire – I remember they were on at the same time as Buzzcocks and Mr Gedge said

The Wedding Present

that it was bad luck, both because it wasn't a huge crowd at their stage and because he would like to go and see Buzzcocks himself. And someone shouted for 'Gazebo', which David found amusing and made some comment about, 'That one not getting requested very often.' I don't think they played it.

LONG DIVISION FESTIVAL

11 JUNE 2011, WAKEFIELD, UK

JON PINDER

I got a press pass to the inaugural Long Division music festival. The Wedding Present were headlining. That got me actually onstage with the band to shoot the sponsor talking to the crowd before they started playing. It was an odd gig, held in a nightclub whose security staff didn't realise that people jumped about at gigs. Once the band started, the crowd were in good spirits and dancing about. Security thought the moshpit was too much and so started dragging fans out kicking and screaming to be thrown out of the venue with a punch or two for good luck.

The gig was stopped until the event organisers could get the venue to remove the security staff. My drunk ex-wife turned up, saw the violence and demanded I take her home. I had to make a decision as to whether to comply with that request or stay to watch the band. The Wedding Present won hands down!

PATRICK ALEXANDER
Wedding Present guitarist 2012–2014

I joined the band through a strange and fortunate sequence of events, none of which had much to do with my ability to play the guitar. Years earlier I had played in different London-based punk bands, including several tenacious, fun years playing every dirty venue up and down the country as the bassist in The Young Playthings. We were good friends with members of the band The Pipettes, and we spent many a wasted Saturday night smoking rollies and drinking cider at house parties in anticipation of our impending fame. When their bassist Jon couldn't do a European tour, I stepped in for a few hedonistic weeks. Over the tour I became close pals with a fresh-faced young Seb Falcone, Jon's younger brother and keyboardist in The Pipettes. Skip forward seven years or so and Seb had become the sound engineer for The Wedding Present. When he knew Graeme was stepping down from playing

2009-2011: At The Edge Of The Sea

guitar, he told me about the opening, and it was an opportunity too good to pass up. I wasn't totally convinced of my ability to play the guitar all that well (I was a bassist, after all), but I didn't let that detail stop me. I also didn't own a guitar at the time. As I say, details…

The band were short of a guitarist with only a few months before the 20th anniversary *Seamonsters* world tour. I sent a few audition recordings over to David, of me playing songs from *Seamonsters* and *George Best*. On a boring afternoon in December 2011, I met David and Jess in a pub in Reading. They were on their way to pick up some T-shirts from their merch person. We talked about the band and the tour, and David subtly interrogated me about my musical tastes – I mentioned Archers Of Loaf, Superchunk, Jawbreaker, Sonic Youth – and they were suitably happy with my disposition to offer me the job a few days later. If being in a band is a lot to do with driving vans, unloading equipment, and dealing with the sweet vicissitudes of life on the road, and also a bit to do with playing and writing music together, then it helps to give the impression that you're reasonably easy to get on with. Playing your instrument is also quite important, so I spent the next three months locked in my freezing shed every night, learning the Wedding Present back catalogue. In the process, I fell in love with the band's music, and especially with *Seamonsters*, which remains one of my favourite albums of all time.

The first few months in the band were a whirlwind that my teenage self thanked me for every day - we flew to LA, I bought a brand-new black-and-chrome Fender Jaguar, we played ten shows over three days at South by Southwest in Austin (including the Iron Bear), and then bounced between the coasts of the US, and then Australia, Japan, and Hong Kong, playing Seamonsters in its entirety every night. It's a moody, introspective album to play live, and every time I hear 'Dalliance', 'Dare' and 'Blonde' in particular, I'm taken back to sweaty, darkened stages across the world. Getting just the right feedback as 'Dalliance' rolls into 'Dare'; stamping on all your pedals to make the quiet parts of 'Blonde' seem even more fragile. Those are priceless memories to me.

I stopped playing regularly live with the band when I moved to New York City for a bit in 2014 and, in the preceding years, we played countless shows (I say countless – ask Charlie and he'll know how many!) and worked on the songs that eventually became *Going, Going…* I'm really proud of all the songs from that album, but 'Bear' and 'Santa Monica' will always be favourites.

The Wedding Present

For me, being in a band has always been as much about the magic that is threaded into the drudgery as the dream-state that you sometimes enter in the best moments onstage. From knowing exactly how to load the van best, to knowing our unspoken pre- and post-show routines and inside jokes; to negotiating foibles, politics, upsets, and intrigues; to the roulette of practice rooms, dressing rooms, riders, and affordable hotels; to hot amps, broken strings, and bloodied picks; to drunken late-night escapades and, in my case, embellishing their re-telling to anyone who will listen; to the thousand mile drives; to looking down at your fingers and knowing it's a millimetre between a good performance and what David might describe as a 'jazz' interpretation of a well-known guitar part; to meeting and becoming great friends with bands and fans all over the world; to playing fast, and light, and loud with people that you're fond of in a way that only a band can. As the man says, 'You can't moan, can you?'

2012: *Valentina* And *Tales*

2012 saw the release of *Valentina*, the band's eighth studio album. And, in March 2012, the first issue of *Tales From The Wedding Present*, David Gedge's biographical comic book series, was published.

DAVID GEDGE

Terry de Castro had this idea to write my biography from the point of her joining Cinerama in 1998 and then being my bass player for the ensuing twelve years. I think she felt that this put her in a unique position. So she researched my scrapbooks and diaries and interviewed me... as well as loads of other people... my parents and Sally Murrell, for example. She did a ton of work on it and even finished a draft but, ultimately, she wasn't entirely satisfied with the results.

We'd originally included a handful of comic book style stories to provide gaps between text and, in the end, this was the one thing that we both thought worked really well. So we came up with the idea of turning the whole biography into a comic book and Tales From The Wedding Present was born. I thought this was a brilliant idea because I've always adored comics. So we started writing stories based on her research and I got an old friend, Lee Thacker, to illustrate them. Lee used to draw cartoons for the old Wedding Present 'fanzine', *Invasion Of The Wedding Present*, between 1987 and 1990 and I'd kept in touch. I love doing the comic! It's great to send off a load of text to Lee and then get it back a few days later and it's come to life through his brilliant drawings. Plus... it's me! In my own comic! How cool is that?!

TERRY de CASTRO

I was always telling David that I found him amusing and fascinating in equal measure and that I wanted to do a kind of 'character study' of him. Even back in the early days of Cinerama, I thought he was like his own comic book character. It would come out in absurd situations, like him telling us how lucky we were to know

The Wedding Present

him because he was taking us around the world... and then promptly losing his boarding pass. And while everyone else was just lollygagging around, he would have to sort out a thousand complicated logistics. When I finished a first draft of the original bio, though, I just didn't think it translated what I wanted to get across, i.e. the semi-legendary phenomenon that is David, modern-day hero/anti-hero! What I like about the comic book series is its everyday-ness, the Harvey Pekar nature of it. At first people don't realise that Tales From The Wedding Present is an official biography, because the covers are usually surreal, fantastical situations. But when you read the text, it's always some ridiculously ordinary scenario, like a late soundcheck or a parking snafu. I like how the dull but somehow heightened tour escapades become kind of epic in their mundanity. It's amazing to see what Lee does with the covers and stories. We'll come up with something we think is funny and Lee makes it even funnier with his interpretation of the text.

> "*Tales From The Wedding Present* is a brilliant comic book demystifying band life, but with charm. Ace"
>
> Ian Rankin, crime writer

SOUTH BY SOUTHWEST
14-17 MARCH 2012, VARIOUS VENUES, AUSTIN, TX, USA

TIM MORTON

I move to Austin, Texas and two months later The Wedding Present grace the stage at the classic Emo's on 6th Street. I meet David briefly, we chat about the benefits of living in the USA, I get a signed CD and I move on. I get to see them two more times over the years – at the Mohawk, an awesome small outdoor venue, and at Emo's again. Then in 2012 they play SXSW. My work studio is downtown, on the second floor on Neches Street, right next to the Hilton and the Austin Convention Center, right in the heart of SXSW events. Open the windows and you could hear music playing in all directions! During those four days in March I get to break out for lunch, get out early and see them play eight times, alas missing their last show. It was a great luxury to see them play two times a day in very different venues – the strangest venue being during the day at a burger place!

2012: Valentina and Tales

At South By Southwest, 2012

JESSICA McMILLAN

South By Southwest is a big festival in Austin, Texas and San Antonio is quite nearby. We were already scheduled to play nine times at South By Southwest and then we were offered this mini-festival in San Antonio. If I remember correctly, it was the only show for which we were going to be paid – most of the South By Southwest events are put on by record labels or radio stations so you don't get a fee. So we said we'd do it if they provided a hotel. They agreed but then they called us about an hour before we left Austin and said, 'Erm, we weren't able to get you a hotel. I hope that's OK?' We said, 'Well... not really' but we were ready to set off so we thought we might as well do the gig. So we went down to San Antonio but as soon as we arrived it all felt a bit weird. There was hardly anybody there, for a start. Some other musicians and the bar staff were around but there didn't seem to be much of an audience. The fee was quite a lot of money for there being not very many people and so I told David that we should probably get paid in advance. It felt bad all night, basically... there were bands playing with nobody watching them. They were supposed to give us a meal

SOMETIMES THESE WORDS **JUST DON'T HAVE TO BE SAID**

The Wedding Present

so we said, 'Where's the food? There's supposed to be a meal provided!' 'Oh yeah, sorry. We've been run off our feet all day.' Then they remembered that there was food in the kitchen but when we got there it was just two inches of leftover, overcooked, frizzled, lasagne. We complained and said, 'You're supposed to be providing a meal and this lasagne's not really going to cut it!' So they said, 'OK, we'll get pizzas in for you.' So they ordered pizzas. I thought, 'Yeah, we should definitely try and get paid before the show!' I chased the promoter around for about an hour and he finally came back and said, 'OK, come with me and we'll go and do the fee.' I did that and then, about half an hour later, David and I went upstairs. We were just going up to have a look around and suddenly there were all these plain-clothes police officers everywhere. They had these hidden police badges and they'd just gotten them out. All of the bar staff were sat on the kerb out front in handcuffs. And we were like, 'Oh, what's this all about?' We had no idea because we'd been in the basement, in the dressing room, all the time. There was a bar downstairs and even the barman down there didn't know that it was going on. So we watched the police for a while. And then it turned out that the guy who was supposed to be in charge of the club wasn't there for some reason and none of the bar staff were licensed to be at that venue for that night. So the senior police officer started yelling, 'If somebody doesn't come forward and say they're in charge right now, I'm taking you all to jail.'

At that point David and I looked at each other and thought, 'We should probably go.' We quickly loaded the guitars back into the van and started to drive back to Austin. Then, as we were leaving, someone ran up to the van and waved at us to stop. We thought we'd been caught. We thought it was another policeman and that he was going to ask us questions. But the guy just opened the door of the van and said, 'Here are your pizzas!'

DAVID GEDGE

When the San Antonio show didn't go ahead we thought our agent would say, 'Hey, that venue you didn't play at wants their money back!' But we never heard anything about it ever again so…. we quietly forgot about it. In the old days, when Simon Smith used to be the Wedding Present tour manager, there were more than a couple of occasions when he'd be in the promoter's room for absolutely ages and then he'd come out looking stressed and say, 'You lot might as well go to the hotel. This is going to take a while.' I wasn't party to the conversations.

2012: *Valentina* and *Tales*

MELLOW JOHNNY'S BIKE SHOP

15 MARCH 2012, AUSTIN, TX, USA

IAN GELLING

In March of 2012 my partner Steph and I went to Austin, Texas for SXSW and met up with a group of US-based Wedding Present fans to support the band in their showcasing of *Valentina* in numerous venues, and to hear *Seamonsters* played in full. We had a great time and saw some other fantastic bands – Toquiwa, The Twilight Sad, Poliça, Dan Mangan and Thee Oh Sees, to mention a few.

As part of this, The Wedding Present were due to play a festival in San Antonio. A group of us decided to make the trip and Steph and I got a lift with the band. After an hour's drive we arrived at some weird campus where three or four bands were playing various stages but there appeared to be no audience.

The promoter explained that it was early and it would get busier later. We found that The Wedding Present were playing late so we left the band to set up and went into town for some fantastic Mexican food and too many Tuna Margaritas.

Feeling suitably refreshed, we headed back to the festival site only to be greeted by blue flashing lights, police, guns, and the promoter being led away in handcuffs. The band was nowhere to be seen so we ran around looking for them until we came across a guy carrying a load of pizzas.

It turned out he was looking for The Wedding Present as well! Knowing the band's legendary obsession with food, and that DLG was not likely to leave without the pizzas, we followed the bloke to find him and the van, which was doors-open, revved up and ready to go. It was a bit like The A-Team leaving the scene of the crime. Four good things about this:

1. We avoided getting led away by the Old Bill of San Antonio– other attendees were not so lucky. The story was something to do with suspected money laundering.
2. The band had been paid in advance – result!
3. On the way back to Austin and as the clock turned past midnight to 16 March, the whole van sang happy birthday to me – DLG included.
4. The pizzas were excellent!

The Wedding Present

VALENTINA
THE EIGHTH ALBUM
RELEASED 19 MARCH 2012

ANDREW SCHEPS
Producer, *Valentina*

I've only worked with the band recently. I missed the first 28 years. My CV is so varied that nobody (or everybody) I work with seems like a natural marriage. You can either say, 'Oh yes, that makes perfect sense' or, 'Well I don't really get why that happened.' I've worked on lots and lots of different music but my love is guitar bands. It's always been my personal preference. I ended up hooking up with The Wedding Present because Pete, a friend of mine, was doing front of house for them.

And he knew that they were working on a record and thought, 'Oh, hello, someone's going to have to mix it and – Andrew should!' And I was like, 'Oh – OK.' So it was that I knew somebody who had worked with the band.

I knew of The Wedding Present but they didn't really make it out in the States that much at all. Everybody had heard of them but it was kind of, 'Oh yes, they're a band from the early Smiths era, in that genre.' And that was sort of all I knew. But as soon as it came up that I might work with them, and I was actually coming over to England (at that point we were still living in LA) I decided to go meet with the band in Brighton. And I immediately started listening to everything, and of course there was a huge discography at that point, and I just loved what I heard. So it worked out great. David is just so easy to deal with and there's no rock star ego in any of it. It's just – this is his day job, it's what he does. So it went great. I went to rehearsals with them on *Valentina* and then they went off and recorded the record and we mixed it at my studio in LA and since then I think I've done pretty much everything they've put out, except for some acoustic stuff.

We managed to sneak recordings into seminars I give in France. So, in the midst of doing a week-long recording seminar, I go, 'We'll have a band come in for a day' and of course they think we're just there teaching, but we also happen to record

2012: Valentina and Tales

half the record in a day. It's perfect for the seminar and perfect for the band. It's been very kind of stealth in a way, which I think is the way David likes to do stuff anyway. Sort of DIY, but not really. They recorded at a studio in France called Black Box and then David did his vocals with a guy with a very small studio in LA. who he's done vocals with for a long time, after doing all the tracking in France so – yeah, we just mixed. It was David and it was also Graeme, who was the guitar player at the time but he had been the drummer. He was on his way out of the band and the very last thing he did was to be there for the mixes of this record.

Basically, the recording process is putting microphones up in front of people and getting the performance and all of that and then, once you've decided that you've recorded everything you need, then you go mix. Mixing is a separate process to the recording. So you just bring up all the elements and balance them and change the sound a little bit here and there and just try and make it all the most exciting version of what's there.

The mix is never actually a conscious discussion. Because I'm involved in the record-making process, I assume that everybody else knows how it works. Every once in a while you'll have a creative discussion before you start a project and say, 'Well OK, we really want it to be this' but it's very hard to force anything to be anything. If ten different people had mixed *Valentina* you would have ten very,

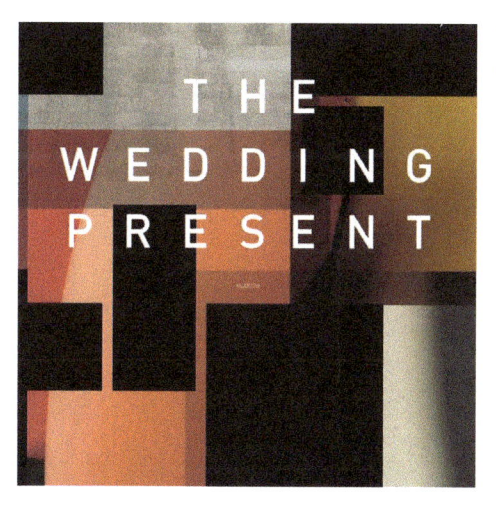

The cover of *Valentina*

very different versions of the record so it obviously goes through my filter but it wasn't ever a conscious decision. When something is loud, I like it to be really loud. I always like to amplify the emotion. And I love things that are aggressive. I love things that are surprising or sad.

I think the end of 'Deer Caught In The Headlights', the big instrumental build there, makes it sad in a proud way, if you had to define the emotion. And not because of my involvement. Just musically, how you react to it. So I was just trying to bring out more of that. And I love things that are heavy.

But I don't think David ever said, 'Oh, this'll be a heavy record.' It just always sounded to me like it was going to be a heavy record because that's what was there. It's such a great jam at the end.

It was David and Jessica and Graeme who came for the mixing. David and Jessica were in LA anyway, so that worked out for them. And Graeme knew that

The Wedding Present

he was going but he felt really personally invested in these songs and recordings, so he really wanted to be there. It was a very simple process. We mixed the whole album in ten days. There were a few days where we finished two songs a day.

GRAEME RAMSAY

Making what became *Valentina*, I had a bit more input and was really trying to make something that kept a thread of Wedding Present Past. David's singer/writer persona has inevitably changed over the years but harmonically I wanted that thread in there.

What I'm most proud of, though, was the song 'End Credits'. During writing and arranging it, it struck me that what we were missing, or at least not showcasing, was David's 'other' guitar sound – the weird tone from Strats with strings tuned in unison. I realised we could take the second guitar right out of the picture and replace it with another drum kit, since there were two drummers in the band, leaving a big space down the middle for David and his guitar. It's a testament to Terry de Castro's knack for melody that the bass 'solo' was made up on the spot, and yet not one note was changed when we recorded it after she'd left. The track came out every bit as raucous as I hoped and, when you hear it, there's no other band it could be. I definitely wanted to be involved all the way through. It's true that I was very keen to be involved in mixing it but leaving the band didn't really enter the equation until quite late on. I was already committed to the production process. Mixing is a really underrated influence on the finished product. It wouldn't affect the song in the 'David Gedge's identity' sense but, aesthetically, the music can sound very different based on someone's mix interpretation.

MIKE BAKER

Inevitably, The Wedding Present returned and it was game on again. *Take Fountain* showed that they were still able to create fantastic soundscapes and soaring melodies, *El Rey* was another triumph with the return of Steve Albini on recording duties and then *Valentina*, probably their best album yet, showing that they are only getting better and better. These latest albums really show the strength in the songwriting, which is more mature, more vulnerable. They know what they want and how it should sound.

I attended a lot of the Brighton gigs and was surprised to regularly see David at the merch stall, chatting with fans and posing for photos. I think this a big part of why people love The Wedding Present, it's the fact they do it all themselves. They keep control of what they do and we all feel a part of it. From personal email replies to personalised notes in with your online purchases, this all contributes to

2012: Valentina and Tales

the closeness we feel to the band. The joyous singing along, the sweaty rough-housing upfront, the immediate assistance when you inevitably fall over, partly drunk and partly swept up in the emotion of the crowd. We are all one at a Wedding Present concert.

GAVIN MORGAN

My girlfriend was a friend of Jessica's – and gradually we began doing more and more for the band, often helping out selling the band's merchandise on tours – if you've bought a T-shirt at a gig over the last decade, there's a good chance I sold it to you. This culminated with the Club 8 promotion for *Valentina*. With the band overseas, David asked me to organise the sending out of the CDs and limited edition 7"s. Suddenly our house was drowning in boxes of records – endless trips to the post office carrying sacks of cardboard packages. Oh, and the vinyl had to be numbered 1-500. A long weekend of writing by hand numbers onto the back of 500 records followed.

But it's all worth it. Highlights must be going to all of the gigs on the *George Best* tour of 2007 – from Stirling to Portsmouth, and beyond – and finally having the time and money for such things. Who'd have thought, as a 14 year old back in the Eighties? Seeing the band in other countries is always fun as well – such as flying to New York for a few dates on the *Bizarro* 21 Tour. Meeting John Peel's wife, 'The Pig', was also memorable, with David introducing me to her after a gig in Stowmarket, completing the circle. The Wedding Present have been a constant feature in my life for 30 years – and have accompanied, and caused, life-changing events for me.

GRAEME RAMSAY

Like any ongoing decision, pros and cons are weighed up along the way and most are subject to change. The novelty, the privileged experiences on stages and in studios, the travel and – if we're honest – the perceived glamour, all outweigh the negatives most of the time. By the end of 2011 I felt I'd probably done everything I could expect to do and didn't foresee so many novel experiences or thrills ahead. I also identified a little less with the songs we were putting all our effort into. In truth, there are more boring reasons like not feeling able to afford being in the band; never being likely to get a mortgage etc. I'm sure I read an online post summing it up as 'eventually they get bored and quit' but it's not as simple as that – you don't think to yourself, while flying home from LA where you mixed your record with a Grammy-winner, 'Man, am I bored of this!' The balance of things just changes over time and you feel Real World things pulling you away.

The Wedding Present

The Wedding Present commute to work

Charlie living in Berlin presents something of a logistical challenge but, even in Cinerama days, Terry was living in America for much of the time. If you value their input you just work around it. And with technology and communication being easier now, it's not too much of a problem.

When Patrick Alexander was in the group, it was easier for Charlie to get to Brighton from Berlin than it was for Patrick to get here from near Oxford. Charlie would go to Berlin airport, fly to Gatwick and half an hour later he'd be here. Patrick was often late because he had to get to Oxford, go into London, cross the city, get on the train to Brighton. He'd say, 'I'm really sorry. I set off at six o'clock this morning but I'm still not there because of delays on the trains...'

And people stay at my flat when we're rehearsing or whatever. It would obviously be easier if we all lived in Brighton. But maybe, in some ways, it's good to have the distance. You're not on top of each other all the time.

David Gedge

ANDREW SCHEPS

Turnover in the band happens quite a lot and it always seems to happen in weird places in the album cycle, where one guitar player will be recording songs written by the previous guitar player while writing songs for the next record which he may not play on. So there's a lot of overlap between musicians' contributions and whether they played the songs they write or write songs for the next people.

DAVID GEDGE

I named the album *Valentina* after a character in a weird Sixties comic book by the Italian writer Guido Crepax. I often steal names from popular culture for my titles and I just loved the word, really.

Valentina is just me exploring what people say to each other, how they say it, why they say it… set against a backdrop of guitar carnage...

The album was written throughout 2009, 2010 and 2011. It took longer than usual because I think the band members, quite admirably, wanted to make sure that we had enough high quality material. It was kind of a new line-up and I think they were worried about being compared to previous line-ups. A lot of what we

2012: Valentina and Tales

do is in the arrangement rehearsals, so when it comes to recording, the procedure is fairly simple. The main difference for this album was that we worked with some new people. It's always good to try different studios and different engineers and this time we recorded the band in Black Box Studios in France with David Odlum and Peter Deimel, and mixed it in Los Angeles with Andrew Scheps. Our requirements are actually pretty humble – good sounding equipment, good sounding rooms, and of course someone there who knows how to choose and place microphones and record the band in a way that captures the vitality and exhilaration in the sound. I think a lot of artists spend too long in the studio and end up with something which doesn't sound as good as the live performance. Andrew is exceptionally talented at doing things in the studio of which I know very little. I'm talking about equalisation, compression, reverb and lots of things of which I have no technical knowledge! The recordings we made in France were already sounding good, but I think Andrew sprinkled a little bit of magic dust over them. He looks like Gandalf from *The Lord Of The Rings*, so that's probably where I'm getting the magic dust metaphor from.

Nowadays I don't write the lyrics until I'm sure the music is finished. It takes me a long time to do the words and so, if the song ends up not being used because it didn't reach a high enough standard musically, then that time has been wasted. I learned that the hard way.

BRIGHTON MUSIC HALL
23 MARCH 2012, ALLSTON, MA, USA

ANDY MASCOLA

I'd seen the music video for the song 'Dalliance' whilst still in high school, and I'd spent a good part of the early Nineties enjoying *Seamonsters* while doing my best to track down the group's earlier releases. One such release, which I was excited to find in my local music shop, was a cut-out, discounted cassette copy of The Wedding Present's second LP, *Bizarro*. Because the 1984 Honda Accord I'd inherited on my sixteenth birthday only had a tape player, the treasured white RCA cassette with a hole punched clear through its case rarely left my car. Even after I'd sold the Honda and moved on to newer vehicles and music media formats through the years,

The Wedding Present

the *Bizarro* cassette was always a happy remembrance of driving around, sharing music with friends. It was this same cassette that I brought with me to the *Seamonsters* anniversary show in 2012.

Although barely spring in New England, the Brighton Music Hall was very hot that night. I was wearing a short sleeve polo along with my prized *Bizarro* cassette and a black Sharpie tucked into the breast pocket in the off-chance I might get an autograph from one of the band's members. After the opening act, the lights came up and I scanned the audience. After only a few minutes I spotted David Gedge walking briskly through the crowd, doing his best to keep a low profile. 'There he is,' I said to my wife. I swiftly pulled the cassette and Sharpie out of my pocket and jumped off the stool I'd been sitting on. 'Pardon me, Mister Gedge,' I said, stepping just in front of him. 'Would you please sign my cassette?' David politely took the cassette and Sharpie from me and opened the case. As he signed the orange j-card inside, he mumbled something about not seeing too many tapes around anymore. I laughed nervously, thanking him profusely after he'd handed the cassette and marker back. He smiled, nodded and continued to make his way through the crowd. I was ecstatic.

The Wedding Present's performance of *Seamonsters* that night was everything a fan of the record could hope for. The band replicated each of the songs in the order they appeared on the album without losing any of the dynamic touches that made each recorded track so special. It was a great night, one that my wife and I still talk about. I will always love The Wedding Present and will forever hold dear my copy of *Bizarro*, made even more special after being signed by the album's creator.

Onstage in Boston, 2012

2012: Valentina and Tales

CASBAH
30 MARCH 2012, SAN DIEGO, CA, USA

ESTHER YBARRONDO

I finally got to see The Wedding Present perform for the first time after all these years. I've been a fan for a long time although not from the very start. Very simply, I love the juxtaposition of David's music and lyrics of relationships, many we all relate to. His music is timeless and to see him in concert – well it could have been one I had attended many, many years ago. He's as youthful today in spirit, and he looks it as well. In this day and age of technology and social media, it's nice to see him engage with his loyal fans, and always accommodating. I'm just thankful he made the additional stop south of LA to San Diego during his 2012 tour. Long live Gedge and company!

Pepe le Moko in Boston, 2012

TROUBADOUR
31 MARCH 2012, LOS ANGELES, CA, USA

TERRY de CASTRO

The first time I saw The Wedding Present perform live was on 31 March 2012 at the Troubadour in Los Angeles, which is odd because I'd actually been at about 300 Wedding Present gigs before that. How could that be? Well, it started in 1998 after David finished recording the first Cinerama album, *Va Va Voom*, and asked me to do a gig and radio session as the bass player. Then, without much ado – or very many rehearsals – we almost immediately went to the States for our first mini-tour, which was a total blast. David wasn't convinced as it was a scrappy, disorganised tour but I was completely on board. The band got better and Cinerama continued to do more tours and recorded two more albums.

The Wedding Present

Correction: three more albums. As time went on Cinerama started to sound more and more like The Wedding Present, and when we recorded *Take Fountain* in 2004, it was initially intended to be a Cinerama record. But David made a decision that seems almost inevitable in hindsight and Cinerama became The Wedding Present circa 2005.

I found the whole thing incredibly exciting. One of the first gigs we did as The Wedding Present was at the Queen Margaret Union in Glasgow and it was by far the biggest concert I'd ever played. We'd just embarked on a massive tour that lasted almost a year and a half. David called it 'The Wedding Present B-to-Z' tour because it started in Belfast and ended in Zaragoza. I think there were 160 gigs on that tour, and we did many, many more over the next few years. It's possible that my gig count is more like 400. And I loved (almost) every minute of it. The camaraderie, the world travel and the gigs were some of the best times of my life. Having said that, the years of 20-hour drives, service-station sandwiches, cold venues, shared hotel rooms, 5am check-ins, 5am check-outs and graffiti-ridden dressing rooms finally wore me down, and I decided to pass on the bass torch. It wasn't an easy decision, but 2010's At The Edge Of The Sea festival ended up being my last Wedding Present gig. I celebrated the moment by jumping into the sea (we were right at the edge of it after all!) with our drummer, Charlie Layton, after the show. Two years went by before I saw my first Wedding Present concert.

The whole time I was touring with The Wedding Present I wondered what the band actually sounded like, which might seem strange, but I think it must be a fairly common experience for band members. Hearing recordings and seeing films isn't the same, and there's no way to re-create the feeling of being in the crowd – a Wedding Present crowd, that is. I have to say that from the perspective of the stage it looks like a lot of fun, and I finally got to be there on that spring night in Los Angeles. I certainly wasn't undaunted by the prospect of seeing the band for the first time after my departure – it felt a little bit like going to an ex-husband's engagement party. I was in high denial, gregarious, chatty, cheerful and let's be honest – absolutely hammered! I'd been to the famous Rainbow Bar and Grill in West Hollywood with my fella before the show and had a quite a bit more than a few. They were performing the brand new album *Valentina*, but as a kind of double-header, they were opening by also playing *Seamonsters* in its entirety. I was somewhat gutted by that, because *Seamonsters* was the one album I would have most enjoyed playing; it was my favourite. In fact, I was gutted about a few things, not least of all that the band members all got pay rises directly following my departure, and David decided to cut out all the hard, grueling drives and take flights to the far-away gigs. Also, rumour had it there

2012: *Valentina* and *Tales*

Those ever-shifting line-ups...

Wedding Present line-ups have been a fluctuating thing since 1988! So I'm used to it. But managing people and their expectations is really one of the hardest parts of my job. Everyone has to work together closely. And even with four people who, one year, love each other and play together really well... something will happen and the next year it'll be, 'It's not really working any more.' And it's hard to sometimes put a finger on why. It's a complicated dynamic within a band. You have these four distinct personalities and they all have varying relationships with each other.

And people change over the years, too... so their relationship with the band alters. And that might affect the way other people in the band are to them. It can also depend on what songs you're working on... are people inspired by the music? Do people like the new direction? There are so many factors. I think every line-up has had little eras where we've been an astoundingly good group. I'll tell people, 'This is the best line-up ever!' And then it'll go sour. You can often sense when someone's on the way out. It's got to the point now where I can almost predict the moment when people are going to leave because you can see their attention waning... they turn up to rehearsals not having properly prepared. Or they're generally miserable or argumentative.

But then something will change, someone else might quit and the unhappy person becomes friendly with the new member and that'll rejuvenate his or her interest. Or we'll go in a different direction musically that they're keener on. It's difficult to understand it sometimes. It's not just the band members, though. It's also their social network – girlfriends and boyfriends and husbands and wives and their mates. They're all part of the eco system. When the band's away for a long time the people left behind can resent it. 'Here's me, stuck at home, going to work to pay the bills while you're at an after-show party in LA!'

David Gedge

---

was now a single hotel room going spare that everyone got to enjoy on occasion. Wow, you look away for one minute and everything gets nice all of a sudden! Ha – I'm exaggerating (but it did amuse me).

The gig itself was looming and *Seamonsters* was about to be played. David made an announcement at the start that he wasn't going to speak in between songs because it was such an intense album that he just wanted to play it right the way through. I missed this announcement however, and was (remember I was completely sloshed) being... ahem... a bit boisterous. Someone in the audience asked me to either be quiet or move away. THAT was embarrassing, the idea that of all people in the audience, it was I who was disturbing someone. I felt guilty about it for a moment, but then

The Wedding Present

The Wedding Present, Rennes, 2012

remembered that David (tipsy) roared and guffawed with a mate through one of my performances – and I play acoustic.

I did feel guilty though, and I apologised to the guy, who seemed fine about it in the end. But here's what surprised me: I loved the gig. It was absolutely brilliant. *Seamonsters* was so exciting to see that I couldn't help myself shouting, 'I LOVE THIS ONE!' as each song started – I shouted it ten times. By the time 'Octopussy' came on I was in tears. Actually, I was nearly in tears the first time I played that song as well, live at Dingwall's in Camden in 2002 or something. I was about to burst into tears because I was so moved by playing the song, but right then someone's spilt beer sailed directly into my face (Dingwall's needed a barrier). But seeing *Seamonsters* live might just have been one of my best ever live gig experiences. And then they played the new songs from *Valentina*, which were absolutely cracking as well. After the gig, I got to hang out with all my mates (my former bandmates), which was genuinely exciting. I had to catch myself, though, when the son of producer Andrew Scheps wanted to meet the bass player. I was about to shake his hand (not really), but of course he meant Pepe. The evening was a bittersweet experience, but it was a huge high as well. In 2016,

378   SOMETIMES THESE WORDS JUST DON'T HAVE TO BE SAID

2012: *Valentina* and *Tales*

I even had the opportunity to dip my toe back in and play a couple of gigs with The Wedding Present again. When we were in the rehearsal room, I was so thrilled to be playing that before every song I'd shout, 'I LOVE THIS ONE!' But in 2012, I finally got to find out what The Wedding Present sounds like: phenomenal, in fact. And each subsequent time I've seen them play since then it has been a similar experience to the first time: like seeing one of my favourite bands play all of my favourite songs.

NORTHCOTE SOCIAL CLUB
14 APRIL 2012, MELBOURNE, AUSTRALIA

MATILDA REID

My partner bought *George Best* which in itself was amazing because there were only a few record stores that would stock or import alternative music in early Eighties Melbourne. We loved it straight away and for me the fast guitars and upbeat lyrics were my new found sound. I travelled to the UK in 1988 and was hoping to see The Wedding Present so when I arrived, and not seeing anything in the gig guides, I wrote them a letter to the address on the record cover. Trouble was, I had no address for myself – just 'poste restante'. I'd had no reply before heading off to Europe and sadly when I returned the post office told me I had received mail but they no longer had it. In 1995/96 my partner, daughter and I were living in London and we finally managed to catch them at some pub in north London. It was fantastic! The Northcote Social Club is not the largest venue but that's irrelevant when you're at the front. When we were all calling out for our faves I yelled '2, 3, Go!' 'Like the girl behind you,' he said. She was wearing that T-shirt. Somehow he suggested that me and the girl in the '2, 3, Go!' T-shirt should kiss – so we did! There's nothing like the joy of hearing your favourite songs live. The joy and love that is rock'n'roll. I bought a *Valentina* T-shirt and scored the setlist. David signed them and for a while I didn't feel 48! They came back in 2013 to do *George Best* and of course we went both nights. I got the setlists for both nights and got them signed. I feel totally personally responsible for the Australian tours and their success. I couldn't believe how he stood behind the merch desk as cool as you come.

The Wedding Present

KENNETH WELDIN

I grew up in Glasgow so it was the Barrowlands – the Barras. Over the years The Wedding Present always seemed to come calling around Guy Fawkes Night, and they always remembered the golden rule: play Glasgow on a Saturday night. I had a couple of brushes with the great man at that time when he visited the merch stall. 'Hi, how are you? Thanks for coming back. Could you sign this please? Could you play 'Go Out And Get Em, Boy!' please?' Seems innocent enough but it was Gedge. In front of me. He spoke to me.

Roll forward 27 years. Home is now Melbourne, Australia. The Weddoes are in town playing their first ever tour Down Under. Over the journey, I am into double figures with them. I cannot be more excited. I pressgang my gig buddy Mitch into coming – a Wedding Present virgin. I met Mitch at an Ian Brown gig in Melbourne and we have the same taste, so gig together. For about six years my wife never met Mitch. He was some bloke I went to concerts with.

Northcote Social Club is basically a room, no bigger than any scout hall you have ever been in but with an inner city hipster beer and deck on the side. Mitch is there, having had a crash course in The Wedding Present history in the preceding few months. *Valentina* has only been out in Oz for a fortnight but all the lyrics have been learned. They play with a vibrancy that belies their longevity. There's a crowd of middle aged balding expats, air guitars on their thighs, just about balancing a bottle of Victoria Bitter with their spare hand in a way that betrays their age. The band is great. The sound is great. The jokes between the songs are to the usual standard. *Valentina* is immense. *Seamonsters* back to back is simply fantastic. They end with 'You Should Always Keep In Touch With Your Friends'. It can't get better than that, can it?

In the far left corner of the room is the merch table. Queuing up I get the *Valentina* book and Mitch the *Hit Parade* double CD. David signs both. Despite the state of my voice after two hours of going full tilt, David recognises my accent. 'Yes, I used to watch you in the Barrowlands.' 'Great place to play – I enjoyed it.' A bit later on, I head off to the gents. On my way in, the door opens and I step aside to let the person out. It's David. He recognises me from the merch stall and then goes on to chat. 'So how long you been in Australia for?' And we chatted. Brilliant. He was basically interviewing me – David Gedge was asking me questions. I am not sure how long it was but it could have been five minutes. 300 seconds. Me. Gedge.

2012: Valentina and Tales

A stairway. Outside the gents. Him asking me stuff. My bladder exploding. To avoid embarrassing myself, eventually I had to say, 'Sorry, but I need to go!' Later, downstairs, we see him sashaying his way through the bar crowd on the deck, glass of red in his hand. Totally cool. My hero.

JOHN PEEL CENTRE FOR CREATIVE ARTS

25 MAY 2012, STOWMARKET, UK

RACHEL BENNETT

I was right at the front and The Wedding Present were immense! Mid-set, David Gedge pointed at me and said, 'I know you, don't I?' He knows who I am!

AT THE EDGE OF THE PEAKS FESTIVAL

26 AUGUST 2012, HOLMFIRTH, UK

JON PINDER

I was lodging with an old school friend in Headingley. I'd recently met my now fiancée and mother of my two children, but at the time we were still in early days of the relationship. The gig was on August bank holiday Sunday. The Friday before was my 40th birthday. We'd been out drinking all weekend and, after two days of solid alcohol intake, we'd fallen out on the Saturday night although I stayed over. I got up really early to drive back to Leeds, leaving before she awoke and not knowing if I still had a girlfriend. I spent a few very nervous hours getting to Holmfirth on public transport not knowing if she'd ever talk to me again. Eventually, I plucked up the courage to text her and apologise for whatever it was I'd said to be greeted with a warmish response, which was the best I could hope for. It cheered me up anyway, as did the beer festival

The Wedding Present

at the local brewery that was also happening that day. I ended up going back to the beer festival after The Wedding Present to watch a blues band, and had to pay £50 for a taxi home. Brilliant day though!

O2 ACADEMY
31 OCTOBER 2012, BRISTOL, UK

KERRY ROSS

It was pouring with rain and, as we walked into the venue, I saw DLG hanging out by the merch stand. I was 39 and had been a fan since I was 17. Ridiculously starstruck, I'd never met or talked to him before but plucked up courage and went in to have my photo taken, which he very graciously agreed to. As he put an arm around me for the photo, he got wet on my sodden jacket. He said to me, 'Still raining then.' I apologised and took my jacket off for the picture, and afterwards, faced with my musical hero of many years, could not think of anything to say apart from, 'I'm sorry I'm wet.' I didn't even realise what I'd said until my friend told me at the bar; I was too chuffed to care!

ROISIN DUBH
3 NOVEMBER 2012, GALWAY, IRL

CHRIS MEEHAN

What a gig! I shook David's hand and called him a legend. I roared at my mate Kev to get a pic. I walked through the crowd holding Gedge's hand as Kev roared, 'It's on video mode you twat.' There I was, walking through the crowd as my hero David Gedge tried desperately to get away from me – ha ha! I used to play 'Mars Sparkles Down On Me' for a year during a tough time. The greatest, most underrated songwriter of all time. 'Brassneck' makes me violent (not really), 'End Credits' makes me silent, and 'Heather' makes me thank God I moved on. My favourite band of all time. I thank God for The Wedding Present and thank David for his lyrics about my life.

2012: Valentina and Tales

GLENN CAMPBELL

Where do I start? I've been listening to and watching The Wedding Present live since 1989. I am from Kildare, Ireland but have lived in Sydney, Australia for the last 19 years. There are so many songs and albums that take me back to my youth or different points in my life and so many highlights, especially my first overseas trips which included both Phoenix (complete with riots) and Reading festivals. One highlight was hearing *Seamonsters* live for the first time at the SFX in Dublin. It was at this gig that I bumped into a guy from Waterford College where I studied that I'd seen around but never knew. We chatted about gigs and bands and continued to bump into each other at Wedding Present gigs. Seeing The Wedding Present live at the Annandale Hotel in Sydney was unreal, an iconic venue that is sadly no longer a rock venue. It was even more memorable as it was *Seamonsters* live and I got to introduce my wife to The Wedding Present live. And to finish with, 'You Should Always Keep In Touch With Your Friends'. It was just so emotional, being so far from home and all the friends I grew up with, seeing them live. We decided to go see The Wedding Present in Ireland as it coincided with my 40th so I got to see them again with my friends in Dublin and Galway. In the mosh near the end of the Roisin Dubh gig, I bumped into the guy from college that I never saw outside of the gigs and hadn't seen in 23 years. I couldn't believe it. The mutual grins on our faces was priceless and we got to swap gig stories once again. Hopefully The Wedding Present keep in touch and it never ends...

O2 ACADEMY
8 NOVEMBER 2012, LIVERPOOL, UK

ALEX BOARDMAN

Two very muscly dudes, shirts off, were dancing aggressively (but knew all the words, surprisingly) and were annoying the fuck out of everyone at the front of the gig. About halfway through, one of them stood on the barrier at the front of the stage and attempted to stage dive on everyone he'd been annoying. He jumped, the crowd parted and he hit the floor with a huge bump right in front of me. He and his mate went and sat, dazed at the side and everyone was very happy. Prick!

The Wedding Present

JUNCTION
21 NOVEMBER 2012, CAMBRIDGE, UK

KARL KATHURIA

I took my eldest daughter – only the second gig she'd been to with me, the first being Busted and McFly. We chatted to David but she was utterly unimpressed by him and didn't immediately become yet another massive fan. Far more exciting to her was getting to speak to the support band, Toquiwa, who she seemed to fall immediately in love with, especially when they said she had 'lovely hair'.

KOKO
23 NOVEMBER 2012, LONDON, UK

ANDY WALLIS

My friends are all big Wedding Present fans. I'm the 'one who gets the tickets'. The Wedding Present to me are just a band that have always been there. I've loved them since I was 14. I remember hearing 'This Boy Can Wait' and being hooked. I have played the music at all times, been to see them live countless times and just had the best times with my friends – taking my vinyl to my friends' indie nights and enjoying people loving hearing 'Kennedy' and 'Brassneck'; getting the landlord of the pub we used to frequent to put more Wedding Present on the jukebox so we could have a jump about and talking to David at his At The Edge Of The Sea festival and ending up talking to him about the mods.

I also remember the *Seamonsters* tour at Koko but for all the wrong reasons. As usual, I had sorted the tickets but, three days before the gig, my elderly cat was trying to wee on the kitchen floor. I grabbed him, and he bit me, causing an infection. My hand was very red so I went to my local minor injuries clinic thinking that antibiotics might be needed. I was sent straight to the Royal Free Hospital where I had to stay in for two nights. The Wedding Present were at Koko playing *Seamonsters* and I was at the top of the hill in a hospital bed and on a drip, with my hand in the air.

2013-2014: EPs And Re-Releases

After releasing the *4 Chansons EP* in 2012, 2013 saw The Wedding Present release a four song EP in German, followed in 2014 by one in Welsh. 2014 also saw the re-release of eight Wedding Present albums in extended editions with rare and previously unheard tracks.

MAXWELL'S

8 FEBRUARY 2013, HOBOKEN, NJ, USA

MATT GRAY

One of my favourite Wedding Present memories began with my friend Dominic calling me at work from Hoboken, New Jersey, USA. Dom had only recently moved to the US from Singapore. I mentioned I was seeing The Wedding Present that night at KOKO, adding 'I think they are playing Hoboken next year.' 'What – Maxwell's? That is four blocks from here' replied Dom. Checking the Scopitones website I confirmed it was Maxwell's. Dominic said, 'Get two tickets.' Like a pre-programmed weak-minded fool I purchased two tickets, suddenly coming to the conclusion that one of the tickets was for me. Three months later I found myself in Hoboken, New Jersey joined by not only Dominic but also Dan and Simon, two other English friends living Stateside. Then there was the blizzard. Well, that is how US news channels described it. We had spent the day in NYC as the snow began to fall. As we made our way back to Hoboken the snow was getting deeper. Twitter confirmed the gig was going ahead. Arriving at Maxwell's the four of us resembled snowmen.

Brushing ourselves down and being typical Brits, we headed to the bar before going into the room where the gig was. On entering the back room one thing came very apparent, either news did not filter through to other

Live at the Tokyo O-Nest, 2013

ticket holders that the gig was on or Americans are just scared of a bit of snow. The gig became quite an intimate show by Wedding Present standards. DLG was in top form, jesting with the audience that the snow was nothing compared to gigs in Scotland and that Americans were soft. He moved on to talking about the Blitz in World War II, with another dig about the Yanks joining too late and trying to take all the glory. Simon dropped his phone while taking a photograph. David told him, 'You don't want to drop that – I heard they are expensive.' This made Simon's night and he said if that had happened when he was 15 years old he would have been the talk of his school. I pointed out that owning a mobile phone in 1989 would have been a bigger deal than David talking to him. The highlight of the gig was a blinding version of 'Deer Caught In The Headlights'. After the gig and a few drinks, we made our way back to Dom's apartment, chucking snowballs at each other. My first experience of seeing The Wedding Present in a different country was fantastic. The next night Dom and I did go the Bowery Ballroom in NYC for the gig there. It was great, but not quite the night before. I did get to speak with David afterwards, something I had not done since writing (very bad) fanzines in my late teens. He was polite and warm, as he was when I was a dim-witted kid asking stupid questions. The Wedding Present's music evolves in a great way, but David still remains one of the most charming 'rock stars' I have had the pleasure to meet.

STEPHEN WARD

I moved to the USA in 2005 as a soccer coach, met Nicole and we got married in 2009. Nicole was a reluctant Wedding Present fan at first but liked a few songs and loved the gigs and banter David had with the crowd. We were expecting our second child. The Wedding Present were touring the States and were playing Hoboken and New York in early February. I got tickets for both nights for me and Nicole. I figured she should have had our child and be suitably recovered by then. I presumed wrong.

The due date was put back and I started to worry as Nicole was taken into hospital on the day before The Wedding Present were to play Hoboken. Do I choose David and the gang over my second-born? A snow storm started and the weathermen were predicting two feet of snow and I figured I wouldn't have to choose. Surely the gig would be cancelled?

Nicole gave birth to our daughter in the afternoon and by early evening – with the blessing of my wonderful wife – I was in the car on the road up to Hoboken as the snow started to get thicker. An hour later I had parked up and was wading through the snowdrifts to an almost empty Maxwell's. All the smart people had stayed home. It was great. I spotted David by the merch stall and headed over for a chat. In an empty venue we chatted for a while before he said, 'Would you mind watching the merchandise stall while I go onstage?' 'Of course,' I replied. And off he went to thrash through the set.

I never sold anything as there were so few people there and, besides, The Wedding Present were onstage and the few that were in Maxwell's were watching. I was kinda hoping/dreaming he would ask me to pick up a guitar and join them onstage for a couple of numbers but it wasn't to be. But for that 90-minute set, I truly felt like a member of The Wedding Present! Sad I know, but after I left and started to dig my car out of the snow drifts with my bare hands, and on the gruelling and stressful three hour long journey through whiteout conditions watching even the snow ploughs slide off the road, I reflected on my day.

A beautiful daughter, Nola, followed by an almost personal Wedding Present gig in which I worked for the band. I felt like it was worth the effort and undoubted grief I would get from the in-laws for leaving my wife in the maternity ward.

The Wedding Present

BOWERY BALLROOM
9 FEBRUARY 2013, NEW YORK CITY, USA

NICOLA JEAKINS

My boyfriend Paul and I booked a romantic weekend in New York City. We love music and decided to have a look to see if there were any gigs on during our stay. To his delight we discovered that The Wedding Present were playing The Bowery Ballroom.

I had never heard of The Wedding Present but Paul explained to me that it was one of his favourite bands, along with The Smiths and The Fall.

When we arrived in the Bowery, we had a walk around the venue and spotted David Gedge standing at the bottom of a stairway chatting to another couple. I said to Paul, 'Why don't you go and say, 'Hi' to him and tell him you have come all the way from Wales to New York to see him and perhaps have a photo taken with him?' Paul said he couldn't talk to him and wouldn't know what to say.

BOTTOM OF THE HILL
16 & 17 FEBRUARY 2013, SAN FRANCISCO, CA, USA

KERRY ROSS

After seeing them in Bristol in 2012, I got a bit obsessed with seeing them again and quickly booked for their next Bristol date the following May, at The Fleece. I then noticed that on my 40th birthday, they would be playing in San Francisco for two nights.

After exhausting various friends as options to come with me, I decided that I'd regret it if I didn't go so booked a holiday to San Francisco on my own. The thing that had put me off holidaying alone in the past is – what to do in the evening? I knew that two of the five nights I had booked I would be seeing my favourite band, in a room with lots of people I had at least one thing in common with. After struggling to book tickets, and tweeting David to ask him whether it had sold out, he messaged me to save me tickets on the door. On the first of the two nights, I walked into the venue and

2013–2014: EPs And Re-Releases

saw David again at the merch. I walked over to thank him for his help with the ticket and he asked what I was doing in San Francisco and I explained I came just to see the band. He then offered me a lift home from the venue in the tour bus which I accepted on both nights. They were all fantastic; made me feel so welcome and introduced me to some fantastic Wedding Present fans who I now consider friends. On the tour bus I started campaigning Charlie to put one of my favourite songs on the setlist for The Fleece in the May and they played both songs that I asked for – 'Niagara' and 'Bewitched' – and David talked to me from the stage during their set. It's not just the music, although that's fantastic. I was on holiday alone and it was my best birthday so far.

KING'S ARMS HOTEL

21 FEBRUARY 2013, AUCKLAND, NZ

BEN PEARSON

I must confess to being a relative newcomer to the band, having been (only very slightly!) too young to have caught them in their Eighties/Nineties heyday. I have since seen David and Co. half a dozen times or so now. Every show really has been wonderful. I think we've been lucky to have nearly always caught Gedge in a good mood both onstage and at merch duties – belying the fabled grumpiness.

My first show was on the *Bizarro* reissue tour and a favourite, if only for being the only time I have ever seen 'Take Me!' played live. We've requested it from Charlie at every show since but to no avail! Three of us had booked a trip to New Zealand for an England cricket tour and, out of the blue, our friend Ellis casually mentions that The Wedding Present are playing in Auckland. Quite how Ellis, who is generally unaware of any gig listings on our doorstep in Reading let alone on the other side of the world, found this out remains unclear. And there was surely no way the gig would coincide with our tour itinerary?

But yes – The Wedding Present would be playing their first ever NZ gig in a pub in Auckland. And we were starting our trip in Auckland and it was our one free evening in the city. It was the most brilliant coincidence.

The Wedding Present

CHINNERYS

11 JULY 2013, SOUTHEND-ON-SEA, UK

LEE MORGAN

I was lucky enough to interview David for his gig in Southend. He was great! Funny, knowledgeable and, even though he had probably been asked the same questions before many times, he answered each one with the same enthusiasm as if it was the first time he'd heard it. He also asked me which was the best chip shop in Southend!

AT THE EDGE OF THE SEA FESTIVAL

24 AUGUST 2013, BRIGHTON, UK

MATT MILLERSHIP
Tensheds

As I've played most of my career solo – in a piano ballad style – when David Gedge saw us at At The Edge Of The Sea, a heavy, punky blues outfit came as a bit of a surprise to him, I think. In a deadpan voice, completely calmly, he said, 'Oh, that wasn't what I was expecting.'

SLADE ROOMS

22 OCTOBER 2013, WOLVERHAMPTON, UK

'GRAMP'

Over the past few years I'd been doing a lot of photography, working with quite a few local unsigned bands both promo and live, mostly in the Slade Rooms. I'd also been lucky enough to shoot some of my fave bands, as there seemed to be an influx of the old guard going out on the road again. So I sent a cheeky email, asking if it would be possible to get a photo pass for the gig, and was

2013–2014: EPs And Re-Releases

Live at the Shepherds Bush Empire, November 2013

dumbfounded to receive a reply from DLG saying yes. A few days before the gig, DLG was saying there may not be vinyl for sale on the tour as TNT had 'lost' them. Via Twitter I messaged him to say that I ran my own transport company. I could send a van to collect the vinyl if it was located and I'd bring it with me to the gig. In the end TNT found the vinyl and the band were able to collect it en route from Brighton to Wolverhampton. At the gig I bumped into DLG, introduced myself, thanked him for the photo pass and proceeded to have a conversation about transport. Here I was, chatting with the singer with one of my fave bands – the band I saw on my 18th – talking about bloody transport!

GLEE CLUB
23 OCTOBER 2013, CARDIFF, UK

PAUL EMANUEL

A group of us were to travel up to Cardiff from west Wales to see the *Hit Parade* tour, effectively a home gig as it was only an hour's travel away. My best

The Wedding Present

One more from the Shepherds Bush Empire, November 2013

mate Dylan rang me after I finished work to say he was in Casualty after injuring his leg in work, and was not going to be able to make the gig. He was gutted. The rest of us travelled up to the gig, and Dylan sent me a text message to say he was home from hospital on crutches, and with some strong pain killers. On arriving at the venue and getting some drinks in, I noticed that David Gedge had assumed his usual pre-gig position at the merchandise stall. I approached him, relayed the story of my friend, and asked if he would mind speaking to him to try and cheer him up. David seemed a little bemused but kindly agreed. So I rang Dylan and, after enquiring about his leg, said there was someone at the venue who would like to speak to him and passed the phone to David. David said, 'Hi Dylan, this is David Gedge from The Wedding Present' and then proceeded to chat to Dylan about his injured leg. Half an hour later, Dylan sent me a text checking that it was not a wind up!

2013-2014: EPs And Re-Releases

O2 ACADEMY

29 OCTOBER 2013, LIVERPOOL, UK

LINDA HALSALL

Every tour David seems to forget or run out of something. In 2013 it was aftershave balm. The tweet went out, unanswered and unfulfilled for a week or so. So when it came to Liverpool I found a shop in Crosby that sold it and took it to the gig. Jessica gave me a now much-treasured beanie hat in return and David thanked me just before playing 'Real Thing'.

NINES

25 MAY 2014, BARROW-IN-FURNESS, UK

DAVID GEDGE

We've always had a policy of seeking out new and interesting places to play. We were offered a concert in Barrow-in-Furness, once. I had never heard of bands playing in Barrow-in-Furness and so I said, 'Yes, I'd love to do that.' And it was a great night. I think sometimes with places where bands don't often play... that aren't on the rock 'n' roll touring map, so to speak... the concerts are better because people are more enthusiastic. If you live in London you can see a hundred bands every night. Having said that our London shows are usually good!

TRAMLINES FESTIVAL

25 JULY 2014, SHEFFIELD, UK

MEL LAMPRO
Braver Than Fiction

Another Wedding Present fan had asked via Twitter if the bands playing Tramlines with The Wedding Present could give David a hug. The gig was at The Leadmill and my band, Braver Than Fiction, were opening up both the

The Wedding Present

venue for the Tramlines weekend and for The Wedding Present. I was a little in awe as I wandered backstage, up the stairs and past the open door of The Wedding Present's dressing room. There was the man himself but I hesitated as I didn't want to disturb him before a show. Instead, I waited until after the gig. When David came over to help out on The Wedding Present's merch stall next to ours, I mentioned to him what had transpired. He was an absolute sweetheart and made sure to make a point of coming to find me at the very end of the night and pose (mid hug) for a quick snap. What a gent!

TRADES CLUB

26 JULY 2014, HEBDEN BRIDGE, UK

MALCOLM WYATT

Before we knew it, David and Pete's homage to Quo's '25 years in the business' had new meaning, the band themselves celebrating a glorious 30 years. The last time I saw them was on a cracking summer's evening at Hebden Bridge Trades Club. I was lucky enough to interview David that night and took a while preparing, only to realise that most of my questions were in fact statements, giving him little to get his teeth into. There's the mark of a man you feel you know so well and respect so much. As it was, the lighting was too dim to properly see my prompts anyway and, pretty soon, the support's sound check drowned us out. It didn't matter though – David was as engaging as I'd expected. Top man all round. And what a night that was, at a characterful venue where you're sweating like hell and being jolted around so much you might as well dance. David definitely felt the heat, while loanee guitarist Sam – in for Patrick – was staring at his tortured fingers, seemingly in shock. Playing guitar so passionately can't be good for the health. Yet bass player Katharine's cool suggested it was all just par for the course. Similarly, there was no respite for Charlie on drums, while Danielle sneaked on and off to add keyboard and sublime harmonies, looking embarrassed as she returned to take the applause. I'm not sure where those four fitted in on the scale of The Wedding Present employee numbers but they all had the spirit of the initial 'Bramley Gateshead Hassocks Middleton' line-up I first witnessed and loved. Another night of Wedded bliss was soon behind me, but I was still on a high as I climbed the Pennines after a perfect night in Yorkshire's Happy Valley.

2013-2014: EPs And Re-Releases

AT THE EDGE OF THE SEA FESTIVAL

23 AUGUST 2014, BRIGHTON, UK

CATHERINE KONTZ
French For Cartridge

I first met David Gedge when I was asked to provide some keyboards for the last couple of John Peel sessions through our friend Kari Paavola, who used to play with Cinerama and The Wedding Present. I had lots of fun at BBC Maida Vale playing the inside of the piano and doing my best at the Hammond while the drummer, Graeme, operated the Leslie speaker.

A few years later we did a tour of libraries with French For Cartridge and David was in the audience (or actually, pretty much the only audience). He thought our set-up of toy pianos, reed organs, megaphones and masquerade costumes would be a great opener for his festival, so we found ourselves in Brighton a few months later for At The Edge Of The Sea. Good memories.

GREENSIDE HOTEL

29 AUGUST 2014, LESLIE, UK

STEVEN GRAY

I've seen The Wedding Present twice in my local pub in Leslie, Fife up in Scotland. Two of the best nights of my life. Not only that, but I got to speak to David after the gig both times. I was absolutely nervous approaching him, but he was so easy to talk to and I also got him to sign stuff and got photos with him. He's a great guy who's always got time to speak to fans and even hangs about at the merchandise stall. Not many front men would do that. The first time was a time machine gig, as David called it, with previous members of The Wedding Present. Paul Dorrington was playing that night for the first time in years and they did an amazing version of 'Flying Saucer'.

The Wedding Present

THE LAST BIG WEEKEND FESTIVAL

30 AUGUST 2014, GLASGOW, UK

PAUL DORRINGTON

It was a weird thing but a nice thing to get a message from David. We were at a garage rock festival called Hipsville down south and I got a text from him saying, 'Emma Pollock who used to be in The Delgados has asked me to take part in this festival in Glasgow. I've turned her down twice already and I really don't want to turn her down again but our drummer, bass player and guitarist are all booked up and completely unavailable. It's a bit of a weird thing but would you want to do it and maybe ask Diane if she wanted to play bass?' And I said, 'Well, she has never played bass before. She plays guitar. But I'll ask her.'

So my girlfriend and I joined the band for about a week, rehearsing and playing a couple of gigs, and Diane got to experience a slice of what it's like being in The Wedding Present. From David's point of view, back twenty years ago, it was always part of the DIY ethic that everybody's girlfriend who wanted to work was in. David's girlfriend at the time was the roadie and driver. Keith's girlfriend did the merchandising. And I think Peter's girlfriend used to do merchandising as well. So it was always like, 'Well, if everyone can just bring their other halves along on tour it all makes life a bit happier and easier.' So when he said, 'Oh, if you want to do this one-off gig and bring your girlfriend as well, she can do it too' it was 'Well, yeah. She'll finally find out what it's like to be stuck in a van driving from Brighton to Edinburgh in one day.'

So we drive up to Edinburgh from David's and stayed in a hotel there. We had a day's practice or perhaps two days and then it was the gig. Because the drummer was based in Scotland, the only way to get this new one-off band to practice for more than one day was to go up to Scotland. The setlist was half *Seamonsters* and half *Hit Parade*. Loads of fans just went mad. They were like, 'It's just like the old days!' It was a very time-travelly few days. It was fun, though. It was good. It was fun hanging out with David and everyone else for a week, a little bit nostalgic, but in a way it felt quite natural just slipping back into it. It had been twenty years since I'd played any of the songs but, weirdly, after about an hour's practice I could remember them all. It's like you can never leave!

2013–2014: EPs And Re-Releases

Left to right: Katharine Wallinger, David Gedge, Patrick Alexander and Charles Layton
Photo: Jessica McMillan

RIVER ROOMS
12 SEPTEMBER 2014, STOURBRIDGE, UK

KAREY PARSONS

I saw them at The River Rooms, a strange unit on an industrial estate under a pizza takeaway but it was bloody brilliant and the sound was surprisingly fantastic. I was on a weird ledge which meant I could see really well and dance in an unusually unrestrained manner, and someone below the ledge tapped me on the arm mid-gig and said I seemed to be enjoying myself. I think he was being nice, although I wasn't too sure. He was probably just worried I'd fall on him and knock him out.

At the O2 Academy in Birmingham, I was at the edge of the moshpit, doing a pitiful job of moshing, and, afterwards a very nice bloke behind me said I'd whacked him in the balls a couple of times with something very heavy in my bag, but he was very understanding about it. Appropriately the 'something heavy' was a copy of The Peel Sessions book that I'd just bought in a charity shop. Watching indie music is still largely the preserve of middle-aged men who can get a bit fighty when they go to see a band from their youth, but I'm delighted that there's a strong female following for the Weddoes, which is always really noticeable at At The Edge Of The Sea. I went on my

The Wedding Present

own in 2014. I'd been with mates before, but no one could make it the next year and it was actually rather brilliant to go alone. Mr Gedge probably won't want to hear this but I went alone this year too and haven't asked anyone else. I loved it so much as a lone music experience!

I was largely skint in the late Eighties and early Nineties. Although I bought all the albums, I couldn't afford many of the singles. So I'm really enjoying gathering 12"s from second hand record shops now and the joy of playing them is sublime. It's hard to think of a favourite song – there are so many! I first became aware of them when I saw the video of 'Why Are You Being So Reasonable Now?' so that's always been a favourite. I love the obvious ones like 'Brassneck', 'Kennedy', 'Dalliance', 'My Favourite Dress' and 'Corduroy'. 'Loveslave' is a favourite from *Hit Parade* – with its extraordinary video! – and 'Make Me Smile (Come Up And See Me)' is one of my favourite covers ever.

I know I'm missing some important ones out but I've been listening to all of these a lot recently – 'Don't Take Me Home Until I'm Drunk', 'Interstate 5' (brilliant videos) and 'Mars Sparkles Down On Me', just because it's beautiful. And I love 'Always The Quiet One', because I so often am.

ELIZABETH EDGE

It was quite a surprise to hear The Wedding Present were playing here in Stourbridge and to begin with I questioned whether it was a covers band. But I was so excited when I realised it was them! Anyway the gig was ace and I lost myself in the black sea of the crowd and indulged in a few tipples. After they left the stage, I migrated over to the merchandise stand where, unknown to me then, Jessica was standing. I smiled and chatted. I then saw David and, with the courage of those aforementioned tipples, I approached him. We exchanged pleasantries. I then just asked him bluntly 'Do you wear jewellery?' When he answered, 'No' with a wry smile, I said, 'Oh, that's a shame. I'm a jewellery designer and maker and I'm especially looking into men's jewellery.' I went on to explain what I was working on at that time, showing him my work on my phone. At points people were coming up to David for photographs and I ended up in a few of them. He then said, 'Have you got a business card?' I hadn't and I was gutted, as so many people had told me to get some done. He then went on to explain that he and Jessica were getting married and would I make the ring? I couldn't believe where this conversation had led! I had to scrawl my contact details on an old receipt I found in my pocket with a Sharpie pen David lent me. I then returned to my husband and friends, not quite registering what had just happened!

I woke up the next day and promptly tweeted The Wedding Present, apologising that I didn't have a business card and was it all real? We then started conversations and it turned out Jessica liked a certain design I did, so I had her finger size and I hand made the gold wedding ring for her. I found a sweet little box for it and we arranged a time to meet up. We met in Brighton, and I stayed with a good friend of mine. I met Jessica and David in a great tea shop where we had lunch and I presented Jessica with the ring hoping that a) she liked it and b) it fitted (which is always my concern when making rings for people). It turned out that a) she loved it and b) it did fit! Phew! We had a great chat and lunch, although I unfortunately was unable to eat as I'd been out the night before around Brighton with my good friend, which amused David. It was great to hear David's stories of early times with The Wedding Present and about staying focused. They sent me a photo of themselves together after the wedding, Jessica wearing the ring that I made.

CLAPHAM GRAND

14 NOVEMBER 2014, LONDON, UK

NICK FROST, ACTOR

How time flies. The year is 1989. Comrade Thatcher's iron grip is finally loosening. Arsenal win the league and Stock, Aitken and Waterman run rampant across the British popscape. I was a gentle soul as a young man. A bit of a mummy's boy; liked a hot bath and the comfort of my own bed. Angsty, fragile. Frequently bathing in the luke-warm gloom of unrequited love.

I stood at a bar in Reading town centre mumbling my order for the obligatory pint of snakebite and black, my long greasy hair acting as a shield from the world. I was here at the festival to see The Wedding Present. Sadly, I never made it that far. I think the biggest mistake I made was drinking too much. The pub had asked us to leave when our collection of plastic pint glasses (by now almost five feet high from the top of the table) had toppled onto a young Maltese glass collector who later, sadly, died. We'd been drinking for six hours and when we got back to the camp it was a lot busier. A lot busier. Not one

The Wedding Present

inch of space was left. Some bigger boys had pitched tents nearby and were playing catch with a tennis ball, loudly calling each other 'helmets'. Nervously, I make an excuse and lolloped off to do a chud. After a 15-minute walk over Somme-like conditions, mud, shit, bodies strewn here and there, confusion reigns now. A bearded man with no pants on is laughing loudly at me while he does the Diavlo really high, really near to me, willy flapping like a sports-sock filled with gravel. It was horrible. And the toilybox itself was a literal shit hole. A pyramid of oily plops peeking at me over the seat as I walked in. No. This isn't right. I'd never done anything like this. I was out of my depth. It was barely 5pm. What was it going to be like after dark? Oh god.

I started to get the wobbles. I wish I was at home with mum washing my hair (something she did till I was 33). Feet up. Smell of the Breville wafting in from the kitchen. A man walks by chewing on what looks to be a chimp's wrist. I heave and there, in my watery-eyed, drunken haze, the idea I'd been searching for, the moment of clarity. 'Fuck this. Go home.' And I did. Right there and then. I left my groundsheet and sleeping bag and I ran. I missed all those great bands, Inspiral Carpets, Ride, Nick Cave And The Bad Seeds... and I regret it. I regretted it, for a long while. As Mum was picking me up from the station, wee sodden and stinking like cider vom, my biggest regret that weekend... I missed The Wedding Present. The only band I really wanted to see. He sang songs about me. About us. About them, about the girls that wiped their mouths after we kissed. Wounded knees, broken hearts and, every once in a while, stopping to take the time to look at the stark architecture of a post- industrial north. And I had missed it.

The year is now 2014. David Cameron has our NHS in a stranglehold. Chelsea run rampant in the Premier League and One Direction continue their assault on hearts and minds. On a cab ride through Clapham I notice a sign hanging off the front of the Clapham Grand. It tells me that The Wedding Present will be here on Friday. I quickly phone my friend and we clear the decks for Friday night. I email David Gedge, excited and babbling. Surely now there is nothing to stop me from seeing them. David emails me a little while later to say the gig is in two months. Oh. I think a homeless person was standing in front of that bit of the sign. Balls.

Two months later... My friend and me are nestled in a nook drinking beer and gin. We are hidden in a corner, watching people. Old people. Older people. A drunk randomly trying to make conversation asks me if I like music. It's such a generic question that we get the giggles. I start to notice familiar faces, not familiar like I know them; it's more like I feel like I knew them. The closer I look, the more I recognise: at first it's just hair, a 46 year old man sporting curtains, soft

2013-2014: EPs And Re-Releases

IT tummies peeping out of tight 'Carter' T-shirts bleached with age.

Often in pubs I get a weird feeling that I don't belong, that I shouldn't be here, a sad by-product of the job I do. But I don't feel that here. I feel a sense of belonging, a sense that we, all the forty something men and woman in this room, are kindred spirits. Once inside my eyes begin to play tricks on me. 'Wow, everyone's so old,' my 25 year old friend pipes up. 'No they're not!' They are. I hate her. She's the youngest one here. I don't know how to feel. It's like I've been swept up in a time fart. My present is here, all right, but, oddly, so is my past, both existing at the same time.

There are good things and bad things about doing films. Being shown to a private box just ten feet above the stage is definitely one of them. There is a large cupboard, which we immediately rifle through. It's empty. Mid-rifle, we're interrupted by a burly soundman. 'Oi! The upper circle's closed tonight, you have to... oh, it's you. Sorry... as you were!' (Another good thing: you can get away with murder. Not literally though, right? Guys?) The lights dim and a wave of excitement ripples through the room. From up here I can't see one Zimmer frame. It's wonderful.

The gang come out and it's on. I'd waited 25 years for this moment and it was worth every second. At first I think it's my eyes and brain and the stench of the time-guff fucking with me but it isn't, it's actually happening – the crowd begin to pogo. For the next hour we dance and sway and sing our hearts out. I look down at the crowd and the Zimmers are gone, smiling faces, hair curtains swaying back and forth and for a brief moment in time we're back. I turn to speak to my friend but she's not there. A baby sits, happily gurgling in a pile of big clothes. The year is 1989...

David with Shaun Of The Dead *and* Hot Fuzz *actor and Wedding Present fan Nick Frost Photo: Jessica McMillan*

SOMETIMES THESE WORDS **JUST DON'T HAVE TO BE SAID**   401

The Wedding Present

2015-2016: *Going Going... Still Here*

2015 saw Cinerama release their version of The Wedding Present's 2012 album *Valentina*, showcased at Islington's O2 Academy. This was followed in 2016 by the release of *Going Going...*, the ninth studio album by The Wedding Present.

O2 ACADEMY ISLINGTON

6 JUNE 2015, LONDON, UK

LEE JAMES HORREY

I have lived in Italy since 1998 so don't get to see The Wedding Present or Cinerama as much as I would like, but I have managed to see them every couple of years, especially since they started doing their 'album' tours (*George Best* in Paris, *Bizarro* in Varese, *Seamonsters* in Cambridge, *Watusi* in London, *Saturnalia* in Cambridge). Often you see the bands only on the stage but, with The Wedding Present, you know you will get the chance to meet David at the merchandise stand. However, what I didn't expect was bumping into him a couple of other times, in a restaurant in Paris before the gig, having the band meal, and then being interviewed; and in Varese, just walking past him and Jessica in the street, a couple of hours before the gig – me with a wider grin of recognition, him looking sheepish and slightly nervous I was going to intrude on his time off. Hearing 'Honey Rider' as it was meant to be in June in London was a definite highlight and something I waited about 17 years for. My holidays are geared around a gig whenever they announce a tour and I am looking forward to introducing my kids to the live shows at some point in the near future.

2015-2016: *Going Going... Still Here*

DAVID POYTON

I can see myself on the Cinerama DVD from Islington. I ended up buying six tickets for that gig – I couldn't remember buying the first two, lost the email reference for the next and bought them again in case the transaction didn't go through. I found four unused tickets in my computer room drawer the other day. Oh well – it was still worth the £400 plus that it cost me in hotel, travel, beer money and, er – extra tickets!

NICKY VIGNOLI

A friend said he had seen this band and never seen guitars played as fast. They were called The Wedding Present and had an LP called *George Best*. I bought it and that was it – off to the Ritz in Manchester and the International on Plymouth Grove!

Our local bowling club ran a race night to raise club funds. I was well into The Wedding Present by this time and you had the option of just betting on the horses or actually 'owning' one, which I paid a donation for. My horse was called 'My Favourite Dress'. I got some strange looks from the organiser and people in the room, me being a man, but I knew what it was all about. The horse came nowhere.

2015 and I'm making my first visit to At The Edge Of The Sea and Brighton, all the way from Derbyshire. Leaving on Saturday at 7am and 'commuting' via Manchester Piccadilly, London Euston, the Tube, London Victoria and onto Brighton, arriving in good time for the 3pm start. With it being bank holiday weekend, Brighton was full of mods. Very few rockers.

There was a raffle each day and David announced that he had left today's prize at home so he had to go back for it, only to be held up for 25 minutes because of all the mods and scooters blocking the road. He said he didn't realise just how popular this bank holiday thing was and he was thinking of not holding it on this weekend again. Talking to David outside, I had my photograph taken with him which topped an absolutely brilliant weekend. David asked me what #vivagne was (long live Glossop North End) and he asked how many we get at matches. I said, 'About 300' to which he replied, 'Oh, about as many as we get for a Wedding Present gig then!' I was full of it – Brighton, Concorde 2, Cinerama, The Wedding Present and a lot of alcohol! I awoke on Sunday morning and texted my stepdaughter to say, 'It's fucking brilliant!'

The Wedding Present

The Wedding Present, 2015
model: David Gedge, Charles Layton, Katharine Wallinger and Samuel Beer-Pierce
Photo: Jessica McMillan

AT THE EDGE OF THE SEA FESTIVAL

29 AUGUST 2015, BRIGHTON, UK

MARK THURMAN

I remember listening to *Bizarro* in a flat with friends in Norwich in 1991. At the time I was working in a factory and it, along with *Seamonsters* and a little Half Man Half Biscuit, was in my earphones all day. I also remember driving home from a first date in May 1993 with this beautiful redhead in the passenger seat whilst I clumsily sang along to 'Silver Shorts' and proclaimed the Wedding Present cover of 'Theme From Shaft' to be better than the original. That beautiful redhead is still with me – she's now my wife. It wasn't until 2015 that we saw David and the band live for the first time. Having explained to David I was popping my Wedding Present cherry, David asked drily, 'So what took you so long?'

2015–2016: *Going Going... Still Here*

MICHAEL KORCHIA
Watoo Watoo

As a musician, I've always been impressed by the way Gedge can write such moving songs with so few chords; like Lou Reed and Dean Wareham do in other styles. I exchanged a couple of tweets with David a few years ago. A week after we played Indietracks with my band Watoo Watoo in 2014, he sent me an email: 'Will you play my festival?' I was madly happy! I remembered all the times I've seen him on stage; how I was happy just to shake his hand and to say, 'Thanks' last time I saw him after a gig in Bordeaux. And now he asks me to play his festival! Two anecdotes spring to my mind: the day before the festival, we all went to an Indian restaurant. I asked someone to take a picture of David with Pascale (the singer in Watoo Watoo) and I. When we looked at the pictures, I told David that he was a magician and that he could do wonders, as the 'play' button on my camera worked again. It had not been functioning for two months. David answered, 'This camera works wonders: it makes you look young!' The day after, the play button didn't work anymore, but the picture with David is still our band's profile picture! David is the head of the At The Edge Of The Sea festival so he usually doesn't have time to attend full performances, but he usually comes to listen to a few songs. When playing with Watoo Watoo, we use my computer to play the backing tracks; I'm at the bass and Pascale sings and sometimes plays percussion or keyboards. He came to see us perform our few first songs. Alas, we had a technical problem that had never happened before. The backing tracks of the first three songs were corrupted so the songs kept skipping, making it impossible to play in time. The rest of the gig went without a problem and the crowd enjoyed our set, particularly our fast, organ driven, version of 'Pourquoi Es-Tu Devenue Si Raisonnable?' After the gig, I went to see David to tell him I was sorry about this technical problem. He answered that he liked what he heard, at least when it worked. Why do these kind of technical disasters only happen when they shouldn't?

ROLO MCGINTY
The Woodentops

I had been aware of The Wedding Present for ages but due to my own activities I had not really listened to their albums, been a fan or investigated them and I felt a little far from The Wedding Present 'scene'. So I went down to At The Edge Of The Sea not sure what to expect. We were hanging around with all the musicians in the area around the back when a group of people came in. Though no one was glam or fashion-wise standing out at that point, I recognised David immediately. I approached him to say, 'Thanks for inviting us' and there

The Wedding Present

A grand day out at Indietracks Festival, 24 July 2015: David Gedge (above); and Danielle Wadey (below) on keyboards

2015–2016: *Going Going... Still Here*

he was, right in front of me. You know when you like somebody straight away. There's nothing to dislike, just a whoosh of character and mutual enjoyment of the moment of meeting. You'd like to know them more but time is tight, there's a show to set up and as we share agents we are likely to meet again – indeed, we have – briefly – once. I saw he has, like me, a big reserve of energy towards what he does. It makes him not dulled by years of gigs and people but, far from that, I can tell he thrives on it. He's sparkly-eyed, on the edge of a giggle and appreciative of people around him. You feel you've known him a while already.

I really enjoyed that evening he invited us to. I played acoustic electric and the bass player, Mal, brought his electric double bass that has... a lot of bass! As we were playing I heard a noise, a kind of metallic rattle and shake. It reminded me of when you stand outside a drum and bass club or a car with the sub-woofer up loud and the body work is sounding like it's going to shatter on certain notes. Our bass had found the resonant frequencies of the Concorde 2. The sound engineer came to me later and said, 'I have never heard anything like that before in this building. Every rivet was vibrating and the glass snarling. And the metalwork – I thought it was going to collapse the place. Sounded great!' he said. That was The Woodentops acoustic. I enjoyed that very much.

ERIC TISCHLER
The Jet Age

I met David a full 20 years ago, when he was touring the States to promote *Mini*. I had only recently embraced The Wedding Present, having initially dismissed them after reading CMJ's review of *Seamonsters* and thinking, 'That sounds like crap.' (*Seamonsters* is now a top-three record for me, rubbing shoulders with *Quadrophenia* and *Revolver*.)

I was interviewing David for a magazine but, being new in my fandom, I didn't have a bottomless reservoir of questions – I was kinda winging it. It turned out we shared a lot of interests, including an intense love of James Bond (and, in particular, Roger Moore) and a similarly intense dislike of celery. Sure, he teased me by insisting there was a TV show starring Roger Moore and Tony Curtis (as if!) called *The Persuaders*, but we had fun and ended up staying in touch. When David launched Cinerama, my band The Hurricane Lamps would share bills in DC and then everyone would retire to my house, where we'd stay up into the wee hours drinking bottle after bottle of red wine.

Over the years, The Wedding Present's make-up has changed regularly, and my current band, The Jet Age, has been fortunate enough to tour with a few iterations of the group. What strikes me now is how many

The Wedding Present

friendships I've built with literally dozens of wonderful people, from The Wedding Present and Cinerama bandmates, to support staff, to other fans – some of whom've adopted my bands, too. All this bonhomie isn't coincidence – beyond David's raw, unbridled, rock-star charisma is someone who's thoughtful and interesting, someone I'm glad I'm friends with. One more story: about five years ago – 15 years after David and I first met – a big package arrived in the mail. In it was a DVD box set of the entire run of *The Persuaders*, starring Roger Moore and Tony Curtis. The Wedding Present is a lovely gift that keeps on giving. And I know, first hand, that David is a gift-giver *par excellence*.

FESTIVAL NO 6
4 SEPTEMBER 2015, PORTMEIRION, UK

DAI HOWELLS

They were touring the '12 singles in a year' show. Before the gig, David was helping out on the merchandising stall and I got chatting to him. I had been to Festival No.6 in Portmeirion the previous two years and asked David if The Wedding Present would ever play there. He said that they would love to but hadn't ever been asked. I was thrilled when I saw the line up for 2015 as The Wedding Present were going to be playing – and in the woods as well! I had seen a couple of bands in the woods previously and the setting is magical and very intimate. The day eventually arrived and I got there early to see them setting up. Obviously it was going to be a low-key acoustic set – fantastic! But there was no sign of Charlie. All was revealed once the set started, as a huge white rabbit was the drummer for this set. Whilst short, at around 30 minutes, the set was fantastic and they played a lot of my favourites including their greatest song 'My Favourite Dress'. I think David felt a bit threatened as, whilst playing that song, he asked Damon Gough (Badly Drawn Boy) to remove the rabbit from the stage!

LORRAINE ROBERTS

It was really close up and personal. Their drummer was missing so we had a white rabbit on the stage, which was surreal. But they were tight and drew a very large happy crowd. It was great to hear 'Brassneck'. Other up-and-coming artists turned up to dance in the woods which was, in my opinion, paying a great respect to them and it made my festival.

INDIE DAZE FESTIVAL
3 OCTOBER 2015, LONDON, UK

MILLIE FAGAN

My dad Pete took me to see The Wedding Present as a rite of passage because they're his favourite band. We met Gedge lurking near the merch during The Wonder Stuff. He was really lovely and down to earth to talk to. The final song was the unmistakable 'My Favourite Dress'. My dad's grin was huge when the first chords struck up as it's one of his faves. One of my favourite gigs and I'm so glad I shared it with my dad!

ENGINE ROOMS
16 OCTOBER 2015, SOUTHAMPTON, UK

RICHARD FISHLOCK

For a couple of years in the late Eighties The Wedding Present produced their own fanzine called *Invasion Of The Wedding Present*, a cut, paste and photocopy newsletter that was always eagerly anticipated by my friends and I, a loyal band of Wedding Present fans studying in London. In amongst the glamorous news updates penned by Keith, the scratchy cartoon strips featuring our heroes in unlikely situations and the latest offers from Grapper & Sons' expanding merchandise empire, there was often a competition to enter. Issue three hit our doormats in summer 1988 and included a competition prize that was surely the ultimate for any diehard fan of The Wedding Present – your name, plus one, on the top of the band's guest list for life. Not just for a one off gig, not even for a tour, but forever! Contestants had to name their three favourite Wedding Present tunes and then guess the combined weight of the band. We sat around

The Wedding Present

for an afternoon forensically studying photos of the group before scribbling our guesses on the back of an envelope and posting them off to Wedding Present HQ in Leeds. Some weeks later came the fantastic news – my girlfriend at the time Tara had won the competition with a guess of a very svelte 592 pounds – one pound out! Deciding that I would make more use of the prize, Tara asked the band whether they'd be happy to transfer the prize to me, to which they graciously agreed. From then on I became indie kid royalty, a Charlie Bucket smugly sailing into Wedding Present gigs here, there and everywhere with my grateful 'plus one'. The first time I was able to catch up with the band and introduce myself was at the BBC television studios in London, where the band were preparing to record their first *Top Of The Pops* appearance – the now infamous performance of 'Brassneck'. Through his contacts at the BBC, a good friend of mine called Paul had managed to secure tickets to the show.

In the BBC bar, before the recording, we introduced ourselves to the band. But David's welcome was slightly wary. 'Are you sure you're Richard Fishlock? We met him at our gig in Manchester recently and he looks nothing like you!' I produced ID from my wallet and we quickly twigged what had happened – because the story of my good fortune was reported in the subsequent issue of *Invasion*, cunning readers were impersonating me to gain access to Wedding Present gigs for free, as naturally I couldn't be at them all. They had even talked to the band about my friends and family, who of course they'd never met. To solve the problem we agreed on a pseudonym to put at the top of the guest list and went down to the studio for the recording. We loved the band's performance. While David's stage presence was a fittingly surly response to the requirement at the time that artists mime to their songs, there was still the music itself, and hearing the chugging rhythm section and Grapper's amphetamine chords in the *TOTP* studio made us grin and dance like idiots. Over the 25 years or so since 'winning' the competition I have often been asked how many times I took advantage of my golden ticket and what I always answer is, 'Not nearly enough.' Happily though, I was able to call upon it recently, having not seen the band live in a long while. I got in touch with David via Twitter and asked if I would still be good for the guest list at the band's upcoming show in Southampton – David laughed and said, 'Well, that was the deal!' The fantastic thing for me was that my 'plus one' this time was my 13 year old daughter Ella and it was great to be able to introduce her to David at the merch stall just before the band took the stage. The set they played was perfect, ending with my all-time favourite Wedding Present song, 'My Favourite Dress'. Ella and I grinned and danced like idiots.

2015–2016: *Going Going... Still Here*

WAKE UP! INDIE ALL DAYER FESTIVAL

17 OCTOBER 2015, NOTTINGHAM, UK

COLIN SIMPSON

I had the ugliest car in the world – a Fiat Multipla. An amazing car, if you don't care about looks. With the seats out I had a double bed in the back. I was in an awful Irish band at the time, so the amount of drink I consumed required lots of nights sleeping in the car. It also meant I could now travel to more gigs without the added costs of hotels – I live right out in Weardale and no bands play here!

The Indie All Dayer featured Echo And The Bunnymen, Brix And The Extricated, The Sultans Of Ping and The Wedding Present. Being a relatively new fan of all these, going to see them all at once would tick a load of boxes on my bucket list. I got there early and parked on the roof of a multi-storey car park right opposite the venue. I got there just in time to see the crowd get let in – from above! I raced down to get to the front and met an ex-music journalist who was stood next to me. She was gorgeous! I fell in love instantly. Beautiful blonde hair, about ten years older than me, skinny with an awe-inspiring smile and the sexiest big eyes I'd ever seen. I told her I used to work at BBC6 Music, filming the acts on Marc Riley's show. We were destined to be together forever and go to loads of gigs all the time. Then her photographer boyfriend came back with the drinks. I got very, very drunk. After the gig I collared David Gedge and slurred, 'You understand me better than ANYONE!' After a short breath, which felt like forever, he replied, 'No, I don't.' I stalked the streets looking for a chicken shawarma, found one, got back to my car and went to sleep. At about 3 AM, a car park attendant woke me up knocking on the windows. Apparently I wasn't allowed to sleep there. I told him I wasn't going anywhere as I was way too drunk to drive, and he said he'd call the police. I've never had much to do with the police, but I'm guessing they're way too busy on a Saturday night to tell someone off for being asleep in a car park they'd paid £13 for the pleasure of parking in all night. I went back to sleep and slept really well and then drove home sometime after midday.

ANDREW FENTON

In the Eighties it was said that The Wedding Present were The Smiths fans' second favourite band. In my case it was the other way round.

The Wedding Present

The Wedding Present were always number one. Lots of people 'into music' claim a particular band make up the soundtrack to their lives. In my case that band is The Wedding Present. The boy Gedge's lyrics kinda make this easier to be honest. Tales of everyday break-ups, love and heartache. To this day I always skip 'Give My Love To Kevin'. My first experience of The Wedding Present was a *George Best* cassette lent to me by my best mate, who is still my gig buddy to this day. I copied it and played it to death. I've since bought the album at least another three times, so I don't feel too guilty about that first pirate copy. First time I saw them, Mr G wore those flowery bright T-shirts, as did I. They opened up with 'Why Are You Being So Reasonable Now?' which had just been released, and they sang half the song in French. I bought a 'Brassneck' T-shirt that day which I still wear to gigs. Mr G stated he had not seen one for a long time when he saw me wearing it at Indie Daze in October 2015. I had never spoken with him until that Indie Daze gig, but I always tell people he gave me 50p once, although I gave him £3 for a copy of the 'Sucker' 7" first!

Until October 2015, it was always just my gig buddy Nige and I going to Weddoes gigs. No one else was interested in that 'racket'. But I finally persuaded my wife of 21 years to come with me to Indie Daze – well, I just bought the tickets without consulting her. That was also the first time I had my picture taken with Mr G and spoke to him. My wife said to him that I loved him more than her. Mr G replied, 'I'm sure he doesn't.' I didn't comment. My wife's verdict was, 'They were not as bad as I thought they would be,' which is high praise indeed.

ACADEMY

14 NOVEMBER 2015, MANCHESTER, UK

CECILIE JOHANNASSEN

When the Manchester Academy 25th anniversary concert was announced in February, I got a text from my friend Dan: 'Get a ticket and come over.' I had it booked within a few days and the waiting began. When November finally came we walked to the venue, stopping at different pubs on the way.

2015-2016: *Going Going... Still Here*

I was surprised that my feet would actually carry me. I'm sure Dan and Dave felt like minders dragging me around, but I couldn't have asked for better company. Suddenly we were there. Inside the Academy.

The stage was right in front of us, and Cinerama entered. I remember turning to Dan – probably with the most ridiculous grin on my face – to make sure it was really happening. And then I got lost in music and happiness. 'Your Charms', one of my favourite Cinerama songs, had my heart in a little happy twirl, and 'Ears' was exquisitely beautiful. Gedge and Emma Pollock created a moment I'll never forget, and it was the highlight of my night. When The Wedding Present entered, the party was definitely on and we got what we all wanted; loud guitars and sounds that made our cores tremble. It was sweaty and bouncy and fun, and I kept pinching myself to make sure it was all real. I loved to see the crowd reaction to the music, and I loved to feel what it did to me. Dan kept running off to bounce in the middle, and even I had to engage in some mini-bouncing where I was stood. And all through the concert I kept looking at Dave and Dan for confirmation this wasn't a dream. Because it felt like that to me. And then it was over. People started to leave, and I remember how much I didn't want to go. I think I even asked if we could rewind and start all over again. Being a bit shy and awkward, I had to be dragged over to the merchandise area (I have a habit of saying embarrassing things to musicians I'm in awe of), and suddenly found myself face to face with Gedge.

In my ear I heard Dan saying I was CJ off the internet and that was my clue to yet again say something I'm not proud of, which will not be repeated here – or anywhere else. However, I got the CD I was missing, and I got it signed by Gedge, who is an absolutely lovely man and one of the most talented writers of words and music I'll ever be in the presence of. I still can't believe this night happened, and I'd probably give up my sanity to relive it. The signed CD and ticket has made it into my treasure cabinet and they will stay there forever. My history with The Wedding Present and Cinerama might not be very long, but to me it's one of the most beautiful and intense experiences of my life. It's a love story I think will last until the end of my days.

ANDY BARTON

I saw The Wedding Present on the night after the Paris terrorist attacks, and there was quite a strange atmosphere beforehand. But once the bands started playing, it was a great night. Cinerama

The Wedding Present

performed, followed by a great, shambling performance by Badly Drawn Boy. My wife Bernie also came with me for the first time, so we took up a position in the centre of the Academy, away from the usual moshpit. From my new vantage point, I was struck by just how good The Wedding Present sounded. They seem to keep getting better with age! It was a great set and the combination of old songs, such as 'You Should Always Keep In Touch With Your Friends' and newer songs such as 'Santa Monica', worked brilliantly. I had a massive smile on my face for the former, and the latter is a great song that shows The Wedding Present are still a vibrant, forward-looking band.

My wife really enjoyed the gig, which made my night too. I bought a new T-shirt and she got a record bag signed by David and had a photo taken with him. David was really friendly as usual, asking if my wife had enjoyed the performance. I think he was even happier we had bought some merchandise too. Looking around the Academy crowd, I could see fathers and sons and mothers and sons, which I thought was quite nice. I know a woman who attends gigs with her son, but he won't stand with her as she embarrasses him with her singing!

The only way is up: David Gedge at Manchester Academy, November 2015

2015–2016: *Going Going... Still Here*

On 18 May 2015 the *Valentina* album was reinterpreted by Cinerama.

DAVID GEDGE

I'm continually trying to think up thought-provoking and challenging projects. My original idea, three or four years before, was to develop and release a set of songs simultaneously as both Cinerama and The Wedding Present and the songs that eventually became *Valentina* just happened to be the 'next' set of songs. That was the extent of my planning! Obviously the LPs didn't come out simultaneously, though. That was a bit over-ambitious on my part.

KYTV FESTIVAL
19 DECEMBER 2015, CIVIC HALL, WOLVERHAMPTON, UK

GLENN

My first ever Wedding Present gig was in Birmingham at the old Hummingbird in October 1988. Support was The Heart Throbs. I remember a few shoes ending up on stage, which David commented on. The last time I saw them was at the Civic in Wolverhampton with Ned's Atomic Dustbin. I was down at the front and, afterwards, I spoke to David and met his dog Doris.

BEACON RADIO
10 JANUARY 2016, SEATTLE, WA, USA

NATE ELLINGSWORTH

My wife Catherine introduced me to The Wedding Present when we started dating ten years ago. She had been a diehard fan for ten years before that. We have seen them a few times and they are always excellent. We saw David play an amazing acoustic set in someone's living room. Afterwards, he was very gracious and took a picture with my wife and signed a Cinerama

The Wedding Present

single for us. This was our favorite show so far (though the tenth anniversary of *Seamonsters* show at the Crocodile in Seattle was a close second). David has always been accessible and kind when we have seen him. The song 'I'm From Further North Than You' always strikes a chord with us, as does 'Dalliance'. Catherine has so many memory burns from their music and, as time goes on, it feels almost like the soundtrack to our life together.

KATY MCCORMICK

My husband and I had just moved to Seattle and were finding our way around all the different live music venues – from dive bars to nightclubs, from community centers to theaters – and having a great time discovering new, mostly American, bands. There is just so much going on in a relatively small city, I think we could be out every night if we had the stamina.

So I was totally up for it when I heard that David Gedge was playing a house concert at a secret location in Seattle. We were quick to apply for three tickets – my husband, me, and my son, who was visiting from the UK. I was super-excited by the opportunity to not only see David up close and acoustic, but also to have a new experience and also (nosy me) get to see inside a Seattle home. We got the details the day before and on the night made our way to a classic Seattle craftsman-style house in the up-and-trending Beacon Hill neighbourhood. It was a winter night just after Christmas and dark and we milled about on the sidewalk for a while in typical British fashion. 'Do you think this is the place?' 'Um, I don't know – what do you think?' Luckily some other concert goers appeared as reinforcements, so up we went. Once through the front door we were in an ordinary living room but cleared of furniture and with about 45 folding chairs in rows. From the front of the 'stage' to the back row must have been no more than 20 feet and the people in the front row were inches away. I'm finding it hard to describe what it's like to hear a great performer in such an intimate setting, sharing an experience with only a few dozen others, but I just loved it. David was relaxed, funny, a bit hoarse from a day's recording at a Seattle studio. He was full of stories and charming intros to one great song after another. I'd never heard The Wedding Present live so it was all completely fresh. Afterwards, my son Bill went up to David to talk to him while I slipped into the kitchen and talked to David's wife Jessica and the couple who were hosting the concert.

2015–2016: *Going Going... Still Here*

David Gedge, Cambridge Junction, 29 May, 2016

O2 ACADEMY

24 MARCH 2016, GLASGOW, UK

KATE SULLIVAN

One of the things that I enjoy the most about seeing the Weddoes live is when, during much-loved old songs, David stays faithful to the recorded version – particularly the 'ohs' on 'My Favourite Dress' ('That was my favourite dress you know, oh!'). Towards the end of 2015, I noticed that David had stopped doing them and I could only hear everybody else singing them. With a couple (or maybe four) drinks in me I took it upon myself, on behalf of all of us, to tell David that the 'ohs' and the 'ahs' were the things we, the fans, had come to expect and please could he remember to do them in future? Obviously I regretted this conversation the next day – it's his song after all and he can sing it however he wants. We got ourselves over to Leicester in March 2016 and again the 'ohs' and 'ahs' were missing. When chatting to David at the merch afterwards, he referenced our earlier conversation and said he had been

The Wedding Present

David Gedge and Danielle Wadey, Valencia, 1 November 2016. Opposite: pointing at The Point, Sunderland, 2 December 2016

thinking about what I'd said when he was singing 'My Favourite Dress' that night. A week later I found myself down at the front in Glasgow. When 'My Favourite Dress' started, I had zero expectation of getting what I wanted but, after the first 'oh', David looked down at me and smiled. I've got to say that this was one of the highlights of my life.

After three years as a two-day event held on the August bank holiday weekend, David Gedge's At The Edge Of The Sea festival reverted to a one day event on 20 August 2016.

2015–2016: Going Going... Still Here

DAVID GEDGE

After At The Edge Of The Sea 2015 we went to the managers of the Concorde 2, the seafront venue in Brighton where we've staged the event since 2009, and said, 'Can we book you for next year's August bank holiday weekend again, then, please?' And they said, 'No.' We said, 'No?! But we've had it for the last seven years!' And they said, 'Sorry but the Mods have beaten you to it.'

The Mods put on bands all through the day and then have a club through the night. Loads of people go to it, so I suppose I can see why the venue did it. They'll make more money from that, even though our fans are more than capable of spending a few quid at the bar. At first I was a bit annoyed. I was disappointed that the venue hadn't told the Mods that we had first refusal over that weekend. I guess I expected some kind of loyalty. Call me old-fashioned! But, in retrospect... I think it was probably a blessing in disguise. Two days is just a bit too much for me really... two different Wedding Present sets, two different Cinerama sets... booking two days' worth of bands. It sounds daft but it is really quite a lot of work. And even for the rest of the group... rehearsing so many songs on top of their extra appearances in 'other' bands at the festival... it's exhausting. I feel guilty putting them through it all. So, in 2016, it reverted back to being a one-

The Wedding Present

day event... like it had been for the first few years. And, I have to say... I much preferred it. A few people complained but it was generally a lot less stressful for me, especially since there weren't 1,000 Mods outside making it difficult to get to and from the venue. So now I say to people, 'Come down for the weekend but on the Sunday go and explore Brighton – there's loads of stuff to do.'

MARTIN NOBLE
British Sea Power

The drummer in my old school band, Ted, was the first one in my group of school friends to get into The Wedding Present. He was a big John Peel head. I didn't quite get them. They weren't considered a 'cool' *NME* band at the time. Maybe they weren't the band to help you get in with the girls? When I split up with my first girlfriend at school, Ted gave me 'Love Will Tear Us Apart' and 'You Should Always Keep In Touch With Your Friends' on 7". A very sweet thing to do. Both songs went straight to the heart in different ways. Neither of these bands was glamorous or hugely popular, but they could bring out deep emotional feelings. It was a significant moment for me. The Wedding Present could also raise a knowing chuckle as well. As well as that blend of pathos and bathos, I loved the guitar sounds and melodies, and also loved the fact they had covered Pavement and The Velvet Underground, two of my favourite bands at the time.

I didn't care if they weren't on the front page of the *NME*, the Weddoes gave me something real and relatable, without cokehead wanker showmanship. A band to have at your side and which you could rely on. From then on I got hold of as much as I could. *Tommy* and *George Best* first, from the Merrion Centre market in Leeds.

What I couldn't get, Ted had. Ted had all the singles on 7" from *The Hit Parade*. I was a bit late and was gutted I couldn't find them all. I went to a show in Huddersfield in the mid-Nineties when my girlfriend and I had gotten back together. I had wooed her back with compilation tapes heavy on the Weddoes. The travelling party that day was me, her and Ted. I'm sure there's a Weddoes song in that.

I saw them play in Reading when I was at uni. My friend John had drunkenly shouted to David on the merch desk, 'Can you give my mate a kiss? He loves your band.' David shook his head, smirked, and said, 'No'. I assumed he was grumpy from then on.

Move on over ten years. I'm playing guitar in British Sea Power. We bumped into David and Jessica at a house party at South By Southwest, Texas. Our singer Jan tried to embarrass me by recounting the Reading Uni story of when my mate had asked David for a kiss. We soon

2015–2016: *Going Going... Still Here*

realised we all lived relatively close to each other in Brighton & Hove and that we were Man United fans and from then on we've watched matches in the local pub, through the Fergie, Moyes, van Gaal and now Mourinho eras. We've met here and there. He's DJ'd at a New Year's Eve party and we played in a kind of supergroup (members of British Sea Power, Brakes, Jim Jones and Field Music) at his At The Edge Of The Sea festival. We did a cover of The Weddoes' 'It's A Gas'. I was acting out a boyhood dream. Jan forgot some of the lyrics and cocked it up. Classic.

GOING, GOING...
THE NINTH ALBUM
RELEASED 2 SEPTEMBER 2016

DAVID GEDGE

It's a concept album. I was initially avoiding using that description because it tends to conjure up images of progressive rock albums about medieval knights. But I've come to terms with it now. Over the 32 years since the band started I've hopefully learnt something about writing but I've also worked with about a dozen very talented co-writers who have often pushed me in very different directions.

We wanted the tracks on *Going, Going...* to be varied. It probably sounds slightly pretentious but I wanted to take the listener on a journey and, because I knew it was going to be something like 70 or 80 minutes long, I knew that we had to keep their interest throughout! So the music is purposely diverse and the album has little ideas – surprises, I suppose you'd call them – tucked away throughout. That was the plan, anyway. If you're listening to a Wedding Present recording you're listening to how the band wanted it to sound not how some businessman with a big bank account wanted it to sound. We're always willing to experiment, even if that means upsetting the existing fans.

The Wedding Present

LANDEI LUGAU

22 OCTOBER 2016, DOBERLUG-KIRCHHAIN, D

DAVID GEDGE

If you play in out of the way places it's often much more of an event. It happens in Germany a lot, for some reason. We were invited to play a concert in a place called Doberlug-Kirchhain, which I had to look up on the map. It seemed like a village but the fee was quite good and so I thought, 'OK, why not?' And it turned out to be one of the best-attended shows on that whole Continental European tour – bigger than Berlin! It turns out that it was an historic venue: people have been loyal to it since the days of the GDR. There was a museum room filled with old photographs of the place. So it has this great reputation and people travel to it from the surrounding area. After the concert there was a disco and we all danced. We'll often play in an unassuming little town like that and it'll end up being a fantastic night. Chatting to the promoters afterwards, it finally dawned on me that they'd approached me after a Wedding Present concert in Newcastle-upon-Tyne a couple of years ago previously. 'We are from a village in Germany and we'd like you to play at our venue.' I remembered smiling politely at the time and giving them our agent's contact details, thinking, 'Yeah, hmmm... that'll probably never happen...'

MARCUS KAIN
The Wedding Present guitarist
2016-

I moved to Brighton from Melbourne, Australia, in late July 2016. A day after arriving I was sitting, jetlagged beyond belief, in Billie's Cafe with my mate Seb Falcone. Seb had worked front of house sound for the band I was touring with in 2014 and we'd kept in touch. I said I was going to tourist my way around the UK for a few months and start looking for work after Christmas, but he told me a band he worked for – The Wedding Present – were auditioning new guitarists, and that there were European and UK tours lined up for

2015–2016: Going Going... Still Here

October, November and December. Despite not having a place to live sorted out, and my guitars being on a ship that was still two or three months away, I accepted Seb's offer to be put in touch with David, and committed to the audition.

After meeting with David and Jessica for a pre-audition coffee, the first thing that struck me about David was how quiet he can be. It was hard to read whether or not he liked my musical resumé or not and I remember leaving thinking, 'Well, I *think* that went OK...' 'Go Out And Get 'Em, Boy!', 'Drive', and 'A Million Miles' were chosen for the audition, so I found a guitar and got to work. When I listened closely to "Go Out And Get 'Em, Boy!' my first thought was, 'Fuck me, that strumming is fast!' but I learned those songs inside out. The audition was at Brighton Electric and the moment we all started playing what struck me was what a great drummer Charlie is. I've always been a very rhythmic guitarist and to me it felt like Charlie and I locked in pretty much straight away. After each song David was classically poker-faced, so I had no idea if what I was doing was hitting the spot. Musically it felt good to me, but that's all I knew. David, you kept me guessing!

A couple of weeks later, I assumed I hadn't gotten the gig. So I sent an email to say thank you for the audition, that it was nice meeting everyone. Shortly after that I got a phone call from David informing me that I had indeed got the job.

02 Academy, Liverpool, 6 December 2016

SOMETIMES THESE WORDS **JUST DON'T HAVE TO BE SAID**

The Wedding Present

That moment was like being shot out of a cannon – I had 23 songs to learn for a gig I was playing in Brighton that Saturday, and another 24 songs to learn for The Wedding Present's 2016 EU tour which kicked off shortly after. But I'm still here, so I guess something went right! The tours that have followed have been awesome. I'm writing this the night before flying to the United States to begin The Wedding Present's 2017 North American tour. Loud shows, long drives, and a different hotel every night; this is what we do, and I love it.

BREWERY ARTS CENTRE
3 DECEMBER 2016, KENDAL, UK

BEN CROMPTON
Actor

I'll be honest – I came to The Wedding Present late. They were a band I was always aware of and I found something comforting in their constant presence, forging on whilst many other bands from the late Eighties and early Nineties packed it in. 'Kennedy' got a regular spin on my turntable as a teenager. But it's *Take Fountain* and *Going, Going...* that grabbed my attention and had me revisit their earlier albums. I love that, in contrast to the drive of the better-known songs, they can produce something of the delicate, reflective nature of 'Marblehead' or 'Sprague'.

My missus and I got tickets to see them in Kendal for my birthday weekend in December 2016. It was our first night away together in over three years since our second child was born. Driving from Newcastle, *Going Going...* was the perfect soundtrack and gave the crossing of county lines a real 'Here Be Dragons' moment. As we wound across the beautiful open countryside and approached the sign telling us we were entering Cumbria, 'Santa Monica' was playing. We crossed from Yorkshire into Cumbria just as the guitar begins its strange ascension halfway through the song. If you ever want to feel a sense of uneasiness entering new territory, time it so that you do so at exactly 3.20 whilst listening to that track.

2015–2016: *Going Going... Still Here*

The Brewery Arts Centre, with its low ceiling, was full of 40 and 50 year olds. David was stood by the merch stall whilst support band Melys reminded me what I loved of the late Nineties and early 2000s. As their song 'Disco Pigs' rang out, they left the stage through the crowd one by one, nicely setting up the main event. When The Wedding Present took to the stage the room started buzzing. My missus was drinking like we wouldn't get another night out together for another three years. The predominately male moshpit grew stronger. I held onto her as we joined the surging crowd, singing at the top of our voices as we were pushed and pulled.

Not many gigs leave you breathless. That one did. All that jostling. I must be out of shape. I picked up the *Marc Riley Sessions* LP and the French version of the 'Why Are You Being So Reasonable Now?' single. Top night.

The Wedding Present

Close Encounters

Being a selection of rapid-fire memories of The Wedding Present or David Gedge from some die-hard fans.

JON PINDER

I saw David Gedge in Amazing Records in Leeds, browsing through Blondie albums. I plucked up the courage to tell him how much I enjoyed the gig and then realised in my starstruck state I had no idea what to follow that opening statement with, so threw out a couple of random questions and then ran off.

GEL MCGARTH

I remember talking to David at the back of the Merrion Centre and he was with his girlfriend. We were only about 15 or 16. I also remember drunkenly approaching them at other gigs and asking if his girlfriend was 'Sally' from one of their songs.

MARK SCOTT

I asked David, 'Good drive up?' David said, 'Yeah, not bad. The M25 wasn't too busy really.' Great conversation!

SIMON GEORGE

I interviewed the band, then had my question repeated (sarcastically!) on stage that evening, on the *Bizarro* tour in 1989.

NICK HALLWORTH

I once spotted Mr Gedge in Morrisons supermarket in the Merrion Centre in Leeds. The cereals aisle, if I recall. Might not have been him though. I'm not sure which brand of cereal he was buying and I wouldn't want to over embellish an already well-rounded story.

PHILIP BEEGAN

Going to see The Wedding Present in London wearing my snug 'Ukrainian Sessions' T-shirt (I could only get size medium and I wear extra large), I got accosted and shouted at by a 70 year old Ukrainian bloke on the tube. He was drunk, I was drunk – it was all good.

Close Encounters

ANDREW EAVES

My Wedding Present-related memories are many: breaking my ribs twice on the *Seamonsters* tour; getting told off by Grapper for wiping my fevered brow on my brother's T-shirt during a gig (my response of, 'He's my brother' placating the now legendary guitarist); and the jaw-dropping times I heard 'Heather' and 'Come Play With Me' played live for the first time. The Wedding Present were gifted to me by one of my first good uni friends. The Northern angst and downright hilarious lyrics immediately grabbed me by the shoulders and said quietly 'This is you. You need search no longer for solace.' Whilst admitting cheerfully that I was clearly a bit of a pretentious tit, I still hold onto that thought. In turn, I gifted The Wedding Present to my younger brother Martin when I returned home from my first term at Sheffield University in about 1989. The Weddoes have been with me ever since, and we've grown older and considerably greyer together. Although, thinking about it, me and our kid have greyed suspiciously more than Gedge has. My fondest memories, however, will always be the inter-song chats from Gedge concerning the weather, flights of significant aeroplanes (Concorde) and countless other irrelevancies. I also miss the silly little dances.

MARTIN POYNTZ-ROBERTS

I used to work in a pub in Bristol called The Prince Of Wales on Gloucester Road. One evening, into the pub walked David with friends or bandmates. I was struck dumb! Faced by my guitar hero, I had no idea what to do or say. So I said nothing but continued to serve him a pint of Butcombe Bitter. [David Gedge: 'I don't drink beer so it wouldn't have been!']

They stayed for a while. I tried not to stare. What a weirdo I must have been. David brought some pint glasses back to the bar. I said, 'Thanks mate' and then garbled this ridiculous sentence, 'You're my favourite pop star!' and probably turned red. David said, 'Thanks!' and promptly left. How pathetic was that? As a journalist I've met plenty of famous folk but none as important as David.

ROB CRILLY

David Gedge once threatened to throw me out of a Wedding Present gig for wearing a Birdland T-shirt, probably entirely justifiably.

DAN BLOOMFIELD

There was a house on Brudenell Road. Six of us – all students at Leeds University moved in. There was a load of old Sinister Cleaners EPs and some broken

The Wedding Present

equipment left in the basement. Then Pete Solowka turned up and asked if he could retrieve his enormous papier-mâché dragon that he'd left behind. I think he and Len Liggins lived there. Anyway, I was deeply into The Wedding Present from years back, when I was at school in Carlisle. This was a fantasy come true for me so I said no. I kept it for a while, but it was enormous and eventually I left it behind in a house in Headingley when it started to fall apart. I also remember being infatuated with a girl studying chemistry who ignored me and shagged all the members of CUD instead.

JANE GAZZO
TV and radio presenter

Gedge and I often joke that he's to blame for my 25 year media career. He was the first international artist I ever interviewed for my radio show (on Melbourne community radio) around *Hit Parade*. He gave me a good deal of his time and I remember laughing a lot. We stayed in touch and in 2000 I landed in London. Before too long, I was presenting on BBC 6Music. I'm forever grateful to David for inviting me to session recordings when John Peel was alive and even taking me to LA cafe Swingers when I was in the US once. I have always admired David's dry humour and his knack for proficient pop with amusing song titles. Who else could write a song called 'Health And Efficiency'? I'm now back in Oz and still a massive Wedding Present fan – and still presenting on radio. I consider Gedge a mate. And I'm grateful he was such a great interviewee all those years ago.

JAMES FRYER

I bumped into Grapper when he was having a Christmas meal with friends at the Java Indonesian restaurant in Sowerby Bridge in December 1988. Probably the last place he'd expect to be recognised by a Wedding Present fanatic and he couldn't hide his embarrassment as I asked him to sign my restaurant bill in front of his mates. One lunchtime I spoke to David outside Jumbo Records in the St Johns Centre in the early years of Cinerama. He was hanging around waiting for Sally, lamenting that he had been dragged to do some last minute shoe shopping for her before they went off on holiday.

PAUL KERSHAW

I went to college in Cheltenham. It is now Gloucestershire University. In the old days we called it Cheltenham University of National Technology. How childish. Whilst at college, the term 'having a Gedge' was often used by friends when someone didn't come out on an evening as they preferred to stay in and be miserable because they were sulking over a girl. For example, 'Where is Paul tonight?' 'Oh, he's not coming out, he's having a Gedge.'

All The Songs Sound The Same...

Favourite songs and albums: a few Wedding Present desert-island discs.

BRIAN BREHMER
Yeah Yeah Yeah Yeah Yeah

I had been listening to a local DJ in Milwaukee at the time named Mot, who did Wednesday nights on WMSE, 91.7FM. He was and continues to be a big fan of The Wedding Present and played them from time to time. One of the songs that he played caught my ears and so I went out and bought the album. The song 'Yeah Yeah Yeah Yeah Yeah' symbolizes what I felt falling in love with a woman from El Salvador and having a long-distance relationship. I called up Mot and asked him to dedicate the song to her and had her listen live online so she could hear it. As he said, it's not a traditional love song but then ours was not a traditional love story either. Every time I hear the song, I think about the early days and how we have now been married almost nine years. Sure, other songs describe or illustrate our love, but none as strong and as poignant as 'Yeah Yeah Yeah Yeah Yeah' by The Wedding Present… it's our song.

COLIN TURNER
Interstate 5

The only single I have ever pre-ordered. I liked it that much. Still do. It's just tinged with sadness when I hear it as it was released around the time of John Peel's death.

STEVEN MACKEY
Seamonsters

Like many musical-loving children of the Eighties, I flirted with The Pixies and The Pogues, The Smiths and The Smashing Pumpkins. I was born just too late for The Jam and The Clash, for ska and Northern Soul, latching on to them retrospectively. I am still excited to hear the new music championed on the likes of 6Music. Most of these bands or genres, however, tend to represent either specific phases of my life, or else I periodically and greedily devour their back catalogue to the point of overkill. Only two have stayed with me since the musical awakening of my early teens. One is Neil Young; the other is The

The Wedding Present

Wedding Present. I have nothing in the way of humorous anecdotes, no stories of sneaking into a Wedding Present gig via the band's dressing room or proposing to a girlfriend just as 'Kennedy' erupts on stage. I rarely tweet, never mind commit to print something this personal, and my Facebook activity can best be described as voyeuristic.

It has been a solitary voyage in many ways; I have been unaccompanied for around 20 of the 30-odd times I have seen The Wedding Present in concert. To my mind, this is absolutely as it should be: anonymous in an audience of more or less like-minded people, free to mouth the words and nod my head unselfconsciously. When I buy the latest album, it is invariably played loud when I am driving or home alone. Bizzarely, although I often feel like grabbing the nearest chart lover by the lapels and asking if they realise what they are missing, if I make a compilation for someone I rarely include a Wedding Present track; perhaps because I can't stand the thought of anyone dismissing it as 'not for them' after one listen.

Alongside albums from The Housemartins, Beastie Boys and Dinosaur Jr., a vinyl copy of *George Best* was being passed among my friends. It was almost certainly stolen from a local record shop, and soon became a staple of the Saturday evening pre-pub drinking sessions. While we also listened to The Fall and The Smiths, the guitar sound of *George Best*, fast and melodic, coupled with bittersweet lyrics that were right up my 15 year old hormonally confused street, had ignited something in me that abides to this day. David Gedge has said in recent years that the album sounds 'tinny' now and, relative to the records that came after it, that may be true. But to me, whether the bold opening statement of 'Everyone Thinks He Looks Daft' or the angst ridden 'My Favourite Dress', it is an album of raw beauty that I immediately identified with.

By late 1989, I had devoured the band's second album, *Tommy*, even though I never really understood why certain tracks appeared on both. I confess that I did not embrace the Ukrainian folk sessions with the same fervour, but the release of *Bizarro*, with the lavish layered guitars of 'Kennedy' and the accompanying visual treat of DLG refusing to play the miming game to 'Brassneck' on *Top Of The Pops*, reaffirmed my faith. Music was by now part of my very fibre; the following year I went to both Glastonbury and Reading. Albums like *Screamadelica* and *Nevermind*, released within a day of each other, were important to me, and remain so. But it was a record released three months previous to those two, a piece of such ferocity and subtlety that it soon became, and remains to this day, my all time favourite 40 minutes of music: *Seamonsters*. It is a majestic record, somehow managing to be both angry and tender, with thrashing distortion next to direct and hypnotic guitar work,

All The Songs Sound The Same...

at times seemingly at odds with Gedge's vocal performance, but somehow working perfectly. Most importantly for me, *Seamonsters* was not an album that you 'got' after one or two listens. It had a slow-burning intensity that demanded attention and, over a period of weeks and months, it seared itself upon my very soul. Like an old and loyal friend, I can play it at any time, in any mood, and it never disappoints.

PAULA WISEMAN
Take Fountain

I found The Wedding Present through a discovery of David's off-shoot project, Cinerama. I have been a fan of The Divine Comedy for many years and a fellow fan and friend told me I should listen to a band called Cinerama because it was the kind of music I liked. I got my hands on a copy of *Va Va Voom* and was totally hooked from day one. I think it was partly the tone in David's voice and partly the beautiful orchestrations on there.

I'd heard of The Wedding Present many moons ago but never really listened to any of their stuff in great detail up to that point. I got myself a copy of *Take Fountain*, the album that was originally intended for a Cinerama release but released under the Wedding Present name, and was smitten from then on. I've been welcomed into the Wedding Present family with open arms and they are a truly lovely bunch!

Left: Paula Wiseman with David Gedge

DEREK PEPLAU
Kennedy

20 May 1990 was the day I would unwittingly begin a long journey of fandom for what would become my favourite band, The Wedding Present. That was the day that the video for 'Kennedy' premiered on MTV's alternative music program, *120 Minutes*, hosted by Dave Kendall. I'd never heard a song like it before. David Gedge and Grapper's lightning fast guitar strumming, Keith Gregory's angry bass distortion high in the mix and Simon Smith's military precision drumming punctuating the track. I'd taped the show and must have rewound it a dozen times to re-watch and re-listen. The Wedding Present sound is a bit like Rush: not for everybody, but if you like it, you really like it. I really liked it. I immediately started trying to track the

The Wedding Present

album down, not an easy thing to do in pre-internet America for an import title like *Bizarro*. Eventually the CD longbox was secured and the album copied to tape and the tape played to shreds in my car. The rest of the album did not disappoint. I was hooked.

Over the next 25 years I would eventually track down nearly every track ever committed to CD or vinyl, see the band live many times, and even become an active member of their fan community, following the band on tour for a stretch. Even though their sound has morphed many times over the years, if I had to point to one track that to me personally sums up The Wedding Present, it's got to be 'Kennedy'. It's not my all-time favorite Wedding Present track, but it's the sound that I fell in love with. Nothing else compares. 'Too much apple pie'? 25 years on, I still haven't come close to having my fill.

MARK MORRIS
My Favourite Dress

A bright sunny day in May 2007, on the way with my best men to marry my wife Leanne Morris with the windows down and *George Best* belting out. My first-ever Leadmill Wedding Present gig – truly awesome. The intensity and passion in Gedgey's voice was amazing! 'My Favourite Dress' – my favourite song. The introduction, the rawness, the words…

RICHARD KNEW, FILMMAKER
Dalliance

I was a final-year film student in 1991 and wrote to David Gedge to see if I could make a B-side or extra video for them as a final-year project as they had been my favourite band for a couple of years. David phoned me back and I ended up producing and directing the official promo video for 'Dalliance', ably supported by my mates on the course, which then subsequently inspired a video for one of the 12 singles in *The Hit Parade* the following year!

NICK PERRY
Corduroy

It wasn't easy being an indie kid without a record player in 1990. Getting at the music meant relying on friends putting together mix tapes and listening to John Peel and recording your own. 'Kennedy' was definitely on one tape, 'Brassneck' too and maybe something off *George Best*. These tracks epitomised the sound that I was beginning to immerse myself in. But they didn't feel like they were mine – my mates with the record players had got there first. Then I found the *3 Songs* EP for sale on cassette in Woolworths. Even in good record shops, the selection of music available on tape was always terrible, so this – a bona fide new release from a quality band – was a score.

All The Songs Sound The Same...

David Gedge and Richard Knew on the set of the 'Dalliance' video
Photo: Tudor Morgan-Owen

And then I got it home and listened to it. On 'Corduroy', Gedge's voice was familiar but the hundred mile an hour guitars had gone, replaced by slow, chiming chords, occasionally overlaid with an atonal dirge. This was a very different Wedding Present. The song sped up at the chorus; closer to how I thought of their sound but, after a pause, the pace dropped again. The slow chords returned with Gedge getting more emotional, more emotional than ever before – 'I worshipped you once before, and you slammed the door' – before a second chorus. Pause. Snare. Then the climax – machine gun drums and squalling lead guitars thrashed out exhilaratingly over the song's opening chimes.

Then the B sides... 'Crawl' was more conventional, but no less intense – 'There were some things I had to do, say that again and I'll kill you.' 'Make Me Smile (Come Up And See Me)' was an inspired choice of cover version, perfectly suited to the band both lyrically and stylistically.

I played both sides of the EP over and over again knowing that, after each track, something else great was coming up. I shared it with my friends, bringing something new to the group for the first time. They were as surprised and excited by this change of direction as I'd been. But I'd got there first this time. Eventually I saved enough from my Saturday job

The Wedding Present

earnings to get myself a stereo with a record player and the world of vinyl opened up to me. When *Seamonsters* came out the following year, it was an obvious addition to my expanding record collection. And what an album that was.

IAN BRITTON
Dalliance

I remember driving my mum somewhere on the Leeds ring road when John Peel was covering for Jakki Brambles on daytime Radio One. Peel played 'Dalliance', which starts nice and slow. But when it kicked off you could see cars suddenly jump and lurch forward as they hit the accelerator pedal to match the band!

GRAHAM WEAVER
Kennedy

The thing I remember was the personal touch. Often you would write and you would get a reply. This was mostly done by Sally on Reception headed writing paper – really detailed information about tours, etc. You would order a T-shirt or something and there would always be a postcard included, which was a really nice touch. The band seemed to care about the fans and this seemed pretty magical at the time. I also remember when 'Kennedy' was released and I couldn't stop whistling it in the office. The office was open plan and I got reprimanded by my manager. He was German and I always remember him saying, 'Do ve ave a canary in the ovvice?'

MIKE GAYLE, AUTHOR
Not From Where I'm Standing

George Best had already been out for over a year when I first fell in love with The Wedding Present. One lazy Saturday morning I happened upon the video for 'Nobody's Twisting Your Arm' while watching the indie top ten countdown on ITV's *Chart Show*. This feisty tale of young love gone wrong spoke volumes to the eighteen year-old me. I bought the 12" single from HMV in Birmingham the same day and when I finally got to listen to it I was blown away. This was the band I'd been looking for all my life and now there was literally nothing in the world that I wanted more than to own everything they had ever recorded. A week later I stood once again in HMV studying the cover of the Weddoes' debut. I was somewhat confused as to what *George Best* was doing there and what I was supposed to make of the fact that the album was named after him. Regardless I paid my money, certain that my new favourite band could never let me down no matter who the album was named after. And

All The Songs Sound The Same...

they didn't let me down. Every song was indeed a corker. Every song made me want to turn the music up even louder. Every song made me want to own more of their music. As soon as I'd saved up enough money I returned to HMV and bought the 12" of 'Why Are You Being So Reasonable Now?' and that's when it happened... that's when I found my all time favourite song by my all time favourite band. I can't quite put my finger on why 'Not From Where I'm Standing' stands out for me more so than, say, fan favourites like 'My Favourite Dress' or 'Everyone Thinks He Looks Daft' but it did. The moment I heard it I knew it was the one. It was the song I used to listen to in the dark while lying on my bed. It was the first song I listened to after splitting up with my first serious girlfriend. It was the song I knew even then would always be with me. And it still is.

Even now as I sit at my desk 28 years later, listening to it via iTunes, it still makes me feel exactly what I felt back when I first heard it, a shudder of excitement and awe, at hearing my all-time favourite song by my all-time favourite band.

TED PICKEN
My Favourite Dress

Late Eighties, mid-teens, some really great friends – but not quite sure how to tell them that. Girls also featuring but what a tangled web of highs and lows that was. I was working hard and wasn't drinking but found a great escapism and release in music. All sorts really – stuff to sit and think to, stuff to sing along to, electronic music actually designed to move you and then the visceral simplicity of guitar rock. I cannot describe how 'My Favourite Dress' used to make me feel, but there was such a joy in the familiarity (you only needed to listen to it twice to pick it all up) and comfort. It didn't ask much of you, but it gave so much. I was falling into and out of love regularly but totally incapable of expressing my feelings in any normal manner so shouting along with David Gedge made so much sense. As a boring, studious lad, I fell for girls who preferred sexually competent rogues – 'Give My Love To Kevin'. I'd treat love as some sort of mathematic formula, not quite understanding why it didn't quite equate: 'It took six hours before you let me down.' What a saddo. And then, rippling through it all, a gentle sense of humour. I got *Tommy* and *George Best* after they had been released but I queued up for my cassingle (yes, I mean cassingle) of 'Kennedy', and took every opportunity to play the cover of 'It's Not Unusual' for laughs (and pathos). The older kids in bands liked it too – street cred! And that was it, I would get every release

The Wedding Present

to ensure I didn't miss that elusive glimpse of levity from the boys. You can just imagine how I responded to the *Hit Parade* releases – like a kiddie in a sweet-shop. I love *Bizarro* and the singles from around that time. I wasn't sure about *Seamonsters* when I listened to it – the first side seemed a bit too indie mainstream but when they hit 'Heather' I knew where I was. I love the futility of it – once you've lost a girl everything is gone, even your special places. It grew on me. 'Suck' was porn in those days. You had to take it where you could find it. I fucking loved it.

My biggest regret is not to have purchased a Wedding Present T-shirt that was doing the rounds at some time. A bloke smiling and saying, 'I love them' and his girlfriend saying, 'I hate them'.

MILLIE FAGAN
The Girl From The DDR

I went to Leeds with someone and bought a signed copy of 'The Girl From The DDR' in Jumbo Records with them. A few months later we were almost seeing each other, but then they told me they had a girlfriend they didn't want to break up with. Probably the most foreshadowing record I've bought: 'I've realised that I don't think I am ever gonna leave my girlfriend for you!' *Valentina* was all I listened to for a good month after.

David Gedge and Millie Fagan

DARREN COLEMAN
Go Out And Get 'Em, Boy!

We were living in Switzerland and when my daughter left school she asked me to write something on her shirt to add to the good wishes that her friends and teachers had written. I wrote 'There's a whole world out there and it's screaming past, why don't you take it all and make it last forever, or maybe just a lifetime.' I realise, after looking the lyrics up, that what I heard and have sung all these years might not be exactly right, but it's been a part of my life regardless.

End Credits

DR WENDY FONAROW
Professor of Anthropology and
The Guardian's Indie Professor

When I was researching the definition and origins of indie music for my book, *Empire Of Dirt*, I came across a review of The Wedding Present in the *NME* that called them 'The Princes Of Indie City'. I included the quote to give scholars an idea of the aesthetics of indie music. It said, 'They talk ordinary. They dress ordinary. They embody the proud discredited dream of indiedom, namely that in every no-hope English ghost town there lurks a poet laureate of disaffected adolescence.' While describing the band, this characterization captured the values of the community, intelligence and the elevation of the ordinary into something extraordinary. The Wedding Present was one of the bands that helped establish a genre that is now taken for granted as a style of music. They appeared on the *NME*'s *C86* cassette compilation, which is widely considered to be a watershed moment of independent music culture in the UK. As an American researcher and fan of indie music, the wit, wisdom, and politics of The Wedding Present was one of the pulls towards making indie music the focus of my research, dissertation and later a book.

My first meeting with David Gedge, poet laureate of indie, was in front of a record store in Leeds. I had travelled there with the band's booking agent, Russell Warby, to see David's newest project, Cinerama. I had seen The Wedding Present play the Reading Festival in 1994 and 1996 while I was researching and making my annual pilgrimage to the cradle of independent music festivals. Twice was not enough. When Russell asked if I wanted to make the trip from London to Leeds see Cinerama, I jumped at the chance. We were introduced against a backdrop of vinyl albums and then went to a nearby teashop to chat before their show. I mentioned that I had completed a PhD on the culture of indie music and had included some quotes about him. He gave a kind and self-deprecating comment that I later came to realize was very much his style. The second time I made the acquaintance of David Gedge was at a short-lived pub quiz I was running at a dive bar called The White Horse in East Hollywood. It was my dream to bring a bit of Britain to the sunshine of Los Angeles. This pub quiz was designed to attract British ex-pats. To that end, I had one round each week called 'British Delight'. This round would feature questions easy for someone from the UK but challenging

The Wedding Present

to Americans. On the first pub quiz I hosted, one of the British Delight questions was, 'Who is George Best and what is he known for?' If your instinct was to answer, 'The name of the first Wedding Present album,' you'd have been perfect for our quiz. At the third pub quiz, I pulled my partner aside and said, 'Dude, I think that is David Gedge of The Wedding Present sitting over there. What is he doing here?' (Yes, in California we really do say 'dude'). The answer was David Gedge was about to win our pub quiz handily. He did have a couple of advantages. He is a Brit and had someone on his team who worked at an embassy. The quiz's visual round was 'National Flags' and this made his embassy friend close to a pub-quiz ringer. Afterwards, to my surprise, David approached me and asked, 'Haven't we met in England?' This strange combination of circumstances (Brit-o-phile pub quiz in Hollywood, fabled indie band from Yorkshire, teashops, record stores, dive bars and clubs) somehow perfectly captured to me the essence of The Wedding Present: strongly English yet global; intellectual while disarming; accomplished yet humble. It was the beginning of the friendship between the prince and the professor of indie rock.

In the years since then, I have seen The Wedding Present countless times in various cities. David subscribed to my indie gig list and would let me know in advance of any Los Angeles visit. I would do the same for Britain. He would answer my questions when I'd be under a deadline for the 'Ask The Indie Professor' contributions for *The Guardian*. When I wrote about band T-shirts, I discussed how Wedding Present fans would show their longevity by wearing an original T-shirt from a tour that was over two decades old to a contemporary show. I was delighted when I made a cameo appearance in one of their comic books. While they play their classic albums in full, something that could be nostalgic, The Wedding Present feature a constantly expanding repertoire at their live shows. David and The Wedding Present continue to move forward with new recordings, albums, and publications. While others might rest on their laurels, indie's poet continues to forge new ground, so the voices of disaffected youth can find a pathway out of any no-hope ghost town in England or abroad.

MARIA FORTE
David Gedge's Business Adviser

I first met David in 2006, originally becoming involved in The Wedding Present world to help sort out the reversion of their publishing copyrights from their past manager's clutches. The role then seemed to expand, as there was a label deal to be done and then a licence and then… just one more thing… and here we are 11 years later! I knew I had aligned with someone just that bit different from other artists I have worked with when typing out the title of the song 'Model, Actress,

End Credits

Whatever...' I asked David, 'How many dots do you want after 'Whatever'?' The response was immediate. 'Three please!'

DAN VEBBER
Writer for The Simpsons, Futurama, American Dad

I am not a music writer. That is to say, I'm not someone who can write about music with any degree of panache or authority, even if the music in question is a band I've obsessively followed for a quarter century. This is largely because, having never played music myself, I lack the terminology to comment on it in a way that makes me sound like I know what the hell I'm talking about. For example, I'm sure there's a good point to be made about how The Wedding Present are arguably better than any other band at exploiting the sudden transition from wistful reflection to furious bombast (see 'Dalliance', '2, 3, Go!' and, most recently, the entire opening suite of *Going, Going...*) but when I try to point that out I just end up saying something like, 'It's cool how they go from real quiet to real loud!' And no one's going to hire me over at Pitchfork if that's the extent of my zesty wordplay.

What I am pretty good at, however, is writing fart jokes for animated TV shows. So I do that, often while something by David Gedge roars out in the background. I flat-out love The Wedding Present more than any other band and have done since I was first introduced to them via *Bizarro* back in 1990. Soon after, I saw them live for the first time, in Chicago on their *Seamonsters* tour. A then-little-known group called Catherine Wheel opened for them – what a double bill! I was young. I had just enough beer in me to make the music transcendent. An astonishingly cute suburban punk-rockette dancing next to me knew all the lyrics, just like me and, during 'Dare', when we joined hands and screamed, 'Yes, all right, I scare you!' into each other's faces, I was certain I'd be getting laid that night. I didn't. Not even close. But, the point is, there was lots of emotion wrapped up in Wedding Present fandom for me from the very beginning.

Years later I had a steady gig writing for that splendid explosion of cartoon sci-fi nerdiness, *Futurama*. I was in Portland, visiting friends similarly ga-ga for everything Gedge, on the occasion of the 20th anniversary *Bizarro* show. The experience of seeing the nine-plus minutes of 'Take Me!' performed live is one of those things I wish I had the writing talent to capably deconstruct. In a move so desperately brazen it can only be explained by my consumption of what I remember as all the PBR in Oregon, I approached the band's adorable merch girl, gave her my card, and invited her and Gedge to attend a table read of one of my upcoming episodes. It seemed like a good idea at the time; when I woke up the next morning and replayed the incident in my head I wanted to jump in

The Wedding Present

front of the nearest logging truck. (Lots of logging around Portland.)

Back in Los Angeles a few weeks later, I was stunned to get an email from the aforementioned merch girl (who turned out to be Scopitones bigshot Jessica McMillan), saying that she and Gedge were in fact huge fans of *Futurama* (or at least its big brother, *The Simpsons*), and that they'd like to take me up on my shitfaced offer. Holy mackerel! I had actually tricked my musical idol into seeing me as some sort of (gasp) peer!

Anyway, I wrote David Gedge into my episode ('Cold Warriors', Season 6, Episode 24) as the only spare character available, a ten year old evil science nerd whose name was eventually changed to 'Josh Gedgie' (alas, Gedge's actual name wasn't deemed 'funny' enough by my showrunner). Hollywood: this town'll murder your dreams! But the point is, as far as I'm concerned, DAVID GEDGE WAS A GODDAMNED CHARACTER IN FUTURAMA! He got to meet Matt Groening and to hear the show's crazy-talented voice actors say, 'Gedgie' over and over as they read the script out loud. And I got him to take a picture with me in which I look really fat, and to sign a dog-eared Wedding Present/Catherine Wheel flyer I had stolen from that first Chicago show all those years ago. All-in-all, a good day for both of us. Buzz Aldrin was also in that same *Futurama* episode, playing himself. But David Gedge wrote 'My Favourite Dress'. All Buzz did was walk on the stupid moon.

STEWART LEE
Comedian

I remember the treble rush of those early singles so vividly. They all make much more sense now... like East European folk music crossed with scratchy funk, which I never felt before. Two rhythm guitars doing different things, like Chic made out of cheese wire.

CLYDE HOLCROFT
TV Producer

Everyone knows that the most important things you need when revising for exams aren't books and a memory – it is things like a revision diary, schedule and a lucky Smurf you can toss on an exam paper and answer the question it lands on. But I needed one more thing and that was a revision soundtrack. In 1988 I found the perfect accompaniment to trying to remember the semi-helical structure of DNA, Oxbow lake formation and what *Jude The Obscure* was all about. It was *George Best* by The Wedding Present.

My mate Ben let me tape his album and I found a picture of George Best in a newspaper and cut it out. I stuck this to a tape label and wrote out the words 'The Wedding Present' in blue biro. Yes, I'd been warned that 'home taping is killing music' but I didn't care. I was Telford's

End Credits

very own Che Guevara.

I listened to the tape constantly as I revised. One side would finish and I'd turn it over and listen to the next, repeating this over and over like an indie Sisyphus. I don't think this is connected but I did really badly in my GCSEs: 7 Ds and 2 Cs. The following year The Wedding Present played the Wulfrun Hall in Wolverhampton. This was a town of mystery and glamour to me, coming from Telford. I went to the gig with a mate who was on crutches. We stood waiting for the band to come on, supping our beers. When the band started, my mate handed me his crutches and jumped into the moshpit. I remember David saying he was going for a curry that night after the show and I just stood there thinking, 'I want to have a curry with David Gedge.' My friend's health was never the same again. I'm not saying David Gedge was 100 percent responsible for this. I mean, he didn't kick his crutches away or anything.

I was hooked. New songs and albums came: mythical songs like 'that apple pie one' as my mate Spag called it. The Status Quo on acid guitar solo of 'Take Me!' The hand-painted sleeve of 'Brassneck'. Then *Seamonsters*, then the pop charts with 12 singles in 12 months. It never stopped... until it did. I thought that was it.

Then, in 2005, *Take Fountain* arrived. When a band you love releases new material, it's terrifying. You know that at best it'll sound like your favourite songs from their back catalogue, only not quite as good. But, no, this was a great album. I couldn't stop listening to it. That same year I found myself producing The Frank Skinner Show and ordering a vast amount of merch off the Weddoes' website. I received an email from Jessica and I invited her and David to the show. We had Ringo Starr as a guest that night but I didn't care. I met Ringo; he hugged me and said, 'Peace and love.' But all I could think was, 'David Gedge is downstairs and I'm going to meet him!' I had ten minutes before having to start the show's recording. Enough time to get nervous, get my 'Brassneck' single signed and tell David I loved his new album. He thanked me, but said, 'That's my job.' It is, I guess. His job is writing brilliant music and he's very good at it.

And I did manage to have a curry with David. Me and my wife have even had dinner with him and Jessica at his house. I spent most of the time in the toilet. But that's another story.

STEVE ALBINI

It's hard to pick a favourite from The Wedding Present and Cinerama material I've worked on. They are pretty prolific and not a band with the one good song and the rest as filler. You can pretty much drop the needle anywhere and get the picture. Most of their songs had a wide dynamic range, very similar themes, sexual or romantic awkwardness, quiet

The Wedding Present

part, loud part, interesting little break in there somewhere. Picking out one of those as opposed to appreciating that they carved out a whole style for themselves seems petty. They are a distinctive and durable band partly because their songs fit together into a complete aesthetic, not because they got lucky with a single tune or riff. A lot of great bands are like that, AC/DC, Crazy Horse, The Sex Pistols, Complete, Kraftwerk... For what it's worth, they had good taste and great execution of cover versions, from Steve Harley to Pavement.

MELYS

We had been fans of the Weddoes for quite some time so when we started bumping in to the band at various Peel shows we were thrilled. What made it better was how lovely they were too and how shy, which is something we didn't expect but just made them more endearing people. They turned up at our bistro in north Wales once and we were gutted to have missed them. We met them again at a joint show we played with them in Amsterdam at the Paradiso venue. It was great to share the stage with them, I remember David being surprised at how loud and aggressive our set was. Unfortunately the next time we played together was at the John Peel memorial gig at Maida Vale. On another occasion there was a birthday party for John Peel at his home. It was a fantastic affair and Andrea (our singer) got pissed and regaled Delia Smith with stories for most of the night. David was on a different table and Andrea kept exchanging rather girly waves with him, toasting each other with their glasses of wine. We can only surmise David was as drunk as we were. Either that or he was laughing at the state of us! Who knows? We were lucky enough to have stayed at Peel's house a few times and whenever we spoke about The Wedding Present, John would always express what lovely people they were, which in our book was high praise indeed.

DANIELLE WADEY
The Wedding Present bassist 2016–

My friend Louise put my name in the hat as a possible keyboard player for Cinerama. I had an email inviting me to come and meet the band for what I assumed would be an interview/trial session. I quickly rehearsed up some songs to dazzle the band with and excitedly made my way to the rehearsal rooms one lunchtime. We went to a cafe for lunch and what I thought would be the 'interview' part of the day. Charlie sat quietly behind a paper, occasionally intervening with a smile or a laugh. David asked me some questions about synthesizers, and Pat filled the rest of the time with amusing tour stories! As lunch ended, I mentally prepared myself to go and strut my stuff on the keys. David paid

End Credits

for my lunch and said, 'So, rehearsals start on Monday.' I looked bit shocked and asked, 'Do you want me to play anything?' and he said, 'No.' That was that! I started the week playing Cinerama and finished it playing Cinerama and a handful of Wedding Present songs... on a variety of instruments! That's where it began and, four years later, I can honestly say I've had the best time!

CHRIS ALLISON

George Best is over 30 years ago now? That makes me feel old! Thankfully I started my music production career early. The Wedding Present was the first band I worked with as a producer. I think we made some great recordings together – almost 50 in total! 'Kennedy' is a bit of a stand out to me. 'Everyone Thinks He Looks Daft' was a very good track. And 'My Favourite Dress'.

ROBIN INCE
Broadcaster

We got through a lot of hair gel then. Every Tuesday, Mark and I would go to Feet First, the Camden Palace celebration of alternative music. It used to be all Dinosaur Jr and Happy Mondays around here in them days. Due to our exuberant haircuts and the shadows they cast over our faces – Spanish students would wrongly guess we may be able to sell them drugs. There were a few songs that would make us vault the ornate bannisters to get to the dance floor. This was not necessary for 'Blue Monday' as you had a good five minutes to get to the floor and still had another five minutes to dance before mumbling, as if the first time, 'This song may be too long' and returning to the bar. Other songs were brisker and gymnastics were a necessity if you wanted at least a verse and chorus to make strange, hyperkinetic shapes to. 'Kennedy' was one that required speed of reaction. One of UK independent music's finest vivid pop stabs. If you were lucky, it may be back to back with 'Debaser'. I remember one *Melody Maker* journalist stating that if The Wedding Present had come from the North West of America, they would be given far more time and far more kudos in the UK. We could always rely on Peel though. I sat in a car park in Beaconsfield reading about Peel's 50th birthday bash with The House Of Love, The Wedding Present and, obviously, The Fall. It seemed Peel was so very old then, and now I'm just two years away from the same. I am older than Mick Ronson ever managed to be.

I saw The Wedding Present on the day Vincent Price died. They were at the Wedgewood Rooms in Portsmouth. Wandering to the toilet, a friend of mine's elbow brushed David Gedge. She was elated. The most recent time I saw The Wedding Present, the audience had a sense of reverence, with a wide variety of outlooks and jobs and haircuts, for

The Wedding Present

those who still had hair to be cut. I will appreciate any set that begins with a Philip Larkin recording: 'I thought it would last my time/The sense that, beyond the town/There would always be fields and farms/Where the village louts could climb.' Larkin suits David Gedge well. The lost or broken loves, the graffitti on walls, the sadness of landscapes.
Walking to the stage, Gedge looks like the boxer brother of Gary Numan (and a boxer who never lost a bout) and the warmth in his spoken voice between songs has a hint of John Shuttleworth. All these things are good to me. It is not a 'hits' set, and I hear some men loudly explaining in droning voices to bored wives that they are perturbed by the lack of 'Kennedy' and 'Everybody Thinks He Looks Daft'. The guitar is still loud and choppy, brittle, yet like granite too. Then, something with a hint of the complexity and beauty of The Durutti Column moves further to the foreground. The latest drummer is in possession of protean facial gymnastics. He out-Moons Moon. I want to hear more of the new – I can always play the old in my head on the train home.

Some audiences demand the songs of their youth, the songs that briefly have a hallucinogenic quality that will make them feel young again. They could feel younger still if, rather than shackling themselves to the hits of the past, they keep moving on, just as The Wedding Present continue to do. Progression doesn't mean you have to leave the old behind, but it gives you more to look forward to. There is no encore: some traditions must always remain for The Wedding Present. As the man in the audience still bleats about the lack of the past in the set, the rest leave content that progress continues. My friend's arm was unbrushed that night... but there'll always be Portsmouth.

MICK HOUGHTON

When Keith left in 1993, David was the only original member left and you can't but respect that David's kept the band going ever since. And the reason he's been able to do that is because he has never lost sight of who his – or rather who The Wedding Present's – fans are, and he knows exactly what they want. So The Wedding Present have become a cottage industry where the company boss knows its product inside out.

MARC RILEY
Broadcaster

There are some points in your life when you have to decide exactly what it is that you're meant to be doing with the rest of your days. Mine came to me at the age of 27 when I considered the time was right to 'grow up'. I got a proper job, which lasted all of three months. After that I became a record plugger. Poacher turned gamekeeper. Although with a toe still in the music business, I had (not for the last time) 'retired' from making music 'due to

End Credits

public demand.' That was it. Over. After a couple of years this toe in show business turned into a size eleven foot covered by a great big clumsy hobnail boot. I somehow eventually ended up on BBC Radio 1 and became firm friends with the man who I grew up listening to. The same man who kept me afloat during my post-Fall years. The man whom I admired so greatly. John Peel. Tragically, John is no longer with us. The man who took it upon himself to change the cultural face of the UK was taken away from us. It was then very appropriate that the then fledgling BBC 6Music was slowly finding its feet and would within the space of three or four years become the kind of station you like to think would have been the perfect home for John. A home in many ways he built.

Throughout my years in The Creepers there were many other bands who benefitted from the 'Peel Effect'. Too numerous to mention. But one of those was – as if you can't see this coming – The Wedding Present. The constant support. Plays. Sessions. Encouragement. Friendship. John's love of the *George Best* LP (which was a heroic support considering John's affiliation to Liverpool, Manchester United's most hated rival) was well known. And until John passed away he remained a firm fan of all things 'Gedge'. So I suppose I'm trying to say that to see the release of Wedding Present sessions done for our 6Music programme over the years is something of an honour. In the great tradition of the Peel/Selwood releases on the Strange Fruit label these session releases prove that even without John the BBC can still be a place where great bands can continue to grow and be creative... amongst friends. We have a running joke with David now that as he leaves the studio after a session he should corner producer Michelle and book in one for the following year. And that is pretty much what happens. As I type there is another Marc Riley/Wedding Present session looming large.

JESSICA McMILLAN

As a grumpy, contrary, introverted teenager, the only real benefit of having an older sibling (vastly more popular and confident than myself) was that boys used to make my sister mixtapes. They would go straight from her beat-up Honda Civic's tape deck (it wasn't even attached to the car, it was a small boombox that we carried around) into my little 15 year old hands. Through these tapes I found The Cure, Joy Division and The Clash. I'm not sure if my sister even ever listened to them but to me they were a gold mine and a lifeline. When my (also smarter and better at school) sister went to University in 1994, she had a boyfriend who, to me, was a bit god-like. He loved Morrissey and The Smiths. I'd never really met anyone apart from my old history teacher who liked The Smiths... it was a small island. This boyfriend was equally obsessed with a band called The Wedding Present (he

The Wedding Present

later split up with my sister by writing the lyrics to Kennedy over and over for pages and pages).

I can't remember exactly where I was when I first heard The Wedding Present or even what song it was... but *Saturnalia* had just come out and I was mesmerised. I loved the soaring chorus of guitars and the woeful but not pitiful lyrics. They quickly became one of the bands I looked for in record shops every weekend in Seattle. I still have that first copy of *Saturnalia* (it says 'KUPS' on it because my sister had a late night radio show and she stole it from the station.) Of course I then 'acquired' it! I also remember standing outside of the Crocodile Cafe in Seattle at the age of 18 listening to The Wedding Present play through the wall because it was a 21 and over show.

Flash forward about five years... I was living in Glasgow, being completely useless in more ways than one... and Cinerama needed a merchandiser. Why not?! They couldn't believe I was just there doing nothing... but that is often convenient for a band... someone who has the time and will work for cheap! After joining Cinerama on the road for four or five dates, it turned out that Sally was thinking of not going on tour any more. Again, I was doing nothing in Glasgow, so I volunteered to learn how to roadie. They called it 'throwing me in at the deep end' and it was a bit of a leap for me, not being a musician or knowing anything about 'backline'. I remember my first solo roadie assignment (Nottingham Social, 2002) and feverishly winding the top E string so tightly that it broke. I wanted a hole in the floor to open up so I could crawl in. Thank goodness I got over that... I still don't really know anything about guitars but I am fairly good at faking it!

When I started touring, the Cinerama line-up was David, Terry, Simon and Kari. One thing to know about touring with bands is that if you do anything slightly annoying, they will pick and pick until you stop doing it or leave the party. On that first tour I would say, 'What?' when I didn't quite catch something. Boy, did that get kicked out of me... a chorus of, 'Whiiiiittttts?' (I'd been living in Scotland) would ring out from the British members of the group. I now say, 'Pardon?' Unfortunately... after more tours than I can think of, my memory fuzzes things together. Where was it that we got all those parking tickets? Which North American tour was it that we saw the world's largest McDonalds (thrill a minute!)? I guess it doesn't matter which one it was, the thing that underlines all of them is how much we laugh at the stupidest things... the most inappropriate things. Sat in heavy traffic in Amsterdam once, the word 'Dutch' before anything suddenly became a source of incredible mirth and, to this day, still makes me titter for no reason. Most importantly, I still love The Wedding Present. We've worked out that I am the person in this world who has seen The Wedding Present more times than anyone else. I feel quite

End Credits

honoured to have this position. During the *Seamonsters* 20th anniversary tour I remember how amazing it was to hear 'Heather' live and so, so loud every night. Even though I have to admit, those fuzzy guitars at close range somehow made me a little bit sleepy!

SHAUN CHARMAN

My daughter Nina's starting to play the drums at school. They went round the group and said, 'How did you learn the drums?' And she said, 'Oh, my Dad used to play.' When she said the name of the band, the teacher turned out to be a really big fan. She'll be better than me soon! I'm very pleased to have made the records I did, with The Wedding Present and with other bands as well. Once upon a time I just wanted to have released something on vinyl, and wanted to be played on Peel once and maybe get a session. So I certainly managed that.

PETER SOLOWKA

If there's one thing I really think back on, to get an overview of all the things that went on there, as far as my life's gone I just feel so lucky. I don't mean that someone's given me a lottery win. You work hard as a musician. All musicians work hard. They're passionate. They put a lot of belief into what they do. I just think that initial combination of four people – for whatever reason, whatever it was, however good or bad we were at our instruments – that combination that started off was something that was lucky. I've been in lots of other bands and that combination wasn't there. There was a certain way that everyone worked together which was lucky, that helped us make those records. – the energy and the dynamism, whatever it was.

If it wasn't for that luck in those people getting together for whatever reason, my whole life would have been so different. I've done things which loads of people dream of, playing on massive stages in front of millions of people, playing your music the way that you want to play it without any interference at all. I suspect that's a dream that people have and luck has given me that dream. And look at the music I'm doing now, the music I'm playing now. I wouldn't be able to do that if it wasn't for those days. I feel quite privileged to have been in the position that I've been in really. It's great. So thank you for all the four individuals I was with also. I recognise that we all worked hard in our own way. We all have strengths and failings. But we were special.

You could always turn around and say, 'Oh Peter was always complaining about David's singing range.' He's only got a range of about fourteen semitones, so he says. I've tried playing notes when we're playing live to try and increase his range but it doesn't sound right. It's a limitation, so you work within it. Shaun was learning to play the drums but we worked within

The Wedding Present

it. That combination of those four people at that time was special. And it's got to be acknowledged and accepted.

What's very humbling about being in The Wedding Present is there aren't many things you can do in life which touch people. The records we made between 1987 and 1991 really touched people's lives. 25 years on, people still play the music to make themselves feel happy. That is such a very humbling thing. So many people I work with – teachers who come up to me, parents who talk to me about their kids – say, 'Oh, you don't mind this, do you?' and they bring out a record for me to sign. It's weird, but it's great.

DAVID GEDGE

I will come off stage after a concert sometimes and people will say, 'That was brilliant, David... you must have really enjoyed it!' And they're usually thrown by my reply, which is, typically, 'No, I actually found it quite stressful.' And it's true. I definitely don't do concerts for fun... I genuinely find it difficult and exhausting and the endless travelling wears me down. So people say, 'Well you must like making records, anyway.' And I say, 'Not really, because there's always that worry that you're creating something which isn't as good as what you've created before.' I spend days working on songs on my own in my room... going over them again and again. I'll try a different approach... which won't sound right... so I'll try something else. Then I'll worry that my time could be spent doing something more constructive. The usual next question is, 'So, why do you do it, then?!' And the answer is that I honestly don't know. I've been driven to do this for so many years now that I think it's become something of an obsession. Or an addiction. Who knows? I'm not really a very confident person so maybe I just like the reassurance that people don't think I'm useless? I don't know. But there's one thing of which I am sure. The thing of which I'm most proud is the way that The Wedding Present seems to have formed some kind of community around itself. Band members, business colleagues, friends and fans have come and gone (and, in some cases, come back again!) but, throughout the years, there's always this weird thread that connects us all.

After the dreadful attack on concert-goers in Manchester on 22 May 2017 The Wedding Present were playing in Glasgow and I asked the audience to take part in a minute's silence for those affected by the tragedy. This was the Friday night of a Bank Holiday weekend and the thousand strong crowd was well oiled and in a celebratory mood. Yet, during that minute's silence, you could hear a pin drop. There was total respect and shared empathy. I felt humbled and proud. Tears began to roll down my cheeks as I nodded to our guitarist Marcus as a sign that he should play the opening riff of 'Brassneck'. All I could think was... 'These are my people.'